D0084631

DATE DUE

NOV 1 9 2009

OCT 2 2 2010

BRODART, CO. Cat. No. 23-221-003

THE SOCIOCULTURAL AND POLITICAL ASPECTS OF ABORTION

THE SOCIOCULTURAL AND POLITICAL ASPECTS OF ABORTION

Global Perspectives

Edited by
Alaka Malwade Basu

Westport, Connecticut
London

Library of Congress Cataloging-in-Publication Data

The sociocultural and political aspects of abortion : global perspectives / edited by Alaka Malwade Basu.
p. cm.
Includes bibliographical references and index.
ISBN 0-275-97728-5 (alk. paper)
1. Abortion—Cross-cultural studies. I. Basu, Alaka Malwade.
HQ767.S65 2003
363.46—dc21 2002072823

British Library Cataloguing in Publication Data is available.

Copyright © 2003 by Alaka Malwade Basu

All rights reserved. No portion of this book may be reproduced, by any process or technique, without the express written consent of the publisher.

Library of Congress Catalog Card Number: 2002072823
ISBN: 0–275–97728–5

First published in 2003

Praeger Publishers, 88 Post Road West, Westport, CT 06881
An imprint of Greenwood Publishing Group, Inc.
www.praeger.com

Printed in the United States of America

The paper used in this book complies with the Permanent Paper Standard issued by the National Information Standards Organization (Z39.48–1984).

10 9 8 7 6 5 4 3 2

ACC Library Services
Austin, Texas

Dedicated to the memory of Bruno Remiche, whose enthusiasm and friendship got this study off the ground.

Contents

Tables

Chapter 1

Introduction: Induced Abortion in a Changing World

John C. Caldwell and Pat Caldwell

Induced abortion is a major phenomenon of the contemporary world. Each year it is practiced by one woman out of every fourteen of reproductive age (World Health Organization 1994, 1–14). With a level estimated at about 45 million per year (World Health Organization 1998), it occurs over one-third as frequently as births and just as frequently as deaths. It probably explains almost two-fifths of all births averted each year and hence is a dominant factor in the global fertility transition.

Yet abortion is far less often or completely studied than fertility, mortality, or contraception. This is partly because it is such a controversial phenomenon. In much of the world, governments and other institutions are hostile to it. In fact, many of the women who practice it do not express themselves as being generally in favor of the procedure.

There is another reason why little research is undertaken into induced abortion, but it is really a reason why it should be a focus of research: around two-fifths of all abortions are clandestine and are carried out in societies where the circumstances of the pregnancy render the abortion illegal or where the provider is not legally qualified. These are the abortions classified by the World Health Organization (1994, 2) as "unsafe," and although not all of them are in fact unsafe, most deaths do occur in this kind of abortion. Abortion accounts for about one-third of maternal mortality, and around 99 percent of this mortality occurs in illegal operations in the Third World. Pick and colleagues,[1] describing Mexico City, write that in most countries where abortion is illegal, the law does not stop women from aborting yet ensures that they can do so only under dangerous conditions. The fact that induced abortion so often occurs with moral disapprobation and in clandestine and illegal circumstances means that women face not only physical dangers but also emotional distress and psychological damage.

THE GLOBAL PICTURE

Few global pictures are more tentative than those of the distribution of induced abortions. This is shown by Frejka's estimates (1993, 211), where the high estimate is almost twenty times the size of the low estimate in the case of Africa and more than double for South and Southeast Asia. There is not only an extreme reluctance to disclose illegal acts but even to disclose legal abortions because of the continuing moral debate. The insecurity of the database has made many demographers reluctant to enter the research field.

The fear of disclosure varies by society. In sub-Saharan Africa it is greatest among married women because society is shocked by a woman who is in a position to have a baby refusing to do so, whereas there is widespread sympathy for the difficult situation of the pregnant single girl. In South Asia, single girls are terrified to admit that they are pregnant and sexually experienced, whereas married women with children receive understanding and sympathy if they do not wish to bear another child.

Another problem surrounding the disclosure of abortion is that many women, when their menstruation is overdue, take herbal preparations or pharmaceuticals without ever knowing whether they have been pregnant or merely prematurely alarmed. This is equally the case with menstrual regulation and is promoted in countries like Bangladesh precisely because the ambiguity presents both a legal and a moral loophole.

Both abortion and menstrual regulation have occurred throughout history. Classical Europe permitted abortion. Premodern abortions were either dangerous physical interventions or, more commonly, less dangerous and potentially less effective attempts carried out by drinking herbal solutions. Both methods have survived in the contemporary world. Menstrual regulation, by both these means, also has a long history, but it has been practiced in Sri Lanka and, as Levin shows, in Guinea, mostly to maintain health, especially reproductive health.

The women most likely to have abortions vary dramatically from society to society (Singh, Henshaw, and Berentsen; Renne; Serbanescu et al.; Caldwell and Caldwell 1994). In the West and sub-Saharan Africa, around three-quarters of abortions are to single women and about the same proportion to persons under twenty years of age. In Eastern Europe, Latin America, and probably much of Asia, the proportions are reversed, with three-quarters of the abortions to married women and to persons over twenty years of age. In the West and sub-Saharan Africa, the majority of women having abortions have borne no children, whereas this proportion falls to 20 percent in Latin America and 15 percent in Eastern Europe. Obviously there are different paramount dangers motivating an abortion. In some societies the greatest obstacle to a potentially satisfactory life comes from premature motherhood or marriage, although in others the increasing load of dependent children poses the greatest threat.

In the popular mind, legal abortions are associated with trained doctors and liberal abortion legislation, and illegal abortions are associated with backyard, untrained practitioners and illiberal laws. This distinction is increasingly being blurred. In sub-Saharan Africa only two countries, Zambia and Burundi, have liberal laws, yet induced abortion is everywhere becoming safer as the number of private medical practitioners increases and as many of them find that abortion provides a substantial part of their income. In contrast, few countries have as liberal abortion laws as does India, but 90 percent of Indian abortions are illegal, clandestine, and not performed by doctors because the priority of both the women most concerned and their families is not safety or cheapness but secrecy, which cannot be guaranteed in public facilities.

Although the proportion of potential conceptions prevented by contraception has grown enormously this century, the same is also true of abortions. Primitive abortions were relatively hard to achieve and very frightening. Furthermore, in spite of today's tremendous rhetoric about abortion, there is now far more moral support for women seeking abortion than there was at the beginning of the century. In regional terms both contraception and abortions are most prevalent where incomes are highest and fertility lowest. Thus, half of all pregnancies are aborted in Europe, compared with 27 percent in Latin America, 25 percent in Asia, and probably under 15 percent in Africa.

These figures demonstrate the inevitability of abortion—even if illegal and clandestine. In Latin America, where governments, religion, and laws are almost universally hostile to abortion, two-fifths of all pregnancies are aborted. This is a measure of economic and social change in Latin America. It is also evidence that repression cannot succeed and that governments, if not the Catholic Church, must accept the fact and come to some realistic and humane compromise.

The need for compromise rests on the very real danger of illegal abortion. When abortion was legalized once again in Romania in 1989, maternal mortality fell by two-thirds (Serbanescu et al.). The suppression of abortion is particularly invidious in the Third World with its limited medical capacity: Mundigo presents figures showing that 90 percent of unsafe abortions take place in developing countries and that over 99 percent of abortion deaths occur there.

ABORTION ATTITUDES

Although there is widespread opposition to abortion solely by choice, majority popular opinion supports permitting abortions in some circumstances in countries ranging from Bangladesh (Amin) to France (Blayo and Blayo) where, as in most Western countries, the level of support stands at over 90 percent of all those polled.

In contrast, opposition comes from most religions. Only in the Catholic Church, which is the sole monolithic and completely organized religion in the world, is that opposition nearly absolute in all circumstances. The church's opposition to abortion has hardened over the last 130 years and has become almost absolute since the publication of *Casti Conubii* in 1930 (Mejia 1996). Nothing in this book suggests that this position is likely to change easily or soon, although it is possible that the Catholic Church will become less outspoken and crusading under a different pope, as has already happened with regard to "non-natural" methods of contraception. The latter change may have occurred to provide greater clarity and focus for the fight against abortion.

In the longer run the debate is not completely closed. There is still some question about when ensoulment takes place; no agreement that abortion is identical with homicide; and a persistence of the argument, in the case when a mother's life is threatened, that it is permissible to choose the lesser of two evils, namely, allowing the fetus to die if that will increase the mother's chance of survival.

As abortion techniques improved in the nineteenth century, both Catholic and Protestant countries brought in harsher legislation against its practice. Subsequently, they reenacted similar legislation in their colonies irrespective of the colonized people's theological or philosophical views on the subject. For well over a century the countries formed from British India adhered to an 1860 British Colonial Act against abortion, although it might be noted that no prosecution was ever launched under this legislation (Amin). The situation did not change until India legalized abortion in 1971; Pakistan liberalized its law to include the health of the mother as a cause for allowing abortion in 1990; and Bangladesh, without legal change, advised in a 1980 memo that menstrual regulation was not illegal because the pregnancy status was not known.

Nothing in Confucian and Shinto ethics or Hindu religion forbids abortion, and modern legal changes have encountered little opposition in East Asia or India. Islam is more concerned with the implication of skepticism that Allah will provide. Different Islamic legal schools give varying interpretations on the moral issue of abortion, especially early in pregnancy, but the latter is not prohibited by the dominant school in South Asia. Buddhism is generally taken to be opposed to abortion, and this is the position usually taken by its monks although not so firmly by many of its adherents.

The striking aspect of the International Conference for Population and Development (ICPD), held in Cairo in September 1994, was the conviction with which the Holy See assumed the prohibition of abortion to be a universal morality. Almost equally striking was the lack of spoken opposition from large Asian countries that adhered to different philosophies and that had no intention of outlawing abortion. Part of the explanation was that most of them preferred contraception to abortion as a method of family limitation, intended to continue their expansion of family-planning facilities, and would take a decline in abortion rates as a sign of their success. What is less often noted about ICPD is that the much-publicized understanding between the Holy See and some fundamentalist Muslim governments was merely a conservative accommodation to oppose radical aspects of the conference's Programme of Action. The Catholic Church's main opposition was to anything that could be interpreted as encouraging abortion, whereas the Islamic governments were against sex education or family-planning provision or advice being made directly to wives or unmarried children without being filtered through the family patriarch.

The most powerful ethical and philosophic challenge to the prohibition of abortion has come this century not from non-Christian religions but from secularism and communism, which dispute the right of a decision to be made purely on religious grounds. This separation of the state and church has widened the grounds for abortion in most Western countries. In all communist countries abortion was at some stage legalized, although these decisions were reversed at times in some countries to promote population growth.

In recent times the secular philosophy has found a strong ally in the women's movement, which has argued the right of every person to act on his or her own ethical philosophy. This is not the only strand to their moral approach, for they have opposed past legislation and theology on the grounds that these were dominated by male decision makers and male viewpoints that should not bind women, especially with regard to events going on in their own bodies.

The legal position is complex, as is detailed by Mundigo. Only 7 percent of countries refuse to permit abortion on any grounds, whereas 84 percent permit it to save the woman's life, to preserve her physical and mental health, and in cases of rape, incest, or fetal impairment. On the other hand, only 22 percent make it a matter of choice without imposing restrictions. Developing countries, at least in theory and legislation, restrict abortion much more fiercely. Only 6 percent allow it on request, and around one-quarter for fetal impairment, rape, or incest. Those developing countries that make it a matter of choice are entirely communist or excommunist, with the singular exception of Tunisia. Thus, Cuba is the only country in Latin America with easy access to legal abortion. Liberal abortion laws now exist in Asian countries, ranging from the communist nations to India and Turkey as well as those central Asian countries that were formerly part of the Union of Soviet Socialist Republics. An interesting exception is Buddhist Sri Lanka, which is liberal on so many other issues but still forbids abortion.

Singh, Henshaw, and Berensten show that where there are accurate statistics, mostly in countries with liberal abortion laws, social attitudes nevertheless result in a wide range of abortion levels. Thus, in the West, the proportion of terminated pregnancies averages 22 percent but ranges from 10 percent in the Netherlands to 26 percent in the United States. Eastern Europe averages 47 percent, ranging from 27 percent in the former German Democratic Republic to 63 percent in Romania. In the communist Third World, China's level is 27 percent and Cuba's, 58 percent, and in noncommunist countries Tunisia records 8 percent and Singapore, 22 percent.

THE MEANS AND MECHANICS OF ABORTION

Legal abortions are carried out either by trained doctors or by trained nurses or health assistants with some kind of further medical backup available. The latter is most often the case when menstrual regulation is performed with manual suction equipment, as in Bangladesh, where the family planning program provides the services. Even in these circumstances the program provides only 40 percent of all abortions, the remainder being the estimated number of clandestine abortions, which, together with the legal abortions, account for about 15 percent of all pregnancies (Ahmed, Sarkar, and Rahman 1996; Ahmed, Haque, Hossain, and Alam 1996).

Currently, the women's movement spearheads the secular demand for more liberal abortion laws, insisting that women should be allowed choice about what goes on within their own bodies. The movement also emphasizes that it must be the woman's choice because it is her future that is so radically altered if she continues with pregnancy, birth, nursing, and child upbringing. This argument is making inroads into male political conservatism and the Catholic laity and even seems to disquiet the church.

Yet sociologically it may be misleading, and we are entitled to ask how often women make the decision to have an abortion on their own. In savanna West Africa, Renne reports that, at least for married women, interfering with fertility is suspect, and the decision to do so is certainly men's business. In Vietnam, Johansson and colleagues (1996) report that wives and husbands always consult each other, if only so that they can provide mutual moral support against the suspicion and opposition of the older generation. In the Karachi slums, Fikree and colleagues (1996) found that few women had an abortion without talking with their husbands first. On the other hand, most of them had even earlier discussed the matter with another woman, possibly to gain information that could influence their husbands. In the urban slums of Brazil, Leal and Fachel (1996) found that unmarried couples disagreed in a significant proportion of these consultations: women were more likely to favor abortion, apparently so that there would be no subsequent complications to their lives, whereas men often advocated fostering, presumably so that they would know they had descendants and possibly so they could later claim these descendants. In southwest Nigeria, Caldwell and Caldwell (1994, 289) found that 8 percent of women did not discuss the decision to abort with partners because they had no stable relationship, whereas of the remainder, only one-quarter did not act jointly with their partners, in almost all cases because they already knew or suspected strongly that their partners would attempt to prevent the abortion. It seems likely that the situation of joint decision making described here is general in most of the Third World and likely that it also characterizes developed countries, at least within marriage or other stable relationships.

The search to identify individual characteristics predisposing women to abort is less fruitful than such investigations of contraceptors often proved to be. In rural Bangladesh, a multiple regression analysis (identifying odds ratios significant at the 1 percent level) found women with three or more living sons 2.4 times as likely to procure an abortion as those with no living sons; previous family-planning users 2.3 times as likely as those who had never used contraception; and those who had conceived within 24 months of the last birth, twice as likely as women with longer birth intervals (Ahmed, Sarkar, and Rahman 1996; Ahmed, Haque, Hossain, and Alam 1996). Education and age were only marginally significant. The last two findings are found throughout much of the world, especially in developing countries.

The fact of contraceptive use selects a subsample of the population more determined to control their fertility. Some may indeed abort because they feel it is their right to remain unpregnant once they have made a choice in favor of family planning, and many family-planning programs agree with them. Women with short birth intervals abort for a range of reasons: to hide the fact that they resumed sexual relations at what their culture regards as an inappropriate time; to protect the last-born from prematurely early weaning and consequent greater risk of death; to protect themselves physically from having two pregnancies close together; to protect themselves from having two small children to bring up at the same time; and to protect the family economy from having to make outlays on education or life-course rituals or ceremonies in close succession. In northern Nigeria, Renne identifies the potentially short birth interval as a cause but noted that its effect was weakening as educated women were less ashamed of it being shown that they had resumed sex early.

In Kerala, India, the likelihood of abortion rose with the number of children (Rajan, Mishra, and Vimala 1996), and this, too, is a frequent finding around the world. But what is surprising is how weak most socioeconomic correlations are. In Romania, Serbanescu and colleagues found only slightly higher abortion rates in urban areas, among the least educated and among the married, but it could be argued that Romania would hardly reach its extraordinary level of abortion without high rates among all sectors of the population. In the Brazilian slums, the only differential identified was that those who started childbearing early had proportionately more abortions (Leal and Fachel 1996). The explanation may be in fact that rural-urban differences could not be investigated and that slum populations are fairly homogeneous.

It is worthwhile stressing Mundigo's point that abortion usually cannot properly be described as a woman's preferred choice but rather as the least bad of various alternatives. Nevertheless, this book brings out the fact that this statement probably should be modified for Eastern Europe, where it is often the preferred method of fertility control. Such has also long been the position for many Japanese women.

In sub-Saharan Africa, most abortions occur to single women. In Nigeria, girls are often faced with the prospect of having sex at short notice as an alternative to the threat of losing their boyfriends (Caldwell and Caldwell 1987, 239–41). At short notice they can take few precautions, and, in any case, the great majority have the most rudimentary concepts of contraception and often little access to contraceptives. The situation throughout sub-Saharan Africa is probably very similar to that found by Stambach in Tanzania, where even sexually active girls were often surprisingly ignorant of the chances of becoming pregnant.

In contrast, abortions in Asia are sought mostly by married women and perhaps unusually, as Icduygu (1996) reported for Turkey, because they want no more children. The reasons are predominantly economic. Yet South Asia at least shares with sub-Saharan Africa a horror of short birth intervals and the evidence they provide of parents prematurely resuming sexual relations and appearing not to care about any danger to the infant already born or the one likely to be conceived. Khan and Patel (1996), reporting on India, and Fikree et al. (1996), on Pakistan, reveal this to be a major cause of marital abortion in South Asia. In Pakistan, and doubtless in India as well, women who have previously had difficult births also have a predisposition to seek abortions.

Latin America presents the most complex picture. Leal and Fachel (1996) report a study in a southern Brazilian slum as showing that pregnancy was often a strategy employed by young women to strengthen a union or force a marriage. Where the pregnancy failed to achieve that aim, an abortion was likely. But other poor women in a Dominican Republic study reported by Mundigo sought an abortion either because their partner was not a good breadwinner or because the relationship was so unsatisfactory that it might not continue but might leave the woman with yet another child. It might be noted that a similar situation exists in many informal unions in Nigeria. In Brazil, where one-quarter of pregnancies are aborted, Rocha (1996) reports a high level of abortions by women who have earlier experienced cesarean sections, both procedures apparently being frequently advised by their doctors.

In contrast, Hutter reports that abortion in Russia is carried out much more for social than economic reasons. Sometimes there, too, the reason is an unsatisfactory and often drunken husband. But as in most of Eastern Europe, the predominant motivator is the housing shortage. This is graphically illustrated by the fact that one-quarter of all married couples are still living with their parents—usually the husband's—eleven years after marriage.

THE IMMENSE IMPORTANCE OF REGION

The only way to understand the contemporary abortion situation is to take a regional approach. Regions differ dramatically in cultural, religious, and historical backgrounds, and the experience of countries in the same region affects them all. This book makes it clear that researchers in any particular region tend to generalize this experience to a greater extent than is warranted for the world as a whole.

The most furious arena of the contemporary debate is Latin America, almost wholly Catholic and with a powerful institutionalized church having a long history of political intrusion. It is no accident that so many of the researchers and contenders in today's abortion debate are Latin Americans. The Latin American papers in this volume report a continent-wide attempt not only to enact and enforce harsh legislation to suppress abortion but also to change national constitutions in order to entrench clauses making future attempts to liberalize abortion legislation difficult to achieve (Rocha 1996; Lerner and Salas).

The West, even at its most Catholic, is now different. In most countries, secular forces have achieved reasonably liberal legislation or have ensured that stricter legislation is rarely enforced. Most women who want an abortion can get one, frequently within a national health service. The most characteristic aspect of the contemporary Western situation is the lack of desire by both politicians and church leaders that this situation should be debated and that the society and polity should be traumatized in a Latin American fashion. The exception is, of course, the United States, but even here the debate is cooling and a similar kind of silent de facto compromise appears to be being sought.

A completely different pattern developed in Eastern Europe's communist countries, where for most of the time abortion was legal, not discouraged, and free (Hutter; Serbanescu et al.; Stloukal 1996). It was resorted to on a massive scale partly because of housing and other difficulties and partly because contraceptives were not easily available. Yet this is not the whole story, for it is also one of philosophy of life and morals. The communist regimes had directly attacked bourgeois morality and its religious basis. What is interesting is just how successful this attack was, apparently disproving any suggestion that people have an innate apprehension of abortion as being the equivalent of taking life or destroying motherhood already under way. Stloukal (1996) goes much further and indicts an induced passivity and a desire to leave the decision to the patriarchal state and the patriarchal medical system. Eastern European doctors came to look upon fertility control as a medical matter.

Much the same picture may be painted for the Third World's communist regimes, China, Vietnam, and Cuba (Mundigo). In Cuba, the only Latin American country with legalized abortion, half of all pregnancies are terminated, even though three-quarters of the population practice—admittedly often badly—family planning. Just as Christianity has offered little opposition to abortion in Cuba, Buddhism has not provided a bulwark against it in Vietnam.

The fact that abortion for any cause is banned in most African countries, while liberal but largely ineffective legislation exists in only two, is often taken to show that abortion in the region is suppressed to a greater extent than anywhere else in the world. The reality is very different (Anarfi; Levin; Orobaton 1996; Renne; Stambach; Caldwell and Caldwell 1984), and effective restriction has largely been confined to South Africa. Elsewhere, pragmatic governments have no wish to argue with the Christian church or with traditional attitudes that abortion is both unnatural and linked to witchcraft, but existing legislation is not enforced. A large proportion of sub-Saharan doctors gain a considerable part of their income from abortion. Indeed, as the number of modern doctors has risen, abortions in the better-off parts of the region have become increasingly medicalized and increasingly safe. They have also become increasingly certain compared with older herbal methods (Anarfi; Levin; Stambach). The reason why Africa probably has the lowest level of abortions of any major world region is not suppression but lower levels of economic development and a continuing acceptance of high fertility. The exact level of abortion is difficult to determine; traditions of postpartum and other sexual abstinence make it hazardous to attempt Orobaton's approach (1996) employing Bongaarts's models. Eventually, laws will begin to follow practice, as Anarfi points out occurred in Ghana during the 1985 legal recodification. As yet, abortion is most likely to be practiced by young women wishing to continue with education or to hold a job in the modern sector of the economy. Strong pressures in southern and East Africa to reduce polygyny levels mean that men cannot take on their young pregnant girlfriends as additional wives in the way that was so easy in the past (Stambach).

South Asia presents a varied picture as portrayed for India (Khan and Patel 1996; Rajan, Mishra, and Vimala 1996), Bangladesh (Amin; Ahmed, Sarkar, and Rahman 1996; Ahmed, Haque, Hossain, and Alam 1996), Pakistan (Fikree et al. 1996), and Sri Lanka (De Silva 1996). Probably over 6 million abortions a year occur in India (Chabra and Nuna 1994), accounting for perhaps one-sixth of pregnancies and one-quarter of all fertility control. Abortion in approved premises is legal and not disapproved by either the state or Hinduism. Yet 90 percent are performed clandestinely by nurses or self-taught women. The reason is that the latter guarantee secrecy, which, given the South Asian family system, is absolutely necessary for the unmarried and preferable for the married. Many rural women do not even know how to obtain a legal abortion. In Bangladesh, government-backed menstrual regulation has overcome this problem, and around 15 percent of pregnancies or supposed pregnancies end that way. Abortion is still illegal, without the law being strongly enforced, in both Pakistan and Sri Lanka. In both countries there is a movement toward greater legalization, especially for menstrual regulation, and indeed the latter is practiced openly in Sri Lanka by the Marie Stopes clinics (De Silva 1996). There seems little doubt that all of South Asia will move toward legalized menstrual regulation and probably to full legalization of abortion without strong opposition.

Elsewhere in the Muslim world, abortion is rarely legal, although Tunisia has offered abortion by choice for thirty years. Another exception is Turkey, where a liberal abortion law came into force in 1983—a reaction to a level of illegal abortions that probably terminated around 13 percent of pregnancies. Now, over 20 percent of pregnancies are legally terminated (Icduygu 1996).

THE GENERAL PICTURE

It is not often realized in the Catholic world just how little ethical and moral opposition there is to abortion in Confucian, Shintoist, and Hindu countries as well as in communist and excommunist ones and widely in the secular West. Opposition in Islam is not firmly rooted, and most Muslim countries will probably eventually accept menstrual regulation at least. The United States and Latin America are almost certain to move to the European position where abortion is silently accepted.

For the demographer, there are other issues of interest. Abortion is clearly now playing a major role in Third World demographic transition and in maintaining below-replacement-level fertility in most industrialized countries and some developing ones. It probably explains 35 to 40 percent of all fertility control in the world. The question arises whether this was also true of the late-eighteenth-century French fertility decline or the more general Western nineteenth-century fertility transition. It may seem unlikely because of abortion's very primitive and dangerous nature in those times, but contraception was also primitive and difficult to practice. This question is central to demographic transition, but we will probably never have a trustworthy answer.

What we do know about the contemporary world is that for countries in the middle of demographic transition, family planning and abortion usually both rise together. This shows that there is an increasing determination to control fertility, often the product of a successful family-planning program. It also shows that couples who have gone so far as to accept contraception are often so annoyed at its failure that they are provoked to an unusual degree to compensate for the failure by having an abortion. This attitude is also frequently taken by governments and family-planning programs in countries where abortion is legal. There is not always a succession of failed contraception and then abortion. In many countries—those of Eastern Europe as well as Japan and Cuba, for instance—a great number of women and couples opt for abortion as the preferred and least intrusive method of family planning.

Abortion directly or indirectly affects much of the world's population. It is spectacularly under-measured and under-researched. The ICPD urged that this situation should be changed, but little evidence exists of more research resources or greater numbers of social scientists being moved toward this important, and often tragic, area. They are restrained by a dislike of the contentious atmosphere and the weak statistical base. Hopefully, these problems will increasingly be seen as a challenge rather than a deterrent.

NOTE

1. In-text citations without dates are to chapters in this book. Other citations have corresponding references that provide the usual details of publication and are listed in the

following section. The papers listed as published in *Demography India* were also presented at the conference on which this volume is based.

REFERENCES

Ahmed, M. K., A. H. Sarkar, and M. Rahman. 1996. "Determinants of Induced Abortion in Rural Bangladesh." *Demography India* 25 (1): 105–18.

Ahmed, S. B. e-Khuda, I. Haque, B. Hossain, and A. Alam. 1996. "Induced Abortion in Rural Bangladesh: What Do We Know?" Paper presented at the International Union for the Scientific Study of Population Seminar on The Sociocultural and Political Context of Abortion, March 1996, Trivandrum, India.

Caldwell, J., and P. Caldwell. 1994. "Marital Status and Abortion in sub-Saharan Africa." In *Nuptiality in Sub-Saharan Africa: Contemporary Anthropological and Demographic Perspectives,* ed. C. Bledsoe and G. Pison, 274–95. Oxford, Clarendon.

Caldwell, P., and J. Caldwell. 1987. "Fertility Control as Innovation: A Report on In-Depth Interviews in Ibadan, Nigeria." In *The Cultural Roots of African Fertility Regimes,* ed. Etienne van de Walle and J. Akin Ebigbola, 233–51. Philadelphia and Ile-Ife, Nigeria: Population Studies Center, University of Pennsylvania, and Department of Demography and Social Statistics, Obafemi Awolowo University.

Chabra, R., and S. C. Nuna. 1994. *Abortion in India: An Overview.* New Delhi: Veerendra.

De Silva, W. I. 1996. "The Silent Cry: Sociocultural and Political Factors Influencing Induced Abortion in Sri Lanka." Paper presented at the International Union for the Scientific Study of Population Seminar on The Sociocultural and Political Context of Abortion, March 1996, Trivandrum, India.

Fikree, F. F., N. Rizvi, S. Jamil, and T. Husain. 1996. "The Emerging Problem of Induced Abortions in Squatter Settlements of Karachi, Pakistan." *Demography India* 25 (1): 119–30.

Frejka, T. 1993. "The Role of Induced Abortion in Contemporary Fertility Regulation." In *International Population Conference, Montreal 1993,* 1:209–13. Liège, Belgium: International Union for the Scientific Study of Population.

Icduygu, I. 1996. "Correlates of Timing of Induced Abortion in Turkey." *Demography India* 25 (1): 131–46.

Johansson, A., L.T.N. Tuyet, N. T. Lap, and K. Sundstrom. 1996. "A Study of Abortions in Two Villages in Thai Binh Province, Vietnam." Paper presented at the International Union for the Scientific Study of Population Seminar on The Sociocultural and Political Context of Abortion, Trivandrum, India.

Khan, M. E., and B. C. Patel. 1996. "Level of Unwanted Pregnancies and Its Consequences: Qualitative Information from Bihar, India." Paper presented at the International Union for the Scientific Study of Population Seminar on The Sociocultural and Political Context of Abortion, Trivandrum, India.

Leal, O. F., and J.M.G. Fachel. 1996. "Abortion in South Brazil: Contraceptive Practices and Gender Negotiation." Paper presented at the International Union for the Scientific Study of Population Seminar on The Sociocultural and Political Context of Abortion, Trivandrum, India.

Mejia, C. M. 1996. "A Critique of the Role of the Catholic Church in the Abortion Debate." Paper presented at the International Union for the Scientific Study of Population Seminar on The Sociocultural and Political Context of Abortion, Trivandrum, India.

Orobaton, N. 1996. "Are Unsafe Induced Abortions Contributing to Fertility Decline in Africa? Findings from Egypt and Zimbabwe." *Demography India* 25 (2): 261–74.

Rajan, S. I., U. S. Mishra, and T. K. Vimala. 1996. "Role of Abortion in the Fertility Transition in Kerala." Paper presented at the International Union for the Scientific Study of Population Seminar on The Sociocultural and Political Context of Abortion, Trivandrum, India.

Rocha, I.B.D. 1996. "The Abortion Issue in Brazil: A Study of the Debate in Congress." Paper presented at the International Union for the Scientific Study of Population Seminar on The Sociocultural and Political Context of Abortion, Trivandrum, India.

Stloukal, L. 1996. "Eastern Europe's Abortion Culture: Puzzles of Interpretation." Paper presented at the International Union for the Scientific Study of Population Seminar on The Sociocultural and Political Context of Abortion, Trivandrum, India.

Sundstrom, K. 1996. "Abortion across Social and Cultural Borders." *Demography India* 25 (1): 93–104.

World Health Organization. 1994. *Abortion: A Tabulation of Available Data on the Frequency and Mortality of Unsafe Abortion.* 2d ed. Geneva: Maternal Health and Safe Motherhood Program, Division of Family Health, World Health Organization.

———. 1998. *Unsafe Abortion: Global and Regional Estimates of Incidence of and Mortality Due to Unsafe Abortion.* 3d ed. Geneva: World Health Organization.

Chapter 2

Abortion: A Worldwide Overview

Susheela Singh, Stanley K. Henshaw, and Kathleen Berentsen

Worldwide, women have always turned to abortion as a last resort to prevent unwanted births, both historically and now. Moreover, they have done so even where abortion has been dangerous or forbidden. Even in societies where large families were preferred, abortion was nevertheless sought out to protect the family's honor by preventing births outside of a recognized union or marriage, to protect women's health by preventing births that were considered undesirable for reasons such as close spacing of births or the age of the mother, and to protect the family from poverty and deprivation. In communities where a small family was desired, women used abortion to limit family size as well as for the other reasons just mentioned. Increasingly, women now seek abortion because they cannot afford more children, because an additional child may prevent them from working, because the timing of a birth may interrupt their education, or because the relationship they are in is unstable. Despite the universality of the practice of abortion, however, it is clear that there are wide variations across countries in access to safe abortion services; in the legal status of abortion; in societies' acceptance of abortion and in the prevailing moral and ethical views concerning its practice; and, according to the limited information available, in the actual level or incidence of abortion.

Abortion techniques are described in some of the earliest medical texts of China and Egypt, and the practice of abortion was advocated by the ancient Greeks to regulate population size. It was used with few if any restrictions in the period of the Roman Empire. In much of the non-Western world, abortion prohibitions were not part of indigenous cultural, religious, or legal tradition but were imported as part of colonial, imperial, or Western influence in the past two centuries, when legal restrictions increased in the colonial countries themselves. In addition, as David (1981) has pointed out in summarizing the research of numerous scholars, the perspective of Western religions on abortion is complex, but "no major religion, with the possible exception of Roman Catholicism, has a unified position on the matter of induced abortion. The overall impression obtained from the historical perspective is that abortion was practiced in virtually every society, despite the great variation in cultural and moral views. As a result, ... distinctions must be made between official, semi-official and non-official religious attitudes and actual behaviors as perceived within the socio-cultural context of a given time.... Some flexibility can be found most everywhere and even the strictest prohibitions are seldom fully enforced" (4).

Perhaps not unexpectedly, historical sources give little sense of the extent of the use of abortion. Although we may not expect to find quantitative information on abortion in the past, the lack of reliable quantitative information on the incidence of abortion even up to the present day is more surprising. Despite improvement in measurement of many other aspects of reproductive behavior, this one remains very difficult to measure with accuracy in most countries. These difficulties persist even in some countries where abortion is legal, even where the level of education is high—normally an indicator of better quality of reporting—and they are found in both developed and developing countries. Clearly there are more factors involved in willingness to report on this aspect of reproductive behavior than with most others. The legal status of abortion is one of them: where abortion is illegal, it is to be expected that fear of repercussions would greatly reduce the willingness of both providers of abortion and of women themselves to report on the topic. But in addition, ethical, moral, and religious values and beliefs are reflected in societal attitudes and public opinion concerning abortion, and they affect women's willingness to discuss and report on abortion. This is seen in the fact that even in many countries where abortion is legal and widely practiced, a high proportion of women will not report abortions that they have had in conventional surveys.

Although this chapter's focus is not on the measurement of the level of abortion, the availability and quality of quantitative information on abortion is likely to be relevant to analyses of many other aspects or issues concerning abortion, be they legal, political, psychological, anthropological, or historical. Reasonably accurate measurement of the level of abortion and of how it may have changed over time would greatly increase our ability to develop and improve theoretical frameworks for understanding the practice of abortion and for understanding the very different role it has played in different social groups. This chapter tries to describe the existing quantitative information on abortion, to highlight the difficulties of obtaining information on abortion, and to point out some of the resulting inaccuracies and limitations of existing data on its incidence.

We first discuss the difficulties of obtaining information on abortion and the different methodological approaches that have been tried. Next we review available information on the level of abortion worldwide. The implications of unsafe abortion for women's health are then briefly reviewed. Finally, we discuss the role of abortion as a determinant of fertility.

METHODOLOGIES FOR MEASURING THE INCIDENCE OF ABORTION

Data on the number of induced abortions are obtained by a wide range of approaches that include registration systems but that also include surveys, reports of complications treated in hospitals, and indirect estimation techniques based on inferences about natural fertility and the contributions of contraception and abortion. All approaches have limitations and problems in the quality and completeness of the estimates they yield, and the problems encountered with a given approach can vary from setting to setting. Two reviews of methodologies for research on abortion include discussion of estimation methodology and suggest the difficulties involved in work in this area (Coeytaux, Leonard, and Royston 1989; Barreto et al. 1992). A brief discussion of the main approaches to obtaining estimates of the level of abortion is helpful because it allows the user to evaluate the resulting estimates and to better judge the range of error associated with different estimates.

Registration Systems

In some countries, providers of abortions (hospitals, clinics, private doctors) are required to complete and submit a form to a governmental body for each abortion procedure that they perform. Examples of such countries are New Zealand, Japan, and most countries in western Europe. In addition, forty-six of the fifty-one administrative areas (fifty states and Washington, D.C.) within the United States have a registration system. One potentially important problem typically encountered with this otherwise very good reporting system is the tendency of some providers (often private doctors but sometimes clinics as well) to either not complete the form for every procedure or to not complete any forms at all. Depending on how important nonreporting providers are in a given country, this can result in a significant level of underreporting. An advantage of this system of reporting, even where it is incomplete, is that some sociodemographic characteristics of the women obtaining an abortion are typically also recorded.

In some areas, including most of eastern Europe, the former Soviet states, Australia, and Quebec in Canada, data are generated from administrative records of providers or of the funding agency. In the formerly communist countries, these systems may miss providers that are not under the control of the Ministry of Health, whereas Quebec and Australia are examples where they miss abortions that are not reimbursed by national health insurance. In Austria, administrative records fail to distinguish between induced and spontaneous abortions.

Surveys or "Censuses" of Providers

This approach is only infrequently applied. One of the better-known cases where it is used, and used successfully, is the United States. Periodic surveys of providers have yielded more complete information on the numbers of abortions than the existing registration systems, which are implemented by the states and compiled at the national level by the Centers for Disease Control (CDC), an agency of the federal government. In 1996, the CDC collected registration data from the central health agencies of forty-six states and the District of Columbia as well as from hospitals and other facilities in four states, but it obtained a count that was 11 percent fewer than that from the survey of abortion providers carried out by the Alan Guttmacher Institute, a private nonprofit agency (Henshaw 1998). This may be particular to the situation in the United States because the registration system is an uneven patchwork across states and also because of the reluctance of some providers (especially private doctors) to complete reporting forms.

One difficulty of this approach is that it requires obtaining and maintaining the trust and cooperation of providers. It also requires continuous maintenance and updating of a name and address list of all providers. An additional and unique difficulty of the approach as applied in the case of the United States is that because the surveys are carried out by a private nonprofit organization, having data collection at regular intervals may not be always possible, depending on the availability of funding and other factors.

Estimates of the number of legal menstrual regulations in Bangladesh were made by surveying a sample of personnel trained to perform vacuum aspiration and the results projected to the country (Begum, Kamal, and Kamal 1987). In Nigeria, a probability sample of physicians and hospitals was surveyed to ascertain the number of abortions performed by doctors and the number of women treated for nonmedical induced abortions. This is the only nationally representative survey of abortion providers conducted in a country where abortion is prohibited under most circumstances (Henshaw et al. 1998).

Other provider surveys carried out in countries where abortion is prohibited under most circumstances have been limited to nonrandom samples. Surveys of traditional providers carried out in Mexico, the Philippines, and Thailand produced useful information about women who have abortions as well as the conditions under which abortions were performed and the methods used (International Fertility Research Program 1981).

Surveys of Women or Community Surveys

Some retrospective fertility surveys have included questions on whether a woman has had any abortions, and some have also asked separately about the number of induced and spontaneous abortions. Various approaches have been taken: questions on abortion have been integrated into a full pregnancy history or probe questions on abortion or pregnancy losses have been asked only when intervals between live births are very long or a few separate questions have been asked about abortion after a birth history was obtained. In general, these approaches, which involve an interviewer directly questioning the respondent about abortion, have obtained estimates of abortion that are implausibly low, often lower even than the expected level of spontaneous abortion. A review of the experience of the World Fertility Survey with collecting data on pregnancy loss concluded that "judged against agreed-upon levels of spontaneous loss in human populations, WFS surveys measured from 50 to 80 percent of recognizable losses. The coverage of induced abortions appears to be much worse" (Casterline 1989, p. 81).

In-person interviews of women in similar surveys in developed countries, even where abortion is legal, have achieved varying results. In the United States, the 1982 National Survey of Family Growth (NSFG) achieved 48 percent reporting (compared with independent external sources), but by 1988, the NSFG obtained only 35 percent reporting of abortions (Jones and Forrest 1992). The most recent NSFG survey, carried out in 1995, introduced two new data collection procedures. The main interview was personal but was conducted through a process called a computer-assisted personal interview (CAPI), in which the interviewer entered responses directly into a computer that immediately checked data so that corrections could be made at that time. In addition, at the end of the interview, an innovative procedure—audio computer-assisted self-interviewing (ACASI), which allowed respondents to listen to questions over an audiotape (or read them from the screen) and to respond confidentially by directly entering responses into the computer—was used specifically to improve reporting on sensitive topics such as abortion. The combined effect of these two new procedures greatly improved reporting: 59 percent of all abortions were reported in the 1995 NSFG, compared with 35 percent in the 1988 NSFG (Fu et al. 1998). Each procedure contributed to this result: reporting was 45 percent in the main interview alone (CAPI) and 52 percent based on self-reported data alone (ACASI).

Surveys done in the Czech Republic and Romania achieved about 45 to 50 percent and 80 percent reporting, respectively, also using a direct in-person interview (Czech Statistical Office, World Health Organization, and Centers for Disease Control 1995; Institute for Mother and Child Care, Bucharest, and Centers for Disease Control 1995). These are both countries where abortion is legal and is at a moderate (Czech Republic) to very high level (Romania); in one case a very high level of reporting was achieved, but in the other, as in the United States, despite the fact that abortion is legal and has been so for many years (the Czech Republic), women's willingness to report abortions was quite low.

Surveys in South Korea (Cho and Ahn 1993) and Turkey (Ministry of Health, Turkey, Haceteppe University Institute of Population Studies, and Macro International 1994) have obtained reports of large numbers of induced abortions, suggesting that reporting was at least fairly complete in these countries. The use of abortion to control fertility is widely accepted in both countries.

Special attempts to assure confidentiality and secrecy of the woman's response to questions concerning abortion appear to have some success. A large-scale 1992 survey of urban households in Colombia, in which women self-administered a short questionnaire, sealed it, and placed it into a special box, achieved a reported annual rate of 24.6 abortions per 1,000 women aged fifteen to forty-nine for the period of a few years before 1992 (Zamudio, Rubiano, and Wartenburg 1994).[1] This rate was 73 percent of the rate estimated for all Colombia for the year 1989, based on an indirect estimation methodology using hospitalization data (Singh and Wulf 1994).

Indirect Estimation Techniques

In this section we discuss the more commonly used approaches to making indirect estimates of the level of abortion. Estimates for any country or subpopulation require understanding the limitations of the type of data on which the estimates will be based and the conditions of abortion provision in that setting. Any number of approaches or combinations of techniques may prove necessary, depending on the particular setting.

World Health Organization's Estimates for the World and for Regions

The basic element in these estimates is the ratio of abortions treated in hospital (both induced and spontaneous) to deliveries occurring in the same hospitals. These data come from hospital-based studies or in a few cases from national level hospitalization statistics. This ratio was adjusted by subtracting .034, the expected ratio of hospitalized spontaneous abortions to live births.[2] Other adjustments are made to allow for the fact that half or more of induced abortions do not result in complications requiring hospitalization and for the fact that abortion ratios are lower in rural than in urban areas. Factors that enter into making assumptions are the total fertility rate (TFR), contraceptive prevalence, and the proportion of deliveries that take place in hospitals or other health care facilities.

Estimates of Abortion Level in Countries Where Abortion Is Highly Restricted

A methodology was developed and applied in 1991 to estimate the total number of induced abortions based on the number of hospitalized abortion cases in three Latin American countries (Singh and Wulf 1991). The reported national number of hospitalized abortion cases (including induced and spontaneous abortions) was adjusted for undercoverage and for misreporting; then the number of spontaneous abortions was estimated and subtracted from the total number of hospitalized cases.[3] The number of hospitalized induced abortion cases in each country was multiplied by a factor that reflects the number of induced abortions that are performed for every one that causes a complication serious enough to result in hospitalization. For example, if one in every five induced abortions resulted in a complication that needed hospitalization, the factor or multiplier would be five. The total number of abortions and the resulting rates were estimated for six countries (Singh and Wulf 1994, data shown in Table 2.3) using factors ranging from 3 to 7. The midpoint factor, 5, was recommended as the most plausible but perhaps somewhat conservative multiplier, given the conditions of provision of abortion in Latin America in the late 1980s and early 1990s, the period for which these estimates were made. Earlier studies in the 1960s suggested that the multiplier at that time was about 3 (indicating that one in every three induced abortions was hospitalized) (Armijo and Monreal 1965; Monreal 1976). Although this methodology produces estimates that give only a rough idea of the level of abortion, they are useful in the absence of more accurate data.

More recently, this methodology was applied to the Philippines and, somewhat modified, to two other countries, Bangladesh and Nigeria. The modification in the latter two countries involved combining indirect estimates based on hospitalized abortion patients with estimates of safe procedures, menstrual regulations (MRs) in Bangladesh, and physician-provided abortions in Nigeria. A representative sample survey of medical facilities was carried out in Nigeria to obtain this information, and in the case of Bangladesh, official estimates of MRs were used and adjusted based on available data on completeness of reporting.

Cross-checking results with other methodologies, always a useful procedure, supports the general findings from this estimation approach. For example, Frejka and Atkin (1996) have estimated that the abortion rate (the number of abortions per 1,000 women aged 15–49 per year) was 41 for the region of Latin America in the late 1980s, a rate that is similar to the results from Singh and Wulf (1994). In this study Frejka and Atkin (1996) used a technique developed by D. Nortman to deduce the number of abortions after calculating the number of births averted by contraception and comparing this with the expected total number of births if there were no contraception or abortion.

Estimates Based on the Bongaarts Proximate Determinants Model

Abortion levels may be inferred from Bongaarts's model of the proximate determinants of fertility in situations where measures are available for the other major determinants (marriage, contraception, and postpartum infecundability) and are lacking only for abortion. Application of the Bongaarts model yields an index of abortion and an estimate of the proportion of fertility reduction that may be attributed to abortion (Bongaarts and Potter 1983). This approach is useful because it is less demanding of data than some other approaches to estimating the role of the proximate determinants of fertility. However, small errors in measurement of the three other main determinants can have large effects on the estimated abortion index; variation from the assumed total fecundity rate of fifteen births would also strongly affect the estimate of the abortion rate, which is obtained by inference, and so would interactions between the determinants. In addition, the Bongaarts model excludes consideration of sexual activity, pregnancy, and abortion among the unmarried, and for this reason the index of abortion obtained from this model would reflect the level among married women only. Nevertheless, this model is often applied with the aim of estimating the relative contribution of the four major determinants of fertility and is sometimes used to estimate the level of abortion. A variant of this approach was developed and applied to married women only in three Latin American cities (Foreit and Nortman 1992).

Estimates Based on Repeat Abortion History

Henshaw (1989) discusses a method that uses information on the proportion of abortion patients who have had prior abortions to estimate the level of abortion. It is based on the observation that the correlation between the abortion rates of geographic areas (states or countries) and the proportion of abortions that are repeat procedures is very high. If, for a sample of women having abortions or being treated for complications of induced abortion, it is known what proportion of the women have had a prior induced abortion, the abortion rate can be estimated within broad limits for the population represented by the women. The estimate utilizes a regression coefficient calculated from countries with reasonably reliable data. The advantage of this method is that it can yield an approximate abortion rate with minimal data input; two important limitations are that the abortion rate is estimated for a period ten years prior and that the estimated rate is applicable only to the population for which the proportion with repeat abortions is available.

Other Approaches

In a country where abortion reporting is complete in some geographic divisions but not others, an estimate of the total number of abortions in the country can be made by assuming that the abortion rate in areas with incomplete reporting is the same as that in similar areas with more complete reporting. This method was used to produce estimates of 225,000 abortions in France in 1993 (Blayo 1985), compared with the reported total of 167,000, and of 333,000 in Italy in 1983, compared with 234,000 reported (Tosi et al. 1985). Yet another approach sometimes used when abortion is legally restricted but where the number of abortion deaths is known is to assume that each death represents a certain number of abortions, ranging from 100 to several thousand.

WORLDWIDE LEVELS OF ABORTION

Any description of the current worldwide incidence of abortion requires piecing together information from a number of sources. In some countries where abortion is legal and available, data collection systems exist, and information on the number of legal abortions is reasonably accurate. In many of these countries, some characteristics of women obtaining abortions are also available. However, in countries where abortion is highly restricted as well as in those with very few restrictions, there are no systems for collecting information on illegal abortion, and the only available statistics are estimates that range greatly in quality and are sometimes so rough as to be potentially misleading. In addition, for most of the developing world, estimates are available only at the regional level. Data-based country-level estimates have been attempted only in a few instances, and examples of these will be discussed. In this section we present an overview of the level of abortion across the world, by region, based on the most reliable of the available estimates. We also present measures for countries with reasonably complete reported information and for a few countries with reliable estimates. In addition, because important variations occur within countries and attention to national-level measures alone can often be misleading, we discuss examples of significant subgroup differences within countries.

Number of Abortions Worldwide

During the past few years, mainly with a focus on clandestine abortion and its consequences for women's health, the World Health Organization (WHO) has been at the forefront of estimating the number of "unsafe" abortions in the world; in making these estimates, WHO considered all abortions in countries where the procedure is highly legally restricted to be unsafe, even though in many of these countries, some abortions are performed by physicians using medically safe procedures in hygienic settings. WHO's most recent published estimate (1998) is that there were 19.9 million unsafe abortions globally in 1995. Combining WHO's estimate of unsafe abortions with separately collected official statistics of the number of abortions in countries where the procedure is legal under broad conditions (adjusted where reporting is known to be incomplete), it was estimated that 45.5 million abortions were performed worldwide in 1995. Approximately 25.6 million were in countries where abortion is legal, and about 19.9 million were unsafe or clandestine abortions. The worldwide annual total number of induced abortions may be put into perspective if we remember that, of the approximately 210 million pregnancies that occurred worldwide in 1995 (including an estimate of miscarriages), almost one-quarter ended in abortion (Alan Guttmacher Institute 1999).

Estimates of the number of unsafe abortions occurring in all developed and developing countries and in each region and subregion are shown in Table 2.1. Estimates of the number of safe abortions in each region have also been compiled using other sources and are shown in Table 2.1 (Henshaw, Singh, and Haas 1999).

Looking at the numbers in Table 2.1, a few less well known facts may be pointed out. It is perhaps not widely recognized that a substantial number of legal abortions occur in Southeast, South, and West Asia—principally in a few

Table 2.1

Global and Regional Estimates of the Total Number of Abortions, of the Number of Unsafe and Safe Abortions, and of the Abortion Rate and Ratio Circa 1995

	Number of abortions (millions)					
Region and Subregion	Total	Safe	Unsafe	Rate per 1000 women 15-44	Rate per 1000 women 15-49	Ratio per 100 pregnancies*
World	45.5	25.6	19.9	34.8	31.5	25.5
More developed regions**	10.0	9.1	0.9	38.9	33.6	41.7
Excluding Eastern Europe	3.8	3.7	0.1	20.2	17.4	26.4
Less developed regions	35.5	16.5	19.0	33.8	31.0	23.0
Excluding China	24.9	5.9	19.0	33.3	30.6	20.3
Estimates by region^						
Africa	5.0	^^	5.0	32.7	30.2	14.8
Eastern Africa	1.9	^^	1.9	41.1	38.1	16.2
Middle Africa	0.6	^^	0.6	35.1	32.4	13.8
Northern Africa	0.6	^^	0.6	17.4	16.1	11.9
Southern Africa	0.2	^^	0.2	18.8	17.2	12.0
Western Africa	1.6	^^	1.6	36.6	33.8	14.8

Asia	26.8	16.9	9.9	33.3	30.4	25.2
Eastern Asia	12.5	12.5	^^	35.7	32.3	34.5
South-central Asia	8.4	1.9	6.5	27.8	25.4	17.7
South-eastern Asia	4.7	1.9	2.8	40.0	36.9	27.7
Western Asia	1.2	0.7	0.5	31.7	29.2	19.5
Europe	7.7	6.8	0.9	48.4	42.1	47.9
Eastern Europe	6.2	5.4	0.8	89.6	78.0	64.8
Northern Europe	0.4	0.3	^^	18.3	15.6	23.3
Southern Europe	0.8	0.7	0.1	24.4	21.3	34.1
Western Europe	0.4	0.4	^^	10.6	9.2	17.2
Latin America	4.2	0.2	4.0	36.7	33.6	27.1
Caribbean	0.4	0.2	0.2	50.1	45.4	35.2
Central America	0.9	^^	0.9	30.3	28.1	20.9
South America	3.0	^^	3.0	38.9	35.5	29.5
Northern America	1.5	1.5	^^	22.1	19.2	25.5
Oceania	0.1	0.1	^^	21.2	18.7	20.4

*Known pregnancies defined as abortions plus live births.

**Developed regions were defined here to include all countries in Europe and North America, Australia, Japan, and New Zealand; all other countries were classified as less developed.

^Regions as defined by the United Nations.

^^Fewer than 50,000 abortions.

Sources:

Populations: United Nations (1997a).
Births: United Nations (1997b).
Illegal abortions: World Heath Organization (1998).
Legal abortions: See text.

countries, Bangladesh, India, Turkey, and Vietnam; the significant number of *unsafe* or clandestine abortions in eastern and southern Europe may also not be commonly recognized. In addition, this table shows some results that fit expectations: the very large number of unsafe abortions in Africa, Asia (other than East Asia), and Latin America and the predominance of unsafe abortion in these regions as well as the large number of legal abortions in East Asia, reflecting the presence of China in this subregion.

Abortion Rates and Ratios Worldwide

The abortion rate, or the number of abortions per 1,000 women of reproductive age per year, enables us to compare regions and countries, as well as subgroups within countries, in terms of the incidence of abortion. A second basic measure of abortion, the abortion ratio, or the proportion of pregnancies that is resolved by abortion, also allows comparisons across populations, in terms of the probability that, given that she is pregnant, a woman would choose abortion and be able to obtain it. The rate is most useful for describing the absolute level of abortion and the ratio for describing the probability that the average pregnant woman will have an abortion. The ratio can be misleading if it is at all construed to be a measure of the level of abortion: for example, the abortion ratio may rise or remain the same even as the abortion rate declines; similarly, one population may have a higher abortion rate than another even when its abortion ratio is lower. Care in interpretation of these two measures is essential.

Abortion Measures, Global and Regional

Abortion rates and ratios were calculated for each region of the world by combining the estimates of numbers of abortions shown in Table 2.1 with U.N. estimates of the number of women of reproductive age and the number of live births occurring in 1995 (United Nations 1997a, 1997b). Rates are shown for two base populations, women ages fifteen through forty-four and ages fifteen through forty-nine, to allow comparison with other studies.

The worldwide average abortion rate around 1995 is estimated to be 35 per 1,000 women aged fifteen through forty-four per year (Table 2.1). This is a moderately high rate and implies that if this rate remained unchanged, the average woman would have about 1.1 abortions in her lifetime (this is the total abortion rate, or TAR).[4] The average rate is slightly higher among all developed countries (38.9) than it is among all developing countries (33.8). This is due to the high rates that are found in the former Soviet Union and in eastern Europe, areas that together constitute about one-third of the total population in developed countries. Other parts of the developed world (the rest of Europe, North America, and Oceania) have much lower abortion rates (an average rate of 20).

Within the developing world, some significant variations are found. East, central, and West Africa (annual rates of 32.7 to 41.1) have notably higher estimated abortion rates than northern or southern Africa (rates of 17.4 to 18.8). There is somewhat less variation across the subregions of Asia, with rates ranging from 27.8 to 40.0, around an average regional rate of 33.3. In Latin America, the Central American subregion has a somewhat lower rate than the regional average (30.3 compared with 36.7), and the Caribbean subregion has a higher than average rate (50.1).

Abortion Measures in Countries with Reasonably Complete Statistics

Although not exhaustive, Table 2.2 presents, separately for countries with reasonably complete statistics (estimated to be 80 percent or more complete in Panel A) and for countries with data that are less than 80 percent complete or of unknown completeness (in Panel B), the number of legal abortions, the abortion rate, the abortion ratio, and the TAR. What is most striking is the extreme range of abortion rates, from a low of 6.5 in the Netherlands to a high of 77.7 in Cuba, considering countries with reasonably complete reporting. The rate is low in the Netherlands even though that country has one of the most liberal abortion laws, ready availability of free abortion services, and low fertility. One writer attributes this low rate to a culture of acceptance of sexuality along with an almost moralistic attitude about sexual responsibility and avoidance of unwanted pregnancy (Ketting 1994). A similarly wide range is found among countries with incomplete reporting, where the rates are, however, underestimates of actual levels. Even so, a few countries have very high rates of over 50—Romania, the Russian Federation, Ukraine, Vietnam, and Yugoslavia (Panel B of Table 2.2).

Most developed countries have rates between 10 and 20, but rates are much higher in eastern and central Europe and the countries of the former Soviet Union. It has been suggested that the high reliance on abortion in those countries developed because contraceptives were not readily available during the period of rapid fertility decline, and consequently abortion became a widely accepted if not preferred method of fertility control.

Official abortion statistics are available for most of the former Soviet bloc countries, but their completeness is uncertain. Before 1990, statistics were considered relatively accurate for most eastern and central European countries, but a large number of unofficial and illegal abortions took place in the Soviet Union. Since the transition from communism, abortion services have become available from private physicians and clinics in most countries of this subregion, and these providers may not report their abortions to government agencies. Therefore, the statistics may no longer be complete in eastern Europe and are probably even less complete in the former Soviet Union countries. The figures in Table 2.2 are therefore minimum estimates of actual numbers and abortion rates. Neverthe-

Table 2.2

Number of Legal Abortions, Rate per 1,000 Women Aged 15–44, Ratio per 100 Known Pregnancies,[1] and Total Abortion Rate[2] by Completeness of Data and Country

	Number[3]	Rate	Ratio	Total abortion rate
Panel A. Statistics believed to be complete				
Australia, 1995/96	91,900	22.2	26.4	0.67
Belarus, 1996	155,700	67.5	61.9	2.04
Belgium, 1996[4]	14,600	6.8	11.2	0.21
Bulgaria,1996	89,000	51.3	55.2	1.55
Canada, 1995[5]	106,700	15.5	22.0	0.49
Cuba, 1996	209,900	77.7	58.6	**2.33**
Czech Republic,1996	46,500	20.7	34.0	0.63
Denmark, 1995	17,700	16.1	20.3	0.48
England & Wales, 1996[6]	167,900	15.6	20.5	0.48
Estonia, 1996	16,900	53.8	56.0	1.63
Finland, 1996	10,400	10.0	14.7	0.31
Germany, 1996	130,900	7.6	14.1	**0.23**
Hungary, 1996	76,600	34.7	42.1	1.07
Israel, 1995	17,600	14.3	13.1	0.43
Kazakstan, 1996	178,000	43.9	41.3	**1.32**
Latvia, 1996	23,100	44.1	53.9	1.33
Netherlands, 1996[6]	22,400	6.5	10.6	**0.20**
New Zealand, 1995	13,700	16.4	19.1	0.49
Norway, 1996	14,300	15.6	19.1	0.47
Puerto Rico, 1991-1992	19,200	22.7	23.0	**0.68**
Scotland, 1996[7]	12,300	11.2	17.2	0.34
Singapore, 1996	14,400	15.9	22.8	**0.48**
Slovak Republic, 1996	24,300	19.7	28.8	**0.59**
Slovenia, 1996	10,400	23.2	35.7	0.70
Sweden, 1996	32,100	18.7	25.2	0.56
Switzerland, 1996[8]	12,800	8.4	13.3	**0.25**
Tunisia, 1996	19,000	8.6	7.8	**0.26**
USA, 1996	1,365,700	22.9	25.9	**0.69**

[1]Known pregnancies are defined as legal abortions plus live births; [2]The number of abortions that would be experienced by the average woman during her reproductive lifetime, given present age-specific abortion rates; [3]Rounded to the nearest 100 abortions; [4]Including abortions obtained in the Netherlands; [5]Including abortions obtained in the United States; [6]Residents only; [7]Including abortions obtained in England and Wales; [8]Includes estimates for two of the twenty-six cantons. Numbers in bold were estimated by multiplying the rate by 30 and dividing by 1,000; all others were calculated using age-specific abortion rates.

Table 2.2 *(continued)*

Armenia, 1996	31,300	35.4	39.4	**1.06**
Azerbaijan, 1996	28,400	16.0	18.0	0.49
Bangladesh, 1995/96[9]	100,300	3.8	3.1	**0.11**
China, 1995	7,930,000	26.1	27.4	**0.78**
Croatia, 1996	12,300	12.9	18.7	0.38
France, 1995	156,200	12.4	17.7	0.37
Georgia, 1996	26,600	21.9	33.2	0.66
Hong Kong, 1996	25,000	15.1	27.9	0.45
India, 1995/96	566,500	2.7	2.1	**0.08**
Ireland, 1996[10]	4,900	5.9	8.9	**0.18**
Italy, 1996	140,400	11.4	21.1	**0.34**
Japan, 1995	343,000	13.4	22.4	0.40
Korea (South), 1996[11]	230,000	19.6	24.6	**0.59**
Kyrgyzstan, 1996	24,600	22.4	17.5	**0.67**
Lithuania, 1996	27,800	34.4	41.5	**1.03**
Macedonia, 1996	14,200	28.5	31.1	**0.86**
Moldova, 1996	38,900	38.8	42.7	0.83
Mongolia, 1996	15,600	25.9	18.2	**0.78**
Romania, 1996	394,400	78.0	63.0	**2.34**
Russian Federation, 1995	2,287,300	68.4	62.6	2.56
South Africa, 1997	26,400	2.7	2.4	**0.08**
Spain, 1996	51,000	5.7	12.6	**0.17**
Tadjikistan, 1990[12]	55,500	49.1	21.2	**1.47**
Turkey, 1993[11]	351,300	25.0	20.5	**0.75**
Turkmenistan, 1990[12]	37,200	44.9	22.9	**1.35**
Ukraine, 1996	635,600	57.2	57.6	**1.72**
Uzbekistan, 1996	63,200	11.8	9.5	**0.35**
Vietnam, 1996[13]	1,520,000	83.3	43.7	**2.50**
Yugoslavia, FR, 1993	119,300	54.6	45.8	**1.64**
Zambia, 1983	1,200	0.4	0.4	**0.01**

[9]Menstrual regulations; [10]Based on Irish residents who obtained abortions in England; [11]Based on surveys of ever-married women ages twenty to forty-four (Korea) and fifteen to forty-nine (Turkey); [12]Includes spontaneous abortions; [13]Excludes an estimated 500,000 private sector abortions.

Source: Henshaw, Singh, and Haas, 1999. Reproduced with the permission of The Alan Guttmacher Institute.

less, the official rates are above 30 in most countries of this subregion and often much higher than this. In Poland the low official rate is the result of legal restrictions, but an unknown number of women obtain abortions in other countries or illegally within Poland.

However, abortion rates have been falling in the majority of eastern and central European countries since the early 1990s, or from the late 1980s in some instances. Though these trends partly reflect the deterioration of the reporting systems, the consensus is that abortion rates are in fact falling largely due to better and increased use of modern contraceptives. Trends in contraceptive use, pregnancy, and abortion need to be monitored, however, to assess whether these positive improvements are continuing or not.

In most countries with incomplete reporting (Panel B of Table 2.2), it is known that many physicians fail to report the abortions they perform. This may be because of oversight, because they do not fulfill all of the legal requirements for performing abortions, or because they do not want to attract the attention of tax officials. India is a special case where, although abortion is legal under broad conditions, most abortions are not registered and not reflected in official statistics. The official reported number of close to 600,000 abortions annually is estimated to be about one-tenth of the actual number. The estimate for India was projected from estimates made in 1966, which had been based on assumptions about the ratio of abortions to live births (Chhabra and Nuna 1994). In Ireland no legal abortions are performed, but over 4,000 women who obtain abortions in England each year give Irish addresses, and an unknown number of other Irish women give local addresses.

Abortion Measures in Countries with Incomplete or No Reported Statistics but with Estimates

Countries that fall into this category are relatively few, partly because creating country-level estimates in the absence of any reported statistics, or where reported information is incomplete, is a time-consuming and difficult task. Yet estimates for countries are very useful for policy makers because policy is made at the country level, and activities to influence the legal status of abortion or service provision tend to be most effective when they are country specific. A large part of the difficulty in making defensible estimates for countries in this category is the gathering of information that does exist on abortion and the development of techniques and assumptions that are unique to each country and that are tailored to the situation in that country regarding the provision of abortion services and the types of information available. Nevertheless, national-level estimates have been made for ten countries with no or only partial reported data on induced abortion (Singh and Wulf 1994; Singh et al. 1997; Henshaw et al. 1998; Huntington et al. 1998).

These estimates are based on the number of women who were hospitalized for abortion complications, building in adjustments for misreporting and un-

Table 2.3
Number of Estimated Abortions, Abortion Rate, and Abortion Ratio for Ten Countries, Based on Indirect Estimation Techniques

Country	Year	Number of abortions[1]	Abortion Rate per 1000 women 15-44	Abortion Ratio per 100 known pregnancies[2]
Bangladesh	1995	730,000	28.0	18.0
Brazil	1991	1,443,300	38.1	30.1
Chile	1990	159,600	45.4	35.3
Colombia	1989	288,400	33.7	26.0
Dominican Rep.	1992	82,500	43.7	27.9
Egypt	1996	324,000	23.0	15.7
Mexico	1990	533,100	23.3	17.1
Nigeria	1996	610,000	25.4	12.0
Peru	1989	271,200	51.8	30.0
Philippines	1994	401,000	25.0	16.0

[1]Rounded to the nearest 100 abortions.

[2]Known pregnancies are defined as legal abortions plus live births.

Sources: Henshaw et al. 1998; Henshaw et al. 1999; Huntington et al. 1998.

derreporting, excluding hospitalized spontaneous abortions, and finally making an assumption about the probability of a woman being hospitalized if she had an induced abortion. In the case of Bangladesh and Nigeria, estimates of unsafe abortions were combined with separate estimates of physician-provided procedures (MRs in the case of Bangladesh and induced abortions in the case of Nigeria). In nine of these ten cases, a range of estimates were made, and the medium-level estimates are shown in Table 2.3. The abortion rate (per 1,000 women ages fifteen through forty-four) ranges from a moderate level of 23.0 in Egypt to a high of 56.1 in Peru. Considering these levels in the context of regional estimates (Table 2.1) and estimates for individual countries (Table 2.2), it is clear that abortion is at a high level in many countries in the Latin American region.

Subgroup Differences in Level of Abortion

So far we have discussed estimates at a very aggregated level, the lowest level of aggregation being the country. Yet there are important differences in both the distribution of abortions and the abortion rate among population subgroups within countries. These differences should be borne in mind when explanatory hypotheses and theories are developed to explain differentials and trends across countries in the national level of abortion. The incidence of abortion or the abortion ratio may vary among population subgroups for many reasons, but two are perhaps most common: differing levels of unintended pregnancy due to differences in family size preferences and in the prevalence and effectiveness of contraceptive use and differences in the prevalence of sexual activity among unmarried women and acceptability of childbearing by unmarried women.

Some striking differences in the age, marital status, and family size of women having abortions are found across countries (Table 2.4). The pattern in North America and western Europe is of abortion being used mainly by unmarried women and by childless women to delay the start of childbearing. Adolescents in these regions also disproportionately resort to abortion when they become pregnant, compared with their likelihood of having a child. In contrast, in eastern Europe (the examples of Bulgaria, the Czech Republic, and Kazakhstan are shown) and in developing countries (data are shown for Latin America) married women, women over the age of twenty, and women with children (often women with several children) are much more likely to resort to abortion because it is chiefly used to space and to end childbearing. In the latter group of countries, either pregnancy among the unmarried is very low, as in India, or if unmarried women become pregnant, they are likely to have the child, and the pregnancy often leads to the formation of a union. In eastern and central Europe, it is common for teenagers who become pregnant to get married rather than to have an abortion, though these patterns are changing. Information from hospital-based studies and community surveys in sub-Saharan Africa shows that unmarried adolescents constitute a high proportion of all women hospitalized for abortion complications and suggests that this subgroup, in urban areas especially, is at increasingly high risk of unplanned pregnancy and unsafe abortion (Kinoti et al.

Table 2.4
Percentage Distribution According to Demographic Characteristics of Women Having Abortions in Selected Countries

Subgroup	Canada 1995	Netherlands 1992	England & Wales 1996	United States 1995	Bulgaria 1996	Czech Republic 1996	Kazakstan 1996	Average of 4 Latin American Countries[1] 1990
Marital Status								
Not Married	73	50	79	84	25	39	7	25
Married	27	50	21	16	75	61	93	75
Age								
Under 20	20	11	19	20	12	11	5	12
Older Than 20	80	89	81	80	88	89	95	88
Number of Children								
No Child	48	49	54	45	na	21	11	19
1 or more	52	51	46	55	na	79	89	81
Total	100	100	100	100	100	100	100	100

[1]The four countries are Bolivia, Colombia, Peru, and Venezuela. The percentage distributions are based on women who were hospitalized for abortion complications and who were classified as likely to have had an induced abortion.

Sources: Bankole, Singh, and Haas 1999; Singh and Wulf 1993.

1995; Konje and Obisesan 1991); however, other investigators have suggested that abortion is also used among women who already have children for spacing and have posited that the overall profile of women obtaining abortion in sub-Saharan Africa may be somewhat similar to that typical of other developing countries, with married adult women who have children accounting for the majority of abortions (Kinoti et al. 1995; Coeytaux 1988). Results reported in Kinoti et al. (1995) show that abortion complication patients had a mean parity of between two and three children and that their mean age was typically twenty-two through twenty-six, based on research in three East African countries and in many hospitals in each country.

Table 2.5 compares some characteristics of women who were hospitalized for abortion with women giving birth in three Latin American countries, Colombia, the Dominican Republic, and Peru. Although adolescents are a very small proportion of women hospitalized for abortion complications, it is nevertheless true that they are a somewhat larger proportion of this group than of all women giving birth. There is also some support for the generalization that women with secondary or higher education are more likely to have an abortion (if subgroup differences in the proportion hospitalized is an indication of differences in the likelihood of having an abortion) than they are to have a child. Women who were not using contraception at the time they became pregnant comprise a very high percentage of all women hospitalized for abortion complications, but contraceptive failure does contribute to abortion, and about 23 to 31 percent of hospitalized abortion patients had been using either a modern or a traditional method at the time they became pregnant.

A few striking examples of subgroup differences in the abortion rate in the United States, a country with reasonably complete reported data, are presented in Table 2.6. The difference in the abortion rate between married and unmarried women is extremely large among all races. The high rates among adolescents compared with all women are also notable. The much higher levels of abortion among nonwhite women overall compared with white women (56.0 versus 21.1) is also remarkable. However, although the abortion rate is higher among nonwhite women, the abortion ratio (the proportion of pregnancies that are resolved by abortion) is lower among both young and unmarried nonwhite women, compared with young and unmarried white women, indicating that the pregnancy rate among nonwhite adolescents and unmarried women is much higher than that among the comparable groups of white women. The abortion rate among non-Hispanic black and Hispanic women in the United States is also much higher than that among white women (Table 2.6).

A second example of large differences within a country is found in the Netherlands. The abortion rate among native-born Dutch women in 1992 was extremely low (3.5); by comparison, the rate among immigrant populations living in the Netherlands was much higher—32 to 35 among immigrants from Surinam and the islands of the Dutch Antilles and Aruba and 14 to 17 among immigrants from Morocco and Turkey (Rademakers 1994).

Table 2.5

Percent Distribution According to Characteristics of Women Having Abortions Compared with All Women Giving Birth in Three Latin American Countries

Characteristics	Colombia		Dominican Republic		Peru		
	Women hospitalized		Women hospitalized	Women 15-49	Women hospitalized		Women 15-49
	for induced abortion complications	with a birth in the past 5 years	for induced abortion complications	with a birth in the past 5 years	for induced abortion complications		with a birth in the past 5 years
	FLASOG 1990	DHS 1986	Paiewonsky 1990	DHS 1992	FLASOG 1990	Alcantara 1992	DHS 1988
	(N=2,696)	(N=1,868)	(N=350)	(N=3,021)	(N=1,342)	(N=333)	(N=2,021)
Age							
<20	14.5	6.9	16.5	10.4	8.9	8.0	5.8
20-24	27.1	27.0	32.7	29.6	21.3		21.2
25-29	25.5	28.1	25.3	26.5	26.5	53.0	25.6
30-34	16.2	19.8	14.8	18.0	19.6		20.6
35-39	11.8	11.8	5.6	9.4	15.7	31.0	14.6
40-44	4.9	4.8	4.3	4.6	7.8		8.4
>45		1.6	0.6	1.6		8.0	3.8
Education							
None	23.1	8.4	7.1	9.9	16.2	5.0	15.9
Primary	27.8	74.0	58.5	73.7	27.4	30.0	53.1
Secondary	30.4	15.0	29.3	10.1	22.9	48.0	25.1
Higher	18.6	2.7	5.1	6.2	33.5	17.0	5.8
Marital Status							
Legal Union		49.5	14.2	23.7			57.0
Consensual Union	66.0	35.0	73.6	59.0	84.9	92.0	31.9
Never married	34.0	6.9	3.1	1.0	15.1	6.0	3.9
Div./Sep./Wid.		8.6	10.0	16.4	--	2.0	7.2
No. of Live Births							
0	21.7	0.0	7.5	0.0	17.7	10.0	0.0
1	22.1	27.2	34.7	24.8	15.3		20.7
2		17.2	26.2	21.2			17.9
3	56.2	32.2	16.7	16.9	67.1		14.9
4 or more		23.4	14.9	37.2		90.0	46.5

Sources: Colombia: FLASOG, 1990 Survey of Hospitalized Abortion Patients. DHS, 1986 Special Tabulations.

Dominican Republic: Paiewonsky, D. (1993) and DHS, 1992 Special Tabulations.

Peru: FLASOG, 1990 Survey of Hospitalized Abortion Patients, DHS 1988 Special Tabulations.

Acronyms:

FLASOG: Federación Latinoamericano de Sociedades de Obstetricía y Ginecología

DHS: Demographic and Health Survey

Table 2.5 *(continued)*

Contraception at time of conception/ current use (DHS)							
None	55.8	40.9	75.0	55.3	60.7	77.0	60.6
Modern	40.3	48.6	8.0	41.2	17.4	11.0	19.3
Traditional	4.0	10.5	17.0	3.5	21.9	12.0	20.0
Total	100.0	100.0	100.0	100.0	100.0	100.0	100.0

Table 2.6
Abortion Rate and Ratio for Selected Population Subgroups in the United States, 1987 and 1991

Panel A. Age and marital status by race, 1987

	Race		
Measure, Subgroup	Total	White	Other
Abortion Rate per 1000 women 15-44			
All Women	26.9	21.1	56.0
Married	9.2	6.9	27.6
Unmarried	45.6	38.2	71.1
Women 15-19	42.2	35.5	71.3
Abortion Ratio per 100 pregnancies[1]			
All Women	28.8	25.2	39.3
Married	8.7	7.0	19.0
Unmarried	57.1	62.0	50.0
Women 15-19	41.0	41.7	41.5

Panel B. Age by ethnicity, 1991

	Ethnicity			
Measure, Subgroup	Total	Non-Hispanic White	Hispanic (Any Race)	Non-Hispanic Black
Abortion Rate per 1000 women 15-44				
All Women	26.3	17.9	36.2	65.9
Women 15-19	37.6	28.4	40.4	80.5

[1]Pregnancies are defined as legal abortions plus live births.

Sources: Panel A: Marital status, Henshaw, Kooning and Smith 1991; all other data, Henshaw 1992. Panel B: Ventura et al. 1995.

IMPLICATIONS OF UNSAFE ABORTION FOR WOMEN'S HEALTH

Legal induced abortion performed under proper medical conditions is remarkably safe. The mortality rate for legal abortions in developed countries ranges from 0 to about 2.0 per 100,000 legal procedures. By comparison, the mortality rate from pregnancy and childbirth (excluding deaths from induced or spontaneous abortion or ectopic pregnancy) was much greater: in the United States in the 1980s, it was about eleven times higher (a rate of 6.6 per 100,000 live births, compared with a rate of 0.6 per 100,000 legal abortions [Henshaw 1993]). Yet, it is widely acknowledged, unsafe abortion has many consequences for women's health, spanning a wide range of severity, from death at one extreme to temporary disability at the other. Immediate consequences of unsafe abortions may include hemorrhage, physical damage to the reproductive organs, infection, sepsis, and septic shock. Longer-term consequences include chronic pelvic pain, incontinence, obstetric complications in the future, and possibly infertility (Ladipo 1989; Liskin 1992). Statistics on most of these consequences are as hard to obtain as actual data on abortion itself. Using hospital studies, WHO has estimated the proportion of maternal mortality that is due to abortion and, considering results for developing countries only, produces a range of between 6 percent (western Asia) to 24 percent (South America) with a world average of 13 percent (WHO 1998). A few studies have suggested that illness from all maternal causes, including morbidity from unsafe abortion, is as much as 15 to 16 times *mortality* from maternal causes: this was suggested in the case of India in the 1970s and Nigeria in the 1980s (Sundstrom 1993). Hospitalization for serious medical complications is important for what it says about the negative impact of unsafe abortion on women's health and also because it consumes scarce medical resources. Even though not all women who need hospitalization obtain it and the number of hospitalized women is therefore an undercount of the extent of this consequence, some statistics are available on hospitalization, and these yield a minimum estimate of the more serious types of morbidity due to abortion.

Data from hospital records were analyzed for ten developing countries, and the results are shown in Table 2.7. The annual count of the number of women hospitalized for induced abortion is calculated after adjustments for misreporting, undercoverage, and exclusion of an estimated number of spontaneous abortion cases. The rate of hospitalization due to induced abortion per 1,000 women per year ranges from about 3 in Bangladesh to about 16 in Egypt. If these annual rates of hospitalization were to continue throughout these women's lifetime, the average woman would have a chance of between one in twelve (Bangladesh) to one in two (Egypt) of being hospitalized for abortion complications during her reproductive years (column 3 of Table 2.7).[5] Another measure of the impact of morbidity due to unsafe abortion is women hospitalized for abortion complications as a proportion of all women hospitalized for deliveries in a year; this proportion is very high in countries where delivery in hospital is

Table 2.7
Hospitalization Due to Induced Abortion in Ten Developing Countries

Country, year	Hospitalization for induced abortion			
	Number of women	Rate per 1000 women 15-44 per year	% Women likely to be hospitalized by age 45*	as a % of women hospitalized for birth
Bangladesh, 1995	71,800	2.8	8.3	60.3
Brazil, 1991	288,650	8.1	24.2	10.5
Chile, 1990	31,950	10.0	30.1	11.3
Colombia, 1989	57,700	7.2	21.5	8.7
Dominican Rep., 1990	16,500	9.8	29.5	8.4
Egypt, 1996	216,000	16.3	49.0	40.7
Mexico, 1990	106,600	5.4	16.3	5.6
Nigeria, 1996	142,200	6.1	18.3	10.3
Peru, 1989	54,250	11.0	32.9	12.8
Philippines, 1994	80,100	5.1	15.3	13.5
Total	1,065,750	7.0	21.1	12.0

*The annual rate (column 2) multiplied by 30 (the number of years lived from ages 15 to 44), expressed as the number per 100 women.

Sources: Singh and Wulf 1994; Singh et al. 1997; Henshaw et al. 1998; Huntington et al. 1998; and unpublished tabulations.

low (Egypt and Bangladesh, 40.7 and 60.3 percent, respectively) and is much lower in all other countries: 10 to 13 percent in five of the ten countries and 6 to 9 percent in the remaining three. Because women hospitalized for induced abortion often have longer hospital stays and need more resources (e.g., blood transfusions) than women giving birth, abortion complication patients probably absorb an even higher relative proportion of hospital resources than these percentages indicate.

With recent improvements in access to safe, though clandestine, abortion services in some parts of Latin America, particularly in major urban areas, the proportion of unsafe abortions that result in serious complications needing hospitalization is believed to have declined substantially (Frejka and Atkin 1996; Paxman et al. 1994). Although conditions are changing everywhere, this may not yet be the case in rural areas of Latin America and in other developing regions, especially sub-Saharan Africa and South Asia, where morbidity due to unsafe abortion is likely to be still at a very high level, especially in rural areas.

Review of the literature by WHO (1998) confirms that in sub-Saharan Africa and Asia, the consequences of unsafe abortion are as important a health issue as they are in Latin America. Women with complications resulting from an unsafe abortion form a high proportion of all gynecological cases admitted to hospitals and in some areas are a substantial proportion of all obstetric and gynecological cases. A 1981 study of Kenyatta National Hospital found one of the highest levels of abortion cases as a proportion of all obstetric and gynecological admissions (59 percent [Aggarwal and Mati 1982]). A 1990 study of the Philippine General Hospital in Manila found that abortion cases were 12 percent of all obstetric and gynecological cases combined (Stewart and Festin 1993), and a 1988 national sample study in Bangladesh found a proportion of almost 16 percent (Begum et al. 1991). A second review of unsafe abortion in Africa highlights the fact that sepsis is still an important consequence of unsafe abortion in this region (Kinoti et al. 1995): hospital-based studies in Kenya show that 12–16 percent of abortion cases were septic, while one South African study shows an even higher proportion (about 25 percent) and a household survey in Ethiopia found that 54 percent of all maternal deaths were abortion related.

Despite the difficulties in documenting mortality and health consequences resulting from unsafe abortion, available studies support the conclusion that the incidence of unsafe abortion and the sheer numbers of women affected are substantial. As a result, the impact of unsafe abortion on women's health and survival continues to be an important concern that demands the attention of policy makers.

THE ROLE OF ABORTION IN FERTILITY LEVELS AND TRENDS

Although varying across countries, abortion is clearly a significant means of fertility control worldwide. However, its importance relative to other direct or proximate determinants of fertility is often not possible to calculate because of the lack of information on abortion in fertility surveys that provide measures of the other proximate determinants. It is even more difficult to calculate the contribution of abortion to fertility decline, because doing so requires information on the level of abortion over a period of time. One comprehensive approach to measuring the role of abortion is to determine the role of all four major proximate determinants, marriage, postpartum infecundity, contraception, and abortion, in explaining the level of fertility (Bongaarts and Potter 1983; Gaslonde and Bocaz 1970; Hobcraft and Little 1984; Moreno 1991). The Bongaarts model, which is less demanding of data than other proximate determinant models and which can be estimated using an aggregate measure of abortion, is often used to measure the contribution of abortion to fertility and to fertility change as well as to measure the role of abortion relative to that of the other three major proximate determinants. The Bongaarts model allocates the amount of fertility control that exists in a population (measured by the difference between the actual TFR and a hypothetical total fecundity rate [TF], usually assumed to be fifteen births)[6] to each of the main proximate determinants and estimates the importance of each determinant in the form of an index or as the percent of overall fertility control that it explains. In this section we summarize results from some earlier studies of the role of abortion in fertility decline and present some new information for Latin America.

Findings from Earlier Studies

Frejka (1985) has reviewed the role of abortion as a determinant of fertility, pulling together the scattered information that was then available. Data for the 1960s and 1970s on the proximate determinants including abortion were mainly available for developed countries, though even among developed countries, information on abortion was often lacking. Two developing countries, Cuba and the Republic of Korea, were included in this review. The role of abortion was estimated by applying the Bongaarts model, calculating the abortion index, using it to infer what the TFR would be in the absence of abortion, and presenting the impact of abortion as the percent increase in the TFR that would occur if there were no abortions.

TARs were quite low in western European countries: rates of under 0.2 characterized this region in the 1960s, and even by the 1970s and 1980s, the TAR was at most 0.6 in this region. However, in some eastern European countries the TAR had reached quite high levels by the 1960s and often continued at these levels or increased further through the 1970s and 1980s (Table 2.8). This was the case in Bulgaria, Czechoslovakia, and Yugoslavia (TARs of between 0.9 and 2.1), and in Romania and the former Soviet Union, much higher rates were observed even from the 1960s onward, estimated to be in the range of 5 to 7.

The abortion index as calculated within the Bongaarts model allows for the fact that it takes more than one abortion to avert a birth: an abortion averts between 0.4 and 0.8 of a birth, with the impact being larger where contraceptive use is higher.[7] Estimating the Bongaarts model for those countries that had both abortion information and data on the other three proximate determinants, Frejka has

Table 2.8
Total Legal Abortion Rates, Estimated Index of Abortion and Implied and Hypothetical Total Fertility Rates for Selected Countries, 1959–1977

Country	Year	Total Abortion Rate	Index of Abortion (C_a)	Implied TFR[1]	Hypothetical TFR (in absence of abortion)	Difference between hypothetical & implied TFR: Births averted by abortion	As a % of Implied TFR	As a % of overall fertility control[3]
Eastern Europe								
Bulgaria	1976	1.9	0.63	2.04	3.24	1.20	59	9
Czechoslovakia	1959	0.9	0.80	2.46	3.08	0.62	25	5
	1970	1.0	0.76	2.13	2.80	0.67	31	5
Hungary	1966	1.0	0.53	1.93	3.64	1.71	87	13
	1977	2.5	0.73	1.91	2.62	0.71	37	5
Poland[2]	1972	1.2	0.88	2.74	3.11	0.37	14	3
Yugoslavia	1970	0.5	0.75	2.36	3.15	0.79	33	6
Other								
Cuba	1972	1.6	0.79	3.89	4.92	1.03	26	9
Korea, Rep. of	1960	0.5	0.97	6.13	6.32	0.19	3	2
	1970	1.5	0.82	3.81	4.65	0.84	22	8

[1]Implied by Bongaarts's model (TFR = $C_m \times C_c \times C_a \times C_i \times 15.3$). The index shown has been rounded; the implied TFRs shown have been computed by using unrounded indices in the equation. Definitions of indices: C_m = index of marriage; C_c = index of contraceptive use; C_a = index of abortion; C_i = index of postpartum insusceptibility.

[2]Reporting of abortions incomplete.

[3]Authors' calculations: (Births averted by abortion)/(TF – Implied TFR) where TF, total fecundity rate, is assumed to be 15.

Source: Extract from Frejka 1985, Table 2, p. 128, and authors' calculations.

demonstrated that in the countries with high total abortion rates, abortion accounted for about 0.6 to 1.7 births averted: the TFR would increase by this amount if there were no abortions. This would be an increase in the TFR of between 25 percent (Czechoslovakia in 1959) to as much as 87 percent (Hungary in 1966). In the case of both Cuba (1972) and Korea (1970), abortion accounted for about 1.0 births averted; its absence would increase the TFR by 22–26 percent.

Frejka (1985) notes an important limitation of the model: in situations where most abortions occurred among unmarried women (such as in the United States), the impact of abortion appeared to be negligible because unmarried women are not incorporated into the model. Yet the total abortion rate in the United States in 1973 was 0.5, increasing to 0.7 by 1976 (the two years analyzed in Frejka 1985), and abortions were 19 percent of all pregnancies in 1973, increasing to 25 percent in 1976 (Henshaw and Van Vort 1992).

Summaries of the few available estimates for Latin America over the period of the 1950s to the 1980s found that the TAR typically ranged from about 0.5 to 2.7, with the highest levels found in Cuba and Chile (Frejka and Atkin 1996). TFRs during the 1960s and 1970s in this region were higher than those shown in Table 2.8 for Europe, usually between 5 to 6 children per woman, and in some cases even higher (Centro Latinoamericano de Demografía 1993). As a result the role of abortion as a determinant of the level of fertility would generally be at the bottom end of the range found for eastern European countries. For example, with the highest reported TAR of 2.7 and contraceptive use at about 20 percent (use at this period was not quite low), the number of births averted would be 1.3, and in the absence of abortion, fertility would increase by 22 to 26 percent if the TFR was 5 to 6 children.

DISCUSSION

There is no doubt that in most developing countries, and in some developed countries as well, estimates of the level of abortion are difficult to make and may have an unknown but often uncomfortably large margin of error. Yet despite these difficulties and limitations, estimates of the incidence of abortion are useful for a number of reasons. At the very least they provide a context for interpretation and generalization of the results from more in-depth research on all aspects of abortion. But such estimates can also help in many other more direct ways. Having them is directly relevant to focusing and furthering the policy debate concerning the legal status of abortion, restrictions on abortion services, and access to safe abortion services. Without defensible estimates of the extent of unsafe abortion, it is harder to be persuasive about the extent of the public health consequences, of consequences for women's health, and about the need to improve the conditions under which women are obtaining abortions or even the conditions of treatment for women who are hospitalized for complications. Accurate information on the incidence of abortion also ties into policy issues that concern the adequacy of family-planning services. Where there are no estimates of abortion, it tends to be ignored in evaluating the effectiveness or success of family-planning services. This means that contraceptive failure that is resolved by induced abortion will probably not be taken into account in determining unmet family-planning service needs. Instead, declines in the birth rate that result from both successful contraception and from abortion are both attributed to the former. One unfortunate consequence of this is that the extent of the problem of incorrect use of effective methods and of nonuse when women need effective protection against pregnancy is often not recognized. Thus the need for better family-planning services that help women to identify the method that is most suitable for them, teach them how to use methods to maximum protective effect, and counsel them on changing methods with a smooth transition rather than suddenly stopping use is often unaddressed.

This worldwide review shows that the actual incidence of abortion neither reflects the legal status of abortion nor public positions that are taken, policies that are stated, or attitudes that are often expressed by governments or by private institutions, including religious bodies. There is clearly a large gap between attitudes and practice that is found even at the individual level, where women themselves express the conflict between their values, which are often opposed to abortion, and their decision to have an abortion nevertheless. Information on the incidence of abortion reminds us that if we were to unquestioningly accept publicly stated positions and values, we would be greatly misled. Concrete information on the actual level of abortion serves a useful purpose: it directs us to examine the contradictions and the complexities that underlie the practice of abortion, rather than accepting the more simplistic positions that are usually stated in structured interviews of women or by institutions as their official positions.

Because of the numerous situations in which estimates of the level of abortion are not only useful but may in fact be essential, there is strong justification for researchers to continue to pursue improvements in data collection approaches and in estimation techniques. The promise that has been opened up by the results of experimental approaches to increasing the respondent's confidentiality in the interview and in the survey process (Zamudio et al. 1994; Fu et al. 1998) is definitely worth pursuing. Making the best use of existing data on hospitalization for abortion complications and improving on this approach also has the advantage of not only yielding an estimate of the level of abortion but of also providing information on the impact of unsafe abortion on women's health.

Even though in relative terms abortion is much less important than the other three proximate determinants (contraceptive use, marriage, and postpartum infecundity) as a determinant of the number of children that the average woman has, it still has a substantial impact on the level of fertility. Current information on the level of abortion worldwide shows that it is practiced at a moderate level in most regions of the world and at a high level in some countries, regions, and subgroups. This is true regardless of the legal status of abortion and even though contraceptive use has increased steadily during the past decades; motivation to control and time births has clearly risen even faster than use of contraception. Given the increasing strength of women's and of couples' motivation to successfully control the number and the timing of their children, it is probably true that abortion will continue to be needed and to be used across the world for some time to come. Women will probably continue to resort to abortion: where contraceptive use is widespread, it will be used as a backup to contraceptive failure, and where effective contraceptive use is not yet extensive, women will continue to resort to abortion as an important means of fertility control. The fact that women are willing to risk their health and in some cases their lives to avoid an unwanted birth also argues that it is very likely that the use of abortion will continue in many parts of the world for some time to come.

NOTES

1. Reporting for periods further back in time was quite poor, however, and self-administration meant that close to 10 percent of women who were illiterate were excluded from the study.

2. Late miscarriages, of gestation 13 to 22 weeks, are assumed to be 3.4 percent of all live births, based on life tables of the survival of pregnancies (the proportion used by Singh and Wulf 1994 and documented in Harlap, Shiono, and Ramcharan 1980).

3. Four different approaches to estimating the number of spontaneous abortions were applied. The first was to assume that 33 percent of hospitalized cases are spontaneous (based on the results of analyses in Singh and Wulf 1993); the second was to assume that this proportion was 25 percent, based on the results of analyses of Brazilian data; the third was to assume that the proportion spontaneous was 10 percent, based on a survey of the opinions of a survey of health professionals in six Latin American countries (Singh and Wulf 1994); the fourth was to apply the biological estimate (see note 2 above).

4. The total abortion rate is calculated as the abortion rate (35) multiplied by 30, the number of years lived between ages 15 and 44, divided by 1,000. It is the average number of induced abortions per woman at the end of the reproductive years if current age-specific abortion rates prevail throughout the childbearing years.

5. These levels do not allow for repeat abortions, and the lifetime chance of hospitalization would be somewhat lower if repeat abortions are taken into account.

6. The maximum total number of births a woman would have if she were exposed to pregnancy throughout her reproductive years and no deliberate attempts were made to control fertility (Bongaarts and Potter 1983).

7. One abortion averts less than one birth because the duration of the period of pregnancy and of infecundity following the abortion is much shorter than the length of a full-term pregnancy and of infecundity following a live birth. On average, one abortion averts 0.4 of a live birth where there is no contraceptive use. The number of births averted is greater where contraception is used because abortion is then used only when an accidental pregnancy occurs. At most, where contraceptive use is at a very high level, an abortion will avert up to 0.8 of a birth. This relationship is seen in the formula for the Bongaarts aggregate index of abortion, which is calculated as follows:

$$Ca = TFR/(TFR+(0.4^*(1 + u)^*TAR))$$

where TFR = total fertility rate, u = proportion using contraception among married women, and TAR = total abortion rate.

REFERENCES

Aggarwal, V. P. and J.K.G. Mati. 1982. "Epidemiology of Induced Abortion in Nairobi, Kenya." *Journal of Obstetrics and Gynecology of Eastern and Central Africa* 1 (2): 54–57.

Alan Guttmacher Institute. 1999. *Sharing Responsibilities: Women, Society and Abortion Worldwide.* New York: The Alan Guttmacher Institute.

Alcantra, Elsa. 1994. "Determinates y consecuencias del aborto en tres ciudades del Peru." Preliminary report on project funded by the World Health Organization, Instituto de Estudios de Población, Universidad Peruana Cayetano Heredia, Lima, Peru.

Armijo, R., and T. Monreal. 1965. "The Problem of Induced Abortion in Chile." *Milbank Memorial Fund Quarterly* 43 (4): 263–80.

Bankole, A., S. Singh, and T. Haas. 1999. "Characteristics of Women Who Obtain Induced Abortion: A Worldwide Review." *International Family Planning Perspectives* 25 (2): 68–77.

Barreto, T., O.M.R. Campbell, J. L. Davies, V. Fauveau, V.G.A. Filippi, W. J. Graham, M. Mamdani, C.I.F. Rooney, and N. F. Toubia. 1992. "Investigating induced abortion in developing countries: methods and problems," *Studies in Family Planning* 23: 159–70.

Begum, S. F., H. H. Akhter, H. Kamal, and G. M. Kamal. 1991. *Hospital-Based Descriptive Study on Illegally Induced Abortion-Related Mortality and Morbidity, and Its Cost on Health Services.* Dhaka: Bangladesh Association for the Prevention of Septic Abortion.

Begum, S. F., H. Kamal, and G. M. Kamal. 1987. *Evaluation of MR Services in Bangladesh.* Mirpur, Dhaka: Bangladesh Association for the Prevention of Septic Abortion.

Blayo, C. 1985. "L'avortment légal en France." *Population et Sociétés,* No. 187.

Bongaarts, J., and R. G. Potter. 1983. *Fertility, Biology and Behavior.* New York: Academic Press.

Casterline, J. B. 1989. "Collecting Data on Pregnancy Loss: A Review of Evidence from the World Fertility Survey." *Studies in Family Planning* 20 (2): 81–95.

Centro Latinoamericano de Demografía. 1993. *America Latina: Tasas de fecundidad por edad, 1950–2025.* Boletín Demográfico (July) 52, Santiago, Chile.

Chhabra, R., and S. C. Nuna. 1994. *Abortion in India, An Overview.* New Delhi: Veerendra.

Cho, N. H. and Ahn, N. "Changes in the Determinants of Induced Abortion in Korea." *Journal of Population, Health and Social Welfare* 13 (1993): 67–79.

Coeytaux, F. M. 1988. "Induced Abortion in Sub-Saharan Africa: What We Do and Do Not Know." *Studies in Family Planning* 19 (3): 186–90.

Coeytaux, F. M., A. Leonard, and E. Royston. 1989. Methodological Issues in Abortion Research. Proceedings of a seminar held by the Population Council in collaboration with International Projects Assistance Services and World Health Organization, December 12–13, New York.

Corporación Centro Regional de Población, Ministerio de Salud de Colombia and Institute for Resource Development/Westinghouse. 1986. Demographic and Health Survey of women of reproductive age in Colombia in 1986.

Czech Statistical Office, World Health Organization, and Centers for Disease Control. 1995. *Czech Republic Reproductive Health Survey: Final Report.* Atlanta: Centers for Disease Control and Prevention, 1995.

David, H. P. 1981. "Abortion Policies." In *Abortion and Sterilization: Medical and Social Aspects,* ed. J. E. Hodgson, 1–40. New York: Academic Press.

Federación Latinoamericano de Sciedades de Obstetricia y Ginecologiá. 1990. Survey of hospitalized abortion patients, carried out in four countries. Special tabulations done by the authors for this paper.

Foreit, K. G., and D. Nortman. 1992. "A Method for Calculating Rates of Induced Abortion." *Demography* 29 (1): 127–37.

Frejka, T. 1985. "Induced abortion and fertility." *International Family Planning Perspectives* 11 (4): 125–29.

Frejka, T., and L. C. Atkin. 1996. "The Role of Induced Abortion in the Fertility Transition of Latin America." In *The Fertility Transition in Latin America,* ed. J. M. Guzman, S. Singh, G. Rodriguez, and E. A. Pantelides, 179–91. Oxford: Oxford University Press.

Fu, H., J. E. Darroch, S. K. Henshaw, and E. Kolb. 1998. "Measuring the Extent of Abortion Underreporting in the 1995 National Survey of Family Growth." *Family Planning Perspectives* 30 (3): 128–33, 138.

Gaslonde, S., and A. Bocaz. 1970. *Método para medir variaciones en el nivel de fecundidad.* Centro Latinoamericano de Demografía, Series A, no. 118, Santiago, Chile.

Harlap, S., P. H. Shiono, and S. Ramcharan. 1980. "A Life Table of Spontaneous Abortions and the Effects of Age, Parity and Other Variables." In *Human Embryonic and Fetal Death,* ed. E.B. Hook and I. Porter, 145–64. New York: Academic Press.

Henshaw, S. K. 1989. "Estimating Incidence of Abortion from Repeat Abortion Histories." In *Methodological Issues in Abortion Research,* ed. F. M. Coeytaux, A. Leonard, and E. Royston, 33–38.

———. 1992. "Abortion Trends in 1987 and 1988: Age and Race." *Family Planning Perspectives* 24 (2): 85–86, 96.

———. 1993. "How Safe Is Therapeutic Abortion?" In *World Congress of Gynecology and Obstetrics: 13th, 1991: Proceedings,* ed. E. S. Teoh, S. S. Ratnam, and M. MacNaughton, 5:31–40. New York: Parthenon Publishing Group.

———. 1998. "Abortion Incidence and Services in the United States, 1995–1996." *Family Planning Perspectives* 30 (6): 263–70, 287.

Henshaw, S. K., L. M. Koonin, and J. C. Smith. 1991. "Characteristics of U.S. Women Having Abortions, 1987." *Family Planning Perspectives* 23(2): 75–81.

Henshaw, S. K., S. Singh, and T. Haas. 1999. "Incidence of Abortion Worldwide." *International Family Planning Perspectives* (supplement): S30–S38.

Henshaw, S. K., S. Singh, B. A. Oye-Adeniran, I. F. Adewole, N. Iwere, and Y. Cuca. 1998. "The Incidence of Induced Abortion in Nigeria." *International Family Planning Perspectives* 24 (4): 156–64.

Henshaw, S. K., and J. Van Vort. 1992. *Abortion Factbook: 1992 Edition.* New York: The Alan Guttmacher Institute.

Hobcraft, J., and R.J.A. Little. 1984. "Fertility Exposure Analysis: A New Method of Assessing the Contribution of Proximate Determinants of Fertility Differentials." *Population Studies* 38 (1): 21–45.

Huntington, D., L. Nawar, E. O. Hassan, and N. A. Tawab. 1998. "The Postabortion Caseload in Egyptian Households: A Descriptive Study." *International Family Planning Perspectives* 24 (1): 25–31.

Institute for Mother and Child Care, Bucharest, and Centers for Disease Control. 1995. *Romania Reproductive Health Survey, 1993: Final Report.* Atlanta: Centers for Disease Control and Prevention.

Instituto de Estudios de Población y Desarallo de Profamilia, Santo Domingo, Oficina Nacional de Planificación, Santo Domingo, and Institute for Resource Development/Macro International, Inc. 1992. Demographic and Health Survey of women of reproductive age in the Dominican Republic in 1992. Special tabulations done by the authors for this paper.

Instituto Nacional de Estadística, Perú, and Institute for Resource Development/Westinghouse. 1988. Demographic and Health Survey of women of reproductive age in Peru in 1988. Special tabulations done by the authors for this paper.

International Fertility Research Program. 1981. *Traditional Abortion Practices: Three Studies of Illegal Abortion in the Developing World.* Research Triangle Park, N.C.: International Fertility Research Program.

Jones, E., and J. D. Forrest. 1992. "Underreporting of Abortion in Surveys of U.S. Women: 1976–1988." *Demography* 29 (1): 112–26.

Ketting, E. 1994. "Is the Dutch Abortion Rate Really That Low?" *Planned Parenthood in Europe* 23 (supplement): 29–32.

Kinoti, S. N., L. Gaffikin, J. Benson, and L. A. Nicholson. 1995. *Monograph of Complications of Unsafe Abortion in Africa.* Baltimore: Johns Hopkins Program for International Education in Reproductive Health.

Konje, J. C., and K. A. Obisesan. 1991. "Septic Abortion at University College Hospital, Ibadan, Nigeria." *International Journal of Obstetrics and Gynecology* 36 (2):121–25.

Ladipo, O. A. 1989. "Preventing and Managing Complications of Induced Abortion in Third World Countries." *International Journal of Gynecology and Obstetrics* 3 (supplement): 21–28.

Liskin, L. S. 1992. "Maternal Morbidity in Developing Countries: A Review And Comments." *International Journal of Gynecology and Obstetrics* 37 (2): 77–87.

Ministry of Health, Turkey. 1994. *Turkish Demographic and Health Survey 1993.* Ankara, Turkey: Haceteppe University Institute of Population Studies and Macro International.

Monreal, T. 1976. "Determinant Factors Affecting Illegal Abortion Trends in Chile." In *New Developments in Fertility Regulation,* ed. H.R. Holtrop et al., 123–32. Chestnut Hill, Mass.: The Pathfinder Fund.

Moreno, L. 1991. "An Alternative Model of the Impact of the Proximate Determinants on Fertility Change: Evidence from Latin America." *Population Studies* 45 (2): 313–37.

Paiewonsky, D. 1993. "Determinantes sociales y consecuencias del aborto inducido en la Republica Dominicana." Unpublished preliminary project report submitted to World Health Organization and Instituto de Estudios de Población y Desarrollo, Profamilia, Santo Domingo, Dominican Republic.

Paxman, J., A. Rizo, L. Brown, and J. Benson. 1994. "The Clandestine Epidemic: The Practice of Unsafe Abortion in Latin America." *Studies in Family Planning* 24 (4): 205–26.

Rademakers, J. 1994. *Abortus in Nederland: 1991–1992.* Utrecht, Netherlands: Jaarverslag van de Landelijke Abortusregistratie.

Singh, S., and D. Wulf. 1991. "Estimating Abortion Levels in Brazil, Colombia and Peru, Using Hospital Admission and Fertility Survey Data." *International Family Planning Perspectives* 17 (1): 8–13.

———. 1993. "The Likelihood of Induced Abortion among Women Hospitalized for Abortion Complications in Four Latin American Countries." *International Family Planning Perspectives* 19 (4): 134–41.

———. 1994. "Estimating Levels of Induced Abortion in Six Latin American Countries." *International Family Planning Perspectives* 20 (1): 4–13.

Singh, S., J. V. Cabigon, A. Hossain, H. Kamal, and A .E. Perez. 1997. "Estimating the Level of Abortion in the Philippines and Bangladesh." *International Family Planning Perspectives* 23 (3): 100–107.

Sundstrom, K. 1993. Abortion: A Reproductive Health Issue. Working paper, Women's Health and Nutrition Work Program, The World Bank, Washington, D.C.

Tosi, S. L., A. Spinelli, M. Pediconi, M. E. Grandolfo, F. Jimpero, and I. Figa Talamanca. 1985. *L'interruzione volontaria di gravidanza in Italie—1983.* Rome: Instituto Superiore di Sanita.

United Nations. 1997a. *World Population Prospects: The 1996 Revision, Annex Tables.* New York: United Nations.

———. 1997b. *World Population Prospects: The 1996 Revision Annex II and III, Demographic Indicators by Major Area, Region and Country.* New York: United Nations.

Ventura, S. J., S. M. Taffel, W. D. Mosher, J. B. Wilson, and S. K. Henshaw. 1995. *Trends in Pregnancies and Pregnancy Rates: Estimates for the United States, 1980–92.* Monthly Vital Statistics Report, vol. 43 (11), Supplement. Hyattsville, Md.: Centers for Disease Control and National Center for Health Statistics.

World Health Organization. 1998. *Unsafe Abortion: Global and Regional Estimates of Incidence of and Mortality due to Unsafe Abortion.* 3d ed. Geneva: World Health Organization.

Zamudio, L., N. Rubiano, and L. Wartenburg. 1994. La incidencia del aborto en Colombia. Paper presented at the Conference on Induced Abortion in Latin America and the Caribbean, organized by World Health Organization, Universidad Externado de Colombia, and the Alan Guttmacher Institute, November 15–18, Bogotá.

Chapter 3

The Challenge of Induced Abortion Research: Transdisciplinary Perspectives

Axel I. Mundigo

Abortion is a social, economic, and demographic reality. Depending on the legal status of abortion, the health impact of induced abortion can be positive or negative. It also has powerful ethical connotations, being condemned by many religions as a sinful act. Societies add to this religious stigma by making induced abortion a criminal act punishable by law. Politicians seldom risk their career or their votes by going public in favor of reforming abortion laws, so the changes in abortion legislation around the world tend to be few and heavily contested. Against this background, the study of induced abortion, especially where abortion is illegal, remains a major challenge to researchers working on reproductive health and women's rights issues.

One of the salient characteristics of induced abortion as a research topic is its transdisciplinary nature. Consequently, induced abortion stands at the intersection of a variety of academic disciplines and intellectual perspectives, cutting across medical and health sciences, the full range of the social sciences, and the legal and ethical professions. The fact that abortion is a relevant subject for so many disciplines, being also a central concern for health advocacy groups, makes research on this topic a rich source for policy discussion and legislative change.

Induced abortion is also multidimensional in nature, having behavioral, social, legal, religious, demographic, service, and policy dimensions among others. This chapter will discuss each of these dimensions, providing relevant research examples. For analytic purposes, these dimensions can be handled from two perspectives: the individual, or micro level, and the aggregate, or macro level. The individual-level perspective concentrates on the study of antecedent and postabortion behavior—that is, the determinants and consequences of induced abortion—and utilizes mainly the concepts and methods of the social sciences.

The aggregate-level perspective requires the application of demographic and statistical analysis, including indirect estimation techniques. The objective is to understand levels and patterns of abortion incidence in a community, region, or country.

Research that follows the microlevel approach would be mostly interested in pursuing questions such as these: Why was the decision to abort taken? Under what circumstances? Who influenced the decision? When was the abortion performed in terms of the pregnancy duration, where, and by whom, using what means? Was it the first—or repeated, in which case which order was it? Macrolevel analysis is concerned, although not exclusively, with the numerical dimension and answers questions such as these: How many abortions take place in a year? Why did the unwanted pregnancy occur? Where was the abortion performed? How is it related to family size and fertility history, in particular to contraceptive use or nonuse? Most individual questions arising in abortion research suggest that a qualitative approach would be most suited to understand behaviors that place women at high risk of morbidity and mortality, whereas the macrolevel questions require, for the most part, quantitative data collection approaches such as population-based surveys, which are extremely difficult, or surveys of specific communities, for example, of hospital clients.

In the discussion that follows, the emphasis will be mostly on the individual dimension. Many of the case studies cited are from a recently completed World Health Organization (WHO) research initiative on induced abortion (Mundigo and Indriso 1999).

LEGAL AND HUMAN RIGHTS DIMENSIONS

Abortion can be spontaneous or induced—resulting from a personal decision to interrupt a known pregnancy. The right to abortion is strongly controlled by governments, and abortion laws tend to delimit the exact situation and gestational duration under which an abortion can take place: for example, to save the mother's life or in case of rape and incest or, under more liberal legislation, on demand up to three months of gestation. Therefore, induced abortion can be either legal or illegal. Of the approximately 20 million unsafe abortions that occur each year in the world, some seventy thousand result in actual deaths. The risk of dying from an unsafe abortion is much higher in the developing countries—1 in 250 interventions—than in the developed world, where the figure is only 1 in 3,700 (World Health Organization 1994).

Only forty-one (22 percent) of the 190 countries in the world have abortion laws that make it available on request. Even countries such as Finland and England and Wales offer abortion only when it is justifiable for health as well as for economic and social reasons, although it is true that in practice abortion is available in these countries virtually on demand. Only 6 percent of the world's developing countries allow abortion on demand, among them Albania, China,

Cuba, the Democratic Republic of Korea, Tunisia, Vietnam, and most of the new countries formerly part of the Soviet Union. The gap between developed and developing countries is very marked when we observe the reasons under which abortion can be legally performed. Abortion to save the life of the woman is legal in 173 countries, or 93 percent of the countries of the world, including 91 percent of the less developed ones. The big difference, however, lies in the fact that the majority of women in the developing world in this situation are unaware of their legal rights, and often even health providers are not aware of the existing legislation. The second reason, to preserve the physical health of the woman, begins to show a larger difference between developed and developing countries: it is a legally valid reason to perform an abortion in 89 percent of the former but in only 52 percent of the latter. The third reason, to preserve the mental health of the woman, only increases the differential: it is valid in 88 percent of the developed countries and in only 35 percent of the developing ones. Lastly, in cases of rape or incest the difference is even more marked: 84 percent in developed countries and 26 percent in developing ones; and for fetal impairment, it is 84 and 23 percent, respectively. For entire world regions, such as Latin America, the option of safe abortion remains largely outside the law (with the exception of Cuba and Guyana). Similarly, in Africa, which contains some of the world's poorest countries, safe abortion is not an option for most women.

Restrictive abortion laws discriminate against women in the area of reproductive rights and also in the right of access to health services. As Cook (1995, 1006) has pointed out: "Reproductive and sexual equality will require that men and women have equal capacities for reproductive self-determination. At a most basic level, it means ensuring that women have equal access with men to reproductive health services." Following this legal argument, which is widely held by advocacy groups working on reproductive rights, Cook adds: "Reproductive equality would bring into question restrictive abortion laws, because these laws criminalize medical procedures that only women need" (1006). The point is then made that no medical procedures for men are subject to similar criminal sanctions. It is also recognized that ethically sound policies should bring about a positive balance between desirable and undesirable consequences. As the Declaration on Ethical Propositions that emerged from a roundtable on these issues (1994) puts it: "An example of a policy that produces a preponderance of unfavorable consequences for reproductive health is criminalization of abortion."

In addition to conducting research on the origins of existing laws, whether they are applied or not, the paucity of information on the behavioral dimensions of induced abortion makes the advancement of work on legal rights and on legislation very difficult. As Nunes and Delph (1995, 16), reporting on the recent change in the abortion law of Guyana, have noted: "A main weakness of public policy formation in many developing countries is the paucity of factual data and the lack of a tradition of using data to inform decision-making. The subject of abortion law reform is perhaps the most vexed of all public policy issues and is prone to be in the absence of facts."

The illegal status of abortion in many societies, the poor documentation of health statistics, the lack of services in others, and the reticence of hospitals to declare abortion complications all conspire to make it extremely difficult to ascertain the real situation, either at the national or subregional levels. The many problems that arise from an illegal act make the study of induced abortion that much more difficult: women refuse to tell the truth; clandestine abortion providers won't give any information; and hospital service personnel often prefer to hide these cases, declaring them spontaneous abortions or another disease just in case someone may suspect that the clinic or hospital might be performing abortions.

THE RELIGIOUS DIMENSION

Among organized religions the most vocal in opposing abortion is the Roman Catholic Church. The Vatican's opposition to abortion at the 1994 International Conference on Population and Development made it one of the central topics in international media reporting of this event. As Cohen and Richards (1994, 150), in their report of the Cairo Conference, commented: "Press coverage, however, was dominated by an abortion debate that, admittedly, occupied a disproportionate amount of time. The protracted negotiations over the final document's abortion language was historic." The Vatican argued that "references to *unsafe abortion* should be deleted because all abortions are unsafe for the fetus" (151). Scholars representing other religions also sided with some of the Vatican positions, especially Muslim leaders supported by Islamic states (Cohen and Richards 1994, 151). It is interesting to note that the official position of the Vatican is not shared equally by all Catholics (Kissling 1995–96).

Muslims have different schools of thought regarding abortion and the beginning of life (see Amin's chapter in this volume). The Shinto religion, by contrast, holds that a child becomes a human being when "it has seen the light of day"; therefore, the issue of abortion does not have major moral or ethical connotations. Neither Hindu nor Buddhist theology contains scriptural prohibitions against abortion (Lader 1966).

THE SOCIAL DIMENSION

Some societies censure abortion based on traditional and religious values, and in others abortion is seen as a better option than carrying an unwanted pregnancy to term. Many Asian societies, for example, place a strong social stigma on single or unwed motherhood, for example, Korea and China. In fact, abortion is much more acceptable from a societal perspective in Asia than it is in Latin America or the United States. This explains in part the growth of sex-selective abortion in some Asian countries, where couples who prefer a boy may abort a female fetus. This practice is condemned by law, but it is still pervasive in several countries, including India (Chandrasekhar 1994).

Another social dilemma with moral overtones is that of the single woman who prefers to risk an abortion than be prepared for sex by using a method when she is not sure there will be a sexual encounter. As Dixon-Mueller (1993, 17) remarks: "Getting pregnant with the option of safe termination enables a woman to test her partner's commitment to maintaining the relationship and raising a child." Dixon-Mueller makes the point that for some women, the option of abortion, at least at some stage during their lives, will be preferable to other alternatives (for example, if they cannot tolerate side effects of contraceptive methods), adding that "some of these circumstances derive from a woman's particular social or personal situations, some from the inadequacies of particular contraceptive methods or delivery systems" (17). In situations where access to modern contraception is not ensured, abortion is simply a backup for failure to obtain or to use a method, as we shall see in the following case study.

CASE STUDY: CUBA

Cuba is the only country in Latin America where abortion has been legal since the 1960s and is performed within the framework of the official health services. The liberalization of the Social Defense Code by the Cuban government in 1964 permitted a broader interpretation of earlier penal codes that had made abortion more restricted. Since then, abortion has become increasingly common, particularly as contraceptives are not always easily available. Its incidence is particularly high among adolescents, a major concern for health authorities.

More than 140,000 pregnancy interruptions are performed every year. In 1990, the number of abortions reached 147,530. The number of live births in that year was 186,658, giving a ratio of eight abortions per ten live births. Since 1968, when estimates of abortion were first reported, the figures have progressively increased from 37.9 abortions per 1,000 women of reproductive age in 1968 to 59.4 in 1990. This latter rate includes abortions as well as menstrual regulation by manual vacuum aspiration.

Contraceptive use is also high in Cuba, about 75 percent. This leads to the obvious question of why abortion continues to play a major role in fertility regulation among Cuban women. This was the question behind the study (Alvarez et al. 1999) reported here. The study was conducted in the Havana municipality "10 de Octubre," which has 239,703 inhabitants and a decreasing birth rate—similar to that of the rest of the country—that was a low 13.7 live births per 1,000 inhabitants in 1990.

The study sample consisted of 1,965 sexually active women, aged 13 to 34, residing in areas covered by the primary health system, and who are monitored by the municipality's System of Family Doctor Care Services. It included all voluntary pregnancy interruptions, whether by standard abortion methods or by menstrual regulation techniques. Private interviews were held with each woman to obtain personal data.

One of every ten women studied had had an abortion in the twelve months prior to the survey, and 54 percent had had at least one abortion during their lifetime. More than one-third of the women explained that their abortion had been a menstrual regulation. The abortion rate (expressed per 100 women) was highest among younger women, especially those under twenty years of age. The abortion experience itself increased with age—for women over thirty, one in three women stated that they had experienced at least two pregnancy interruptions.

Seventy percent of women with a sexual partner were using some form of contraception. Remarkably, 58.5 percent of women without a sexual partner were still using a method. Three out of every four women who had an abortion in the past twelve months had been using a method of contraception. Looking for clues in contraceptive use patterns to explain abortion leads to the inescapable conclusion that there is a high level of method failure, discontinuation, and inconsistent use. There seems to be also a fair amount of method switching, perhaps as a result of intermittent contraceptive supplies. This has been a major problem in Cuba.

From what has been learned about the Cuban abortion situation, it would seem that a major improvement in family-planning services is needed. The main reason for the high abortion levels clearly is contraceptive failure, either through poor use of modern methods or the failure of the methods themselves.

THE DEMOGRAPHIC DIMENSION

The contribution of abortion to fertility change is a topic central to demographic interests, especially the role of abortion in the early stages of the demographic transition. Furthermore, the extent to which induced abortion contributes to the maintenance of advanced or posttransitional fertility patterns, in contexts with varying contraceptive prevalence levels, also needs additional study. Frejka (1993) has estimated the possible contribution of abortion to fertility decline in each region of the developing world. Starting from an overall figure of around 30 million induced abortions annually, he broke it down as follows: up to 3.4 million induced abortions in Africa (high-range estimate), 11.9 million abortions in eastern Asia, between 5.2 and 12.5 million in southern and Southeast Asia, and between 4.4 and 6.2 million in Latin America. This in turn means that of all births averted by either contraception or abortion, up to a third are averted by induced abortion in Africa, 22 percent in eastern Asia, between 11 and 23 percent in southern and Southeast Asia, and between 21 and 28 percent in Latin America.

In areas of the world where abortion is severely restricted by law, as is the case in most of sub-Saharan Africa (Coeytaux 1988), there is a growing awareness among experts that the actual numbers of clandestine abortions may be much larger than previously thought. As Frejka (1993) has noted, the role of abortion becomes more evident because the total amount of fertility regulation is small.

The same is true in Latin America. Paxman et al. (1993) have called the situation in that region "the clandestine epidemic." The following case illustrates the situation in the Dominican Republic. This hospital-based study has the limitations of a nonrepresentative population sample, but it approaches its subject with rigor, seeking patterns of contraceptive use and linking them to the abortion situation.

CASE STUDY: THE DOMINICAN REPUBLIC

The main objective of the Dominican study by Paiewonsky (1999) was to explore the possible impact of the basic sociodemographic determinants on decision factors affecting women's reproductive behavior, focusing on abortion decision making. The study was conducted in two large maternity hospitals in Santo Domingo, the capital of the Dominican Republic, between March and May of 1992. The data were collected through structured interviews with 352 abortion patients seeking services, mostly for postabortion complications, at these hospitals. Three hundred and nine women were interviewed at the country's largest public maternity hospital, the Maternidad Nuestra Señora de la Altagracia (MNSA), which provides services to low-income people. Another 43 cases were interviewed at the Santo Domingo Maternal and Child Clinic, a maternity clinic of the Social Security System, which provides services to workers and their families.

The hospital data were supplemented with detailed qualitative information derived from in-depth interviews with nineteen lower-class and thirteen middle-class women who had previously obtained abortions. The middle-class women were included not only for comparison purposes but also to counter the lower-class bias of most hospital-based abortion research in the region.

As is usually the case in research on induced abortion, two methodological problems arose that may affect the interpretation of the hospital data. The first was the respondent's reluctance to acknowledge the voluntary nature of their abortions. The second was the negative impact of the hospital surroundings on the interview process, which was detrimental in terms of building trust with the respondents. The hospital environment is characteristically overcrowded, noisy, and lacking in adequate office or other secure space to conduct personal interviews on a sensitive issue. Therefore, one major problem was the lack of peace and privacy necessary to conduct the interview.

There was also an internal problem arising from the negative attitudes of the hospital staff toward women who arrived with abortion complications. Because abortion complications are not among the normally assigned routines of a maternity hospital, the staff attitude is one of general rudeness, which is one of many inconveniences these patients must endure in public facilities.

The profile of women who arrive with induced abortion complications suggests that they are mostly younger, married women who have completed childbearing and have at some time worked outside the home. Their occupational status shows no significant association with their reproductive behavior, and neither, surprisingly, does their educational level.

Contraceptive histories of the women in this sample are a good part of the answer to the question of why they decided to terminate their pregnancies. The fact that these women had abortions indicates that this population is particularly motivated to regulate their fertility. When unable to do so efficiently through contraception, they resorted to abortion to attain their goal.

Although the national contraceptive prevalence rate is relatively high—56 percent of all married women are using methods—the fact that 38.5 percent of all married women have been surgically sterilized must be taken into account. In fact, surgical sterilization is the method used by two out of every three current users. Mean age at the time of sterilization has been falling steadily so that one in four women underwent the procedure before the age of twenty-five and six out of ten before the age of thirty. The small proportion of women using reversible methods indicates that large population groups do not employ contraception as a means of postponing or spacing childbirth but instead resort to sterilization once the desired parity has been achieved. The minority that does adopt modern contraception to postpone or space their pregnancies usually resorts to the pill, the use of which is characteristically inefficient and of short duration. There is a curious pattern of moving away from a potentially effective method, the pill, to a less effective but less troublesome one from a health viewpoint, withdrawal. The low effectiveness of withdrawal, combined with a high motivation to limit family size, leads to induced abortion.

The in-depth interviews revealed very inefficient contraceptive practices. In fact, many low-income women's stories disclose a fatalistic outlook on the ultimate inevitability of pregnancy and childbirth. Unlike middle-class women, who regard fertility control as both feasible and desirable, poor women often express the feeling that pregnancy is ultimately unavoidable, even if contraception can help prevent it at a given time. From this point of view, only surgical sterilization and celibacy provide any real assurances against unwanted pregnancy.

In summary, the study in the Dominican Republic showed that although the majority of women were interested in regulating their fertility, their contraceptive practices were very inefficient. It is precisely the discrepancy between a high degree of contraceptive motivation, on the one hand, and inadequate choices and practices, on the other, that creates the conditions for unwanted pregnancies and abortion.

THE ANTHROPOLOGICAL DIMENSION

Although the tools of mathematical demography allow us to extrapolate from hospital data the dimension of abortion in a community, city, or country (see, for example, Alan Guttmacher Institute 1994; Remez 1995; Singh and Wulf 1991, 1994), the behavioral dimension of induced abortion remains largely a question mark. It is clear from the cases cited that the best methodological options are techniques used in anthropological research. Among these are in-depth interviewing (utilizing interview guides), subject-focused one-on-one discussions, and group discussions, in particular focus-group discussions. The Indonesian case (discussed later) relied on data from direct interviews with health care providers whose opinions could not have been obtained using standard survey approaches. The same is true about the women interviewed by Elu (1999) in her study of Mexican women. In many ways, the anthropological approach and method is one of the best ways to reverse what Barreto et al. (1992, 159) have noted, that "in most developing countries, the consequences for women's health, the social and cultural context within which induced abortions are performed, and even the levels and data characteristics of women resorting to abortion are unknown." They also add that "the neglect of induced abortion research extends to methodological issues" (160). It is precisely here that the combined approaches used by many of the studies quoted in this chapter have opened and explored new avenues, mixing quantitative and qualitative methods. The Mexican study to which we now turn demonstrates the value of qualitative data to reveal the complexity of personal situations and how they affect the decision to terminate a pregnancy. It vividly illustrates the social and cultural circumstances that affect abortion.

CASE STUDY: MEXICO

Elu (1999) has explored the social and economic factors that contribute particularly to lower-income women's decision to interrupt a pregnancy under unsafe, often dangerous conditions. The study was conducted at the Hospital de la Mujer (Women's Hospital) in Mexico City, one of the oldest public health institutions in the country. Induced abortion appears to be increasing in Mexico, judging from the number of women who seek help from public hospitals for complications due to unsafe procedures. The study population consisted of a purposive sample of 300 women admitted to the Hospital de la Mujer for abortion complications between August 15, 1990, and January 15, 1991.

There is little doubt that poverty itself contributes to the decision to terminate an unwanted pregnancy, as the following example illustrates:

> Doña Esperanza was born in a small town, a journey of two hours from the capital city. She was 14 years old when she came to Mexico City and since then has been working as a housemaid. She lives with her husband, a 19 year old daughter and a 17 year old son; both children are from her first husband, who died in an accident. She had her first abortion just after she arrived in Mexico City and a second after the birth of her eldest daughter. In both cases, the reason for the abortion was her unstable economic situation which made even getting proper nourishment difficult. During the past eight years, Doña Esperanza, now 44 years old, had been having sexual relations with a man 16 years younger.

At the beginning of their relationship she took oral contraceptives, but then he insisted that she stop taking them so that they could have a son of their own. When she got pregnant, her other children got angry. They reminded her that it was risky to give birth at her age and that both her economic situation and relationship with this man were too unstable. After a great deal of reflection, she decided to end her pregnancy. She took a "tea" and a few hours later she began to bleed and to feel unwell. At the clinic (Centro de Salud), five blocks from her house, they suggested that she go immediately to the Hospital de la Mujer, where they managed to save her life. At the Hospital, Doña Esperanza did not accept a contraceptive injection, because her companion left her when he found out that she had an abortion. But her children predicted that he would return because she supported him financially. (1999, 248–49)

The study concluded that not all women who face induced abortion suffer all the attending traumas with similar intensity. Women in higher income groups can afford a safe abortion. However, there is growing agreement that abortions under the conditions in which most low-income women have them constitutes a serious problem for public health.

Women such as Doña Esperanza are often caught in a conflict when they perceive the need to have a child as a means to hold on to a man or stabilize their marital or sexual union. Furthermore, men are often a major barrier to the use of modern contraception. But when an unintended pregnancy results and abortion follows, men often react in ways that are detrimental to the relationship and to the woman, especially to her own emotional stability. The psychological and the economic dimensions of abortion are additional areas for research.

THE SERVICE DIMENSION

The Mexican study points to the critical role of maternity hospitals in treating abortion complications and saving lives, but the Dominican study highlights the complexity that arises from these cases within maternity hospitals. The staff frequently feels overwhelmed by these cases and, as a result, often neglects them, complaining that abortion complications represent an additional burden for which they receive no compensation. This burden is seldom taken into account when the hospital budgets, supplies and staff, and other needs are planned. Thus, another challenging area for study from a health services research perspective is the role and the attitudes of service providers, especially men and women, doctors and midwives, and nurses and nurses aides, as well as of others who work in maternity hospitals. Where abortion is legal, other service issues arise, as, for example, whether family planning and abortion services should be integrated, and if so, how. One of the World Health Organization studies conducted in Istanbul, Turkey (Bulut 1999), showed that the staff wanted the services functionally integrated through a system of appointments and referrals but that the actual abortion service should be kept separate. In fact, as a result of the study, the family-planning clinic was given responsibility for the first screening and for making appointments, whereas the abortion clinic was moved to another location within the hospital. In other countries, for example, China, a very important concern for women was the training and capacity of the clinic and hospital staff to perform abortions and whether or not they used anesthesia. In China the issue of pain associated with abortion was paramount (Zhou et al. 1999; Gui 1999). The number of concerns regarding the providers, their training and opinions, are many. The Indonesian study that follows highlights just a situation in which the abortion debate has been raging for a long time and where official pronouncements have avoided the issue even when heath law reforms were being approved.

CASE STUDY: INDONESIA

The long-standing Indonesian abortion law originated in the Criminal Law of the Netherlands of 1918, making abortion for purposes of terminating a pregnancy a criminal act. Although efforts to discuss the problem of unsafe abortion in Indonesia have been sporadic since the 1960s—when a symposium on reproductive health issues recommended increased research on induced abortion, changes in the law, and improved family-planning services—the situation did not really change until 1992. In that year, the Health Code of Indonesia was reformed, yet the legal status of induced abortion was left unclear. The study (Djohan et al. 1999) contributed important information on the attitudes of health providers on the issue of abortion.

During the 1980s, menstrual regulation (including vacuum aspiration, suction curettage, and injection of hypertonic saline solution) became increasingly available in Indonesia. In the hospitals that provided these services, the rate of septic abortions decreased. This was done while the legal status of abortion remained unchanged, although the legal injunctions were not applied.

The study consisted of a total of seventy-six interviews with health providers: fifty-four with women and twenty-two with men, and included general practitioners (fourteen), gynecologists (fourteen), family-planning workers (sixteen)—these three groups were equally divided between both sexes—plus sixteen midwives and sixteen traditional birth attendants (TBAs). All the personnel interviewed were Muslims, and most were Javanese. The study was conducted between October 1990 and April 1991 and used in-depth interviews that followed a standard interview guide.

Religion appeared to be the strongest determinant influencing health care providers' attitudes toward abortion. Although this was particularly the case among TBAs and family-planning workers who viewed abortion as a sin, many of the other providers interviewed also shared this opinion. The physicians and midwives pointed out that according to Islam, *roh* (life, spirit, soul) is infused in a fetus after 120 days of pregnancy, even if there is life in the biological sense before that. In this respect, most of the respondents did not consider menstrual regulation as abortion, and this probably helped to overcome any ambivalence they may otherwise have felt. Although this point of view is correct from a religious point of view, it is not held by all Muslims.

Almost all of the gynecologists, general practitioners, and trained midwives approved of abortion for medical reasons if performed by a gynecologist. In cases of rape, the gynecologists believed a psychologist should also be involved. A female doctor said that when she first became a gynecologist, she was strongly against abortion. But experience and the many problems faced by her patients had completely reversed her attitude. She was now willing to perform an abortion if the patient's menstrual period was no more than two weeks late. Most of the gynecologists were in favor of reform of the existing law on abortion. One midwife said that the law should also protect physicians who perform abortions for medical reasons.

Family-planning workers and TBAs felt that if a woman was poor and could not afford another child, or if she was in poor health or had too many pregnancies spaced close together, these should be valid reasons for abortion. In that way their opinions were more receptive to the needs of the clientele they attended in their daily work. Half of the TBAs said they would perform an abortion, but five said they would not and gave religious reasons for their position; in fact, four of these said they would refuse to help a woman with a botched abortion.

The study concluded that at least among many of the health care providers in the formal service sector, the use of menstrual regulation early in pregnancy appears to be increasingly accepted, though not by everyone and not without many provisos and ambiguities. Given these limitations, the role of TBAs remains central in assisting women whom the formal sector does not help.

THE POLICY DIMENSION

Few topics in the reproductive health research agenda have greater potential for policy impact than induced abortion. The challenge is particularly difficult in contexts where abortion is illegal, given that here the pressure to change existing laws and regulations is stronger. Policy makers, program managers, and other public personalities who influence policy are often unaware of the reality of induced abortion among their own constituencies. For abortion research to have an impact on policy, it becomes necessary to state the key findings in a style and precision that can be relevant to officials and their needs for information.

Some research on induced abortion may in fact contribute, along with other information, to strengthen a national debate on a proposed change in abortion legislation, but new information may also fuel a counterreaction, as, for example, from organized religious groups. When a public debate does lead to changing existing legislation, it may not be possible to assess a project's exact contribution to this outcome. As Mechanic (1995, 1492) remarks: "The findings from research studies and recommendations from social science evaluations are rarely translated into practice immediately. The impact of social science research is likely to come over a longer time span by influencing the way in which the informed public thinks about issues and defines relevant considerations."

There are inherent tensions between the producers of scientific information, who may be eager for their results to be applied, and the users in the policy world with regard to how, when, and through what means research findings may be used. The political environment in which policy decisions are made is also very important, particularly for sensitive subjects such as induced abortion. In pluralistic societies with traditions of open debate on social issues, bringing research findings on abortion to public attention is easier than in others where such discussions are not tolerated by the political system. In such cases, the health advocacy community can have an important role in clarifying distortions when anti-abortion forces oppose proposed changes to liberalize existing laws. Several of the projects sponsored by the WHO research initiative on induced abortion had an impact on national legislative processes or on institutional reforms. Among them, the study on abortion in Mauritius brought about a major legislative discussion in that country's parliament by pointing at the magnitude of the problem there; the Dominican Republic study led to formalize a congressional proposal to depenalize abortion; and in Korea, labor unions were interested in the findings to improve access to family-planning services to women in factories. Another set of studies that contributed to strengthen national debates that were already in motion were those in Indonesia, Colombia, and Turkey.

DISCUSSION

Although induced abortion research lies uniquely at the intersect of several disciplines, researchers—especially in the social and health sciences—are often reluctant to undertake studies. This is due in part to the inherent methodological difficulties but also to the strong social and political connotations of the topic (Rosenfield 1992; Kulczycki, this volume). Much of the difficulty, from a methodological standpoint, is the problem associated with obtaining accurate information from women who have acted outside the law and feel stigmatized or, in contexts where abortion is legal, feel the pressure of social, moral, and religious reproof.

In contexts where abortion is illegal, hospitals and clinics do the same—they hide abortions (including abortion complications) under other rubrics. As Henry David (1993, 2) has remarked: "One reason for the difficulty of estimating the incidence stems from the fact that in many countries abortion has long been shrouded in secrecy, enmeshed in cultural taboos, and surrounded with personal value conflicts."

The lack of safe, reliable abortion services in many countries makes the problem much more complex. When an unwanted pregnancy occurs, a woman will go ahead with her decision to abort regardless of whether safe services are available. Penetrating the network of illegal abortion providers from a research point of view is often (but not necessarily) difficult and potentially dangerous. Yet the issue of services, their adequacy, the quality of care, their staffing, and the attitudes of personnel toward women suffering from abortion complications are important areas where research is needed. The economic cost of abortion for services that attend complications as well as for the women who undergo clandestine procedures should also receive increased attention.

Similarly, studies are needed on the determination of the pathways that women follow once they decide to terminate a pregnancy. In contexts where abortion is illegal, its practice can include attempts at self-inducing the abortion, ingestion of drugs and herbal preparations, and resorting to the services of clandestine abortionists (followed by hospital assistance for incomplete abortion, sepsis, or other complications). When abortion complication cases are not treated in hospitals, the extent of postabortion morbidity and mortality will never be known.

Another challenge in abortion research is finding out who has had an abortion to then probe further into more difficult experiential terrain. Abortion among adolescents requires particular attention. The most common way to identify a population at risk of abortion or a population with proven abortion experience is through hospital or clinic records. Starting from populations of known cases or potential cases of induced abortion, the researcher can then proceed to investigate the underlying factors, applying quantitative and qualitative techniques, either singly or in combined research designs. In all cases, researchers undertaking abortion studies should pay careful attention to the ethical aspects of the situation, taking special care to preserve the women's confidentiality and anonymity, especially if clinic records are used as a starting point. The options to the researcher are determined largely by the policy context regarding abortion.

REFERENCES

Alan Guttmacher Institute. 1994. *Clandestine Abortion: A Latin American Reality.* New York and Washington: Alan Guttmacher Institute.

Alvarez, M. L., C. T. Garcia, S. Catasus, M. E. Benitez, and M. T. Martinez.1999. "The Determinants of Abortion Practice in the Municipality 10 de Octubre, in Havana, Cuba." In *Abortion in the Developing World,* ed. A. Mundigo and C. Indriso. New Delhi and London: Sage Publications and Zed Books.

Barreto, T., O. Campbell, J. Davies, V. Faveau, V. Filippi, W. Graham, M. Mamdami, C. Rooney, and N. Toubia. 1992. "Investigating Induced Abortion in Developing Countries: Methods and Problems." *Studies in Family Planning* 23 (3): 159–70.

Bulut, A. 1999. "Abortion Services in Two Public Sector Hospitals in Istanbul: How Well Do They Meet Women's Needs?" In *Abortion in the Developing World,* ed. A. Mundigo and C. Indriso. New Delhi and London: Sage Publications and Zed Books.

Chandrasekhar, S. 1994. *India's Abortion Experience.* Denton: University of North Texas Press.

Coeytaux, F. 1988. "Induced Abortion in Sub-Saharan Africa: What We Do and Do Not Know." *Studies in Family Planning* 19 (3): 186–90.

Cohen, S. A., and C. L. Richards. 1994. "The Cairo Consensus: Population, Development and Women." *International Family Planning Perspectives* 20 (4): 150–55.

Cook, R. 1995. "Human Rights and Reproductive Self-Determination." *The American University Law Review* 44 (4): 975–1016.

David, H. 1993. "Realities in Abortion Research." Discussion of the session on health and social aspects of induced abortion, Twenty-Second Conference of the International Union for the Scientific Study of Population, August 24–September 1, Montreal, Canada.

Declaration of Ethical Propositions. 1994. Ethics, Population and Reproductive Health Roundtable, New York, March 8–10.

Dixon-Mueller, R. 1993. "Abortion Is a Method of Family Planning." In *Four Essays on Birth Control Needs and Risks,* ed. R. Dixon-Mueller and A. Germain. New York: International Women's Health Coalition.

Djohan, E., R. Indrawasih, M. Adenan, H. Yudomustopo, and M. Tan. 1999. "The Attitudes of Health Providers towards Abortion in Indonesia." In *Abortion in the Developing World,* ed. A. Mundigo and C. Indriso. New Delhi and London: Sage Publications and Zed Books.

Elu, M. C. 1999. "Between Political Debate and Women's Suffering: Abortion in Mexico." In *Abortion in the Developing World,* ed. A. Mundigo and C. Indriso. New Delhi and London: Sage Publications and Zed Books.

Frejka, T. 1993. "The Role of Induced Abortion in Contemporary Fertility Regulation." In *Proceedings of the International Population Conference of the International Union for the Scientific Study of Population,* 209–14. Liège, Belgium: International Union for the Scientific Study of Population.

Gui, Shi-xun. 1999. "Factors Affecting Induced Abortion Behavior among Married Women in Shanghai." In *Abortion in the Developing World,* ed. A. Mundigo and C. Indriso. New Delhi and London: Sage Publications and Zed Books.

Kissling, F. 1995–96. "Responding to Religious Conservatism." *Conscience* (Winter), 7–10.

Lader, L. 1996. *Abortion.* Boston: Beacon Press.

Mechanic, D. 1995. "Emerging Trends in the Application of the Social Sciences to Health Medicine." *Social Science and Medicine* 40 (11): 1491–96.

Mundigo, A., and C. Indriso, eds. 1999. *Abortion in the Developing World.* New Delhi and London: Sage Publications and Zed Books.

Nunes, F., and Y. M. Delph. 1995. "Making Abortion Law Reform Happen in Guyana: A Success Story." *Reproductive Health Matters* 6: 12–23.

Paiewonsky, D. 1999. "The Social Determinants of Induced Abortion in the Dominican Republic." In *Abortion in the Developing World,* ed. A. Mundigo and C. Indriso. New Delhi and London: Sage Publications and Zed Books.

Paxman, J. M., A. Rizo, L. Brown, and J. Benson. 1993. "The Clandestine Epidemic: The Practice of Induced Abortion in Latin America." *Studies in Family Planning* 24 (4): 205–26.

Remez, L. 1995. "Confronting the Reality of Abortion in Latin America." *International Family Planning Perspectives* 21 (1): 32–37.

Rosenfield, P. L. 1992. "The Potential of Trans-disciplinary Research for Sustained and Extending Linkages between Health and Social Sciences." *Social Science and Medicine* 35 (11): 1343–57.

Singh, S., and D. Wulf. 1991. "Estimating Abortion Levels in Brazil, Colombia and Peru, Using Hospital Admissions and Fertility Survey Data." *International Family Planning Perspectives* 17 (1): 8–13.

_______ . 1994. "Estimated Levels of Induced Abortion in Six Latin American Countries." *International Family Planning Perspectives* 20 (1): 4–13.

World Health Organization. 1994. "Abortion: A Tabulation of Available Data on the Frequency and Mortality of Unsafe Abortion." WHO/FHE/MSM/93.13, Geneva.

Zhou Wei-jin, Gao Er-sheng, Yang Yao-ying, Qin Fei, and Tang Wei. 1999. "Induced Abortion and the Outcome of Subsequent Pregnancy: Client and Provider Perspectives." In *Abortion in the Developing World*, ed. A. Mundigo and C. Indriso. New Delhi and London: Sage Publications and Zed Books.

Chapter 4

Demographic Research and Abortion Policy: Limits to the Use of Statistics

Andrzej Kulczycki

The 1994 International Conference on Population and Development (ICPD) marked a major shift in the basic rationale for population programs, from a concern with demographic aggregates toward the reproductive health of individuals. However, it was the topic of abortion, or rather what to do about induced abortion, that dominated conference proceedings. One might expect, therefore, renewed interest in abortion among population scholars. Although a cursory glance through recent volumes of such journals as *Studies in Family Planning* or *International Family Planning Perspectives* suggests that abortion has featured more often as a paper topic since the late 1980s, basic and applied research in this field continues to be hindered by factors similar to those that reduce the chances of rational policy making. In most areas of the world, statistics on abortion are incomplete and faulty and thereby unresponsive to policy issues and inadequate for use in social science research. There is not enough locally specific data that is timely and of good quality. Moreover, abortion remains deeply emotive, socially and politically divisive.

We know that the growing body of information and social science efforts to understand the causes and effects of population growth helped persuade governments to adopt policies benefiting family and national welfare (Harkavy 1995). The influence of research on abortion may be harder to assess. There are instances where it has proven influential in policy making and many examples where it has been less effective. The subject of abortion commands minuscule research budgets, and there is much that we still need to learn about it; yet the stock of available knowledge is sufficient to inform policy makers as to the general direction of measures to reduce the incidence of abortion and make its practice safer. It is important to investigate why statistics are not used more effectively to affect such policy changes.

It is pertinent to ask what accounts for the apparent neglect of this topic by demographers. The disdain for studying abortion might be compared to the contempt shown by many academic social scientists for conducting research that could be used to improve family-planning programs. This chapter will examine some of the reasons for this neglect as part of a broader attempt to assess the limits to using statistical data in advancing knowledge and policy in this area. The chapter begins by briefly reviewing the methodological limitations to collecting and using abortion statistics. It points out that despite these and broader reasons why demographers have devoted little attention to studying abortion, a considerable body of knowledge can be drawn upon to inform public policy. This chapter moves on to consider why statistics are not more influential in this area and questions whether demographers are focusing too much effort on attempting to pin down the incidence and prevalence rates of induced abortion and too little attention on the processes that lead to it. The final part of the chapter describes social and political limits to the use of abortion statistics and examines how elastic are such constraints. The chapter draws on the author's own research in Kenya and Poland (Kulczycki 1999) and places greater emphasis on the contributions of demographers, although the work of other social science and public health researchers is also discussed.

METHODOLOGICAL AND DATA CONCERNS

As with any other phenomenon, a thorough understanding of abortion demands the collection and dissemination of accurate information. We need to quantify the frequency and characteristics of abortion so as to analyze it. Statistical analyses can help define a coherent research agenda and improve policies intended to reduce unwanted pregnancy. Relevant statistics may make up a part of the background against which the moral, as well as the social and health aspects of abortion, are discussed. But unlike most phenomena, research reports on many aspects of abortion are flawed or otherwise reduced in value due to deficiencies in the recording of such events (see the chapters by Singh, Henshaw, and Berensten and Mundigo in this volume).

The sensitive and personal nature of abortion makes it difficult to employ the demographer's standard toolkit, built upon the conduct and analysis of large-scale sample surveys. Underreporting of abortion is common in retrospective fertility surveys, even where abortion is legally available and widely practiced. Comparisons with more reliable data show that the 1988 cycle of the U.S. National Survey of Family Growth captured about 35 percent of known abortions (Jones and Forrest 1992). World Fertility Survey (WFS) data, pertaining mostly to countries where abortion is unlawful and stigmatized, captured at most 80 percent of recognized spontaneous fetal losses and largely missed induced abortions (Casterline 1989), even in countries such as South Korea where abortion carries greater acceptance. The Demographic and Health Survey (DHS) First Round surveys did not carry questions about non–live birth outcomes, chiefly due to political objections. This is all the more regrettable at a time of renewed interest in the wanted/unwanted fertility continuum and because well-executed surveys such as the DHS carry weight among policy makers. It also underscores the need for developing more innovative approaches to collecting abortion statistics (Coeytaux, Leonard, and Royston 1991; Barreto et al. 1992; Huntington et al. 1993).

A TOPIC OF DEMOGRAPHIC NEGLECT

But demographers have neglected the study of abortion for more than methodological reasons. A senior Canadian statistician, commenting on how the codirectors of the 1984 Canadian Fertility Survey avoided questions in their questionnaire design that would have shed light on abortion, considers this neglect to be rooted in embarrassment over the high incidence of such a crude method of birth control "in such a gadget-minded society as Canada" (Krótki 1990, 15–17). Polish demographers are embarrassed that their country's abortion rate is high relative to European norms and that this is primarily due to poor familiarity with modern methods of family planning. Demographers may be little different from people in most societies who hold conflicting beliefs and emotions about abortion.

There is also the discomfort that many demographers feel about researching a phenomenon that tends to be a very private act and often is politically and ideologically sensitive at the societal level. Demographers may sense, often with some justification, that their statistics and reports may somehow be manipulated; they are more comfortable with their role as scientists, which, to some extent, includes raising doubts about simple answers to complex questions.

Research efforts on abortion are further stymied by the limited funds available for such studies. There has recently been more programmatically funded abortion research, though even this is minute compared to the funds allocated to population programs. Yet research on what makes a good abortion policy is less ambiguous than what makes for a good population policy; and should research arrive at familiar policy conclusions, then such findings would be more firmly grounded than before with the prospect that both the public and decision makers might be better informed. There is understandable frustration over the political obstacles to implementing the policies needed to reduce the incidence of abortion and the ill health associated with unsafe procedures. However, demographers have shunned away from tackling research questions that mesh with the political world. For example, the directory of the Population Association of America does not even list political science as an area of specialization among its members.

THE CONTRIBUTION OF DEMOGRAPHERS TO ABORTION RESEARCH AND POLICY

Even after allowing for the comparative neglect of abortion by demographers and the technical difficulties that limit the availability and use of abortion statistics, there is still a substantial body of knowledge on abortion. This is based on sociological, demographic, and epidemiological analyses; surveys of public opinion and attitudes; comparative legal studies; assessments of the provision and utilization of abortion services; and the relative merits of different abortion procedures. Although this information is not as exact as one would like, the broad outlines of a well-directed strategy for reducing abortion are clear and center on strengthening the provision of family-planning services.

For North America and Western Europe, somewhat reliable statistics on the incidence of abortion began emerging in the 1960s. They provided evidence that abortion was more frequent than had been thought, safer than had been the case, and more widely accepted than had been assumed. Legislators drew upon this evidence when revising laws and policies. In the 1970s, French demographers persuaded legislators that the declining national birth rate was not related to the growing practice of illegal abortion (Mossuz-Lavau 1986). A number of countries, including India, have justified the decriminalization of abortion on public health grounds, the case for which is incontrovertible. In Romania, after the Ceausescu regime restricted access to abortion and contraceptive services during the late 1960s, the maternal mortality rate rose to a level far higher than elsewhere in Europe. Until a new government relegalized abortion in 1989, abortion-related deaths accounted for at least 84 percent of all maternal deaths throughout the 1980s (Hord et al. 1991). However, contraceptive use still lags. Most recently, the ICPD Plan of Action addressed the issue of unsafe abortion as a public health problem. From a broad policy standpoint therefore, statistics can help map out the directions of public policy, but how useful are they to fine-tuning its details and to filling in research gaps? Let us consider examples from the United States of America and sub-Saharan Africa.

UNDERSTANDING THE IMPACT OF PUBLIC POLICY ON ABORTION RATES IN THE UNITED STATES OF AMERICA

In the United States, there are two major sources of abortion data. Nearly all state health agencies report annual numbers of abortions to the Centers for Diseases Control (CDC), but their reporting requirements vary widely. More complete statistics are available from the Alan Guttmacher Institute (AGI), which periodically surveys all identified abortion providers and through them gathers data on the characteristics of abortion patients. This enables some quite sophisticated research, although there have been few studies on the determinants of abortion rates.

Most work on the impact of public policy on abortion rates has used cross-sectional estimates of state abortion rates. Typically, state abortion rates are regressed against selected demographic and social characteristics such as marriage rates, median education and income levels, religious affiliation, and metropolitan provider share as well as policy-related variables such as the number of abortion providers and public funds for abortions (e.g., Singh 1986; Garbacz 1990). Public funding of abortion may generate some extra demand for the procedure, although it is difficult to distinguish this influence from other effects at the state level.

Blank et al. (1994) used a panel set of state abortion rates over thirteen years and found that restricting Medicaid funding for abortion leads to substantial cross-state migration for abortion services.[1] Their analysis employed two-stage least-squares models with fixed state and year effects. The study indicates that limiting Medicaid funding of abortion is correlated with a 14 percent decline in state abortion rates. However, only a 5 percent decline occurs in actual abortion rates among state residents, indicating that enforcing such laws leads to substantial cross-state migration. This qualification is seemingly lost on lawmakers. Blank et al. (1994) have also found that a larger number of abortion providers within a state increases the abortion rate, chiefly by promoting cross-state migration to nonhospital providers. In contrast to restricting Medicaid funding, parental consent laws for teen abortions have little influence on aggregate abortion rates.

Using a pooled time series from 1982 to 1988 with the fifty states as units of analysis, Meier and McFarlane (1994) have shown that state Medicaid funding of abortion is associated with more abortions, lower teen fertility, fewer low-birthweight babies, fewer births with late or no prenatal care, and fewer neonatal and infant deaths. Higher state expenditures for family planning are linked to significantly fewer abortions and only marginal reductions on teenage birth rates but otherwise yield similar outcomes. Meier and McFarlane (1994) used state-specific dummy variables to control for the confounding due to systematic variation among states in levels of abortion or family-planning funding. The authors estimated that family-planning funding over the 1982–88 period prevented a total of 670,000 abortions—in other words, without such funding, there would have been about 6 percent more abortions nationally. However, the authors conclude with this salutary caution: "States seldom make policy on abortion funding based on public health benefits" (Meier and McFarlane 1994, 1471), the reason being that political considerations dominate.

WHAT WE DO AND DO NOT KNOW ABOUT ABORTION: THE SITUATION IN SUB-SAHARAN AFRICA REVISITED

A number of studies indicate that complications related to abortion are a major cause of maternal deaths in many African countries. This, alongside publicity about unwanted adolescent fertility, the opportunity costs of schoolgirl pregnancies, and conflicting cultural influences, has led to greater awareness of abortion. However, not much has been added to our comprehension of the situation since Coeytaux (1988) reviewed what is and what is not known about induced abortion in the region. There is little reason to think that the situation will change without better statistics and a more favorable context for research, just as policies are unlikely to become more responsive unless acceptable language is found, along with a more conducive political atmosphere. The issue of abortion in Africa is at a prepolitical stage and still does not command the attention of policy makers.

With the possible exception of Nigeria, Kenya has seen more research on abortion than any other sub-Saharan African country, a function of its relatively strong research tradition and greater donor accessibility. With funds from the Swedish International Development Administration, the Population Council has helped sponsor a research initiative on abortion in Kenya. This has included an insightful community-based study of thirty low-income, urban women known to have had an abortion from providers who did not keep records (Baker and Khasiani 1992). The study yielded information on the reasons why women terminate their pregnancies, the stages by which they make such decisions, and how these abortions are carried out.

Nevertheless, despite such useful studies, there remains a chronic lack of in-depth, qualitative, and community-based data elsewhere in Africa and an almost complete absence of reliable statistics beyond those from hospital-based studies. Community-based studies are costly, particularly if scaled up to a regional or national level.

WHY STATISTICS ARE NOT MORE INFLUENTIAL

Deficiencies in the measurement of abortion are but one reason why statistics are not more influential in determining priority research areas and informing public policy. Ideological and perceptual positions are invariably more important considerations. During the recent conflict over abortion in Poland, statistics were dismissed by opponents of abortion who equated the procedure with an external ideology and naively thought that upon the downfall of a despised regime, all would be well in the new order. Abortion was situated within a heavy political and moralistic context, almost totally divorced from social truths. It proved difficult to impress on policy makers the implications of Romania's disastrous experience with outlawing abortion, its relevance discounted on the premise that the procedure had been banned by a dictator for demographic-nationalist reasons.

Even if there are reasonably good statistics available, they may not be available to the right people at the right time, or they may not be clearly interpreted. Statistics can inform debate, but policy decisions are invariably based on other considerations. That statistics might carry little weight is evinced by the ideological blinders of the U.S. right-to-life movement. In the 1980s, this social movement succeeded in sharply restricting U.S. government funding for family-planning programs overseas, leading to cutbacks in contraceptive services and increasing the number of people resorting to abortions—the very behavior those opposed to abortion wanted to discourage. A decade later, U.S. support for family-planning programs overseas was again drastically cut back.

The meaning given to data may depend upon perceptual considerations, especially one's position on the overall issue of abortion, which is why it is possible to base competing arguments on estimates of the frequency of abortion. For those ardently opposed to abortion, statistics may simply confirm their beliefs. To those who support legal abortion, statistics underline how many women have been relieved of the risks of clandestine abortions or of the stress of unwanted parenthood. Statistics may merely reinforce one's perceptions and increase controversy unless demographers and public health researchers put them into perspective. This raises the issue of whether demographers are always asking the right questions.

ARE DEMOGRAPHERS FOCUSING ON THE RIGHT QUESTIONS?

Demographers have concentrated their efforts on estimating the incidence of abortion. This focus is both important and laudable, but should this be the most appropriate locus of their activity? In Poland, the magnitude of abortion is unknown and became even more difficult to ascertain as access to services was restricted. Within a few years, the official records showed that the number of abortions fell from about 130,000 to 60,000 and less, but the proportions between illegal and legal abortions had changed and private medical business had grown so that the total abortion level was probably not very different from that before. Regardless of the true level, it was widely accepted that abortion was a mass phenomenon; opinions differed on how to reduce its scale. In fact, determining the true magnitude of abortion remains not only impossible but also less important than that it is high and could be lower if couples practiced contraception better. This should have been and needs to be the focus of more research and discussion in Poland and neighboring countries, along with the need to improve sex education and contraceptive practice.

Abortion should have been considered against this background because as in most developing countries, society remains poorly informed about these matters. The overconcentration on measuring the incidence of abortion is understandable, given the demographer's penchant for numbers. Information like that is needed, but such numbers also change and depend on many interrelated variables whose interaction needs to be better understood, both to advance knowledge and to plan preventive measures.

In this context, the report by the U.S. National Academy of Sciences (Brown and Eisenberg 1995) on the determinants and consequences of unintended pregnancies is particularly apt. It goes beyond reviewing contraceptive use patterns as they relate to unintended pregnancy and considers the dynamics of the processes that lead to unintended pregnancy and possibly to abortion. That such research may be hard to conduct in countries where there is considerable ambivalence about sexuality need not mean that it is impossible. Such research could also produce knowledge that is more useful for designing programs and services and for reducing the chances of repeat unintended pregnancies. Again, a comparison could be drawn to what has happened with research on family planning. This now evinces more concern with the quality of services and how they are delivered from the perspectives of both the clients and providers and not just with quantifying how many people need services.

HOW ELASTIC ARE THE SOCIAL AND POLITICAL LIMITS TO THE USE OF ABORTION STATISTICS?

The prevailing political and social climate, including both domestic and international conditions, significantly affects the availability and use of abortion statistics. However, there is no clear correlation between the type of political system and the use of abortion statistics, even if it might seem easier to change legislation in a country ruled by edict. Left-wing governments have traditionally been more amenable to adopting permissive abortion policies (Brooks 1992), but national leaders must be convinced that a problem is serious enough to demand their attention. Statistics may facilitate such an awareness, but in democratic polities, especially, national leaders are more likely to move on an issue if it commands public support. Without this, policy changes are difficult to implement, particularly when strongly opposed by powerful lobbies, such as religious or medical groups.

Where religious groups are powerful and hostile to discussing abortion, statistics are less likely to be effectual. In postcommunist Poland, abortion became framed as an ideological and moral question, leaving little room for statistics. A senior bishop from the Catholic Church stated that "statistical data in front of morality... have no meaning."[2] The goal was to tidy up the country's social laws in accordance with religious doctrines; the central concern was to establish that an embryo constituted a human being. The new political elites had a very low understanding of statistics and, beholden to church authorities who had earlier sustained their opposition activities, were willing to link state policy to the Catholic Church's social program.

The formulation of policies is typically a highly complex process that needs critical intermediaries. It can be initiated by governments, interest groups, and political parties but rarely by researchers. Kenyan researchers not only lack more accurate data on abortion but also find it difficult to understand the policy formulation process, how it is made and how it can be influenced (Rogo 1989). Moreover, there is a lack of pressure groups to make known to decision makers the implications of high rates of unwanted pregnancy and abortion. The only activist physicians are at the Kenyatta National Hospital in Nairobi. The Centre for the Study of Adolescence has generated some studies and reviews of abortion in Kenya and sub-Saharan Africa, made this information more accessible, and shown that research on this subject is both practical and politically feasible. However, it has proved impossible to maintain the initial momentum, and researchers feel overwhelmed by their inability to find footholds in the policy process.

Kenyan decision makers have mixed perceptions of the abortion situation. They lack base data but not anecdotal information, and their impressions may be further shaped by traditional societal disapproval of abortion. It is unclear what their views are and how far they can be pushed; it took the government almost twenty years to wholeheartedly embrace family planning. An innovative study that estimated a total of 10,000 pregnancy-related, schoolgirl dropouts each year (Fergusson 1988) helped sensitize policy makers and the general public to the need for dealing with unwanted adolescent fertility. However, there is still a heavy moralistic overlay to such discussion. The cultural and social constraints to addressing abortion remain strong. Even senior personnel of family-planning organizations have reservations about discussing abortion; the Family Planning Association of Kenya only began to provide postabortion contraception counseling to young people in the early 1990s in Mombasa and Nairobi. Politicians and most health care providers alike would prefer that the problem of abortion be avoided.

An awareness of where the public stands on abortion may provide useful policy guidance, but for many parts of the world, public opinion on abortion has yet to be reliably gauged. Many methodological issues need to be considered when making such measurements (Cook, Jelen, and Wilcox 1992). In the United States, attitudes on this issue have remained quite steady since 1972. Most citizens are situationalists, believing that abortion is a correct choice in some cases but not in others. They hold that the government should not determine the moral choices of people at the same time as they tend to think that too many women elect to proceed with abortion. Politicians may take stock of such facts, but other considerations may weigh more heavily in their minds. They may seek to attract votes by assuming strong positions about making access to abortion services difficult. Publics in many countries are ambivalent about abortion, but the opinions of elites are more important in shaping abortion policies.

It is unlikely that statistics will play a role in influencing policy unless greater concern is placed on improving the lives of women and children. This requires not only that many male decision makers stop dismissing abortion as a woman's issue but that women, too, must perceive a grievance and feel an urge to ameliorate it. In Kenya, Mexico, and many other societies, women have more important priorities, not least simply getting by in a time of growing economic hardship. There are more pressing health problems to contend with, including the escalating AIDS epidemic. Also, as in many African nations, prominent Kenyan women are not tackling this problem because they do not want to be construed as opposing a government in a country that still does not encourage freedoms of association.

The international environment may significantly influence the quality of abortion statistics and the content of policies. For example, shifts in the policies of the U.S. Agency for International Development, until now the largest source of aid for population and family-planning activities, may influence funding for abortion research. The so-called Mexico City Policy, intended to thwart any abortion-related activities, had no direct impact on the level or quality of abortion services abroad because no U.S. government funds were earmarked for such purposes. However, it may have increased the frequency of abortion and related complications by restricting the flow of funds to family-planning organizations that might have otherwise addressed such problems. The policy was also more broadly interpreted than warranted, setting back research on abortion (Blane and Friedman 1990).

The restrictive climate affected donor activities and even prevented the United Nations Population Fund (UNFPA), World Health Organization (WHO), and International Planned Parenthood Federation (IPPF) from disseminating the proceedings of a major European meeting (held in Tblisi in 1990) on reducing unwanted pregnancy and abortion through family-planning services. Most of the papers were published several years later (Newman 1993). This occurred after President William Clinton had revoked the Mexico City Policy only days after his inauguration, thereby initiating a second policy volte-face by the U.S. government within ten years. In 1996, federal funds were again barred for any family-planning agencies giving information on abortion. This latest policy reversal is testimony to the strong reach of the Christian Coalition, a well-organized social movement made up of evangelical Protestants fervently opposed to abortion and a powerful voting bloc within a resurgent Republican party.

Groups opposed to abortion have hindered the introduction of mifepristone into the United States, threatening to organize a boycott of all pharmaceuticals produced by the drug's manufacturer. Such pressure similarly impedes the diffusion of mifepristone to other countries. In like manner, African and Central American governments that have launched family-planning programs do not want to jeopardize their fragile base and limited budgets. Decision makers are almost certainly aware of the dangers posed by abortions performed under unsanitary conditions, but they are at least equally aware that abortion politics led the Reagan administration to defund UNFPA and IPPF and caused problems for many other organizations. Multilateral donor agencies may likewise be influenced by nongovernmental actors. For example, UNFPA, WHO, and the IPPF have shown greater interest in dealing with abortion since the late 1980s. They have been stirred in large part by women's health advocates and networks that have become far more active on the international stage, as amply illustrated at the

ICPD (Cairo, 1994) and the United Nation's Fourth World Conference on Women (held in Beijing, 1995).

Women's groups have been especially influential in repackaging abortion as part of a wider concern for reproductive and women's health. In some cases, they have supported more rigorous applied research to buttress their claims. For example, clinics run by the Bangladesh Women's Health Coalition provide menstrual regulation services at one-sixth the cost of those administered by government hospitals and offer individual counseling as well (Kay and Kabir 1988). Such knowledge can be used to improve the allocation of resources and quality of care. There is a need for more service- and policy-oriented abortion research in nearly all countries. For the United States, studies show that recent medical school graduates know little about the procedure, which only a limited number of abortion providers and facilities are now willing to perform. The proportion of residency programs in obstetrics and gynecology offering first-trimester abortion training declined from 23 percent in 1985 to 12 percent in 1991–92 (MacKay and MacKay 1995). By then, 84 percent of U.S. counties had no known abortion provider (Henshaw and Van Vort 1994). Such studies clearly indicate declining access to abortion services and that the medical profession has avoided responsibility to train physicians in this legal procedure. This reluctance has been strengthened by the unwillingness of insurance companies to cover providers and of physicians to risk constant hostile demonstrations and even murder.

DISCUSSION

There are numerous gaps and statistical problems with existing abortion statistics. Many countries even lack baseline information. This underscores the need for more resources and attention to be devoted to this problem generally, although little may come about without the political will to achieve it. Specifically, progress in measuring and researching abortion is more likely to come about through greater interdisciplinary borrowing and the adoption of mixed-method approaches. There remains an urgent need to expand the international coverage of abortion statistics and to improve their quality and comparability.

That basic statistics for much of the world are so limited makes policy changes unlikely, but demographic data and analysis on abortion exists and can be brought to bear on policy makers. Furthermore, if the ultimate goal of research is to improve the human condition, then such estimates need only be sufficiently accurate to indicate broad policy and programmatic directions. Instead, we find that in most areas of the world, the issue of abortion lacks credibility and the strong support of powerful interest groups, although the Cairo conference has given greater legitimacy to efforts aimed at making the practice of abortion safer.

More research is needed not only to improve understanding of the abortion situation but also to see how policy makers consider this issue and how they weigh statistics in that process. It seems that as with many other public issues, statistics are often not used when policy makers consider abortion. Opinions are formed on the basis of other realities and perceptions. This is not to say that statistics have no role—on the contrary, they can provide a useful corrective to poor policy making and can be used to buttress sounder policy. Abortion statistics define problems and suggest policies and are essential to monitoring and evaluating their performance. However, their policy impact to date has been significantly smaller than that of statistics in the population field more generally. Moreover, sociopolitical concerns exert a very influential role in abortion policy making.

This chapter has additionally stressed that demographers should be concerned not only with the exact total of abortions but also with the processes that bring it about. The issue of abortion should not be separated from contraceptive availability and use, other aspects of birth control, and the realities of unintended pregnancies. Those opposed to such research and discussion may try to prevent it taking place. They will be indirectly assisted in their efforts if demographers continue to neglect this area of interest.

NOTES

1. Medicaid is a public health insurance program available to low-income U.S. citizens. Under the 1976 Hyde Amendment, the U.S. Congress prohibited the use of federal funds to pay for abortion except when a woman's life would otherwise be in danger. Many states continue to fund abortions under Medicaid, although by 1989, thirty-one states had imposed some restrictions. This means that poor women in states that do not pay for abortions under Medicaid may be unable to pay for them.

2. Bishop Jerzy Buxakowski, testifying in parliament on behalf of the Episcopate and quoted in *Trybuna Ludu* (1989).

REFERENCES

Baker, Jean, and Shanyisa Khasiani. 1992. "Induced Abortion in Kenya: Case Histories." *Studies in Family Planning,* 23 (1): 34–44.

Barreto, T., O. M. R. Campbell, J. Lynne Davies, V. Fauveau, V. G. A. Filippi, W. J. Graham, M. Mamdani, C. I. F. Rooney, and N. F. Toubia. 1992. "Investigating Induced Abortion in Developing Countries: Methods and Problems." *Studies in Family Planning* 23 (3): 159–70.

Blane, John, and Matthew Friedman. 1990. *Mexico City Policy Implementation Study.* Occasional paper no. 5. Washington, D.C.: Population Technical Assistance Project.

Blank, Rebecca M., Christine C. George, and Rebecca A. London. 1994. *State Abortion Rates: The Impact of Policies, Providers, Politics, Demographics, and Economic Environment.* Working paper no. 4853. Cambridge, Mass.: National Bureau of Economic Research.

Brooks, Joel E. 1992. "Abortion Policy in Western Democracies: A Cross-National Analysis." *Governance* 5 (3): 342–57.

Brown, Sarah S., and Leon Eisenberg, eds. *The Best Intentions: Unintended Pregnancy and the Well-Being of Children and Families.* Washington, D.C.: Institute of Medicine, National Academy of Sciences.

Casterline, John B. 1989. "Collecting Data on Pregnancy Loss: A Review of Evidence from the World Fertility Survey." *Studies in Family Planning* 20 (2): 81–95.

Coeytaux, Francine M. 1988. "Induced Abortion in Sub-Saharan Africa: What We Do and Do Not Know." *Studies in Family Planning* 19 (3): 186–90.

Coeytaux, Francine, Ann Leonard, and Erica Royston, eds. 1991. *Methodological Issues in Abortion Research.* New York: Population Council.

Cook, Elizabeth A., Ted G. Jelen, and Clyde Wilcox. 1992. *Between Two Absolutes: Public Opinion and the Politics of Abortion.* Boulder, Colo.: Westview Press.

Fergusson, Alan. 1988. *Schoolgirl Pregnancy in Kenya.* Nairobi: Division of Family Health—GTZ Support Unit, Ministry of Health.

Garbacz, Christopher. 1990. "Abortion Demand." *Population Research and Policy Review* 9 (2): 151–60.

Harkavy, Oscar. 1995. *Curbing Population Growth: An Insider's Perspective on the Population Movement.* New York: Plenum Press.

Henshaw, Stanley K., and Jennifer Van Vort. 1994. "Abortion Services in the United States, 1991 and 1992." *Family Planning Perspectives* 26 (3): 100–106, 112.

Hord, Charlotte, Henry P. David, France Donnay, and Merrill Wolf. 1991. "Reproductive Health in Romania: Reversing the Ceausescu Legacy." *Studies in Family Planning* 22 (4): 231–40.

Huntington, D., B. Mensch, and N. Toubia. 1993. "A New Approach to Eliciting Information about Induced Abortion." *Studies in Family Planning* 24 (2).

Jones, Elise F., and Jacqueline Darroch Forrest. 1992. "Underreporting of Abortion in Surveys of U.S. Women: 1976 to 1988." *Demography* 29 (1): 113–26.

Kay, Bonnie J., and Sandra M. Kabir. 1988. "A Study of Costs and Behavioural Outcomes of Menstrual Regulation Services in Bangladesh." *Social Science and Medicine* 26 (6): 597–604.

Krótki, Karol. 1990. *Why Are Canadians Dying Out?* Research Discussion Paper no. 85. Edmonton, AB: Department of Sociology, University of Alberta.

Kulczycki, Andrzej. 1999. *The Abortion Debate in the World Arena.* New York: Routledge.

MacKay, H. Trent, and Andrea P. MacKay. 1995. "Abortion Training in Obstetrics and Gynecology Residency Programs in the United States, 1991–1992." *Family Planning Perspectives* 27 (3): 112–15.

Meier, Kenneth J., and Deborah R. McFarlane. 1994. "State Family Planning and Abortion Expenditures: Their Effect on Public Health." *American Journal of Public Health* 84 (9): 1468–72.

Mossuz-Lavau, Janine. 1986. "Abortion Policy in France under Governments of the Right and Left (1973–84)." In *The New Politics of Abortion,* ed. J. Lovenduski and J. Outshoorn, 86–104. Newbury Park, Calif.: Sage Publications.

Newman, Karen, ed. 1993. *Progress Postponed: Abortion in Europe in the 1990s.* London: International Planned Parenthood Federation.

Rogo, Khama. 1991. "A Multidisciplinary Approach to Policy-Oriented Research: An Example from Kenya." In *Methodological Issues in Abortion Research,* ed. Francine Coeytaux, Ann Leonard, and Erica Royston, 115–19. New York: Population Council.

Singh, Susheela. 1986. "Adolescent Pregnancy in the United States: An Interstate Analysis." *Family Planning Perspectives* 18 (5): 210–20.

Chapter 5

Kutoa Mimba: Debates about Schoolgirl Abortion in Machame, Tanzania

Amy Stambach

Kutoa mimba—"to take out a pregnancy" (Kiswahili)—is one option that pregnant schoolgirls living in Machame, Tanzania consider to avoid being expelled from school. This chapter examines the social and cultural circumstances that compel and motivate schoolgirls to seek abortions, and it considers the significance of schooling in affecting students' reproductive decisions. Three cases involving unwanted pregnancies are presented: two concern young women who have had abortions (one a Form 3 student, another a secondary school graduate), and the third, a secondary school student who left school to give birth to her baby instead of having an abortion. Rather than describe the exact events and people involved in each case (subjects' rights to privacy demand that people remain anonymous and that pseudonyms be used), our discussion focuses on what was made public to villagers, teachers, neighbors, and students. By looking at the cultural concerns abortion raises, this chapter explores broad issues of social organization and change as they pertain to schooling and Chagga reproductive practice.[1]

Debates about abortion are closely connected to local perceptions of the demographics of secondary schooling. Many people who live in Machame contend that abortion rates are higher and are increasing more rapidly among secondary school students than among any other group of girls or women. Although no quantitative data support or disprove this assertion, public perception that abortion rates and secondary schooling are interrelated warrants examination for the insight it suggests into cultural ideas about connections between education and reproduction.

A number of studies have addressed the subject of abortion in sub-Saharan Africa, among them a study of abortion among unmarried Kenyan women of low socioeconomic status (Baker and Khasiani 1992); a comparative review of literature on abortion and marital status (Caldwell and Caldwell 1994); and a study of marriage preferences and generational changes in an Akan (Ghanaian) matrilineage (Bleek 1978). These works provide insights into the socioeconomic positions of women who choose, or are compelled, to abort. They motivate discussion here about the cultural meanings of maternity, paternity, and marriage, and they prepare the way for exploring links between abortion practices among young women and the sociostructural positions of secondary schoolgirls.

RESEARCH SETTING

Machame is located on the southwestern slopes of Mount Kilimanjaro, approximately thirteen miles northwest of Moshi, the regional capital, and approximately thirty miles east of Arusha. The area—roughly fifty-five square miles—ranges in elevation from 1,000 to 5,000 feet above sea level and corresponds to the territory once ruled at the turn of the century by a hereditary chief (*mangi*) who controlled trade in and out of the region and who oversaw the distribution of land and food in exchange for the clientage of nonroyal lineages.

With a population of about 63,000 in 1992,[2] Machame is one of the most densely settled nonurban areas in Tanzania. Despite its proximity to Moshi Town, Machame is geographically and culturally distinct from the regional capital in several ways. It is located on the slopes of the mountain, away from the dry, dusty plain below. The mountain is lush with banana trees and coffee shrubs, and the air is cooler and damper at higher altitudes than in the lowlands near Moshi. Unlike in Moshi, land in Machame is identified culturally with Chagga history and ritual life. Past generations are buried in banana groves that surround Chagga houses on the mountain, and rites of passage and of intensification are associated with the sacred groves.

Historically, the people of Machame trace their ancestry to migrations from Shambaa territories in the south and Meru territories in the west. Legend has it that two brothers, Mashami and Nro, fought at the foot of Mount Meru (near present-day Arusha) and as a result went their separate ways. Mashami migrated east to the western slopes of Mount Kilimanjaro; Nro remained in Meru. Today, people living in Machame are considered to be part of a larger cultural group, Chagga. Although this ethnic label is largely a reflection of colonial census categories, the population shares a cultural history that extends through three centuries of intermarriage, warfare, and trade networks. This cultural history is today a key component of regional identity, and it facilitates the sentiment among people in Machame that they are culturally connected to a broader community.

DEBATES ABOUT ABORTION

The exact number of abortions taking place in Machame is difficult to assess. Statistics are scanty and, where available, of poor quality. This is true not only of Tanzania, as elsewhere, but of other sub-Saharan countries as well (cf. Baker and Khasiani 1992; Caldwell and Caldwell 1994, 275; Ladipo 1978, 112). The 1991–92 Tanzania Demographic Health Survey (Ngallaba, Kapiga, and Boerma 1993) reports on women's reproductive histories and knowledge about contraception, but it does not provide information about abortion. Nor is abortion addressed in Omari's otherwise detailed study (1991) of social problems among Tanzanian youth. As Caldwell and Caldwell (1994) note, surveys generally are unsuitable for investigating the subject, and casual conversation with an outsider to the community rarely touches on the issue. Nonetheless, abortion plays a significant role throughout sub-Saharan Africa in decisions about family planning (Bleek 1978; Caldwell and Caldwell 1994; Mashalaba 1989). A number of reports suggest that pregnant girls resort to abortion in order to remain in school (see Barker and Rich 1992; Gyepi-Garbrah 1985; Nichols et al. 1986) and that as many as a quarter of all reported abortions are performed on young women ages fifteen to nineteen (Mashalaba 1989, 17)—roughly the age of secondary school students.

Insofar as abortion rates in Tanzania appear to be increasing (Tanzania Gender Networking Programme 1993, 147; Nyirenda 1992),[3] and insofar as abortions are easier and safer to obtain these days than in the past, public awareness—and debate—has reached a new peak as well. One need only look at several editorials and articles from the official Tanzanian press to understand the public scrutiny directed toward this subject. In an article entitled "What the Law Says on Abortion," journalist Abdulrahaman O. J. Kaniki cites the Tanzanian Penal Code, sections 15.0–15.3, as stating unequivocally that "any person who, with intent to procure miscarriage of a woman, whether she is or is not with a child, . . . is guilty of a felony and is liable to imprisonment for 14 years" (Kaniki 1993). Several months earlier, Isaac C. Nyirenda (1992, 4) wrote to the editor of the same press, stating that he had "followed with interest the debate on contraceptives and realized that something ha[d] not been tackled properly." He referred to the "current economic situation" of schoolgirls who were dependent on their parents and who fell easy prey to "sinful men or fellow male students with money." The solution to this problem, he argued, was to legalize abortion for schoolgirls. His argument, typical of others who favored abortion, held that "if abortion [were] legalised, it [would] reduce the number of students, especially girls, who [were] forced to terminate their studies because of becoming mothers."

In Machame and within the broader Chagga community, secondary schoolgirls figure prominently within debates about abortion. The 1978 National Education Act, which calls for interventions against student "misconduct" and "offenses against morality," is frequently invoked by school authorities to expel pregnant students (Tanzania Development Research Group 1990, 3), and the code for behavior at nearly every secondary school is formulated to the effect that students engaged in sexual relations be dismissed. A number of anthropological works on the contemporary life of East African women has examined the cultural tendency in the region to figure young women of reproductive age as irresponsible agents who represent, as a category, the ambiguities and uncertainties of development (see Kerner and Cook 1991; Mbilinyi 1972; Stambach 2000; Weiss 1993; White 1990). The association of abortion and schooling with the sociomoral degeneracy of young, upwardly mobile women reflects another instance of this tendency. On the one hand, educated young women represent the hopes and dreams of a community working to incorporate the exterior world in ways that augment and improve fundamental qualities of Chagga society; on the other, they represent the possibility of opening out and overextending Chagga society and losing control of fundamental cultural values. Part of the uncertainty can be understood by looking at the demographic and sociostructural considerations surrounding schoolgirl abortion.

Demographically, girls outnumber boys in local Machame secondary schools: according to my 1992 household and education survey, 60 percent of the secondary school enrollment in Machame is female. As a fraction of the total number of primary school students who graduate from Standard VII, this figure is small (fewer than one in ten girls goes on to secondary school), but as a percentage of the number of students enrolled, the number is large. Girls and young women who graduate from secondary school are more likely than their less-schooled counterparts to marry in church (as opposed to marrying traditionally), and secondary school graduates are more likely than their unenrolled age mates to bear their first child later in life. In 1992, in one southern Machame community, three out of four church weddings that occurred within a two-month period involved women who had attended secondary school for at least two years—and in one of these cases, the woman involved had earned a post-secondary teaching certificate. By contrast, all of the women who married traditionally (i.e., whose suitors offered banana beer gifts to young women's patrikin),[4] were primary school leavers or graduates. Levels of formal schooling and delay in age of formal marriage appear to correlate with contraceptive patterns among schoolgirls: according to medical practitioners in one of Machame's busiest clinics, secondary schoolgirls more frequently request (and are provided) contraceptive pills than any other group.

The disproportionate enrollment of girls compared to boys in secondary school, and the social premium placed on church weddings and childlessness-at-time-of-marriage for educated young women, reflects a social commitment among Chagga parents to provide daughters with an avenue for upward social mobility.[5] Chagga girls and women sustain lifelong ties with natal families. They represent one of a general category of women living in East African patrilineal societies who "maintain socially sanctioned identities and jural, ritual, and economic rights and obligations in their natal family and lineage throughout life" (Hakansson 1994, 517). Like Luyia, Sukuma, Nyamwezi, Ganda, Sogo, and Toro women (among others), Chagga women contrast as a group with women who are socially "detachable" from their natal families and who acquire social status and recognition primarily through marriage.[6] By investing in girls' education, Chagga parents invest in their own lineages (Kerner 1985; TADREG 1990, 28).

This social investment comes at a price, however. At the same time that schooling positively represents the opportunity for Chagga women to develop and improve themselves and their natal patrilineages, it negatively represents the possibility that educated women will become too independent, too autonomous in their decisions and actions to the point of detaching entirely from natal households. When schoolgirls "get rid of a pregnancy" (*kutoa mimba*), their actions are seen by many in Machame to represent one of the negative consequences of schooling. This is not to say that formal schooling is dismissed entirely as useless; to the contrary, local interest in schooling is extremely great. Nonetheless, schooling is associated with a number of problems, among them the potential for schoolgirls to acquire "too much" social freedom, to become pregnant, and (in order to remain in school) to seek abortions.

ABORTION PRACTICES

Several options present themselves to girls and young women looking to obtain an abortion. The most desired among schoolgirls with whom I spoke in Machame are procedures offered privately by medical doctors in Moshi or Arusha Towns. Although no professional is licensed officially, some provide abortions (usually dilation and curettage, or D&C) for young women whom they know or who have been referred to them by friends and acquaintances. The cost of a D&C in 1992 was 20,000 Tanzanian shillings for a first-trimester pregnancy and 27,000 Tanzanian shillings for a second- or even third-trimester pregnancy. (At the time, these rates were roughly equivalent to 80 and 100 U.S. dollars, respectively.) The sheer expense is daunting to most schoolgirls, who typically have no income of their own. Some are able to accumulate the cash, often by relying on trusted older sisters or friends to pay (schoolgirls said they would be less likely to ask the genitor of the pregnancy to pay; see the following discussion for reasons); others are forced to purchase abortifacients from local herbalists at a fraction of the cost; and still others choose to buy abortifacients as the first course, contending that herbs are less invasive, less expensive, and equally as effective as medical intervention, particularly if administered early in the pregnancy.[7] Some students mentioned that male medical students-in-training at a nearby hospital provided abortion services free of charge, particularly for their own girlfriends; and others mentioned that self-administered concoctions of extremely strong black tea or bicarbonate of soda (*magadi*) would effect the result.

Older Chagga women are familiar with many of the abortifacients and techniques used to terminate unwanted pregnancies, including the juices of certain herbs that induce miscarriage and the instrumental methods of inserting the midrib of a leaf into a woman's body (see Raum 1940, 68, 113). Judging from conversations with them and from ethnographic accounts, abortion has never been considered a desirable option in Chagga society but has been viewed as a necessary action taken to avoid social ostracism and, in some cases, death. In the past, uninitiated couples found to have conceived were said to have been taken to the forest, laid on top of one another, and their bodies pierced through with a stake (Raum 1940, 69). Women who conceived before weaning an older child were said to have put the household to shame by "growing" two children at once (Raum 1940, 106). Abortion was thus a way of dealing with social relations gone awry, a way of amending mistakes and avoiding public scrutiny, as indeed abortion is regarded in many cultural settings.

Local understandings about the risks associated with abortion often conjoin discourses of education, health, and morality. At the time of my field research, many older Chagga women connected the numbers of abortions obtained by secondary schoolgirls with girls' refusal to be circumcised and with the larger dangers of acquired immune deficiency syndrome (AIDS).[8] In their opinions, uncircumcised girls were by nature more sexually active than their circumcised age mates and therefore more likely to become pregnant and have an abortion; uncircumcised schoolgirls, they believed, were also at greater risk of HIV and other infection by virtue of their active sexual lives. Among students, the argument that circumcision reduced chances of HIV infection carried little weight. Many students challenged the logic of the argument by noting that exposure to the virus during sexual intercourse, not the state of being circumcised per se, effects infection. Abortion—or pregnancy—was not, to them, a post hoc sign of increased risk of HIV, as it was for many older women with whom I spoke—although some women of reproductive age did mention that obtaining an abortion in a medical clinic (like being circumcised by traditional practitioners) could put one at risk of infection (HIV and other) if the equipment used were not sterile.

To understand more of the cultural considerations that surround abortion in East Africa, I would like to look at three cases that came to my attention in 1992 and through them to think about the sociostructural factors that influence students' decisions to stay in school or to have children and leave. The cases I encountered were a great deal less bound and clear-cut in their unfolding than I present here. I have reduced events and comments to basic forms to illustrate some of the normative ideals and moral values that inform conversations and decisions. Even so, taken together, the cases illustrate that no single profile fits an abortion event and that normative ideals and moral values, even when reduced to simple forms, are often multiple and contradictory.

CASE 1: A FORM 3 SCHOOLGIRL

One of the first incidents of abortion I encountered involved a Form 3 secondary schoolgirl. Upon returning home one afternoon from working at a nearby secondary school, I found one of my Chagga housemates sitting at a table, speaking with some of our neighbors about "a blue plastic bag" that had been found in the center of the main tarmac road. I later learned that this bag contained an aborted fetus. The young woman who had left it there, my housemate and neighbors explained, was communicating to her partner through this sign the message that her partner's procreative potential was to her rubbish, best left to be run over by buses and cars on the road. Their conversation led to discussion about the predicament of "secondary schoolgirls these days" who are "tricked into" consorting with men and male classmates; about the audacity of a young woman who would dare to leave an aborted fetus in the middle of the road; and about the deplorable state of Chagga tradition and the threats that an action such as leaving an aborted fetus in the road posed to socially acceptable ideas about marriage and lineage alliances.

Schooling, Marriage, and Abortion

It is interesting to note before anything else that my neighbors and housemate immediately assumed that the young woman who put the bag in the road was a secondary schoolgirl. I, too, talk here of the owner of the bag as though "she" were a "secondary schoolgirl," but I want to reflect first on the significance of this attribution to the women's discussion. I mentioned in the previous section that some people in Machame view schooling as a means for investing in daughters and, by association, for investing in patrilineages. Some older, less educated people also believe that secondary schoolgirls are kept in an unnaturally puerile state when they are in school and that girls of secondary school age ought "normally" to have children and be married, as are their unenrolled age mates. The implication of this assumption is that one undesirable consequence of schooling is the emergence of a group of young women whose sexuality is physically developed but not normatively integrated into the adult community. According to this line of thinking, secondary schoolgirls who abort depart from expected processes of social development; they invert normative ideals about the need physically to produce children to maintain the well-being and social-reproductive health of the community; and they "pollute" (in Mary Douglas's terms) the Chagga social body by literally and figuratively aborting the reproductive potential they control. By contrast, young women who are not enrolled in school and who carry pregnancies to term signify the health and well-being of the Chagga community. Even if they are not advancing socially within institutions of higher learning, they are serving as the mainstays of Chagga tradition and stability by reproducing what their grandparents and parents have done before them.

News of the bag in the road raised questions for my neighbors about the nature of the schoolgirl's relationship with the genitor and about whether or not she was, in a sense, married to him or not. Ideally, Chagga marriage is exogamous and virilocal: it is a relationship between two people of unrelated lineages (*ukoo,* Kiswahili) and their extended families, and it involves (for women) moving to husbands' patrilands. As in other parts of Africa, marriage in Machame is a temporally extended and culturally ambiguous process, a relationship that ranges from the casual and fleeting to the ritualized and elaborated.[9] In the past, when polygynous relations were more socially accepted than they are today, it would have been comparatively easy for an older man to establish a socially recognized union with a younger woman as a second wife, provided he could supply the beer and bridewealth payment (*masaa a ukwe,* Kimachame) that would have accompanied the marriage process. Assuming the genitor of this issue was a married man (the possibility my neighbors considered most likely), he would have been able to marry this young woman openly by offering three, possibly four, gifts of beer to the woman's kin in the past. Today, however, when monogamy is the ideal marriage form promoted by the church and subscribed to by persons who regard themselves as educated and up-to-date (this is the majority in Machame), and today, when young women are increasingly enrolled in school and expected to defer marriage until after graduation, polygyny is more socially difficult to sustain as a viable form of marriage. Instead, monogamy is publicly presented as the ideal marriage arrangement, even if multiple unions are pursued and sexually consummated privately.

Speculation among these women that the man who had impregnated this schoolgirl was an "older man seeking a second wife" illustrates normative connections people make between schoolgirl pregnancies and men. The scorn with which these women spoke of such men indicated that they sympathized in large part with the schoolgirl but that they also saw the difficulties faced by upwardly mobile, and ostensibly monogamous, men: older men who *preferred* to take second wives were *prevented socially* from marrying polygynously and instead had to deny and distance themselves from conceptions arising from the union. My neighbors were ambivalent about who categorically could be blamed. On the one hand, they believed that the schoolgirl had been careless in dealing with the genitor, but on the other, they blamed the genitor for lording his power over the secondary schoolgirl. Simultaneously, they acknowledged that the girl had likely gained access to luxury items, money, and exciting dates through this man and that she could not be entirely blamed for wanting to benefit from his power, and they recognized that the man was pursuing a relationship that was in keeping with what Chagga in the past considered perfectly acceptable and legitimate.

My neighbors' ambivalence in defending completely neither the genitor nor the schoolgirl turns upon a cultural tension in Machame between Chagga ideals about children and patrilineality, on the one hand, and current thinking about legitimacy and descent, on the other. In the past, the birth of offspring—particularly of boys—socially legitimated marriage alliances to a greater extent than did beer presentations or changes in residence (Raum 1940). They continue to do so today. Had the schoolgirl gone through with the pregnancy, she likely would not only have been expelled from school but would also have also been forced to raise the child on her own father's compound (unless the genitor—whom my neighbors presumed was married—would commit to having a second wife openly, in which case she would reside with him and his first wife). At the schoolgirl's natal household, her child would likely be considered the child of another patriline and would be given second-class status to children born into her own patriline to one of her male agnates. In choosing to abort this fetus, my neighbors concurred that this student had made a deliberate choice not to pursue alliances with this man (at least not at that time) and not to foreclose the possibility that in the future she may marry, in socially accepted and open ways, a man of a patriline other than her own (including possibly this man) and raise children who would be considered legitimate heirs to the man's lineage.

Mobility

But if my neighbors and housemate sympathized with the schoolgirl's predicament, they were critical of her decision to leave the aborted fetus in the middle of the road. Such a thing, they said, was unfair to the many passersby (on foot and by car) who came into proximity with the bag and who, although not likely to have been "cursed" by its contents, may have been "dirtied" or "unsettled" by it. Certainly, they agreed, the bag was intended to send a strong message—what they called a curse (*kuloga,* Kiswahili; *itanywa,* Kimachame)—to the genitor, but it had the unfortunate effect of causing discomfort in the village and giving people the sense that something menacing was among them. To my housemate, who self-identified as Lutheran, and to her fellow Christians, this menace was the work of the devil (*shetani*); to less avid churchgoers, it was a sign of witchcraft (*uchawi*).

The full significance of the location of the bag is best appreciated by thinking about schooling in connection with social and geographical mobility. Girls who go to secondary school are mobile in two ways: in terms of the distance they physically travel (many walk five to eight miles daily to and from school) and in terms of the "foreign" knowledge they bring home with them from school. Unenrolled age mates generally remain near their homes on any given day, and although many walk to and from market once or twice a week or to and from lowland maize farms some five or six miles away from their homes, most do not follow a fixed schedule that keeps them on the move daily, as do secondary school students. And neither do they traffic in the social capital associated with the abstract and advanced lessons of school. As Kerner (1995) has noted of ritual transactions on Mount Kilimanjaro, and as others writing about transportation and roadways in Africa have described,[10] social relationships in eastern and central Africa socially inhere in (among other things) geographical movements and objects that have undergone transport—including, for instance, a bag left in the middle of the road. And as Serpell (1993) has noted of schooling in East Africa and as others writing about education in postcolonial contexts have described,[11] cultural ideas about development and modernization are frequently associated with cultural transfers and the movement of ideas and practices from one group to another. In the sense that schooling is about mobility and social change and insofar as movement and transfers effect changes in persons and their relationships to one another, schooling on Mount Kilimanjaro brings about a transformation not only in the status of a person but also in the quality of her or his social position and relationship to other people.

The obstructed movement of the schoolgirl along the educational course—from primary to secondary school, to postsecondary, and eventually to work—parallels the obstructed movements of the people who travel the road where the aborted fetus had been left. Quite possibly it hindered the spatial movements of the person who had impregnated the girl. Chagga footpaths (*vichochoro*) and roadways are frequently marked in subtle ways with medicines (*dawa*) that are intended to influence particular persons, depending on their relationship to the person who "set the trap" or depending on the quality or nature of their person (i.e., whether they are thought to be witches, thieves, strangers, enemies). I was told that visible signs (*alama*) were more common in the past than today, yet people pointed out to me ways that traps might secretly be set. Among the more widely known traps is a small copper coin tossed at the intersection of two paths. An unwelcomed person who crosses over this coin may suffer from *usinga,* an illness characterized by paralysis or disfigurement of the legs. In a similar fashion, blood found on a path may be considered an ominous sign: a young woman whom I knew contemplated whether she had inadvertently stepped over a drop of blood and whether this action may have led to her physical illness. These signs are not limited to footpaths and roadways but are found at other points of spatial transition as well, as when entering a house or a residential compound. Several of the oldest men in the community, for instance, secured their houses against unwanted visitors by setting up a kind of alarm system: they placed a thick metal bar at the foot of their doorway, over which all persons would have to step. Those visitors who had ill intents, they said, would be physically barred from entering the house. Similarly, some families protected their compounds with medicines from certain plants that were rubbed into fence posts and gateways or tied in a cloth and hung discreetly near the entrance.

In light of the significance of secret signs strategically placed along roadways and at points of spatiotemporal transition, the position of the bag—or, more precisely, my neighbors' comments about the position of the bag—suggests that the disposal of an aborted fetus is as vexing as the issues surrounding abortion. Some possible reasons for leaving the bag in the road, my neighbors said, might have to do with the schoolgirl's desire to bring misfortune to the genitor. "Perhaps the schoolgirl put it there so the man would not do this to another schoolgirl," one woman said, referring to the possibility that should the genitor encounter the bag (either knowingly or not), he would become the object of its intention, which may be, they reasoned, that he be rendered impotent. Other speculations included the possibility that the sign was intended to harm the genitor directly, that it might make him physically or mentally ill and that he would have to seek out the person who put the bag there in order to make amends, ask for forgiveness, and in some way compensate for the unwanted pregnancy. Ultimately, these women agreed, the message was likely known only to the person who put the bag there and to the person for whom the message was intended.

The position of the bag some 300 yards from the place where the tarmac road ended led one of my neighbors to think that perhaps the man responsible for impregnating the student was a pickup truck driver or a bus conductor—someone who traveled on the main road frequently and would likely encounter the bag on this particular day. The implications of this possibility would be known to many in the community: that this was a man of comparative means who traveled daily to town, who was on the fast track both in the sense of wielding above-average prestige (driving a car is a sign of status in Tanzania from the perspective of many living in rural communities) and in the sense of moving with women. For the women discussing the incident, all were signs that the man involved would not take social responsibility for the child and that the schoolgirl involved had done well to sever further entanglements.

Whatever their exact identities, the schoolgirl and the genitor were assumed in this case to be people on the move both physically and socially. They controlled the means to position themselves among the comparatively rich and powerful, and they moved in social circles that traveled far socially and geographically. As such, they risked exposing themselves to the dangers of open roads and pathways. One danger, in this sense, was the possibility of being "derailed"—either from the course of matriculation through the educational system or literally from the tarmac road that takes one to town and back. Beyond this, the case also demonstrates cultural ideas about human biology and development: some of the language these women used to describe the blue plastic bag suggests ways in which Chagga conceptualize physical growth and what it means to be human. I briefly look at these views next.

Cultural Ideas about Human Growth, 1

In the past, people living on Mount Kilimanjaro believed that children were conceived through the coagulation of blood and semen: women provided the fleshy tissues that were full of milk, fat, and blood; men, the bones that created structure to the new fetus in the woman's womb (Raum 1940, 75–78). Fetal growth was considered dependent on a constant supply of semen, and regular intercourse was necessary to bring a child to full development. Although some with whom I spoke described conception in Western medical terms (i.e., the terms used in schools today), others used images and metaphors for fetal development that suggest a different view. Adolescent secondary schoolgirls repeatedly called early pregnancies "grains of sand." A young woman whom I describe in the next case, for instance, called the fetus she had aborted *chembe ya mchanga tu*—"only a grain" or "only a speckle of dirt." In contrast, one of the women who described the blue bag to me described its contents as *nyama* (meat). As she expressed it, the bag had been left in the middle of the road "like so much meat" (*kama nyama tu*). Her disgust and sorrow were evident in her tone, although the fuller implications of her comment were more deeply embedded in the specificities of the mundane activity of purchasing meat and transporting it in a blue plastic bag.

That the fetus was like a bag of meat led to two lines of argument among these women: one, that the aborted fetus was socially not a person (*mtu*), and two, that in disposing of the tissue in the bag, the *nyama* had a market value—it had been purchased, or disposed of, for a price. Regarding the former, my neighbors did not agree as to what, if not a person, the fetus was. In contrast to Western conceptions of an unborn child as consisting of equal shares of both genitors' chromosomes from the moment of conception, Chagga maintain (as do other Bantu peoples) that the growth of the unborn proceeds through incremental contributions of male and female fluids. Some of these women maintained that the fetus was only the tissue or blood of the woman, not the structural matter of the man, and that it had not been properly nurtured in a socially accepted and (re)productive way by the genitor as pater. Others said that it was *nyama,* the meat or bones that the man had contributed, and that it had been "firmed up" and grown by the male genitor.

I learned from this and other conversations that these debates about who contributed how much to the pregnancy were important for reckoning the extent to which the man was implicated in the pregnancy. Or, to put it another way, arguments about the role of men in pregnancies have implications for the degree to which the aborted fetus is thought to be a life form that issues from the man's patriline. If, as some maintained, there was "very little of the man in the fetus," the bulk of the tissue was the schoolgirl's, the fetus was not a person, and the male genitor had little role to play in the abortion. If, on the other hand, the fetus had been firmed up by contributions from the genitor, then the aborted fetus was a product of him and by extension could eventually be claimed by his patriline. The decision to abort, in the second scenario, would concern him more directly, for as a significant contributor, he would be morally and socially connected to the unborn child—at least in the eyes of my neighbors.

Regarding the second point—that in disposing of the tissue in the bag, the *nyama* had a market value: women commented knowingly on the ways meat was purchased in the village and on the kinds of people (namely, the comparatively wealthy) who put meat in plastic bags rather than in banana-leaf-thatch wrappers. *Nyama,* the word used to describe animal muscles or organs, including humans', has loaded connotation. The cost of buying a pound of *nyama ya ng'ombe* (beef) at the time was 250 Tanzanian shillings or roughly one U.S. dollar—too expensive for most Chagga to afford on a daily basis but a commodity many associated with the good life and good times. Indeed, Chagga pride themselves on their fondnesses for eating roasted meat; it is one of the distinguishing foods (along with *mbege,* banana beer) that captures the essence, in the opinions of many, of what it means to be Chagga (see also Moore 1986, 131–33). For an additional 5 or 10 shillings, meat purchased at local butcheries is placed directly into a blue or yellow plastic bag for easy transport. At the time, these plastic bags were imprinted with Marlboro cigarette commercials, and even though it was impossible to purchase Marlboro cigarettes anywhere on Mount Kilimanjaro (or, for that matter, in the regional capital, Moshi), these advertisements, along with the 5- or 10-shilling bag itself, were signs of social prestige and, again, of the ability to consume and traffic in the signs of faraway and fast-moving places. Thus, the women's remark that the fetus was placed in a bag, like meat, was loaded with insinuation that the girl who had abandoned it was wealthy, that she was of a class that purchased meat and carried it in Marlboro plastic bags, and that on this particular day she had paid a price and purchased meat of another kind—an abortion—and had carried it off and abandoned it like an unwanted parcel in the middle of the road. By implication, she was *not* a primary school leaver or graduate who ended her studies at Standard VII. Although there exist plenty of Standard VII graduates or primary school leavers about whom people talk, primary school leavers would not, in their accounts, dispose of an abortion in such a way, for they would not have the social or economic capital to put it in a bag in the road. To the contrary, the woman involved in this incident was (to my neighbors) the archetype of a secondary schoolgirl who carried expensive bags and rode buses. The fact that the bag was found at the bus stop near a local girls' school only served to buttress their presuppositions.

The irony of my neighbors' assumptions were striking to me, for most of these women were themselves wealthy; only a few of them went without eating meat for any longer than a few days, and most of them had stashes of blue plastic bags. Yet the point of their conversation was neither to acquit or condemn people like the student involved in this incident nor even to present a statistical picture of who had abortions and how they managed them but rather to reaffirm collective values about (among other things) the symbolic meaning of going to school and the social consequences of abortion.

CASE 2: A SECONDARY SCHOOL GRADUATE

The circumstances surrounding a second incident of abortion are quite different from the first, yet there are important similarities. This case involved a young woman, whom I shall call Monica. Monica had recently graduated from Form 4 and was without formal employment. Like more than three-quarters of her classmates that year, she had failed all of her final examinations and did not qualify for placement in Form 5. Nonetheless, she was hopeful that she would be able to secure an office job by relying on contacts she had made with friends who already had jobs in town or on contacts through her parents, who themselves worked in town much of the week. To her surprise, Monica found herself pregnant, and "to protect her reputation"—as she put it—and to ensure that she still might find a job and formally marry, she chose to have an abortion rather than carry the pregnancy to term. Her reasons for doing this, she explained, were several. I describe them here with reference to schooling and lineal relations and, again, to cultural ideas about human growth.

Schooling and Lineal Relations

First, as a secondary school graduate, she said she was expected to have a job—or to marry someone who did. As she portrayed it, bearing a child as a secondary schoolgirl would undermine the hopes her family had placed in her—namely, that through schooling, she would better her life chances and be in a financial position to remit resources home to parents and extended kin. Had she dropped out of school to have a baby, Monica said she would have disrupted the course of events that concerned her entire family. She explained that she would have had to rely on her father and brothers for food, shelter, and financial assistance in raising the child and in so doing would have prevented or delayed her oldest brother from marrying. I did not at first understand why Monica's oldest brother's marriage was contingent on Monica's marriage and relocation, though I later recalled that this is a common phenomenon in unilineal descent systems involving relocation upon marriage. Marriage among the Chagga, as mentioned previously, involves the transfer of bridewealth from the groom's to the bride's family and is marked, at some stage in the extended process, by the shift in residence of the bride from her natal household to her husband's. For a man to marry, he needs a requisite amount of bridewealth—be it in the form of *mbege,* cattle, goats, or, increasingly these days, money. Often, men obtain this wealth from marriage payments made to their fathers' lineages (which are, of course, also their own lineages) from the marriage of one of their sisters.[12]

But bridewealth payments—at least in the form of beer and cattle—are viewed increasingly as antiquated, particularly among those who consider themselves educated and upwardly mobile. Monica, whose older brother was himself a secondary school leaver, was not in fact planning to marry with bridewealth in the sense that his father had. Instead, Monica said, her brother would likely marry by offering his fiancée's family one or two gifts of beer and then finalizing the marriage in church. He was not directly dependent on the wealth that Monica's prospective husband would bring to the lineage. Why, then, I asked, was Monica's marriage a precondition for his own? To this Monica answered that it is *mila na desturi,* "tradition and custom to do it this way," and indeed it would seem that although the economic basis of bridewealth has shifted in Machame and in much of the Chagga area (again as a function of schooling),[13] the principle of sibling-linked marriage remains the ideal norm.

The birth of a child outside of marriage posed yet another problem for Monica and was another reason she chose to abort: if the genitor did not claim paternity and if she remained living at her father's compound, her father, and eventually her youngest brother, would be considered responsible for feeding and sheltering Monica and her child. This is so for two reasons. First, Monica's *youngest* brother would eventually inherit his father's house and compound and would be responsible for caring for all of the persons who resided in the compound, including, quite possibly, his aging mother and, most likely, his wife and children. Any of his sisters who remained unmarried, and any children these sisters had outside of marriage, would likely fall to his charge. The anticipation was that these responsibilities would prove financially burdensome. Monica pointed to several households in the area in which youngest brothers (heirs to their fathers) were struggling financially to support their unmarried sisters and their children. These cases illustrated that indeed households in which unmarried sisters continued to reside were less wealthy than their fully married counterparts. Moreover, Monica's father had sent her to school for the explicit reason that she would eventually either find a job or marry a man who could support her—or both. As mentioned, schooling is viewed by many in this community as a means for girls to augment the wealth of the patrilineage and to gain increasing social autonomy, either by marrying hypergamously as a consequence of their prestigious schooling or by securing jobs on their own that will enable them to support themselves and (at least some of) their natal kin.

In short, Monica was fearful that should any of her brothers or her father discover she was pregnant, they would beat her and behave cruelly toward her, each of them for various reasons: her oldest brother for the delay or disorder this might cause him in his own marriage, her youngest brother for the future financial burden the child was likely to cause him, and her middle brothers and father for the general shame that she would have brought to the family. When I naively suggested she confront her parents and family with her situation and ask for their advice, she was quite firm in arguing that this was an issue she could never discuss with them and that in general one's immediate family was never to be involved in discussions about unwanted pregnancies or about ways of resolving them. Not even her mother could be consulted about the subject, for Monica felt her mother would also beat and punish her and, potentially, curse her. When I asked Monica to whom she might turn for advice, she said that her school friends and older women (*bibi,* singular; *mabibi,* plural: people of her grandmother's generation) would be the best sources of support, the first insofar as she knew several of them who had had abortions and who could advise her where to go to obtain one and the latter because older women generally knew the medicinal abortifacients that could be used and provided counsel to adolescent-aged girls about sex, marriage, and abortion.

After seeking the counsel and support of those whom she could trust, Monica decided to have the procedure performed at a private clinic in Moshi Town by a licensed medical doctor for 20,000 Tanzanian shillings (eighty U.S. dollars). The procedure was D&C performed under general anesthetic. Monica had no complications or unusual pain.

Interestingly, however, the genitor of the conception refused to pay for the procedure for reasons Monica related to cultural ideas about marriage, lineal rights, and procreation. Among the cases Monica knew about in which her friends' male partners had paid for the procedure, all had intended eventually to marry the schoolgirls and felt that the conception of a child had merely been premature. In paying for the procedure, these male partners were acknowledging not only their biological roles as genitor but also their hopes for future social roles as pater by agreeing to a "secret engagement." That is, they were accepting the social role of father, if not to this pregnancy, then for future children born from this young woman. As noted earlier, the inclusion of the offspring within the pater's lineage is socially recognized in one of the later stages of the extended marriage process—in the past through economically valuable transactions of goats and cows from fathers' households to wives' natal lineages, though today more often symbolically in the form of a beer presentation, small cash gifts, or meat. In light of the many possible ways that gifts and payments can be interpreted (as bridewealth, as payment for a service, or simply as a gift), payments for abortion are potentially interpreted by the young woman involved (and by her family, if they are aware of her situation) as a man's intentions to retain a degree of control over a young woman's reproductive future. This is a very important point, one that may account for why so many schoolgirls have abortions without their partners knowing they have conceived or why, if partners do know, many girls prefer to pay for the procedures themselves if at all possible. Monica chose to use her own resources and resources lent to her from friends for this reason, that is, to prevent her partner from retaining future claims over her and her reproductive capacity. To be sure, Monica harbored some anger and resentment toward this male who had impregnated her, calling him a "thief" (*mwizi*) for having taken off the condom he said he was using (or for never having put it on, she later considered), but she made little to do about his lack of commitment toward taking financial responsibility.

Cultural Ideas about Human Growth, 2

Related to Monica's preference that the genitor *not* be involved in paying for the procedure is her comment about what the fetus was in conceptual terms. Monica described her pregnancy as *chembe ya mchanga tu,* which describes pieces of stone or soil that appear in sacks of rice or in bags of beans as well as dirt that is swept up from the floor and bits of grit that one finds in freshly picked fruits or vegetables. Her choice of term in calling her pregnancy *chembe ya mchanga* suggests that Monica did not have any more attachment toward the "piece of sand or stone" in her body than she did for the "thief" who had impregnated her. Indeed, in light of the fact that human development is understood culturally in terms of the coagulation of female blood and male semen and that the constant supply of the latter is thought necessary for fetal growth, Monica's comment suggests that she considered her pregnancy to contain only a few grains of sand, *mchanga,* and indeed not very much of that.

It also seems that despite the sex education and biology lessons Monica had received as a student, her ideas about human reproduction continue to be informed by a combination of what she learned in school and church and by what she had been taught at home and from older Chagga women (*mabibi*) who counsel girls. Initially, Monica did not think it possible that she was pregnant (*mimba*); she said she had had intercourse with this person only two or three times and had bled slightly with what she thought was menstrual discharge after the last. She seemed to imply that more insemination would have been necessary for conception and that blood in her body, not blood expelled from her in what she thought was a period, would be necessary to feed and contribute to the growth of a fetus.

Two possible interpretations emerge from this: one, that her schooling and general knowledge were not mutually incompatible with what she had learned from the *mabibi* in the village but had been synthesized in a way that made it possible for her to think about human physiology in terms of both; another, that when faced with her situation, Monica chose to rely on local ideas because they facilitated her decision by casting the aborted fetus in nonhuman terms, thereby making the decision less morally vexing for her. Either way, the school model of biology, in which conception is understood in terms of probability, and the church model of humanity, in which life is said to begin with conception, are in play with local ideas that human life grows as a function of the coagulation of bodily fluids and that what it means to be human is socially recognized in terms of lineages.

The implications of this are important for understanding connections between abortion and education. Many studies of schoolgirl abortion imply that schooling instills in students a particular view of human biology that replaces traditional ideas. This view is much too simple, not only because it assumes that students interpret their lessons in ways that are identical with the intended lessons in official curriculum but also because it overlooks the possibility that ideas about human biology and growth derive from many sources. Teachers are not the only culture brokers involved in educating students; *mabibi* and other respected persons in the community likewise play a role in shaping students' ideas about procreation and biological development, and it is in understanding the unity of what are often analytically conceptualized as two distinct epistemological realms (the traditional and the modern, and the home and the school) that one can begin to understand Chagga students' underlying motivations for choosing, or being forced, to abort or not.

CASE 3: A SCHOOL LEAVER WITH CHILD

Finally, I would like to describe a situation in which a secondary schoolgirl found herself pregnant and dropped out of school to have her child. This case illustrates local views of children born to schoolgirls and of the second-class status of student-mother and child. "Neema's" case was regarded as unfortunate by everyone with whom I spoke. Neema said herself that she did not know she was pregnant until it was too late, and too risky, to have an abortion. Unlike Monica, she was not able to raise money through friends to have a safe but costly (and technically illegal) abortion at a medical clinic in town, and she did not want to go to a local *bibi* (old woman) for medicines (*dawa*) to make her miscarry. Indeed, Neema's schooling had taught her that locally procured abortions were dangerous, and although she felt she would have trusted taking local medicines earlier in her term, she did not want to risk infertility by aborting in the second half of her pregnancy.

Neema had been living and working for a wealthy family in the community who, in exchange for her labor, paid Neema's secondary school fees. Her domestic duties were seen as fair exchange for her schooling, and Neema was regarded by many in the community as someone who could make the best of her situation by graduating from school and going on to find a well-paying job. Like many young women who live and work for wealthy families, Neema's natal family was poor. Her mother was a single parent of four children and had encouraged Neema to live and work for this wealthy family, who were in fact distant relatives of Neema's patrilineage (*ukoo*).

Neema's case needs to be understood in the context of domestic labor on Mount Kilimanjaro. As Moore notes (1986, 86), in the past Chagga sent their children to relatives living in other compounds, and children were lent as depositors for debt. Debt incurred by families lending children was returned to the creditor in the form of bridewealth paid when the girl married. Today in Machame those who provide school fees receive only the child's labor in return, not a portion of bridewealth payment (which, as noted, is often not a large factor in the marriage of those who have attended school). The power dynamics of child fosterage are highly unequal. Neema felt she was to an extent at the mercy of her employers/relatives for financial assistance. Unlike some of her wealthier schoolmates, she did not have extra cash with which to purchase luxury items or with which to buy school accessories. In the face of this poverty, she began accepting money and gifts from a man. Some speculated that it was from one of the young men who lived in the household where Neema lived and worked and, as such, was one of her relatives. As with other schoolgirls who accepted gifts from wealthier men,[14] Neema later found that this young man expected sexual favors from her in return. Neema obliged him during times of the month she felt were safe and inserted a rag into her vagina or "drank strong medicines" (as she put it) to prevent conception and regulate her menstrual cycle. Such methods, as Raum (1940, 67) notes, have been used by Chagga women for many generations, although according to the Tanzanian Demographic Health Survey (Ngallaba, Kapiga, and Boerma 1993, 35), Neema's choice of birth control is considered unreliable by well over 90 percent of the women they interviewed in 1991–92.

When Neema found she was pregnant, she dropped out of school (she would have eventually been expelled, people said), left her place of employment, and returned home. If, as some speculated, the genitor of her child were in fact a member of the Neema's extended lineage (*ukoo*), her child would have been regarded by some as the product of an incestuous relationship, and Neema's chances of marrying in socially acceptable ways in the future would have been highly unlikely, at least as considered by these villagers. Thus, to an even greater extent than schoolgirls who are expelled or who drop out of secondary school when discovered pregnant, Neema would have been criticized and ostracized by her neighbors and peers had she carried the pregnancy to term. In my conversations with her, she considered that it was possible that her neighbors and peers would eventually forget or downplay her social violation and that she would marry or have children in the future in a more socially accepted way, but she recognized that should people believe that the male genitor was a relative of hers, the immediate response of the community would be that her actions had been shameful and that she had violated normative ideas about exogamy.

As in many cases involving schoolgirl pregnancy, the genitor of the pregnancy was never identified. Monica—the young woman involved in case 2, discussed previously, and with whom I discussed Neema's situation—reasoned that Neema did not identify the genitor either because (1) Neema did not want him to have future control over her reproductive capacities, much as Monica had not wanted the genitor of her pregnancy to have control over hers; or (2) because if the genitor were in fact a distant relative and if Neema named him, the certainty of this information would most likely prejudice even the members of the community who now knew nothing of what may have been regarded as an immoral, incestuous relationship.

In Machame, where early-term pregnancies are sometimes thought of as grains of sand and where the absence of a socially recognized genitor in some cases fails to define the fetus as human (or, alternately, where the blood has issued from a woman's body and is thought to signify that no part of the woman contributed to the fetus, as in Monica's case), decisions to abort can be cast by those involved in moral or even nonmoral terms. Morally, abortion among schoolgirls preserves normative ideals about marriage and inheritance and leaves open the possibility that schooling will have its intended effect, that it will advance young women economically and socially by delaying marriage and reducing fertility and thereby freeing up educated women for monetarily productive work. Nonmorally, that is, in terms that judge the situation as neither right nor wrong, abortion appears to be conceptualized by some women as an extrasocial, nonmoral concern. In cases where the "grain of sand" is neither "of the woman" nor "of the man," decisions about what to do with the pregnancy are considered beyond the realm of social scrutiny. Even though anthropologically, nonmoral decisions cannot be understood independently of the social relations surrounding them, understanding how people frame their decisions extrasocially is important for understanding how abortion can be simultaneously justified and condemned.

DISCUSSION

Taken together, these cases suggest that schooling symbolically is identified with a transition from one kind of family to another—from one that is formed over an extended period of time through negotiations between lineages and through the birth of one or more children to one that defines itself instantaneously through a wedding ceremony and establishes an economically stable household before coparenting "legitimate" children. This demographic transition—itself cultural in nature—coincides with a number of changes in ideas about marriage and children: marriage is a contract between individuals, and children are raised by mothers and fathers who share equally in the parenting process. Contemporary practice may well differ from this image, for nuclear households are but one new ideal. Nonetheless, cultural ideals appear to have shifted, and schooling appears to be one reason associated with change.

In light of this, schoolgirl abortion represents for some a flaw in the new social order. Young women who have abortions are visible markers that schooling forces otherwise mature and healthy young women to remain an unnaturally long time in school, in a social state of extended youth, where they are required to suppress their fertility and where they risk jeopardizing the social health of the larger community. For others—not least schoolgirls who seek, or are compelled, to have an abortion—the chance to "take out a pregnancy" (*kutoa mimba*) enables them to continue their upwardly mobile social course. The danger for schoolgirls is that they will not be able to terminate their pregnancies before they are visibly discovered and expelled.

Struggles that surround abortion debates touch on much more than the safety of the procedure or on the pros and cons of schooling. Like debates about abortion in any social setting, the issue calls into question fundamental cultural ideas about social reproduction, human biology, and growth, and it illustrates changing understandings about gender, social organization, and generation. In Machame, abortion debates reflect Chagga concerns that educated schoolgirls marry hypergamously and monogamously, that they remain economically and socially autonomous from older men and fellow male classmates, and that they marry and bear children in ways their families consider appropriate. These relatively new ideals for educated daughters constitute an extension of an older cultural problematic, namely, that Chagga daughters maintain lifelong ties with natal kin and support and invest in their patrilineages.

Unlike many accounts of population change and fertility practices that interpret student abortion in terms of women's socioeconomic status and identity or of the rational knowledge they have learned in school, I have emphasized here how the gendered and age-ranked positions of girls and women in families and how cultural ideas about human growth bear upon decisions to abort or not. I have also argued that any impulse to view schoolgirl abortions as a reactive response to modernization and Westernization overlooks the cultural context in which young women seek to control and transform the particular relations that describe and define them as social persons in Chagga society.

ACKNOWLEDGMENTS

I am grateful to many schoolgirls and women on Mount Kilimanjaro who shared their information about abortion with me. I hope that some of what they wanted to convey is reflected in these pages. I am also grateful to the Tanzanian government for providing research clearance, to the Mellon Foundation for research and write-up support and to participants of the 1996 International Union for the Scientific Study of Population conference for comments and suggestions on this work.

NOTES

1. Discussion is based on observations and interviews conducted during sixteen months of research in Machame, Tanzania (September 1991–January 1993). Ethnographic observations were made as part of a broader study on the culture of secondary schooling in Machame and were informed by (1) extended participant observation in one secondary school over the course of an academic year; (2) site visits to twenty-six other secondary schools in Kilimanjaro Region; (3) more than 300 household interviews; (4) full-time residence in northern Tanzania; and (5) review of anthropological and educational literature on Tanzania prior to and upon completing research in Tanzania.

2. This number is figured at an annual growth rate of 2.8 percent and based on the United Republic of Tanzania (1988, 301–3) census figure of 56,000 persons in 1988.

3. See Mascarenhas and Mbilinyi's (1983) annotated bibliography for more references.

4. This is an extremely simplified version of Chagga marriage. For a more elaborate explanation, see Stambach 2000.

5. This social commitment should not be interpreted to mean that Chagga girls attain overall higher levels of schooling than boys. According to my 1992 survey, at least two in ten male primary school graduates (as opposed to one in ten female graduates) attend secondary school. The discrepancy between the high level of enrollment of girls locally (60 percent) and the higher level of overall educational attainment for boys is attributable to the fact that Chagga parents more frequently send their sons than daughters to study in the urban areas of Arusha and Dar es Salaam, where the quality of schooling is thought to be better than in the rural areas of Machame.

6. Among the latter group are Gusii, Teso, Luo, Acholi, and Karamojong women (Hakansson 1994, 519).

7. Hans Cory (also known as Hans Koritschoner) identifies several medicinal plants used in the 1930s as abortifacients in the western Usambara mountains, a mountain range located some 140 miles southeast of Mount Kilimanjaro. Among Cory's list are *Grewia holstii* (*mkole,* Kiswahili), *Impatiens walleriana* (*tulanange,* Kiswahili), *Withania somnifera dunal* (*mageda,* Kiswahili), *Kalanchoe orenata* (*soporua,* Kiswahili), *Kalanchoe glaucescens* (*mkerampindi,* Kiswahili), *Jussiaca pilosa* (*myaria,* Kiswahili), and *Loranthus holstii* (*ngulukesi,* Kiswahili). It is reasonable to expect that many of these plants were—and continue to be—used as abortifacients on Mount Kilimanjaro, where flora and fauna resemble those found in the Usambara mountains at similar altitudes (Tanzanian National Archives 1936, 43–50, 186–92). My thanks to Sheryl McCurdy for providing me with Cory's list.

8. For a broader discussion of this, see Stambach 2000.

9. Anthropological literature on this subject is vast. For examples, see Bledsoe and Pison's edited volume (1994) and Comaroff 1980.

10. See Auslander 1993; Beidelman 1993, 142; and Weiss 1993 for examples.

11. See Bloch 1993 and Swatridge 1985 for examples.

12. Again, this is an extremely simplified version of Chagga marriage. In anthropological literature, the Nuer are famous for sibling-linked marriage (Evans-Pritchard 1951, 77–78; Hutchinson 1992), but sibling-linked marriage is common among many people in sub-Saharan Africa.

13. Bridewealth payments are not going by the wayside everywhere. They remain important in other parts of Tanzania, including the Dodoma area.

14. Bledsoe (1990) discusses this phenomenon as it occurs in Sierra Leone.

REFERENCES

Auslander, M. 1993. "Open the Wombs!: The Symbolic Politics of Modern Ngoni Witchfinding." In *Modernity and Its Malcontents,* ed. Jean and John Comaroff, 167–92. Chicago: University of Chicago Press.

Baker, J., and S. Khasiani. 1992. "Induced Abortion in Kenya: Case Histories." *Studies in Family Planning* 23 (1): 34–44.

Barker, G., and S. Rich. 1992. "Influences on Adolescent Sexuality in Nigeria and Kenya." *Studies in Family Planning* 23 (3): 199–210.

Beidelman, T. O. 1993. *Moral Imagination in Kaguru Modes of Thought.* Washington, D.C.: Smithsonian.

Bledsoe, C. 1990. "School Fees and the Marriage Process for Mende Girls in Sierra Leone." In *Beyond the Second Sex,* ed. P. R. Sanday and R. G. Goodenough, 281–310. Philadelphia: University Press.

Bledsoe, C., and G. Pison, eds. 1994. *Nuptiality in Sub-Saharan Africa: Contemporary Anthropological and Demographic Perspectives.* Oxford: Clarendon Press.

Bleek, W. 1978. "Induced Abortion in a Ghanaian Family." *African Studies Review* 21 (1): 103–20.

Bloch, M. 1993. "The Uses of Schooling and Literacy in a Zafimaniry Village." In *Cross-Cultural Approaches to Literacy,* ed. B. Street, 87–109. New York: Cambridge University Press.

Caldwell, J., and P. Caldwell. 1994. "Marital Status and Abortion in Sub-Saharan Africa." In *Nuptiality in Sub-Saharan Africa: Contemporary Anthropological and Demographic Perspectives,* ed. C. Bledsoe and G. Pison, 274–95. Oxford: Clarendon Press.

Comaroff, J. L. 1980. "Bridewealth and the Control of Ambiguity in a Tswana Chiefdom." In *The Meaning of Marriage Payments,* ed. J. L. Comaroff, 161–96. New York: Academic Press.

Douglas, M. 1966. *Purity and Danger: An Analysis of Concepts of Pollution and Taboo.* New York: Praeger.

Evans-Pritchard, E. E. 1951. *Kinship and Marriage among the Nuer.* New York: Oxford University Press.

Gyepi-Garbrah, B. 1985. *Adolescent Fertility in Sub-Saharan Africa: An Overview.* Boston and Nairobi: Pathfinder Fund.

Hakansson, N. T. 1994. "The Detachability of Women: Gender and Kinship in Processes of Socioeconomic Change among the Gusii of Kenya." *American Ethnologist* 21 (3): 516–38.

Hutchinson, S. 1992. "The Cattle of Money and the Cattle of Girls among the Nuer, 1930–1983." *American Ethnologist* 19 (2): 294.

Kaniki, Abdulrahaman O. J. 1993. "What the Law Says on Abortion." *Sunday News,* January 10.

Kerner, D. O. 1995. "Chaptering the Narrative: The Material of Memory in Kilimanjaro, Tanzania." In *The Labyrinth of Memory: Ethnographic Journeys,* ed. M. C. Teski and J. J. Climo, 113–27. Westport, Conn.: Bergin and Garvey.

Kerner, D. O., and K. Cook. 1991. "Gender, Hunger, and Crisis in Tanzania." In *The Political Economy of African Famine,* ed. R. E. Downs, D. O. Kerner, and S. P. Reyna, 257–72. Philadelphia: Gordon and Breach Science Publishers.

Ladipo, O. A. 1978. "Abortion among Nigerian Youth." *Nigerian Behavioral Sciences Journal* 1: 112–16.

Mascarenhas, O., and M. Mbilinyi. 1983. *Women in Tanzania: An Analytical Bibliography.* Stockholm: Swedish International Development Authority.

Mashalaba, N. N. 1989. "Commentary on the Causes and Consequences of Unwanted Pregnancy from an African Perspective." *International Journal of Gynecology and Obstetrics* 3 (supplement): 15–19.

Mbilinyi, M. 1972. "The 'New Woman' and Traditional Norms in Tanzania." *Journal of Modern African Studies* 10 (1): 57–72.

Moore, S. F. 1986. *Social Facts and Fabrications: 'Customary Law' on Kilimanjaro, 1880–1980.* New York: Cambridge University Press.

Ngallaba, S., S. H. Kapiga, I. Ruyobya, and J. T. Boerma, eds. 1993. *Tanzania Demographic and Health Survey 1991/1992.* Dar es Salaam, Tanzania and Columbia, Md.: Bureau of Statistics, Planning Commission and Macro International Inc.

Nichols, D., O. A. Ladipo, J. M. Paxman, and E. O. Otolorin. 1986. "Sexual Behavior, Contraceptive Practice, and Reproductive Health among Nigerian Adolescents." *Studies in Family Planning* 17 (2): 100–106.

Nyirenda, I. C. 1992. "Legalise Abortion for School Girls." *Sunday News,* May 31, p. 4.

Omari, C. K. 1991. "Some Youth Social Problems in Tanzania: General Trends." In *Social Problems in Eastern Africa,* ed. C. K. Omari and L. P. Shaidi, 12–25. Dar es Salaam: University of Dar es Salaam Press.

Raum, O. F. 1940. *Chaga Childhood: A Description of Indigenous Education in an East African Tribe.* New York: Oxford University Press.

Serpell, R. 1993. *The Significance of Schooling: Life-Journeys in an African Society.* New York: Cambridge University Press.

Stambach, A. 2000. *Lessons from Mount Kilimanjaro: Schooling, Community, and Gender in East Africa.* New York: Routledge Press.

Swatridge, C. 1985. *Delivering the Goods: Education as Cargo in Papua New Guinea.* Manchester, U.K.: Manchester University Press.

Tanzania Development Research Group. 1990. *Girls' Educational Opportunities and Performance in Tanzania.* Copies available, P.O. Box 71612, Dar es Salaam, Tanzania.

Tanzania Gender Networking Programme.1993. *Gender Profile of Tanzania.* Copies available, P. O. Box 8921, Dar es Salaam, Tanzania.

Tanzanian National Archives, List of Native Medicinal Plants Collected by Mr. Koritschoner in the Makuyuni District. W., Usambaras, Tanganyika Territory. File no. 23496.

United Republic of Tanzania. 1988. *Population Census, Regional Profile, Kilimanjaro.* Dar es Salaam: Bureau of Planning and Statistics.

Weiss, B. 1993. "Buying Her Grave": Money, Movement and AIDS in North-west Tanzania." *Africa* 63 (1): 19–34.

White, L. 1990. *The Comforts of Home: Prostitution in Colonial Nairobi.* Chicago: University of Chicago Press.

Chapter 6

Cleaning the Belly: Managing Menstrual Health in Guinea, West Africa

Elise Levin

Women in rural Guinea use local drugs to cure a variety of menstrual problems, including those associated with irregular timing of the monthly cycle. The plant-based medicines are ingested most frequently in the form of a tea or infusion or are added to the daily meal. This manner of inducing late menses, often with the advice of local healers, provides women an acceptable alternative to risking clandestine abortions. Abortion in Guinea is not only illegal[1] but also thoroughly unacceptable to most people. However, as this chapter will show, paying close attention to the details of one's menstrual cycle is a highly *socially acceptable* activity, and through attentive menstrual management, women can avoid unwanted or mistimed childbearing. This form of menstrual management has received almost no attention in research on fertility in Africa, most likely because it does not correspond precisely to biomedical categories of reproductive health or fertility control. It is neither abortion nor contraception; its stated purpose is to correct menstrual problems, not to end a pregnancy.

Although the practice of menstrual management was not initially a part of my research,[2] its importance emerged during work with healers about the use of local plants for fertility control. What had begun as field research for a dissertation on intentional pregnancy avoidance in a high-fertility context expanded over time to investigate some related issues, which included the maintenance of menstrual health. Although the preliminary results presented here may be more suggestive than conclusive, there are some indications that this cultural process of fertility control is important throughout West Africa. The significance of managing menstruation in fertility lies in the interaction between culture and the intentions of women who manage their cycles in the course of managing their lives within a social context that promotes high fertility.

Defining the practice is no easy task. It defies standard Western medical categories, in part because women who take medicines to induce their menses do not consider themselves pregnant, and there is no way for us to know in hindsight whether or not the women were in fact pregnant when they used them.[3] In this community, many women acknowledge a pregnancy only after the fetus begins to move or when the pregnancy is visible; thus, they do not see this practice as abortion.

This chapter lays out a framework in which to place the practice of menstrual management relative to other anthropological and demographic work on fertility and abortion. Following a brief description of the local context, I argue that many women actively manage their fertility without resorting to abortion by monitoring their menstrual cycle and quickly resolving irregularities. With the help of knowledgeable specialists and locally available plants, women remedy a variety of health problems, which can include late menstrual periods. The paper then reviews the notion of a high-fertility context as aptly described by Caldwell and Caldwell (1987) and places the practice of menstrual management within this context. Although anthropologists and demographers who have written about the culture of high fertility have elaborated on abortion as a violation of norms in African societies, they have overlooked menstrual inducement and its potential effect in reducing unwanted pregnancies in that region. Similar practices have been observed in other parts of the world, and this chapter briefly reviews some scholarly work that documents the use of drugs to induce menstruation in other places and times. Moving then from anthropology to biomedicine, I review the mainstream biomedical definitions of reproductive interventions including abortion, contraception, and the so-called morning-after methods. It is important to spell out these definitions because the lay (or "folk") definitions of biological processes used by anthropologists may impose Western biomedical categories, despite efforts to accommodate local categories. Here, we see that menstrual inducement for the purpose of managing menstrual health is different from biomedically defined abortion but can result in a similar outcome—the ending of a pregnancy.

Abortion, often described in anthropological and demographic literature as an aberration or a violation of norms, is uncommon although not unknown in the local context of Muslim West Africa. Contrary to this, menstrual inducement is not forbidden; rather, it is a means of maintaining good reproductive health, which is encouraged. The information presented here is not complete, and much of the argument is pieced together from various sources.[4] Yet interviews as well as abundant circumstantial evidence point to Guinean women's strategic use of this practice, an activity that represents a new area for research on the intentionality of fertility practices that potentially challenges much conventional wisdom on fertility in Africa.

BACKGROUND: GUINEA AND DABOLA

Dabola, a community of about 10,000, lies along a geographical border separating the savanna of the Haute Guinée region and the Fouta Djalon highlands. Most of Dabola's inhabitants claim ancestral origins either in the Fouta Djalon or the Mande centers to the east, and most therefore speak either Maninka or Fula.

As in the past, this rural area is dominated by the cultivation of rice, groundnuts, and the local cereal, fonio. Now a part of the Haute Guinée region, the town of Dabola is an administrative seat for a prefecture (district) of 75,000 people. Dabola has always been a market town, and many people are engaged in commerce. The road to Conakry was recently rebuilt, shifting commerce toward the capital.

Guinea gained independence in 1958, the first of the French African colonies to do so, and established a revolutionary government led by President Ahmed Sékou Touré. The postcolonial period is divided into two eras for Guineans: Touré's regime (1958–84) and the years following. During "Sékou Touré," the new nation was generally aligned with the Soviet Union and therefore was for the large part closed to Western Europe and the United States. The present era is characterized most prominently by the country's slide into "democracy" (the term used locally to describe the post-Touré era and its accompanying feeling of chaos and economic hardship). However, many residents of Dabola were hopeful that the newly paved road to Conakry will lead to economic improvements.

All residents of Dabola are Muslims, except for approximately twenty civil servants and their families from the Forest region who run their own small Catholic church and several other foreigners who are Christians. There are two main mosques, the Fula mosque and the Maninka mosque, whose names refer to their founders rather than the attendees. There are also numerous smaller mosques, including one in which a small group of followers of Wahhabiyya pray.

The local population has a number of options in seeking medical cures, and *fida toubabou*, "white man's medicine," is one of them. Dabola has both a hospital and a clinic for pregnant women and children, which since 1993 has provided contraceptives as part of a U.N. and U.S. government-funded program. The presence of the hospital since colonial times has likely diminished but not eliminated the appeal of a wide variety of other specialists, including healers who deal in magic; Koranic scholars, or marabouts, who also have healing powers; fetishists; herbalists; traveling healers who sell medicinal powders; and other people known for their capacity to heal.

CULTURAL NORMS AND THE CONTEXT OF REPRODUCTIVE DECISIONS: THE CULTURE OF HIGH FERTILITY

In West Africa, it is well known that high fertility is the desired outcome of a cultural system that encourages women to begin childbearing early and to fulfill their conjugal role by having large numbers of children. This cultural system applies to Guinea as well[5] and is supported by both civil and Islamic law. Pronatalist laws dating from the colonial period were still in effect in 1995[6] that implicitly place the family-planning program in violation of the civil code. Having or assisting an abortion is strictly against the law, except in the case that a woman's life is in danger.

In Dabola, as well as the rest of Guinea and West Africa, fertility rates reflect the cultural system; the total fertility rate for Guinea is 5.7, and for the region of Haute Guinée it is 6.6.[7] Due to the high value placed on children, the health of a newborn is protected through societal rules that dictate a wait of at least eighteen and preferably twenty-four months before the mother may again become pregnant. Anthropologists—and demographers—explain this practice and the high fertility level by emphasizing that they stem from strong societal norms that women willingly follow for several reasons. Among these are the desire to add their husband's lineage and to provide children to help in agricultural and household work and as a form of wealth.

Similarly, ethnographies from the early twentieth century describe African societies that strongly favor large families, in which people do everything they can to realize their greatest possible fertility potential. Abortion was rare, according to the early studies, and was practiced only in exceptional departures from normal behavior: a pregnancy before a marriage, as a result of incest, or a situation where a pregnancy would reveal a woman's unfaithfulness (Fortes 1949; Colson 1958; Schapera 1966; Devereux 1955). In other cases a woman who became pregnant during the two-year postpartum period might resort to abortion (Caldwell and Caldwell 1994).

The norms prohibiting abortion are deeply embedded in the social life of Maninka and Fula families; the national and Islamic laws that criminalize abortion reflect existing cultural values. People are extremely reluctant to talk about abortions, either their own or those of others. But talking about contraception was quite another matter during my research. Women were quite willing to discuss the contraceptive measures they take, both in surveys and in daily conversation. Apparently they were not inhibited by the lively public debate on the evils of contraception, which included frequent warnings from imams who went on the national radio to tell people to stay away from family-planning clinics.

Differences can be observed not only in the levels of secrecy about abortion and contraception but also along gender lines in the importance of religion in the matter of contraception. Men are more likely to talk about Islam and the imams' warnings, whereas those women who express a lack of interest or reluctance to use contraception draw attention to their desire to have more children or concerns about side effects. However, not all women are disinterested in contraception: community-level data indicate that an estimated 14 percent of women in the town of Dabola and the immediately surrounding area are using clinical contraceptives only two years after the commencement of family-planning services.[8] The rapid adoption of new contraceptive technologies in Dabola is surprising, even to the national family-planning program staff, precisely because the high-fertility norms are expected to discourage contraception. This rapid uptake is one indication that the predominant cultural rules are not uniformly dictating anticontraceptive behavior.

The difficulties encountered by researchers studying abortion in the region have resulted generally in very little data of good quality. This dearth of reports on abortion, I will argue, appears to be masking extensive menstrual inducement activity, which is acceptable when undertaken for reasons of good maternal health. But by focusing on Western definitions of pregnancy and abortion, many researchers have missed the menstrual management activity and have concluded that normal, married women do not intentionally control childbearing in high-fertility societies. One of my objectives in doing in-depth research on reproductive intentions and practices was to move beyond assumptions of this kind and to learn about local women's management of their own fertility. This necessitated moving beyond official discourse and trying to understand a system different from my own.

MENSTRUAL MANAGEMENT IN DABOLA

Women in Dabola are keenly aware of their *fanka,* their physical robustness (in Maninka language), which determines their ability to withstand hardship, disease, pregnancy, and childbearing. All people are born with a certain level of *fanka,* and one must be conscientious about one's own physical and spiritual limits. Women with more *fanka* are able to withstand a greater number of pregnancies, particularly difficult pregnancies and miscarriages. Women who have suffered illness and difficult pregnancies must safeguard their health. An important indication to a woman of her general health status is the condition of her menstrual health, which she measures in the regularity of the menstrual flow and the amount and quality of the blood. Good menstrual health represents physical well-being both to the woman in question and to others, primarily her husband's family. By being closely attuned to her menstrual cycle and acting quickly to treat problems, a woman can avoid serious problems that are common in this region, such as infertility, difficult pregnancy, miscarriage, hemorrhage, and death—her own or the child's.

Menstrual problems are usually caused by a blockage, which must be removed promptly. Blockages effect the color, quantity, and consistency of the menstrual blood but can cause more serious damage as well. For this reason, women who notice changes or problems in their cycle or in the menstrual blood will get help from one of several sources. They can go to the hospital, where there is a reputable gynecologist, or to the clinic, where a well-known and trusted nurse can cure a variety of problems. Islamic specialists can help women, as can others who use charms to heal. Although the medically trained doctors and nurses are willing and able to help women who are pregnant, women who want to avoid pregnancy, and to a lesser degree women who are having difficulty becoming pregnant, they have less to offer women who come to them with menstrual complaints. This is why many women seek the help of qualified herbalists who rely mainly on their knowledge of local drugs to treat both men and women for many illnesses. Although my data on the use of specific healers is incomplete, in my survey more than 20 percent of women reported having used plant medicines either to help them become pregnant, to avoid pregnancy, or to induce late menses. This chapter deals with the work of herbalists rather than marabouts or fetishists.[9]

Among the most common complaints for which women seek help from herbalists are painful menstrual periods; menstrual blood that is too dark, too light, too thin or thick, too much or too little; flow that is too heavy or too light; and a period that is expected but has not yet begun. As in many other societies, the Maninka word for menstruation is the same word used for "month" or "moon": *karo.* Both the Mandinka and Islamic calendars use a twenty-eight-day month, which corresponds to the average length of a menstrual cycle. Women count months by cycles of the moon, and any cycle longer than twenty-eight days represents a potential problem. (Another term used for menstruation is *mm'bolo ye gi ro:* "my hand is in the water," referring to the large quantities of water needed to clean oneself.) Being able to get pregnant when one wants to is extremely important; anything that would impair one's ability to do this indicates a possible *nyama,* or blockage, and must be corrected immediately. This concern is similarly expressed by some women when talking about contraceptive methods; the injectable Depo-Provera is known to stop menstrual flow during its use and to delay fecundity even after its use is suspended, which is an unfavorable quality of medicines otherwise seen as useful. Even the slightest hint that something is amiss in a woman's reproductive functioning is motivation to consult an herbalist and to take medicine.

Late menstrual periods are one of the most frequent complaints for which herbalists treat women; another is a delay in becoming pregnant. The local herbalists have a well-developed pharmacopoeia, including plants that can help women who have menstrual complaints and others to help in becoming pregnant. Women who seek treatment for "bellyaches" are questioned about their symptoms so that the herbalist can determine whether the bellyache is a menstrual complaint (including lateness), a pregnancy, or something different. The medicines that are used to treat menstrual lateness act by inducing flow (medicines that induce menses are referred to as "emmenagogues" in some of the medical literature). "Cleaning the belly" is one way of expressing menstrual inducement locally, although the term has other meanings as well. Having a regular menstrual flow of the proper quantity, color, and consistency is seen as a sign of good health, which must be achieved before a woman can become pregnant. Most of the herbalists refuse to help women who want an abortion.

Menstrual lateness, if one is not expecting to be pregnant, can be a sign of a blockage. Many women do not expect to be pregnant during a given time, for reasons that must be understood in local terms. The need to maintain a two-year interval between pregnancies provides an incentive to married women to carefully monitor their cycle; some women violate the rule that forbids sexual relations during this time by allowing their husbands to "visit" them (women generally have a room or a one-room house for themselves and their young children). In some cases, it is the fear that a husband will take a second (or third) wife that propels a woman to allow this transgression of rules. Women whose husbands are away for extended periods (men who work in the mines are typically away from home for months at a time) or travel frequently for work or are very old or sick as well as women who are visiting their own relatives for an extended time may find themselves in a relationship in which they do not want to have a child. The incentives for young women in school to avoid pregnancy are well known. And a woman who intends to leave her husband, or who expects her husband to leave, also tries to avoid having more children with him. All of these are reasons for married women not to be pregnant during specific times. As outsiders, it is tempting to regard menstrual management simply as a form of early abortion when a woman has violated rules. Locally, however, the periods of pregnancy avoidance are highly charged with meaning; one must avoid pregnancy and tend to menstrual health so that upon the end of the period of avoidance, pregnancy will be easily achieved and carried through to birth.

The literature on blood and menstruation gives some guidance on the symbolic significance of menstruation and menstrual rituals (cf. Douglas 1966; Gottlieb 1988). Most of this literature, however, deals with menstrual blood as a dangerous force that must be kept separate from society rather than a symbol of health and fertility. In many societies, menstrual taboos dictate seclusion of women in menstrual huts during menses or that they avoid certain activities such as farming, cooking, or hunting.[10] Although the symbolic meaning of the menstrual blood as a *positive* sign of good health and fertility has drawn little anthropological work, some recent writers have dealt with menstruation as a powerful force that women can use to advantage (Sobo 1993) and as a symbol of productivity and health (Setel 2000).

In Dabola, it is worth noting that menstruating women are not secluded, although they observe Islamic prohibitions against entering a mosque, praying, or observing the fast during Ramadan. Beyond the lack of obvious taboos, menstruation is a sign of good health, representing a woman's potential for future pregnancies and successful childbearing.

Herbalists distinguish clearly between helping women to induce menstruation and abortion. All of the herbalists stated emphatically their unwillingness to help a woman with abortion, yet all of them frequently help women by curing menstrual problems, including lateness. Not only healers but also most other people distinguish between the practices of improving or inducing menstruation and intentionally aborting a fetus. In fact, intentional abortion is a very distinct action, which is translated from Maninka to mean "bringing down a baby" or "spoiling a baby," not at all similar to "washing the belly." It is also distinguished from a miscarriage, "a baby that has fallen." The importance of the different meanings occurred during a visit to the market with two other women when one of them pointed out to me a pile of seedpods for sale, telling me it was *kanin*. "When you give birth," she explained, "that's the first thing you eat. It cleans the stomach, the kidneys, everything." Both women then said that they had eaten it after each time they had given birth. "Even now, I take it," the other woman told me. "When?" I asked. "From time to time. It can also be taken to cause an abortion. The healer told us that it wouldn't but if you don't see your period, you can use it." At this point, the first woman who spoke, a nurse, exclaimed that it was the same thing—taking it to see your period or to cause an abortion. The second woman reminded us that the healer had emphasized that menstrual inducement and cleansing were not the same thing as abortion. This conversation made clear the importance of distinguishing between the two practices in conversation. It also highlights the tension between the nurse's biomedical views, which do not recognize the practice of menstrual inducement as a means of enhancing reproductive health, and local views, which insist on it. This tension is played out even in the local arena, where medical staff lives as part of the community and brings a discourse that at times collides with other healing discourse.

Women also distinguish between contraception and abortion: women use menstrual management for the purpose of resolving a late menses, and not to intentionally avoid pregnancy, according to their own explanations. Indeed, survey questions on pregnancy avoidance and induced abortion did not elicit responses about the use of plant medicines, but several women did discuss local medicines in response to a question about inducing late menses. A survey by UNICEF found that 44 percent of women "knew at least one traditional means of child spacing" (UNICEF 1990, 132), but that the "techniques indentified were limited to... talismans or fetish charms" (132). Child spacing refers to pregnancy avoidance in this context. The UNICEF study did not cover the use of plant medicines or abortion.

The practice of inducing a late menstrual period as part of a wider spectrum of menstrual management practices is not unique to Guinea or, apparently, to West Africa, although it is rare in the contemporary literature on Africa. Many examples of similar practices are found when one looks more widely across geographical space and time.

In northern India, women practice menstrual regulation, or cleansing, to cure late periods. Citing Jeffrey, Jeffrey, and Lyon (1988), Anthony Carter (1995, 70) presents cleansing as an "opportunity provided by concepts of pregnancy to maneuver between menstrual regulation and abortion" mediated through body symbols about pregnancy. The three-month point, where pregnancy is said to begin, also divides the practices of "averting a baby" or "causing a baby to fall." Carter also cites work in China by Ngin (1985): "The sign of a warm and healthy womb is regular menses.... Great efforts are made to ensure menstrual regularity." These efforts include the use of Chinese "indigenous fertility regulating preparations" that are used as "abortifacients and emmenagogues" (Carter 1995, 70).

In ancient Greece, a variety of drugs were available to women suffering irregular menstruation. Riddle (1991) has identified numerous medicinal plants that he argues were used widely as emmenagogues both in antiquity and during the medieval period in Europe.

In Jamaica, there is a distinction between "menstrual washout," which favors fertility, and abortion, which does not. "Fertility is never certain in Jamaica, which supports participants' arguments that menstrual 'washouts' are indeed menstrual 'washouts' and not intended as abortions" (Sobo 1996, 501). The author also refers to the distinction between "restoring the menses" and "mak[ing] a baby turn into blood and wash out" and explains that the "multiple-use medications are especially helpful when individuals desire privacy regarding their intentions" (503). Ambiguity can serve as a kind of secrecy and is a strategy that women can employ.

LOCAL DRUGS USED FOR MENSTRUAL MANAGEMENT

Knowing that one must beware of quacks, people in Dabola do rely on some reputed herbalists to treat different kinds of bodily complaints. The herbalists who spoke with me took every opportunity to explain their conservative approach to healing and their caution in curing menstrual problems. First, an herbalist makes a diagnosis only after obtaining a very precise description of the woman's problems, including the length of time she has had the symptoms and how they have changed over time. They prescribe plant medicines, often mixing them in ways that are specific to the problem being treated and its severity. Many plants can be prepared in different combinations with others to achieve various cures; for example, one plant called *sunsungbe* locally, which can help a woman become pregnant, is also used in combination with some other plants to cure sexual impotence in men.

Some medicinal plants known to treat late periods are available at the market, and others must be obtained from a knowledgeable herbalist. In the market, I found two remedies for sale—one is purchased as strips of bark from a tree (*popa*) and the other as seed pods (*kanin,* mentioned previously). Both of these plants grow in Guinea, although far from Dabola, and traders bring them from other regions. *Kanin* is widely known to be "good for women." It is taken immediately following childbirth and induces the expulsion of the placenta. Local physicians recognize that *kanin* induces expulsion of the placenta. Some women take it regularly, merely to maintain good flows and good health. The other plant is known simply as a "bitter" medicine. Both are prepared as a broth or tea.

Herbalists can be consulted with far more privacy than is possible shopping at the market. Both male and female herbalists treat women's problems; they diagnose an individual woman's problems carefully, focusing not only on the main complaint with which she initially arrives but a range of symptoms that she might reveal over time. Most of these consultations, therefore, take place over a period of weeks or months; healers generally want more than one session with a woman. The local herbalists in Dabola with whom I spoke do not accept monetary payment before or during treatment. Other healers, including traveling herbalists from Niger and some traditional medicine specialists in other towns, not only accept but require payment. However, once the treatment has been accomplished, a woman may offer a gift such as six meters of cloth or a bag of rice to the healer.

I collected eighteen plants that are used for reproductive purposes.[11] Of them, five can be used to clean the belly, and of these, three were reported either by doctors or herbalists to be effective in inducing an abortion. All four herbalists with whom I worked claimed knowledge of such plants. One herbalist also claimed to know of a plant that would prevent conception. Other plants are known to help women to become pregnant; those that help women who have previously had a child are distinguished from those that help women who have never given birth. All of the medicines that are used to clean the belly are also used to help ensure a good pregnancy. However, these medicines must not be used once a woman becomes pregnant, according to the herbalists. An important aspect of some of the medicines that help a woman become pregnant is that they induce menses as part of their cure. This procedure rids the body of problematic blood and blockages, and the medicines then correct the problem, the results of which are seen in the next menstrual period.

Herbalists treat a range of reproductive problems, and individual women often come to them with more than one complaint. By considering several problems at once, the herbalist does not have to single out the fact that a woman's period is late. Neither is there a reason to determine whether the lateness is due to an early pregnancy or some other problem. Instead, all aspects of the functioning of her reproductive system are treated simultaneously; the specific plant or plant mixture is chosen to remedy all of the problems.

LOCAL ABORTIONS

Although research on contraception (my central research focus) was not difficult in Dabola, conducting research about abortion was a different matter. A survey of 170 women resulted in virtually no information about abortions. Yet from the beginning of my stay, women and men provided anecdotal evidence of abortions, their own and others'. Some clear patterns emerged from these stories: although abortion is neither a new practice nor confined to unmarried school girls, it is seen in a negative light, and either the woman who resorts to it or the man who caused the pregnancy against her will are named as the culprit. Also, abortion takes place late, by Western standards, usually after the fourth month of pregnancy. Here, I use the term *abortion* according to local use in Guinea, referring to procedures undertaken after the pregnancy is acknowledged privately at least, or the fourth to fifth month in biomedical terms. Thus, abortion does not include the practice of menstrual inducement discussed earlier.

In this section I present kinds of evidence of abortion in Guinea: verbal accounts of abortions told to me in Dabola and nearby towns, reports from local doctors and nurses in Guinean hospitals, and two companion studies on maternal mortality in Conakry (Touré et al. 1992; Cantrelle, Thonneau, and Touré 1993) that take up the problem of home abortions resulting in maternal death. Taken together, these varied pieces of data are further evidence of a cultural logic that places abortion quite separately from menstrual inducement.

One of very few firsthand accounts came from a woman who told me that she had had two hospital abortions during visits to her sister in Sierra Leone. She was married at the time and had given birth to six children, including four "for" her current husband, yet was unhappy in the marriage and simply did not want to have any more children with him. The decision was explained to me very matter-of-factly, in hindsight; the woman had no visible feeling of guilt or shame, and she eventually had succeeded at getting out of the marriage.

Although accusation of abortion is a common insult, the following story may be more believable because it reached me through several paths. A young woman I knew, still in secondary school, had become pregnant the previous year after being seduced by a man from Conakry. As I was told the story by her sister:

> It was her first sexual experience, and she did not even know what was happening. He just took advantage of her and then left. Afterwards, she was afraid, and did not tell anyone that she was not seeing her period. Eventually the pregnancy became obvious, she could no longer hide it, and her father sent her to another town for a hospital abortion. By the time of the abortion, the pregnancy was quite advanced, and she lost most of the year of school. At school, people only know that she was sick. (Hawa, T. E. L. field notes, January 1995)

Other evidence of abortions comes from reports by doctors at various hospitals in Guinea and a series of studies conducted in Conakry and in Moyenne Guinée (a neighboring region) on maternal mortality in 1989–90. One physician reported that every month, one or two women come to his hospital with complications from home abortions. He listed for me the different methods women use to induce an abortion at home, and most of these involved plants that I had learned about from herbal specialists. Abortions are performed legally in hospitals only in the case that it is deemed medically necessary for the woman. One doctor in Conakry also indicated to me that in some cases, doctors perform abortions in the hospital based on their own judgment about the woman's situation but that this is rarely done and only under the most extreme circumstances.

Who are the women who get abortions? According to the doctors responsible for treating women who present at the hospital with incomplete abortions or infections suspected to be due to abortions, many of the women are married, although some are not. The methods used to induce abortions at home include some of the medicinal plants used to clean the belly, or induce menses. Other methods known to induce an abortion are ingesting large amounts of honey or very small amounts of gunpowder. The use of contraceptive pills for abortions was not reported.

The restrictions on doctors regarding abortion are taken seriously; accusation of abortion can have serious consequences for doctors at government hospitals, virtually their only source of employment. One doctor who had been in Dabola about ten years earlier had been reassigned to a less desirable post when he became embroiled in an abortion case. In this case, a woman from another town had requested an abortion, following an extramarital affair, and she died as a result of the abortion. Her husband subsequently charged the doctor with her death, and following a court case, the doctor was transferred.

Because doctors see women suffering the dire results of incomplete abortions, it is not surprising that there is growing interest in the medical community, within Guinea and abroad, in studying the level of abortions and their consequences. No comprehensive data on the incidence of abortion have been collected in Guinea. However, a study of maternal mortality in Conakry concluded that the third most frequent cause of mortality related to pregnancy and childbirth was complications of abortion (Touré et al. 1992, 93; Cantrelle, Thonneau, and Touré 1992). However, it is worth noting that thirteen of the nineteen cases that were described as abortions were actually induced, the others having been spontaneous abortion (miscarriage). Secondly, most of the abortions occurred after twelve weeks of amenorrhea, or supposed pregnancy. This finding is consistent with the distinction in timing, according to the local Dabola logic described earlier, between menstrual management or "cleaning the belly" and abortion or "causing a baby to fall." It also suggests that the early practice of menstrual management may not be as dangerous, in terms of mortality, as later abortions. The articles do not provide data on the method used to induce abortion, although the authors state that 66 percent of reported abortions in Conakry health facilities were induced by the use of "abortifacient medicinal plants" without providing data on the results of those abortions. My point here is not to claim that the use of medicinal plants is not as dangerous as the use of mechanical instruments to induce abortion but merely to point out that some abortion is indeed occurring in Guinea despite norms and laws to the contrary, and that most of its reported occurrence by health facilities places abortion after the third month of pregnancy.

Based on substantial anecdotal evidence and some preliminary studies on maternal mortality, we can only conclude that some women have voluntarily terminated pregnancies in this area for a long time. However, there is no basis to conclude that abortion per se is practiced widely. In fact, if there were many more abortions, I would have expected to hear about more of them during nearly a year of intensive fieldwork. In fact, abortions are clearly not available to anyone who wants them, a fact that was brought home by a case of infanticide that occurred in 1995. It is possible that the need for abortions to end unwanted pregnancy is partially reduced by the widespread practice of menstrual management, including the inducement of late menses. Abortions, when they are induced, remove unwanted pregnancies, pregnancies that arise from incest, extramarital relations, or a marriage that the woman hopes will end.

DISCUSSION

In this chapter, I have argued that in Guinea, women are actively seeking help in treating menstrual problems in a deliberate effort to maintain their reproductive functioning and their ability to have a successful pregnancy. This activity includes the work of skillful and knowledgeable herbalists, whose involvement is important in legitimizing the activity as well as in providing essential medicinal plants and advice about their preparation and use. One element of menstrual treatment is the inducement of late menses, which women are eager to do, fearful that a late period may indicate blockages or other serious problems in their reproductive systems.

Attention to the precise moment that pregnancy begins is a feature of Western obstetrics that is not found in Dabola. There, pregnancy is not tied to the moment of implantation; rather, a pregnancy is established only when a woman believes she can feel it or can no longer deny it. Therefore, an abortion can not be possible before the fourth or fifth gestational month. Indeed, it is well known that rural African women often fail to report being pregnant for several months. Although women know that a pregnancy may well have begun by the time of a first missed period, it is not acknowledged until much later. Similarly, women in Kiti, Nigeria, claimed that a real child develops only after the fourth month of pregnancy (Renne 1996, 489).

Not surprisingly, members of the Guinean medical community (medically trained personnel at hospitals and in the Ministry of Health) equate menstrual inducement with abortion, as I initially had done. One doctor told me that a woman's complaint of stomachaches *(maux de ventre)* usually means pregnancy. "She tells her friend she has a bellyache. The friend says, 'Here, take this,' and gives her a root. Then she aborts." Yet nonmedical people insist that menstrual management, including inducement, was completely different from abortion; it is a positive thing to do, "it is good for women." As discussed earlier, herbalists were especially explicit that treating menstrual complaints is done to maintain good health, avoid blockages, and ultimately to have a successful pregnancy. Abortion, to the herbalists, is an unfortunate outcome of misused medicines or an intentional practice in which they did not engage. The negative meaning of abortion is important if one is to understand it as a counterpoint to menstrual management.

On the other hand, abortions as abortions are the last resort in cases of premarital sex, particularly the seduction of young girls by older men; of incest; of extramarital sex that would be revealed by the pregnancy, where a marriage is about to dissolve; or other situations where the pregnancy is seen as misfortune. Abortions are done in secret; menstrual management may not be discussed publicly, but it is not subject to the same level of secrecy as abortion.

In herbalists' and women's own terms, the inducement of menses is done as a way of "cleaning the belly"; to begin anew, to remove clots and blockages, to improve the quality of the blood, and to restore and maintain one's health and strength. Not knowing of the presence of a fetus and not even wanting to know when one seeks to "clean the belly" helps to establish this activity as conceptually different from abortion.

It has not been my intention to claim that there is widespread abortion in Guinea; to the contrary, it is to explain that practicing menstrual management lessens the need for abortion. As Sobo states (1996), the Western researcher should not conclude that menstrual inducement is something that the women themselves insist it is not. However, there is substantial evidence that the practice of menstrual management can be understood only as part of a broader category of enhancing reproductive health. Although it is not the same as abortion, menstrual inducement, if as widely practiced as it appeared during my field work, would reduce by some margin the number of unwanted pregnancies that would otherwise lead to abortions, miscarriages, or births, with potential demographic significance. If this practice also effectively hides some intentional management of fertility, which it almost certainly does by providing an acceptable way of ending a very early pregnancy (biomedically defined), then there is much more to be learned about intentional fertility management outside of, and prior to, modern contraception.

NOTES

1. Abortion is legal in Guinea only "if performed to preserve the life and physical and mental health of the pregnant woman. For all other reasons abortion is generally illegal under the Criminal Code of Guinea.... A woman inducing or attempting to induce her own miscarriage or allowing someone to do so is liable to imprisonment for a term ranging from 16 days to a year and a fine of from CFA 3600—15,000" (United Nations 1993, 39).

2. This chapter is based on research conducted in the Republic of Guinea during 1994–95. I gratefully acknowledge financial and institutional support from the U.S. Fulbright Commission, the Sociology Department of the Université de Conakry, the Ecole Nationale d'Agriculture et des Forets in Mamou, the Program of African Studies at Northwestern University, and the Prefecture of Dabola. I also wish to thank Alaka Basu, the International Union for the Scientific Study of Population conference attendees, and the following persons for comments on earlier versions of this paper and for library assistance: Caroline Bledsoe, Robert Launay, Helen Schwartzman, Fatou Banja, Karen Andes, Mette Shayne, Patricia Ogendengbe, Mohamed Fofana, Paola Scommegna, and Gil Stein.

3. Although the medical community, including doctors and nurses at the local hospital and clinic, recognize that the local practice of inducing menstruation can cause an abortion as understood in biomedical terms, menstrual management is not equated with abortion locally, outside the hospital and clinic.

4. The data presented are based on a household pregnancy history survey of 170 women; ethnographic interviews with healers, medical staff, women, and other specialists; participant observation during eleven months in Guinea; and national population data.

5. Desired family size in all of Guinea is 6.2 on average for all women, 6.2 for Haute Guinée, and 7.9 for all men (Demographic and Health Survey 1994).

6. Article 317 of the Napoleonic Code of 1810 and amended in 1939 and again in Guinea in 1966 prohibits abortion, and the French law of 1920 (United Nations 1993, 39), prohibits contraception.

7. The estimated total fertility rate for the town of Dabola is 7.2 based on a sample of 170 women, too few for a reliable estimate. However, there is no reason to believe fertility is lower in Dabola than elsewhere in the region.

8. This estimate is supported by three data sets: a survey of the community conducted as part of my research and family-planning clinic data used in conjunction with population data on the town. A complicating factor is the degree to which women use contraception for very short periods.

9. The herbalists' activities are not necessarily limited to the prescription and preparation of medicinal plants. Most of the herbalists claimed to have powers that enabled them to work, and at least one of them employed charms as part of her healing process.

10. Gottlieb does describe the social world of the Beng in which menstrual rituals and taboos are played out, and she places emphasis on the fertility symbolism in menstruation in opposition to agricultural work. However, her main concern remains the separation of menstruating women from certain activities.

11. The plant specimens collected during fieldwork are in the process of being vouchered by the Missouri Botanical Garden, an herbarium of African plants. Once the identifications are vouchered, the next step will be the determination of active compounds. This information will provide more of a basis for understanding the connection between women's intentions and efficacy.

REFERENCES

Caldwell, John, and P. Caldwell. 1987. "The Cultural Context of High Fertility in Sub-Saharan Africa." *Population and Development Review* 13 (3): 409–37.

———. 1994. "Marital Status and Abortion in Sub-Saharan Africa." In *Nuptiality in Sub-Saharan Africa*, ed. C. Bledsoe and G. Pison, 274–95. Oxford: Clarendon Press.

Cantrelle, Pierre, P. Thonneau, and B. Touré. 1992. *Mortalité Maternelle: Deux études communautaires en Guinée.* Paris: Centre Français sur la Population et le Developpement, EHESS-INED-INSEE-ORSTOM.

Carter, Anthony. 1995. "Agency and Fertility: For an Ethnography of Practice." In *Situating Fertility: Anthropology and Demographic Inquiry*, ed. Susan Greenhalgh, 55–85. Cambridge: Cambridge University Press.

Colson, Elizabeth. 1958. *Marriage and Family among the Plateau Tonga.* Manchester, U.K.: Manchester University Press.

Demographic and Health Survey. 1994. *Enquete demographique et de sante: Guinee 1992.* Conakry, Guinea: Direction Nationale de la Statistique et de Informatisation.

Devereux, George. 1955. *A Study of Abortion in Primitive Societies.* New York: International Universities Press.

Douglas, Mary. 1966. *Purity and Danger.* London: Routledge and Kegan Paul.

Fortes, Meyer. 1949. *The Web of Kinship among the Tallensi.* London: Oxford University Press.

Gottlieb, Alma. 1988. "Menstrual Cosmology among the Beng of Ivory Coast." In *Blood Magic,* ed. Thomas Buckley and Alma Gottlieb, 55–74. Berkeley: University of California Press.

Jeffrey, Patricia, Roger Jeffrey, and Andrew Lyon. 1988. *Labour Pains and Labour Power.* London: Zed Books.

Ngin, Chor-Swant. 1985. "Indigenous Fertility Regulating Methods among Two Chinese Communities in Malaysia." In *Women's Medicine: A Cross-Cultural Study of Indigenous Fertility Regulation,* ed. Lucile Newman, 25–41. New Brunswick, N.J.: Rutgers University Press.

Renne, Elisha. 1996. "The Pregnancy Doesn't Stay: The Practice and Perception of Abortion by Ekiti Yoruba Women." *Social Science and Medicine* 42 (4): 483–94.

Riddle, John. 1991. "Oral Contraceptives and Early-Term Abortifacients during Classical Antiquity and the Middle Ages." *Past and Present* August (132): 3–32.

Schapera, Isaac. 1966. *Married Life in an African Tribe.* New York: Sheridan House.

Setel, Philip. 2000. "Someone to Take My Place: Fertility and the Male Life Cycle among Coastal Boiken, East Sepik Province, Papua New Guinea." In *Fertility and the Male Life Cycle,* ed. C. Bledsoe, S. Lerner, and J. I. Guyer, 233–56. New York: Oxford University Press..

Sobo, Elisa. 1993. *One Blood: The Jamaican Body.* Albany: State University of New York Press.

———. 1996. "Abortion Traditions in Rural Jamaica." *Social Science and Medicine* 42 (4): 495–508.

Touré, Boubacar, P. Thonneau, P. Cantrelle, T. M. Barry, T. Ngo-Khao, and E. Papiernik. 1992. "Level and Causes of Maternal Mortality in Guinea." *International Journal of Gynecology and Obstetrics* 37 (2): 89–95.

UNICEF. 1991. *Situation Analysis of Women and Children in Guinea.* Conakry, Guinea: UNICEF.

United Nations. 1993. *Abortion Policies: A Global Review.* Vol. 2. New York: U.N. Department for Economic and Social Information and Policy Analysis.

Chapter 7

Changing Assessments of Abortion in a Northern Nigerian Town

Elisha P. Renne

Duniya mace da ciki ce. [The world is a pregnant woman.]
—Hausa proverb

For many women in the old, walled section of the town of Zaria in northern Nigeria known as Zaria City, the perception that interference with fertility is morally suspect casts both contraception and abortion in a negative light. In this predominantly Muslim Hausa section of Zaria, the ideal of men's authority over their wives' fertility and the practice of seclusion prevail. Nonetheless, in the past, induced abortion was considered morally preferable to pregnancy prior to weaning a nursing child. Women then used medicinal herbs and other organic materials as abortifacients.

However, changing patterns of postpartum abstinence appear to have affected the practice of abortion in Zaria City. This shift is attributed, in part, to women's attendance at government schools beginning in the 1960s and Islamic schools in the late 1970s where they learned that postpartum abstinence over forty days and two years of nursing were not necessary and that pregnancy soon after giving birth was not shameful. Induced abortion now appears to be uncommon for married women, although the fact that many have had spontaneous abortions

This chapter is based on a study conducted during my stay in the Department of Sociology, Ahmadu Bello University, Zaria, Nigeria, as a visiting Fulbright lecturer. I would like to thank Philip Ahire; Labo Abdullahi; and my colleagues in the Department of Sociology, Ahmadu Bello University, and Dr. Dapo Shittu, Department of Gynaecology and Obstetrics, ABUTH-Zaria, for advice and Zaineb DanLadi for research assistance. Additional thanks go to Alaka Basu, Mairo Mandara, and James Trussell for their constructive suggestions.

suggests that some Zaria City women may be attempting to control births through abortion even while religious leaders deplore the practice. That is, although education (whether modern or religious) has led to a modernization of some aspects of behavior (a relaxation of postpartum abstinence controls in this case), it has led to greater conservatism in others (a stronger disapproval of abortion by married women in the present context).

Moreover, if education has led to a decline in abortion among married women, it may be responsible for an increase in abortion among young women, particularly unmarried schoolgirls. Based on field research in Zaria City in 1994–95, this study examines the changing assessment and practice of abortion in relation to women's educational opportunities, to religious beliefs, and to the political economy in northern Nigeria. However, before examining these changes, the research setting and methods of this study are briefly described.

RESEARCH SETTING AND METHODS

Zaria City[1] is the capital of the old Hausa Emirate of Zazzau, and the palace of the present emir, Alhaji Shehu Idris, along with the adjacent Friday mosque and local government offices, dominates the central area of the city. Kwarbai Quarter, where this study was conducted, consists of a large area surrounding the palace and has benefited from this location. Electricity is generally available; many houses have piped water, pit latrines, and some access to a paved road frequently plied by public transport buses. With its many concrete-block houses as well as traditional Hausa mud-block houses for which Zaria City is renowned, Kwarbai Quarter is the largest and one of the more affluent areas of the city. It has a government primary school, several Islamic schools, a chemist shop, and a small open market where cooked meat is sold. Men from the quarter are employed as government workers, teachers, vendors, traders, drivers, and farmers, whereas women who are secluded prepare foods and repackage bulk commodities (both sold outside by young girls) and embroider to generate income, although a few younger women now go out to work as nurses or teachers.

Compounds vary in size and layout depending on whether they are of the older, traditional or more modern style. The former type of housing is entirely walled in, with a common entryway that leads through a maze of passages, first to the resident men's rooms and then to a common courtyard with women's rooms in the back (see M.G. Smith 1954, 28). The more modern concrete-block style often has a veranda or porch from which one enters a main entranceway, with individual rooms situated around the circumference of an interior courtyard. Some houses were owned and occupied by related kin, whereas others were rented from owners.

Research in Kwarbai Quarter began in November 1994, when I moved into a house very close to the emir's palace where one other family was living at that time. Through the help of this family and a young female research assistant, we began interviews of 100 women residing in the quarter using a survey (in Hausa) on childbirth histories and delivery practices. Because abortion and family planning, particularly the latter, were extremely controversial issues in this community, only questions about spontaneous abortion (*bari*) were included in this first survey.

Women were selected for interview according to the snowball method; in other words, women in one compound whose husbands permitted interviews were asked to refer (and recommend) us to another house in the quarter.[2] Having this introduction, we interviewed all consenting married women in the compound. Thus, although this and subsequent surveys do not represent a statistical sampling of the quarter, the women interviewed exhibited a range of ages, occupational, and educational backgrounds. From this initial group of women we selected the majority of the thirty women who were subsequently interviewed using a short questionnaire on changes in postpartum practices and abortion. Their comments about abortion and their explanations of changes in postpartum practices, along with interviews with four Islamic scholars (two who resided in Zaria City, one who taught Islamic law at Ahmadu Bello University, and one who taught Islamiyya classes in a village just north of Zaria), provide the basis for the following discussion.

PRACTICES AND BELIEFS REGARDING ABORTION

In the well-known life history of the Hausa woman Baba of Karo, recorded by Mary F. Smith (1954) in the early 1950s, Baba describes an incident where a young wife, Dantambai, became pregnant only eight months after she had delivered her first child. This event evoked considerable consternation, as is evident from Baba's remarks:

> When Dantambai knew she was pregnant they sent for her mother, but she was angry and said she would not come. Dantambai and her husband were delighted, but their parents were angry. They said they would give her medicine so that the pregnancy should lie down but he [the husband] refused, he said "Here is one child, let's have the other one too!" If you go back to your husband's hut, what do you expect? (M. F. Smith 1954, 149)

This incident would have taken place sometime probably in the 1920s, and from Baba's response it appears to have been shocking, if uncommon, behavior. Yet it was not going "back to your husband's hut" that was viewed as the crux of the problem. Rather, it was the pregnancy conceived soon after an earlier birth and its effect on the mother's milk and subsequent health of the newborn child that was at issue:

> It is not sleeping with the husband that spoils her milk, it is the pregnancy that does that.... But it is not right that she should sleep with her husband for two years; if he insists she should wear a kolanut charm. As you know, there is medicine to make the pregnancy "go to sleep," but that is not a good thing. (M. F. Smith 1954, 148)

This incident is also interesting because it mentions two methods of controlling unwanted pregnancies—wearing a kolanut charm on a waist string and taking medicine to make the pregnancy "go to sleep" (Kleiner-Bossaller 1993). When these methods were unsuccessful, women could take a range of herbal decoctions and medicines to abort the pregnancy (Madauci, Isa, and Dauro 1968, 5), avoiding the shameful and dangerous condition of feeding a newborn child "pregnancy milk" *(sha ciki)*.[3] One older Zaria City woman described such an occurrence:

> There was a woman who wanted to abort her pregnancy because at that time, she had not yet weaned the baby and at that time, it was a shameful thing. So she asked me what to take to abort the pregnancy. So I said, anything that is bitter *(daci)*, so she took *madaci* [*Khaya senegalensis*, mahogany]. Then she had a fever and started bleeding and that's how she aborted the pregnancy.

Another woman suggested that this approach to abortion has been updated:

> When the pregnancy is small, if you take *madaci* and *saiwa lalle* [*Lawsonia inermis*, henna], it will abort the pregnancy. That was what people were using before. But now that hospitals are established, they go there to abort pregnancy. But before it was in the house.

Although some women apparently do go to clinics for abortion, interviews with other Zaria City women regarding abortion suggest that many types of nonclinical local methods for aborting unwanted pregnancies are widely known and still in use (I attempt to list these in Table 7.1). Of these, three of the most commonly mentioned plants used for abortion—*madaci, lalle,* and *tafashiya*—contain active pharmaceutical substances that have emmenagogic or oxytocic effects.

The association of bitter substances and abortion relates to an underlying Hausa medical principle, namely, the necessity of balancing opposing physical characteristics to maintain health (Wall 1988, 288). To maintain this balance, illness caused by excess heat is treated with cooling substances, whereas diseases attributed to excess moisture are treated with things associated with dryness. Similarly, excessive sweetness can be balanced by taking sour things, and excess salt can be allayed by taking bitter ones. Maintaining a balance between sweet, sour, salty, and bitter substances is particularly important during pregnancy, or else certain conditions that are harmful to a pregnancy and subsequent childbirth may ensue. If too many sweet things are taken during pregnancy, a condition known as "sweet" *(zaki)* (Masquelier 1995, 884–86; Mu'aza-Alti 1992, 152; Trevitt 1973, 224; Wall 1988, 185) may result. In this case, the amniotic fluid (also called *zaki*) is believed to accumulate, blocking the birth canal and causing painful and protracted delivery. Sweet was most often countered by taking sour things such as *zobarodo* (sorrel) and *bariketa* as well as bitter things such as *lalle* (henna) and *tafashiya* (African peach) during the seventh or eighth month of pregnancy. Yet taking too much of any of these bitter (or sour) substances may jeopardize a pregnancy—particularly during the

Table 7.1
Some Substances Used as Abortifacients by Zaria City Women

Type of Substance	Active Ingredient	References
PLANT MATERIALS		
Azadivachta indica *dalbeghia*	nimbidin, nimbin (bitter principle)	Oliver-Bever 1986, 140
Cassia sieberiana *marga* or *gama fa'da*	(diuretic, emetic)	Wall 1988, 317
Khaya sengalensis* *madaci**	"Calicedrin" emmenagogue	Oliver-Bever 1986, 86 Wall 1988, 299
Lawsonia inermis* *lalle**	Lawsone, gallic acid, napthaquinone (oxytocic)	Oliver-Bever 1986, 53 Wall 1988, 317
Leptadenia hastata *yadiya*	Asclepin intestinal problems	Jinju 1990, 42 Oliver-Bever 1986, 23
Mormodica charantia *garahuni, garafunu*	Charantin (abortifacient)	Oliver-Bever 1986, 236 Etkin and Ross 1982, 1565
Nauclea latifolia (Sarcocephalus esculentus) *tafashiya*	(alkaloid) Saponoside	Ayensu 1978, 226–28 Oliver-Bever 1986, 63,76
Vernonia colorata, V. amydalina *Shuwaka*	Vernonin (bitter glucoside)	Oliver-Bever 1986, 28
INORGANIC SUBSTANCES		
Potash (*kawa*)*		Wall 1988, 298–300
Bitumen (*kwali*)		
Indigo paste (*shuni*)		Wall 1988, 317
Laundry bluing*		
Injection*		
Match heads		
TABLETS		Etkin, Ross, and Muazzamu 1990
APC (aspirin-phenacetin-caffeine)*		Wall 1988, 281
M&B*		
Cafenol		
Family Planning		

*Abortifacients also reportedly used by Akan women in southern Ghana (Bleek and Asante-Darko 1986, 343–44).

first few months when a pregnancy is believed to be fragile. Taking an excess of bitter things may result in an imbalance that will lead to miscarriage, a belief that appears to be behind the association of excessive bitterness with early abortion made by one third one-third of the women questioned.[4] Timing is important as well. A few women were skeptical about the use of some bitter things such as *madaci* as an abortifacient, in part, because of its use as a medicine to counteract sweet. However, when so used, bitter things are taken late in a pregnancy, long after these substances are believed to be effective as abortifacients.

The Extent of Spontaneous Abortion

The Hausa terms for induced abortion, *zuba da cikin* (literally, "pour or throw out something from inside") (Newman and Newman 1977, 140), and spontaneous abortion, *bari* (miscarriage), which refers to dropping something accidentally (17), are indicative of the way they are distinguished. Induced abortion is intentional, whereas miscarriage is viewed as an act of God. Although 26 percent of the 100 Zaria City women interviewed in the childbirth survey reported having at least one miscarriage, as Leridon (1977, 48) has observed, it may be difficult to assess the extent of intrauterine mortality, in part because distinctions between spontaneous and induced abortion may be obscured when the situation warrants it. Well-known abortifacients such as *lalle,* commonly used cosmetically to color the hands and feet, are easily available to women who could use them to abort an early pregnancy (after missing one or two periods) when a pregnancy is considered to be weak. Unless the woman involved said that she had intentionally aborted a pregnancy, it would be difficult for others to know if the bleeding was caused by a local herb, whether it was the will of God, or whether it was actually delayed menstruation. This ambiguity provides women with a certain leeway in their actions, which are otherwise constrained by moral condemnation and legal restrictions.

Repeated miscarriages are referred to as *wabi* (see Last 1992, 805–6) and are attributed to several factors including hard work, emotional stress, crossing a river, or the spiritual machinations of others. In the case of the latter, religious rather than medicinal help is needed, as one woman whom I interviewed explained:

> Some miscarry, some women that's how they've been having miscarriage continuously. They will never have children, only miscarriage. So that kind of miscarriage, they will be looking for help for the person from mallams.

A variation on this idea of repeated miscarriage caused by particularly precarious pregnancies is the belief that some pregnancies can become so "strong" that they may withstand attempts to abort them (Darrah 1980, 294), thereafter remaining dormant for several years. This condition, known as a "sleeping pregnancy" (*kwantacce;* Madauci, Isa, and Dauro 1968, 5; Kleiner-Bossaller 1993, 17; Last 1979, 315; Wall 1988, 190), refers to the more general belief that some pregnancies can continue for more than nine months. Sleeping pregnancies can be brought about through the use of herbal medicines, and women with this condition may die along with the fetus unless the pregnancy is reanimated by taking countervailing herbal treatments.[5] Mentioned in the earlier comments made by Baba of Karo, medicine used to put a pregnancy to sleep or make a pregnancy lie down might also be used to delay a pregnancy so that proper social conventions can be maintained.

After a spontaneous abortion, women may go to clinics or hospitals to "wash" the remains of the pregnancy, although many did not:

> Some, they wash the stomach for them in the hospital but the Hausa they use these *boka* people [herbalists] and the *boka* people will give them medicine. There is one man in the Gwari area [west of Zaria], he normally puts medicine on his hand, then puts it in the private parts and removes the baby.

Of the twenty-six women who reported miscarriage (in the earlier childbirth survey), 50 percent went to a clinic or hospital at least once for subsequent treatment. Relatively little is known about the reproductive health consequences of spontaneous abortion for these women or about how current economic constraints are affecting their access for postmiscarriage treatment. It is becoming prohibitively expensive for many Zaria City women, as one woman who had the following experience during a recent miscarriage explained:

> It was [Naira] 500 for the washing and N100 for the bed; then they wanted to charge N900 for the blood transfusion and they brought three plastic bags of blood for the drip.[6] But her husband said that he didn't want to pay for anything else, that the money was too much. This was after the washing, he didn't want to pay for the blood transfusion so she said she would be eating things that would make her blood come back.
>
> She was watching the "washing" and was shouting and they even told her to stop screaming. [They didn't use anesthesia because she hadn't paid the money.] So she saw three things they used to wash, they really washed it. The first was like a big syringe, then they had an iron that was thick like her hand, then another iron thing that had three prongs—they used all three to wash. Now there's swelling of her legs and hands, and some water is coming out. She's not going back to the hospital because they will charge her.

The amount just for bed and treatment came to N600, almost an entire month's pay (N700) for a primary school teacher.

Taking traditional medicine in the house was one alternative that some women used:

> In the house, you only give medicine that will wash the dirt from the stomach. They wash it so later it won't turn into another *wahala* [trouble]. But washing of the stomach [D&C or manual vacuum aspiration (MVA)], that is in the hospital, not in the house.
>
> The medicine taken for washing the stomach—you can take *madaci [Khaya senegalensis]* and the bark of *dorawa [Parkia filocoidea]* and even *tsamiya [Tamarindus indica]* bark, you will cook it and then take it.[7]

Although there is some overlap in medicines taken as abortifacients and as postmiscarriage treatments (e.g., the bitter bark of the *madaci* tree was mentioned for both), more commonly the latter have general laxative or tonic effects (Etkin and Ross 1982, 1565–66).

Present Practice of Induced Abortion

Actual levels of induced abortion in Kwarbai Quarter or in Zaria City more generally are unknown. None of the women interviewed mentioned aborting pregnancies,[8] although as discussed earlier, the number of women reporting miscarriage suggests that some had induced an abortion. Several women from my survey group knew examples of women, mostly young and unmarried, in Zaria City who had aborted pregnancies:

I've heard stories of girls aborting pregnancy. Even some of them live in Zaria. There is one of their neighbors, she didn't get a husband because she was just sleeping around. She had three abortions—their family has taken her to Kaduna to abort these pregnancies.

There is one of my uncle's children, she got pregnant and she was a student. So the mother was trying to terminate it for her. So they gave her different types of medicine so she would abort it—but nothing happened. So they told her there is a hospital where they normally abort pregnancies. So when she went there, they told her N6000 because she was 6 months pregnant and it was N1000 a month. So she said that she didn't have that kind of money. Now the girl is at home, she's not yet delivered.

These stories suggest, among other things, that as school attendance among young women in Zaria City increases, so may the need for abortion. Yet it is important to distinguish between abortion induced by unmarried schoolgirls anxious to remain in school and abortion induced as a way of maintaining child spacing as in the past. This shift in the rationale for abortion is related not only to increasing numbers of young women attending schools (both Western and Islamic) but also to what they have learned there. Zaria City women's changing assessments of abortion reflect recent developments in postpartum practices, in Islamic religious beliefs, and in the political and economic situation in northern Nigeria.

Changes in Postpartum Practices and Religious Beliefs

Koranic references (Suras 2:233, 31:14, and 46:15; see also 'Abd al 'Ati 1982, 212) make specific reference to nursing:

Mothers should breast feed their children two full years, provided they want to complete the nursing. The family head must support women and clothe them properly. Yet no person is charged with more than he can cope with. No mother should be made to suffer because of her child, nor family head because of his child. (Sura 2:233)

This practice was widely followed until recently and provided a moral basis for abortion. However, more recent interpretations of this Koranic passage, such as the following interpretation made by one Islamic legal scholar, suggest that although spacing is recommended *(mandub)*, it is not mandatory *(fard)*:

The Muslims here in Nigeria they adopted this two years, within this two years the mother will continue to suckle her own child.... [Those who advocate change,] their argument is that the Qur'an is just advising, because at the end of the verse . . . "to him who wants to complete the two years suckling period," so they say it is not compulsory, it is optional. (Waines 1995, 76)

Zaria City women gave several explanations for this change in the importance of child spacing. For example, some saw the change as related to modernity *(zamani)*—women have become educated and know what to do if children are born within short intervals:

This change started about twenty years ago. They started because before, people were not educated. During that time, women were ignorant, only men went to school. So that's why now, most women know what is happening, that's why these changes started.

One woman described educated women who could afford to do so taking special medicines that would prevent children weaned within a year from becoming ill. With these medicines and with better nutrition, children can thrive without an extended period of nursing:

These changes started around twenty years ago or maybe more than twenty years ago. Before they didn't used to wean a child before it was two years, two years two months. Then, after weaning the child, the mother will take a long time before getting another pregnancy. But now it's not like that. Some get pregnant when the child is eight months—and the maximum is one year.

I don't know what brought these changes but some people are saying it's part of improvement [progress] because in just a few years, you'll have plenty of children.

Women associate education not only with reduced intervals between births and shortened periods of nursing (see Rehan and Abashiya 1981, 234) but also with a variety of changes related to childbirth including attendance at antenatal clinics, hospital delivery, and the use of Western medicines. A reduction in polygyny does not appear to be the impetus for these changes.

Education for Zaria City women is available in two forms. There are Western-style secular primary schools instituted by the state through the universal primary education (UPE) program begun in 1976 (Clarke 1979), and there are Islamiyya schools, which emphasize Islamic learning along with instruction in more secular topics (Reichmuth 1993, 187). Although Islamiyya schools had been set up as early as the 1930s, the first such school in Zaria began in the 1950s (Barkindo 1993, 102), with a real blossoming of their popularity in the late 1970s. One aspect of Islamiyya education was the establishment of adult education classes for married women (Barkindo 1993, 103),[9] some of which were organized in Zaria City in connection with the Islamic reform movement known as Izala.

Izala, Religious Reform, and Women's Education

The history of Islam in northern Nigeria has been marked by a series of religious movements headed by charismatic Muslim leaders who have envisioned the rebirth of society through religious reinterpretation and reform. But during the postindependence era, such new practices—both religious and political—came under criticism by a new wave of religious leaders,[10] one of the most prominent being Mallam Abubakar Gumi. Gumi was instrumental in formulating the goals of the anti-Sufist Jama'atu Izalat al-Bid'a wa Iqamat al-Sunna ("Movement against Negative Innovations and for Orthodoxy," known as Izala) which was formally organized in 1978.

Three aspects of this movement are important for understanding its contribution to changes in women's perceptions of postpartum and abortion practices in Zaria. First, Gumi emphasized the primacy of the Koran and Hadith in prescribing proper Islamic conduct:

> There are no intermediaries in Islam, every Muslim enjoys free access to God as spelt out in the Holy Qur'an and the traditions of the Prophet [Hadith]. If one seeks for help, it should be from God Himself the Lord of all, and not through a Sheikh or saint. (Gumi 1992, 139)

Second, he made his views widely available to Hausa women and men through both radio broadcasts and audio cassettes of preaching sessions (Umar 1993, 167). Third, Izala leaders stressed the importance of education, not just for men but also for women and children, because for individuals to know the truth as written in the Koran and Hadith, they must be literate. Thus, religious teachers *(mallamai)* associated with the Izala movement organized schools and classes that emphasized the reading of the Koran and the Hadith along with discussions of how these readings could aid believers in the correct conduct of their everyday affairs. This scheme was described by M. S. Muhammad, the Izala executive secretary, in 1986:

> It has now become imperative to mention the achievement of the movement [i.e., Izala] as of today.... But [our] great achievement has been teaching in modern schools. We have reached the stage whereby in every corner in this country today we have [established] schools for adult classes, primary evening schools, and also schools for married women. (Umar 1993, 167)

What is significant about this development is the stress on individual knowledge of the Koran and the implicit power that such knowledge could bring to women. Indeed, there was considerable opposition to married women's attendance at adult Islamiyya classes when they were introduced to Zaria in the late 1970s (Y. Tanimu, personal communication), and several women said that their husbands refused to let them attend:

> I would have loved to go but my husband didn't allow it so I just stay at home. He said why didn't I tell him to teach me himself—since he knows how to teach—so I don't need to go.

Nonetheless, many Zaria City women have attended Islamiyya classes at one time or another, and some younger women go to Islamiyya classes as well as Western-style schools.

In Zaria City, women cited both types of education in explaining changing childbirth practices. Some attributed changes to the introduction of Western education:

> The year that these changes started was the year these schools were established, not Islamiyya [schools]. They say that it doesn't matter if you are nursing a child and you get another pregnancy, it doesn't matter. And there is nothing that will happen to the person.

But others mentioned attendance at Islamiyya schools:

> What brought change is the introduction of religion. These Arabic schools, before people were ignorant then. Now they will say that even though a woman is nursing, a husband can meet his wife.... Before, women, normally would go to their parent's house if their husband wants to meet them but now they don't do it.

Because both forms of women's education began in the late 1970s and became more common in the early 1980s and because young girls might attend classes in both, it would be fair to say that both may have contributed to these changes. Attention is given to Islamiyya schools in the following section because they were more often attended by the Zaria City women interviewed in this study.

Instruction in Postpartum Practices at Islamiyya Schools

> Even in school, in their Islamiyya, the *mallamai* will say that after the woman has finished the period of bathing for forty days, the husband can meet her. If the husband should meet her, it's nothing—but before they didn't know anything like that.
>
> —Zaria City woman

Islamiyya education classes for women taught by mallams included instruction on a range of family matters. Some mallams include specific instruction for married women on proper postpartum conduct. One mallam described teaching his married women students:

> In the women's classes, I teach them how to read the Qur'an, the Hadith, then Fiqh—things relating to Islamic law and how to conduct your personal life. We teach them to read it, how to write it, and also to know the meaning.

He instructs them on matters pertaining to postpartum behavior, including that they should not meet their husbands before the birth blood had finished flowing but that this was, at maximum, sixty days. After that, they could have intercourse, but they should avoid pregnancy by using two methods:

> One is that the husband can be controlled; there are certain women who will not allow their husbands to meet them when they are nursing, the husband also may want to meet the woman because he needs it but then in order to, in order not to make him go outside and commit adultery he is allowed to freely play with the woman, she can even masturbate him so that he can feel satisfied and stay at home.

[The other] is that it is prohibited in Islam for a person

to abstain from his wife simply because he does not want a child because the law states it is God who gives anybody anything so it is not allowed for a man to abstain from meeting his wife simply because he does not want her to get pregnant. Now in that case, a man is allowed you know to meet his wife but then before he ejaculates the sperm inside he can withdraw it [*azal*], that one is allowed.

If a woman were to get pregnant during this period, it is more likely that she would be encouraged to carry the pregnancy to term rather than to abort as in the past when such pregnancies were considered shameful. This decline in the stigma surrounding closely spaced births was reinforced by another recent teaching. Several women mentioned having been instructed that extended periods of breast-feeding were detrimental to the infant:

Because the teachers used to say in Islamiyya that too much breast-feeding blocks the brain of the child. That is why they are telling the parents to wean the child when it is one year, eight months or some say when they are one year.

This medical justification of early weaning counters prior beliefs about the need for extended breast-feeding to build up the child's strength (*karfi*) prior to weaning, helping to legitimate shortened nursing periods. One woman, however, described being taught that extended breast-feeding was good:

I go to Islamiyya. I've been going for fifteen years now. They usually tell us that it's good to breast-feed their children, that girls should breast-feed for two years, while boys should breast-feed eighteen months.

Her remark suggests that there is some variation of views among Islamiyya teachers on this topic; nonetheless, women more often mentioned shortened breast-feeding periods.

If attendance at Islamiyya classes by Zaria City women has tended to reduce childbirth intervals and the stigma of closely spaced pregnancies and hence the need for abortion, it also has, to some extent, expanded women's knowledge of Koranic interpretations of abortion.

Schoolgirls and Abortion

If they [young unmarried girls] get pregnant some of them drink henna [*lalle*], they vomit and they get diarrhoea and they usually miscarry. If they take indigo [*shuni*], they get very ill indeed. (Baba of Karo, in M. F. Smith 1954, 179)

If abortion is no longer necessary for child spacing, the need for abortion by young women to avoid premarital pregnancies (as indicated by Baba of Karo's statement) has been compounded by unmarried schoolgirls' need for abortion if they are to complete their education (Caldwell and Caldwell 1994, 282; Oronsaye, Ogbeide, and Unuigbe 1982). In these cases, whether women know of Koranic interpretations of procreation and different Islamic views of abortion is somewhat immaterial as ideals may be overridden by necessity. Unmarried school girls who become pregnant must leave school and often hope of prestigious white-collar or professional employment.

The extent of abortion among matriculating young women—married or unmarried—is presently unknown, although Zaria City women's comments suggest that such abortions (or attempts) are not uncommon:

> We hear stories of girls aborting pregnancy. They abort it so they won't say they are in school and pregnant. But it is not just like that they abort it, they abort it in the hospital. If it is one month, they will charge N1000, two months, N2000, seven months N7000. And these girls can be found anywhere. It is not only school girls, there is a girl in our house in primary school—she's four months pregnant.

Indeed, with more young girls attending primary and secondary schools, it seems possible that induced abortion may actually be increasing among this group.[11] Although some might go to clinics or take traditional Hausa medicines, this pharmacopoeia has been expanded to include modern bitter things such as APC tablets, laundry bluing powder, match heads, Coca-Cola, and family-planning tablets.[12] One middle-aged woman suggested that knowledge of such things was commonplace, judging from her own school experience:

> I've heard [that] blue and lots of salt [will cause abortion]. During school if they see you with blue, they will say, "So, you are experimenting with this type of thing!"

Yet although young women (often with the support of their families) may take medicines in an attempt to abort, the prevailing belief that ultimately all decisions about the fate of a woman's fertility are made by Allah casts human agency with respect to contraception and abortion in a particular moral light. An understanding of this ideology helps to explain why abortion, despite its earlier assessment as a relatively moral alternative to closely spaced births, is unlikely to be reinterpreted in a more positive fashion in the immediate future.

ISLAMIC INTERPRETATIONS OF ABORTION

Most Zaria City women interviewed believed that Islam did not allow abortion under any circumstances, but debates among Islamic scholars suggest a range of learned opinions on this topic. Although there is general agreement that any prohibitions on abortion may be overruled in instances when the mother's life is in danger (Sachedina 1990, 109), there is considerable disagreement about the morality of abortion at other times. These debates relate to arguments over when life begins and the interpretation of the passage from the Koran (cited here in one Hadith [An-Nawawi 1997, 26]) that describes the stages of fetal development:

Verily the creation of each one of you is brought together in his mother's belly for forty days in the form of seed, then he is a clot of blood for a like period, then a morsel of flesh for a like period, then there is sent to him the angel who blows the breath of life into him.

A literal reading of this Hadith suggests that because life begins only after the spirit has been breathed into "the morsel of flesh," abortion may be interpreted as morally acceptable until this time, although there is some variation in the period after which abortion is no longer acceptable, ranging from 40 to 120 days (Makhlouf Obermeyer 1992, 43; Musallam 1983, 57–59). However, more recent readings by some scholars suggest that life begins at the moment of conception and therefore that abortion is never permissible (Sachedina 1990, 110). This view coincides with the federal law which states that unless performed to save the mother's life, abortion is illegal in Nigeria (see Sections 232 and 233 of the Nigerian Penal Code (for details, see United Nations Population Division 2002), which applies to Northern Nigeria; Okagbue 1990, 197–98; Pittin 1986, 45).

Among the Zaria City women interviewed, none had knowledge of the stages of fetal development outlined in the Hadith or of the different scholarly interpretations of abortion. Almost two-thirds of the thirty women in the abortion interviews said that Islam categorically forbade abortion. However, women attending (or who had attended) Islamiyya classes were more knowledgeable and were significantly more likely to say that abortion was allowed if the mother's life was threatened than women who did not attend:

If you are pregnant and if it is giving you problems, especially if you are fainting then you can abort it. Or you can go to the hospital and they will remove it. It happened to one woman, she used to have problems with her pregnancy, so she went to the hospital and they removed it for her. If it's going to kill the mother, it is allowed.

This view is similar to the interpretation of abortion described here by one Islamic legal scholar in Zaria:

Islamically, that as a general rule, procreation is one of the aims and objectives of marriage in Islam but as they say to every general rule there is an exception so this is also the case with Islam. For example, where an expectant mother's own health will be impaired, then Islam makes it an exception that if actually there is not any other way of delivery without impairing the health of the mother, well as an exception to the general rule, to save the life of the mother then the mother is advised to stop the creation. This is one.

But secondly this exception also applies to a situation whereby even if the mother can be delivered of the child but with difficulty still, on that basis, again she will be advised to stop the creation. Whether it will lead to the loss of her life or she can still deliver but with difficulty there and then Islam actually [allows abortion].

How far exceptions that protect the health of the mother might be taken is, to a certain degree, debatable, underscoring the flexibility of Islam as a system of thought. Conceivably, through their increasing knowledge of the Koran, educated Islamic women might eventually propose interpretations in support of women's reproductive health, including that of young girls who are still in school.

DISCUSSION

Presently, many Islamic teachers frown on the use of modern contraceptives, in part because they are not specifically mentioned in the Koran, as explained by one such scholar:

> It's always good for people to stick to their understanding of what the Islamic law is saying or what the Prophet said, now the Prophet showed a lot of things. First of all, he didn't talk of these things coming, these tablets, condoms, and so on and so forth.... And second, even the pills and the condom they also have their own dangers and problems, so certainly the Prophet wouldn't have recommended them.

However, some Islamic teachers, including the one just cited, are neither categorically opposed to married men and women making personal decisions about the timing of births nor about taking certain steps to control births—as long as one recognizes that such decisions are ultimately up to God. Many cite *azal*, withdrawal, as a legitimate form of birth control not only because it is mentioned by the Prophet but also because it leaves open an element of chance that is the best way of showing humility in the face of a higher power, according to one mallam:

> Everything is written. Man cannot change this. So what God has written, that a woman will give birth or will not give birth, it is ultimately God who decides no matter what people may do in the way of family planning. The Qur'an mentions withdrawal (*azal*) as a way of limiting births but this is an example of man proposing.

This particular view of contraception—that certain forms mentioned in the Koran are acceptable but that they should only be viewed as a proposal—is related to present views of induced abortion. Under the prevailing strict readings of the Koran, aborting a pregnancy would be forbidden (except if the life of the mother was at stake) first, because abortion is not mentioned in the Koran as an acceptable way of controlling births, and second, because such an action would be viewed as an intentional attempt to overstep the bounds of human agency and hence as an offense to God.

This current assessment of both contraception and abortion in Zaria City relates to religious reform movements such as Izala that emerged in the 1960s and became popular in response to increasing disparities of wealth that developed during the oil boom years (1974–81). The call for a return to orthodoxy and to the strict reading of the Koran and the Hadith by Izala leaders represented a moral critique of northern Nigerian traditional rulers who, through their inordinate wealth and political alliances with colonial and postcolonial governments, were viewed as corrupted by secular sentiments. The uneducated status of Muslim women was also part of this reformist critique (Umar 1993, 158). The emphasis on women's Koranic education implied that women's religious ignorance contributed, in part, to prevailing superstitious and un-Islamic practices associated with Tijaniyya and Qadiriyya Islam followed by many traditional rulers. Thus, women's attendance at Islamiyya classes was encouraged by Izala leaders in order for them to become literate in the Koran and hence better Muslims. Yet it did not represent a fundamental change in the perception of women's primary roles in Hausa society as mothers and wives. This point is supported by one Zaria City woman's explanation of why she attends Islamiyya classes:

> The reasons I go are to know: 1) how to live with my husband, 2) how to raise my children, and 3) how to say my prayers. And before, women didn't know these things.

Although learning to read and having freedom to attend classes outside their homes may enhance Zaria City women's self-esteem and sense of autonomy, readings of the Koran as taught in Islamiyya schools reinforces their present social position. For example, although the control of fertility is ultimately up to Allah, the Koran states that the control of a wife's fertility is the husband's prerogative: "Your wives are [meant] for you to cultivate: so go to your cultivation whenever you wish" (Sura 2:223; see also Delaney 1991, 30). The subordinate status of women is not questioned because their distinctive role is written in the Koran.

Furthermore, the belief that moral behavior, particularly the strict observance of the Koran, will bring forth the blessings of Allah is combined with a disdain for what is considered to be Western immorality. This moral laxness is associated, among other things, with Western women's legal access to abortion, which is seen to foster "so many unwanted pregnancies in Europe," as one Zaria City Islamic scholar put it. Indeed, the strong anti-Western element of Izala and other Islamic reformist movements in Nigeria suggest not only that increased autonomy for women might be viewed as a Western innovation (see Moghadam 1991) but also that equality in gender relations is considered to have contributed to the moral decline associated with the West.[13]

Moreover, if having children in the context of marriage is viewed as the ideal primary role of women in Hausa society, legalizing abortion and thereby suggesting that other sorts of roles might, in some situations, take precedence (Luker 1984, 205) is an unsettling idea for many Hausa women as well as men, as one Zaria City woman's comments suggest:

> I don't go to Islamiyya. People were telling me to do it but I refused. I won't go. But I'll try to stop doing what is not good and be doing what is good. Because some of the women who go to Islamiyya, if their husbands are talking to them, they will talk back. Is that going to Islamiyya? It is better for them to stay in the house.

Nonetheless, the increasing numbers of women attending Islamiyya classes as well as primary schools and colleges, resulting in literate women better equipped to observe Koranic teachings, may have some unintended consequences as such women will also be better equipped to support their own readings of Koranic texts. Although support for a reassessment of abortion as permissible during the first trimester seems unlikely under the present religious and political context, the actions of young unmarried schoolgirls who attempt abortion even when they know that such behavior is forbidden according to current strict readings of the Koran suggest a way that practice may interpolate ideology. This point is expressed in the Hausa proverb *Duniya mata da ciki ce*—"The world is a pregnant woman." This proverb expresses the idea that the uncertainty surrounding the course and outcome of a pregnancy is similar to the uncertainty of the world. How abortion is controlled and interpreted by Zaria City women and men in the future is similarly uncertain and susceptible to unexpected events.

NOTES

1. The word *city* is used here to refer to Zaria City's political status as the capital of Emirate of Zazzau rather than to its size in population.

2. See Renne 1996a for a discussion of some of the problems encountered in this survey. Trevitt (1973, 221), who interviewed Zaria City women in Unguwar Kusfa, another quarter of the city, hints at a similar reticence encountered and the difficulties of obtaining a random sampling of informants in 1971:

> After an initial visit to collect demographic data, we returned to those compounds where the women seemed willing to talk freely about their customs.... Some people were reluctant to talk of local remedies and customs to us, whom they regarded as "strangers from the hospital."

3. According to Baba of Karo, if a nursing woman becomes pregnant, "the child gets thin, he dries up, he won't get strong, he won't get healthy" (M. F. Smith 1954, 148). Or as one older Zaria City woman put it, "the child will just be squeezed like a cocoyam leaf.... You will see the child going and the legs will be shaking."

4. According to Ekiti Yoruba women, sourness is the primary characteristic of abortion medicines (Renne 1996b). Alternately, Akan women in Ghana believe that an excess of sweet substances can bring about an abortion (Bleek and Asante-Darko 1986, 337).

5. A recipe for reanimating a sleeping pregnancy is given by Jinju (1990, 42):

> Soak 7 roots of *sanya* [*Securidaca longepedunculata;* violet tree]. Squeeze citrus juice into the concoction. Add *kantu* [sugar cube] to the medicine (in preparation). Mix up this medicine with *hura* [fura] and milk... Then drink some of it every morning.

This medicine may also be used for "cleaning the inside" after a miscarriage. Small doses of the roots are said to be a "drastic purgative" (Oliver-Bever 1986, 108).

6. Normally, women who come to register at a clinic or hospital for antenatal sessions are told to give a bag of blood as part of the admission fee.

7. Other types of medicines given after miscarriage include *rai dore* roots (*Cassia occidentalis,* coffee senna; Etkin and Ross 1982, 1562), black soap *[sabalu salo]* used for drinking, and *rubutu* (portions from the Koran, written on a slate and washed off with water that is then drunk). One Zaria City woman described what she knew of medicine for "washing" after miscarriage:

> You can soak *tsamiya* [tamarind] and lemon and bitter garden egg in water, then the next day, they will strain it and the woman will be taking it. Some normally take that black soap, the one meant for drinking called An Kotonou [from Kotonou]. Sometimes women will just drink *tsamiya* to wash the stomach.

8. This response differs from abortion research in southwestern Nigeria (Renne 1996b) and from interviews with women at family-planning clinics in Cote d'Ivoire (Huntington, Mensch, and Toubia 1993, 123). There are also difficulties of estimating the incidence of induced abortion from fertility, marriage, and contraceptive data (as proposed by Bongaarts [1978]) because changing periods of lactation and extended postpartum sexual abstinence were not taken into account in his model (see Reinis 1992, 315).

9. In Kano, a mass education program was set up by the state government with women's literacy as one of its goals (Callaway 1984, 446). Married Zaria City women interviewed in this study attended secondary and postsecondary Western schools or Islamiyya schools; none mentioned attending adult education classes.

10. Other reformist, antiestablishment Islamic leaders include Alhaji Mohammed Marwa, who led a group of followers known as 'Yan Tatsine, and El Zakzaky, who leads a Shi'a group that advocates the creation of an Islamic state.

11. Northern secondary school policies regarding female student pregnancy varies, but it appears that some girls' secondary schools in Zaria with predominantly Muslim Hausa women students allow students to be married and to continue their studies if they become pregnant, taking pressure off their need to abort. A study of secondary students from one school in Zaria is in progress.

12. See Etkin, Ross, and Muazzamu (1990) for a discussion of the ways that the uses of modern pharmaceuticals are being reinterpreted in a Hausa context. Good (1980, 152) describes the use of family-planning tablets as abortifacients in rural Iran:

> Women also attempt to use the contraceptive pill to induce abortions. It is not uncommon for women to take a month's supply in a day to bring menstruation when they suspect they are pregnant with an unwanted child.

13. For example, Gumi (1992, 187–88) cites the ordination of women ministers in England and the United States as contributing to moral decline:

> This is how the original revelations in the religion suffered many important modifications in the past, leading to the mix-up and erosion of values which one easily observes at present.

REFERENCES

'Abd al 'Ati, H. 1982. *The Family Structure in Islam.* Lagos: Islamic Publications.

An-Nawawi. 1997. *Forty Hadith.* Cambridge, U.K.: Islamic Texts Society.

Ayensu, E. S. 1983. "Endangered Plants Used in Traditional Medicine." In *Traditional Medicine and Health Care Coverage,* ed. R. H. Bannerman, J. Burton, and C. Wen-Chieh, 175–83. Geneva: World Health Organization.

Barkindo, B. 1991. "Growing Islamism in Kano City since 1970." In *Muslim Identity and Social Change in Sub-Saharan Africa,* ed. L Brenner, 91–105. London: Hurst and Co.

Bleek, Wolf, and N. K. Asante-Darko. 1986. "Illegal Abortion in Southern Ghana: Methods, Motives, and Consequences." *Human Organization* 45 (4): 333–44.

Bongaarts, J. 1978. "A Framework for Analyzing the Proximate Determinants of Fertility." *Population and Development Review* 4 (1): 105–32.

Caldwell, J., and P. Caldwell. 1994. "Marital Status and Abortion in Sub-Saharan Africa." In *Nuptiality in Sub-Saharan Africa: Current Changes and Impact on Fertility*, ed. C. Bledsoe and Gilles Pison, 274–95. Oxford: Clarendon Press.

Callaway, B. 1984. "The Ambiguous Consequences of Socialisation and Seclusion of Hausa Women." *Journal of Modern African Studies* 22 (3): 429–50.

Clarke, P. 1979. "The Religious Factor in the Developmental Process in Nigeria." *Geneve-Afrique* 17: 46–63.

Darrah, A. 1980. "A Hermeneutic Approach to Hausa Therapeutics: The Allegory of the Living Fire." Ph.D. diss., Northwestern University.

Delaney, C. 1991. *The Seed and the Soil*. Berkeley: University of California Press.

Etkin, N., and P. Ross. 1982. "Food as Medicine and Medicine as Food," *Social Science and Medicine* 16 (17): 1559–73.

Etkin, N., P. Ross, and I. Muazzamu. 1990. "The Indigenization of Pharmaceuticals: Therapeutic Transition in Rural Hausa Land." *Social Science and Medicine* 30 (8): 919–28.

Good, M. D. 1980. "Of Blood and Babies: The Relationship of Popular Islamic Physiology to Fertility." *Social Science and Medicine* 14B (3): 147–56.

Gumi, A., with I. Tsiga. 1992. *Where I Stand*. Ibadan, Nigeria: Spectrum Books.

Huntington, D., B. Mensch, and N. Toubia. 1993. "A New Approach to Eliciting Information about Induced Abortion." *Studies in Family Planning* 24 (2):120–24.

Jinju, M. 1990. *African Traditional Medicine: A Case Study of Hausa Medicinal Plants and Therapy*. Zaria, Nigeria: Gaskiya Press.

Kleiner-Bossaller, A. 1993. "*Kwantacce*, the 'Sleeping Pregnancy,' a Hausa Concept." In *Focus on Women in Africa*, ed. G. Ludwar-Ene and M. Reh, 17–30. African Studies Series 26. Bayreuth University, Germany.

Last, M. 1979. "Strategies against Time." *Sociology of Health and Illness* 1: 306–17.

———. 1992. "The Importance of Extremes: The Social Implications of Intra-Household Variation in Child Mortality." *Social Science and Medicine* 35 (6): 799–810.

Leridon, H. 1977. *Human Fertility*, trans. J. Helzner. Chicago: University of Chicago Press.

Luker, K. 1984. *Abortion and the Politics of Motherhood*. Berkeley: University of California Press.

Madauci, I., Y. Isa, and B. Dauro. 1968. *Hausa Customs*. Zaria, Nigeria: Northern Nigerian Publishing Company.

Makhlouf Obermeyer, C. 1992. "Islam, Women, and Politics: The Demography of Arab Countries." *Population and Development Review* 18 (1): 33–60.

Masquelier, A. 1995. "Consumption, Prostitution, and Reproduction: The Poetics of Sweetness in *Bori*." *American Ethnologist* 22 (4): 883–906.

Moghadam, V. 1991. "Islamist Movements and Women's Responses in the Middle East." *Gender and History* 3 (2): 268–84.

Mu'azu-Alti, M. 1992. "Women as Providers and Consumers in the Traditional Birth Delivery System." In *Women's Health Issues in Nigeria*, ed. M. Kisekka. 149–68. Zaria, Nigeria: Tamaza Publishing Co.

Musallam, B. F. 1983. *Sex and Society in Islam: Birth Control before the Nineteenth Century*. Cambridge, U.K.: Cambridge University Press

Newman, P., and R. Newman. 1977. *Modern Hausa–English Dictionary*. Ibadan, Nigeria: University Press.

Okagbue, I. 1990. "Pregnancy Termination and the Law in Nigeria." *Studies in Family Planning* 21 (4): 197–208.

Oliver-Bever, B. 1986. *Medicinal Plants in Tropical West Africa.* Cambridge, U.K.: Cambridge University Press.

Oronsaye, A., O. Ogbeide, and E. Unuigbe. 1982. "Pregnancy among Schoolgirls in Nigeria." *International Journal of Gynecology and Obstetrics* 20 (5): 409–12.

Pittin, R. 1986. "The Control of Reproduction: Principle and Practice in Nigeria." *Review of African Political Economy* 35 (May): 40–53.

Rehan, N. and A. Abashiya. 1981. "Breastfeeding and Abstinence among Hausa Women." *Studies in Family Planning* 12 (5): 233–37.

Reichmuth, S. 1993. "Islamic Learning and Its Intersection with 'Western' Education in Ilorin, Nigeria." In *Muslim Identity and Social Change in Sub-Saharan Africa,* ed. L. Brenner, 179–97. London: Hurst and Co.

Reinis, K. 1992. "The Impact of the Proximate Determinants of Fertility: Evaluating Bongaarts's and Hobcraft and Little's Methods of Estimation." *Population Studies* 46 (2): 309–26.

Renne, E. 1996a. "Perceptions of Population Policy, Development, and Family Planning in Northern Nigeria." *Studies in Family Planning* 27 (3): 127–36.

———. 1996b. "The Pregnancy That Doesn't Stay: The Practice and Perception of Abortion by Ekiti Yoruba Women." *Social Science and Medicine* 42 (4): 483–94.

Sachedina, Z. 1990. "Islam, Procreation and the Law." *International Family Planning Perspectives* 16 (3): 107–11.

Smith, M. F. 1954. *Baba of Karo.* New Haven, Conn.: Yale University Press.

Smith, M. G. 1954. Introduction to *Baba of Karo,* by M. F. Smith. New Haven, Conn.: Yale University Press.

Trevitt, L. 1973. "Attitudes and Customs in Childbirth amongst Hausa Women in Zaria City." *Savannah* 2: 223–26.

Umar, M. 1993. "Changing Islamic Identity in Nigeria from the 1960s to the 1980s: From Sufism to Anti-Sufism." In *Muslim Identity and Social Change in Sub-Saharan Africa,* ed. L. Brenner, 154–78. London: Hurst and Co.

United Nations Population Division. 2002. *Abortion Policies: A Global Review.* New York: United Nations.

Waines, D. 1995. *An Introduction to Islam.* Cambridge, U.K.: Cambridge University Press.

Wall, L. 1988. *Hausa Medicine.* Durham, N.C.: Duke University Press.

Chapter 8

The Role of Local Herbs in the Recent Fertility Decline in Ghana: Contraceptives or Abortifacients?

John K. Anarfi

The most recent Ghana Demographic and Health Survey (GDHS) report (Ghana Statistical Service 1994) indicates that the total fertility rate (TFR) has declined from 6.4 children per woman in 1988 to 5.5 in 1993, a decline of almost 1.0 in the five-year period. Within the same period, the rate of current use of contraception among currently married women increased from 13 percent to 20 percent. The use of modern methods doubled from 5 percent to 10 percent, whereas the use of traditional methods increased from 8 to 10 percent.

A U.N. estimate puts the TFR of Ghana at between 5.91 and 6.29 in the 1990–95 period (United Nations Population Division 1995). Based on a sample data set from countries with characteristics similar to those of Ghana, a target setting model of the Futures Group, a nongovernmental research organization in Glastonbury, Connecticut, estimated a target level of TFR decline of 1.0 over a fifteen-year period (1990–2005) from 6.5 to 5.5. The contraceptive prevalence level required to achieve the target-level TFR was calculated to be 28 percent. The methods of contraception included a shift in method mix to more effective methods, resulting from increase in average effectiveness from 85 percent in 1990 to 89 percent in 2005. A direct application of the target model to Ghanaian data indicated that assuming a moderate decline in fertility (considered more plausible), achieving a decline in TFR from 6.4 in 1989 to 4 in 2019 would require a rise in the contraceptive prevalence rate to 27.7 percent (with 18.07 percent use of modern methods) by 1994.

It is worth noting that traditional methods of contraception have played and continue to play a significant role in birth control practices in Ghana. The 1993 GDHS indicates that the main traditional methods used in the country are periodic abstinence (7.5 percent) and withdrawal (2.1 percent). That makes the former by far the most commonly used method by women. But according to the survey, only 28 percent of all women and 55 percent of those who have ever used periodic abstinence knew the correct fertile period during the ovulatory cycle. The implications are that more than 40 percent of those who rely on this technique of birth control are probably using it incorrectly. The other method, withdrawal, has not been very popular because traditionally it was considered a crime that was severely punished. In addition, many consider it humanly impossible to practice withdrawal very effectively (Bleek 1976).

The indications are that the current method mix of contraception in Ghana is heavily tilted toward methods whose effectiveness is suspect. That implies that the current level of contraceptive prevalence and the method mix in Ghana do not adequately account for the drop in fertility observed by recent surveys. We may, therefore, have to look elsewhere for an explanation of the significant decline in fertility within a relatively short period of time.

In this context it is worth pointing out that no reference at all was made to abortion or to the use of local herbs for contraception in the GDHS. This chapter attempts to throw the searchlight on these two issues. Specifically, it looks at the possible role of herbs in birth control in Ghana, identifying whether they are contraceptives or abortifacients. It is based largely on a review of the existing literature. Information from a pilot survey, in-depth interviews, and focus group discussions are used to supplement some of the findings in the literature.

THE PILOT SURVEY

The pilot survey was conducted in August 1996 in some parts of Accra, the capital and major city of Ghana. The choice of Accra was mainly purposive: to test whether Ghanaian women willingly give information on a sensitive issue like abortion now unlike in the past (see Bleek 1976). To add a rural dimension to the study, Suhum, in the eastern portion of Ghana, about seventy kilometers north of Accra, was chosen as a second study area. The selection of the sample was accidental. Only women who were willing to cooperate were interviewed.

A total of eighty-seven women were interviewed: fifty-eight in Accra and twenty-nine in Suhum. Nearly two-thirds were aged twenty to thirty-four. A few (5 percent) were aged fifty and above. About 61 percent were currently married, and a little over one-third were single. They had very little or no formal education (three-quarters had no education or up to basic education only). The respondents were predominantly Christian (87 percent), and the rest were either Muslim (8 percent) or practiced traditional religions (2 percent). The women were largely traders/farmers (48 percent), seamstresses (14 percent), and hairdressers (12 percent). Only 6 percent reported being unemployed, and another 8 percent were students/apprentices.

ABORTION IN GHANA

In Ghana, it is almost impossible to guess the magnitude of induced abortion. Nearly three decades ago Ampofo (1971) estimated the average yearly number of abortions from 1963 to 1967 in the country's leading hospital, Korle-Bu, to be around 2,500.

Research by Bleek (1976) in southern Ghana indicates that, although illegal, abortion is widely practiced. He suggests that induced abortion in Ghana is a modern development brought on by the need to complete education and the postponement of marriage. Pellow (1977) reports that leafing through the nation's leading daily newspaper, a prominent paramount chief from the Ashanti Region of Ghana remarked that every young girl listed in the obituary section had died of abortion. Records from a rural hospital in the south of Ghana show that from 1990 to 1992, there were a total of 2,228 maternity admissions, and of this number 335 were abortion-related complications. The theatre records also show that a total of 451 evacuation of uterus procedures were done. These are apart from those that were done secretly outside the hospital and were successful. In the pilot survey conducted specifically for this paper, forty-eight (55 percent) of the eighty-seven respondents stated that they had had an induced abortion.

Touching on the problems of research on abortion in Ghana, Bleek and Asante-Darko (1986, 335) remark that "this practice is not only considered shameful, it is also illegal and, therefore, carried out in secrecy. There are no written records which tell us how frequently abortion occurs. Most abortions carried out in hospitals do not appear in the annual reports because they are illegal and punishable. Moreover, most abortions occur outside the hospital."

Earlier research has observed that people find it difficult to talk about abortion (Bleek and Asante-Darko 1986). It is to be expected that during interviews, people try to avoid the topic as much as possible. Caldwell (1968, 161), in his 1962–63 research on the Ghanaian elite, decided at the eleventh hour to cancel most questions on abortion because he feared that they would jeopardize the entire research project. Similarly, no specific question on abortion was asked in any of the fertility surveys in Ghana in the recent past. Observers believe that the country's abortion laws have contributed to the near blackout on information on this method for birth control.

ABORTION LAWS

The original abortion laws in Ghana had their roots in the United Kingdom's Offences against the Person Act of 1861. Initially, the law imposed the death penalty as maximum punishment for abortion. In 1969 the maximum punishment was reduced to ten years imprisonment and further reduced to five years in a 1985 amendment. Ampofo (1970) reveals that in practice most doctors who are in a position to provide therapeutic abortion are guided by the Justice Macnaughten ruling of 1938, which holds that abortion need not be unlawful if it is done in good faith to save the mother's life and if in the opinion of the doctor the pregnancy will make the woman a physical or mental wreck. This has been embodied in the 1985 Criminal Code (Amendment) Law.

Ampofo (1970, 301) again observes that "the application of the abortion laws in Ghana suffers a great disability because of certain defects in the law." Only an insignificant number of cases brought to the hospitals is reported to the police. One reason for this is that doctors prefer to retain the patient–doctor relationship so as not to scare away women who otherwise can be helped. This is perhaps in line with the Ministry of Health's protocol on the clinical management of Safe Motherhood in Ghana (Ghana Ministry of Health 1993), which includes Good History Taking in the case of unsafe abortion. The protocol suggests that "the patient must be reassured, treated with respect and not chastised for their actions at this time. Always provide privacy and ensure confidentiality during history taking" (Ghana Ministry of Health 1993, 34). A second reason is that the police tend to rely on the doctor's report in order to frame their charges. Incidentally, most induced abortions are done without any sign of complications; hence, doctors' reports cannot incriminate most abortionists. Added to this is the fact that the women tend to shield the abortionists by refusing to give the name, address, and place where the abortion was performed.

REASONS FOR TERMINATING PREGNANCIES

Despite restrictive laws and lack of adequate services, women continue to seek to terminate unwanted pregnancies. Studies in parts of Ghana have unearthed a number of reasons for abortion. The most important cause is financial. An informant in a study in southern Ghana observed: "Most of the cases result from hardships, especially when no one wants to take responsibility. Also, their inability to cater for the pregnancy financially in terms of money is a major factor" (International Planned Parenthood Federation 1993, 40). Another added: "At times too, the woman may not have anybody to help her financially, even for preparation towards delivery. This can compel her to get rid of the pregnancy" (40).

A group of secondary school students blamed it on lack of adequate financial support from their parents, saying: "And some of the parents too don't give their children enough for their needs. The boys will give them money and that is why they have sex with them" (International Planned Parenthood Federation 1993, 47). They also added: "Some of the parents will say 'go to your boyfriend' *(Enye wo nkoaa na mehwe wo)*, meaning 'You are not the only one I am looking after.' They will discourage you, then the issue of 'sugar daddy' comes in" (47).

A second cause of abortion observed by the International Planned Parenthood Federation (1993) study is women having multiple sexual partners and therefore not being able to pinpoint the man who was responsible for the pregnancy. The financial underpinnings of this factor cannot be lost in an informant's remarks: "This is very true. The women around are highly money-conscious. So they have so many lovers. So in times of pregnancy, they are unable to identify the one responsible. So what they do is to collect money from the boys which they use for abortion" (42).

Other reasons cited by informants in the International Planned Parenthood Federation (1993) study include men's refusal to accept responsibility for the pregnancy, fear of or insults from parents, and fear of losing the company of one's friends. Additional reasons for abortion included cases when pregnancy has been the result of adultery, when child spacing is an issue, and the need to seek religious and social approval. Some of the findings in this earlier study were confirmed by the pilot survey reported in this chapter. The reasons given by those who had ever had an abortion included "previous child still breastfeeding" (twelve out of forty-eight), "still schooling or learning trade" (eleven out of forty-eight), "didn't want the baby" (ten out of forty-eight), and "young and unmarried" (seven out of forty-eight).

CLIENTS AND PROVIDERS OF ABORTION

The evidence shows that women from all walks of life—young and old; single, married, or divorced; students and those acquiring a profession, religious or otherwise—resort to abortion. Those that were more frequently mentioned by focus group discussants were unmarried women, including those in educational institutions and other teenagers.

Divorced women also came up for mention. In the words of an informant, "Divorced women are also fond of committing this act. Usually when they are divorced, money and material gains become their major priority. So they wouldn't want any pregnancy to hinder them" (International Planned Parenthood Federation 1993, 43).

It was also mentioned that some circumstances force women of all types to seek abortion. On married women, an informant remarked: "Some who have husbands also do it. There are some men who quarrel with their wives when they are pregnant. So when the women see that their husbands are at loggerheads with them because of pregnancy then they abort it" (42).

Said another: "Their husbands after travelling may one way or the other stop sending them money. This situation can lead the woman to engage herself in an affair which may result in pregnancy. In order to avoid disgrace, she may terminate it" (43).

From his study in a rural setting, Bleek (1976) has observed that abortion is usually induced by people themselves rather than by real or supposed experts. Quite often, people who want an abortion do not have the financial means to pay a doctor's fee and are forced to rely on cheaper methods. Bleek (1976, 248) constructs the process of seeking an abortion in the following words:

> The usual pattern is that as soon as a woman thinks she is pregnant and she does not want it, she or the man responsible for the pregnancy start making careful inquiries among intimate friends. The friends mention some pills or herbs which they have heard to be effective and the man or woman goes to get them. The woman takes the pills or prepares the herbs and uses them in the way that has been explained to her.

In the study reported here, respondents mentioned as abortion service providers are: the pregnant woman herself, herbalists, older community women, medicine men and doctors, and pharmacists. This list of abortion providers gives us some idea of the methods that are used to induce abortion in Ghana.

METHODS OF ABORTION IN GHANA

Based on their research in southern Ghana, Bleek and Asante-Darko (1986) conclude that young people in particular have an extensive knowledge of abortion techniques. Informants reported to him fifty-three different methods, which they divided into three categories: modern methods, indigenous herbs, and miscellaneous.

Modern Methods

The modern methods could further be categorized into two subgroups: direct interference with the pregnancy through intrauterine instrumentation and the use of abortifacient medicines. The safest available intrauterine instrumentation is dilation and curettage (popularly known as D&C). This is reserved for those who have the means to pay for it and the social connections to approach a medical doctor who is willing to perform it. Because many people do not have the means in both financial and social terms, they rely on modern pharmaceuticals for sale in local drugstores or pharmacies in the bigger towns. Studies have observed that only a few of the drugs popularly used in Ghana have abortive effects. Drugs like Meniscol Capsules, Dr. Bongeans Pills, and Ergometrine are said to be effective as they induce uterine contractions that result in abortion (Ampofo 1970; Bleek and Asante-Darko 1986).

The therapeutic value of many others is very doubtful. Included among these is Alophen, used both as a contraceptive and as an abortifacient but which is in fact a purgative. Experts believe that when this drug is used in large doses, the resultant purging can produce strong peristaltic movement that in turn stimulates uterine contractions. Apiol is another popular drug but is of doubtful therapeutic value and has severe toxic effects (Bleek and Asante-Darko 1986). An overdose of certain medicines such as analgesics and antimalarials may trigger abortion as a secondary effect. Added to these are sugar in very high concentration, alcohol, bluing, and purgatives such as castor oil.

Indigenous Herbs

According to Bleek and Asante-Darko (1986), indigenous herbs constitute the largest group of abortifacients. The use of these local herbs could be grouped under four methods. Some are used for intrauterine instrumentation as a stick, which abortionists call the "twig." According to Ampofo (1970, 296), "When these are inserted the conceptus is either punctured or partially separated from the uterine wall. After a period of time, bleeding and pain occur followed by the expulsion of the conceptus."

Two types of twigs have been extensively described by Ampofo (1970, 296). One is the dried stem of the commelina plant, which is believed to work mechanically as it takes up moisture in the uterus, swells up, and dilates the cervix of the uterus, resulting in abortion. The other is from the jathropha plant, the stalk of which is inserted in its fresh state. Its action is believed to be partly chemical and partly mechanical. "The jatropha contains sap which is mildly corrosive and in the indigenous medical practice, the sap is used for the treatment of warts of the skin. When it is inserted into the uterus the sap causes local chemical reaction in the cervix which may start the bleeding from the uterus. In addition to this the stick can cause damage to the conceptus and the combined effect causes abortion" (Ampofo 1970, 296).

Some of the herbs are also used as pessaries. Either the seed, bark, or leaf of a plant is ground, shaped into balls, and inserted deep in the vagina. Most herbal pessaries are said to contain caustic salts such as potassium chlorate in high concentration. They are capable of causing ulceration in the lower genital tract, which can stimulate abortion.

The leaves of some plants are ground, mixed with other herbs or ingredients, and applied as an enema. With yet other plants, the leaves or other parts are prepared as a drink after grinding and mixing them with other ingredients such as sugar, alcohol, and other herbs. Some plants are used as chewing sticks. Users of these methods acknowledge that some of them, especially the use of twigs and the consumption of the ogyamma leaves in particular, are very dangerous. The danger of the twigs lies in the fact that they can cause perforation of the uterus, hemorrhage, sepsis, and tetanus. With the oral abortifacients, the danger lies with the fact that some of them may contain toxic substances unknown to the users.

Miscellaneous Methods

Bleek and Asante-Darko's list (1986) contains various other techniques classified as miscellaneous. They include, among other things, the consumption of sweet substances, which are generally believed to be capable of causing abortion. Strong coffee with excessive sugar is often used. It is also believed that intoxication and exhaustion are conditions conducive to abortion. Guinness stout is used quite often for this purpose, used alone or with lots of sugar. In the pilot study for this paper, some women mentioned Guinness and malt drink; these two are seen as a blood tonic in Ghana. It is believed that the combined effect of the blood tonic and the intoxicating effect of the Guinness can cause the fetus to melt. As Bleek (1976) observed, exhaustion can be achieved by beating and strong sexual intercourse.

The lists by Bleek (1976) and Bleek and Asante-Darko (1986) are by no means exhaustive. It is significant to note that the latter list is far longer than the former. In an unpublished paper, Kumekpor and Kumekpor (1977) mention other methods in addition to those listed by Bleek and Asante-Darko (1986). They sum up a number of herbs and other ingredients that are prohibited to pregnant women because of their potential abortive effects. Indeed, many of these preparations are openly advertised as being harmful to pregnancy, which may be seen as a covert way of advertising their abortive properties. It is an open secret that women who desire an abortion will purposely take the prohibited ingredients, which include the following:

1. An infusion of leaves of certain plants (guava, lemon, mahogany, etc.)
2. An infusion of tobacco and tobacco-based products
3. Very sweet things (such as sugarcane), very hot foods (such as ground cassava powder), alcohol, or guinea pepper
4. The use of strong purgatives or laxatives

I have also encountered other herbal methods that are not included in Bleek's lists. All the herbs assembled have a dual purpose: as contraceptives and as abortifacients. The commonest is the *achampong* leaf, which is listed in almost every leaflet of different herbal medicines that has appeared on the Ghanaian scene of late. For example, on one leaflet with the heading "Some Selected Herbs by Herbal Dr. E. K. Darko, Koforidua," it is listed as number twelve with the following instructions: "FAMILY PLANNING: Cook the fresh leaves of *achampong* together with saltpeter and drink a cupful every morning or before going in for sex." Another advertisement mentions that if one cannot take it regularly, at least she should take it one week before menstruation. Or if one fails to take it and misses her period, she should drink it and use it as enema at the same time to induce an abortion.

Another one that has gained popularity lately is the bark of a tree called *sabrabisie,* which is mainly used as an abortifacient. It is ground, mixed with water and the juice of one lime, and used as enema. If it is to be used as a contraceptive, then it must be used the same way as just described three days before menstruation. Users with whom I spoke recommended it highly, all saying that it had never failed them. The same plant can be used to cure chronic menstrual pains and scanty flow during menstruation. It is also supposed to cure infertility, particularly if related to menstrual pain and scanty flow of menstrual blood. In that case, it is to be used as described three days after menstruation; this is supposed to open up the birth canal to allow pregnancy. A herbalist who comes to the city regularly to peddle medicinal herbs conceded that it is always the last two uses that are mentioned in advertisements, but these add as a warning that pregnant women should not use it. An average of thirty people buy this medicine weekly on each visit.

The third is from a tree called *namba.* For contraception, a little of the bark of this tree is chewed by either the male or the female or both, not less than ten minutes before sex. It is supposed to dilute the man's sperm or weaken the ova of the woman to prevent pregnancy. It is said to be so powerful that in the early stages of pregnancy the scent alone, which is very strong when fresh, can cause an abortion. As an abortifacient, it is ground, mixed with lime juice, and taken orally. Herbal medicine peddlers revealed that this particular medicine is not sold openly and that girls often call them aside and inquire about it. On the average, ten people per week buy this herbal medicine from a peddler who was interviewed. He added that the supply of this particular medicine is always below demand because the tree is not very common and the few available have been overexploited.

Western-trained medical doctors have much doubt about the efficacy of most abortion methods apart from those that involve direct instrumentation of the fetus. They are convinced that a well-settled fetus cannot be removed by, for example, the consumption of herbal concoctions or application of an enema. But as Bleek and Asante-Darko (1986) have rightly noted, the properties of indigenous herbs are unknown to most medical doctors. I have initiated a chemical analysis of some herbs, but the results are not yet ready for this paper. At this stage, therefore, we can only speculate about the efficacy of the traditional methods of abortion in Ghana.

One pertinent question is this: If the methods are not effective, how can we account for the abortions that are alleged to have been caused by these ineffective means? In his study, Ampofo (1970) suggests that girls taken to the hospital under critical conditions mention harmless techniques to conceal the genuine ones. He adds that many presumed pregnancies could actually be cases of delayed menstruation. The arrival of menses would then be taken as proof that the method is effective, which may not be the case. Bleek and Asante-Darko (1986) do not agree entirely with this assertion, adding that "certain abortion cases which look implausible to medical doctors cannot be disregarded as delayed menstruation" (337). Evidence that I have gathered suggests that some of the herbal methods are quite effective, and increasing numbers of women are using them both as contraceptives and as abortifacients. Why then are they not mentioned at all in any national surveys on fertility?

WHY IS THERE NO MENTION OF HERBS IN THE LITERATURE?

Given the overwhelming evidence presented so far about the increasing use of local herbs for birth control purposes, it is difficult to understand why no mention is made of these in big national surveys. In the view of one study informant, an herbalist, people may not want to be associated with local herbs because many still associate them with fetishism. In fact, some Christians still feel that it is sacrilegious to use local herbs, no matter who supplied them. This feeling may stem from the idea held by many people that the herbalist and the fetish priest are one and the same person. The situation has improved of late following the formation of the Ghana Psychic and Traditional Healers' Association (GPTHA) under the auspices of the government. The association was formed at the peak of the country's economic crisis to promote traditional medicine to fill the unmet need for drugs. One study shows that the increase in user charges in 1985 precipitated a halving of utilization of hospital facilities in the urban areas of the Volta Region of Ghana. This gradually rose back to its 1984 level in subsequent years. In the rural facilities, however, the fee increase exacerbated a decline that had already begun before the increase and never recovered (Waddington and Enyimayew 1990). If we consider the fact that about 70 percent of Ghana's population lives in the rural areas, then we can imagine the number of people who depend on traditional medicine.

Another factor is related to the fact that until the formation of the GPTHA, the practice of traditional medicine was shrouded in secrecy. At present, products of herbalists are protected by patents. In addition, they are encouraged to give their products as much publicity as possible. This includes the printing of leaflets, radio and television advertisements, and open advertisements in public places and in vehicles. Peddling of medicinal herbs is now a common scene in most towns of the country.

The dual purpose of most local herbs as contraceptives and abortifacients at the same time, may also explain the silence over their use. In most Ghanaian societies, people still consider the practice of abortion to be bad and shameful and also illegal. No one will therefore want to be associated with abortion. If the mention of local herbs for contraception will create uncertainties in the minds of people, then they will avoid them altogether.

There is also the possibility that women who use herbs may take them for granted. This is because to the typical Ghanaian woman, the use of local medicinal herbs has become a routine that may not require special mention. At the premarital stage of their life, women use various types of medicinal herbs either to present a good look or to make sex pleasant for prospective partners. Methods to achieve the former objective include various forms of enema and oral potions to help them eat well and not to retain bad blood in them. The latter objective is achieved through preparations that are mostly inserted in the vagina. A woman may use an abortifacient if pregnancy comes before a preferred suitor is encountered.

In marriage, women use various kinds of herbal preparations for what they call "maintenance." Sex is considered an important aspect of marital life, but women think that regular sex could be exacting and therefore require regular maintenance of the genital organs. Without that, there would be inflammation of the genitalia, which would make the woman appear dull and generally feel unwell. A common method of maintenance is a mixture of ginger and other hot spices made into a ball and inserted into the vagina; this is supposed to cure all internal sores. The main preoccupation of the woman at this stage is to maintain good health to be able to provide for the husband's sexual needs. Other herbs used at this stage may include those said to regulate menstruation.

Use of medicinal herbs continues even during pregnancy. Most of the herbs used are supposed to help the retention of the fetus and to aid its healthy development. The methods for ingestion include regular enemas and occasional drinking of herbal preparation. Close to the end of gestation, the pregnant woman switches to the use of herbal methods that help the fetus to descend and eventually aid easy delivery. After delivery, the woman is immediately put on herbal medicine that helps to expel bad blood and to heal internal wounds. Most of these induce contraction of the uterus and could therefore be used to achieve abortion. Regularly, the woman eats herbal preparations that are supposed to generate the production of breast milk and also help her recover quickly from the trauma of childbirth. From the foregoing, it could be seen that the life of a typical Ghanaian woman is a switch from one form of herbal medicine to the other in almost a routine order. A study with a specific focus is needed to determine the exact role of local herbs in birth control in Ghana.

DISCUSSION

A study of the role of local herbs in birth control is certainly not an easy task at this stage. Despite the display of a reasonable measure of openness following the formation of the GPTHA, many still keep their herbal medicines secret. The secrecy becomes tighter if the medicine is for a therapy about which little is said traditionally or for which there is a serious stigma.

The case of the late Nana Drobo, who claimed to have a cure for AIDS, illustrates the point. At a certain point he became suspicious that certain scientists wanted to steal the formula for his drugs. Having lost faith in local scientists, he accepted an invitation by some interest groups in Japan to have his drugs scientifically tested. He came back home under strange circumstances, accusing the Japanese of wanting to kill him and take full ownership of the formula. Two months after his return, he died mysteriously, and the police suspected suicide. So far that has been the end of the AIDS drug because he was the only person who knew the formula.

Such formidable circumstances notwithstanding, we can still hazard some speculations about the role of local herbs for birth control in Ghana.

As already mentioned, apart from the numerous herbal preparations said to be used for abortion, most of the others used for contraception also have a dual purpose. That aside, very few are used on as regular a basis as the oral contraceptive pill. The usual method is to use them either one week or three days before the expected start of the next menstruation. The chances are that pregnancy might have taken place already before the use of the medicine. At that stage, the pregnancy may not have been firmly established yet, and removing it with herbal preparations may not be as difficult as Western-trained doctors think.

Another issue is that for most Ghanaian women, especially those in the rural areas, the habit of taking a daily dose of medicine for the purpose of contraception is unknown. Like most other women, their concern is to maintain good health but, unlike Western women, for example, through corrective instead of preventive measures. If the Ghanaian woman feels that her health is threatened, she finds a way to restore it. But all said and done, pregnancy is never seen as a health problem. Even where a woman is hospitalized for pregnancy-related conditions, her situation is described as good. "Oh, she is suffering from a good ailment," people would say.

Related to the nonpreventive stance of most women is the concern for birth spacing instead of birth limitation. Pregnancy will be terminated if it is felt that the health of a breast-feeding child is threatened. Any therapy that could have a permanent effect on a woman's fertility is shunned. Incidentally, many women perceive contraceptives taken regularly to have such an effect in the long run. The fear becomes meaningful if it is seen against the fact that traditionally, every Ghanaian man is a potential polygamist, and thus there is a high probability that every married woman eventually becomes a serial polygamist either through divorce or widowhood. And there is still the notion that every conjugal union must beget a child, that a relationship without an issue is not yet conceivable in Africa, including Ghana (Oppong 1977).

In conclusion, it has been established that a large number of known medicinal herbs are being used for birth control in Ghana. There is overwhelming evidence that most of the herbs act as abortifacients, although this conclusion still remains speculative. In collaboration with GPTHA, known herbal medicines should be scientifically analyzed to determine not only their efficacy but also their toxic content so as to advise users accordingly. If this is carefully done, local herbs stand the chance of filling in cheaply the unmet needs for contraceptives in Ghana and hopefully, much of Africa in the medium term.

REFERENCES

Ampofo, D. A. 1971. "Abortion in Accra: The Social, Demographic and Medical Perspectives." In *Symposium on Implications of Population Trends for Policy Measures in West Africa,* ed. N. O. Addo et al., 79–105. Legon, Ghana: Demographic Unit.

Bleek, W. 1976. "Sexual Relationships and Birth Control in Ghana: A Case Study of a Rural Town." Unpublished Ph.D. diss., Antropologisch-Sociologisch Centrum, University Van Amsterdam.

———. 1978. "Induced Abortion in a Ghanaian Family." *African Studies Review* 21: 103–20.

Bleek, W., and N. K. Asante-Darko. 1986. "Illegal Abortion in Southern Ghana: Methods, Motives and Consequences." *Human Organization* 45 (4): 333–34.

Caldwell, J. C. 1968. *Population Growth and Family Change in Africa.* Canberra: Australian National University Press.

Ghana Ministry of Health. 1993. *Clinical Management Protocols on Safe Motherhood in Ghana.* Fourth draft, August, Ministry of Health.

Ghana Statistical Service. 1994. *Demographic and Health Survey 1993.* Accra: Ghana Statistical Service.

International Planned Parenthood Federation. 1993. *The Dimensions of Abortion in Ghana: An Explanatory Case Study of Kwahu South District.* London: International Planned Parenthood Federation.

Kumekpor, T. K., and M. L. Kumekpor. 1977. "Contraception and Abortion: Practice and Change." Paper presented at the Annual Meeting of the Ghana Sociological Association, Legon, Ghana.

Oppong, C. 1977. "Family Type and Size: Some Recent Evidence from Ghana." In *Social and Economic Supports for High Fertility,* ed. L. Ruzicka, 345–54. Canberra: Australian National University Press.

Pellow, D. 1977. *Women in Accra: Options for Autonomy.* Algonac, Mich.: Reference Publications.

United Nations. 1995. *World Population Prospects—The 1994 Revision.* New York: United Nations.

Waddington, C., and K. A. Enyimayew. 1990. "A Price to Pay, Part 2: The Impact of User Charges in the Volta Region of Ghana." *International Journal of Health Planning and Management* 5: 287–312.

Chapter 9

Menstrual Regulation in Bangladesh

Sajeda Amin

Early termination of pregnancy is known as menstrual regulation (MR)[1] and is widely available in Bangladesh from doctors and family planning paramedics through the network of government health centers. The extensive availability and use of services and the lack of any obvious opposition to the MR program on legal, religious, or other moral grounds has been a puzzle because Bangladesh is generally regarded as a conservative Muslim society and abortion is prohibited under the country's criminal code. Dixon-Mueller (1988) attributes the success of this program to the widespread clinical practice of MR and to ambiguity in legal, medical, and folk definitions of the positive identification of pregnancy.

This chapter examines the factors identified by Dixon-Mueller's analysis as determinants of the successful MR program—programmatic innovation that rests on a maze of ambiguity around the reproductive physiology of pregnancy. I argue that Bangladesh has been able to exploit the legal and religious ambiguities associated with MR. There is less evidence of women being confused by the ambiguities or exploiting them as Dixon-Mueller seems to suggest: women who seek MR are well aware that the procedure terminates a pregnancy rather than merely restoring menstruation. The state has been able to legitimize MR because part of the legal ambiguity rests on establishing pregnancy, and independent pregnancy tests that could constitute critical evidence to establish a criminal case of abortion are not routinely done in Bangladesh.

The first section gives a brief history of the program. The second section gives some highlights of the legal status of abortion and related debates on legal reform. The third section discusses the religious status of abortion in Islam, the majority religion in Bangladesh. The fourth section explores anthropological data on folk beliefs around menstruation and pregnancy. The final section contains a discussion on why abortion by another name came to be widely acceptable and officially provided in a seemingly adverse legal context.

A BRIEF HISTORY OF THE MR PROGRAM IN BANGLADESH

There is indirect evidence that the incidence of induced pregnancy termination is high in Bangladesh. A 1978 study estimated that 800,000 abortions were conducted annually, implying that one in every five pregnancies ended in an abortion (Rochat, Jabeen, and Rosenberg 1981). This estimate confirmed suspicions that clandestine, unsafe abortions were partially responsible for the high level of maternal mortality and strengthened the rationale for an initiative to introduce an MR program in Bangladesh.

The MR program began in 1974 when the government allowed one nongovernmental clinic to provide MR services in Dhaka. The Mohammadpur Fertility Services and Training Center (MFSTC) was established as a project under the Population Control Wing of the Ministry of Health and Population Control. In 1978, the mandate of this clinic and another training organization was expanded to allow government doctors and paramedics to be trained to conduct MR (BAPSA 1985). Subsequently, MFSTC has become officially part of the government's health program upon being granted the status of a semi-autonomous organization affiliated with the government.

At present, five organizations (one government, one semi-autonomous, three nongovernment) are engaged in providing logistic support, training, monitoring, and evaluation services to the MR program. MR kits are imported and provided to trained personnel free of cost. The program remains focused on training doctors and paramedics employed by the government and operating out of government facilities and the total numbers who are now equipped to provide MR services has risen steadily as a result as shown in Table 9.1.

It is probably significant that a large number of those trained are female providers, including paramedics and family welfare visitors employed in the Family Planning Program, who are posted all over the country and equipped to provide MR services even in remote rural areas. The provision of services through female paraprofessionals is believed to be an important aspect of increased accessibility of services because women are usually reluctant to be examined by male physicians. Close to 50 percent of the trained providers are women—the decision to train paramedics in the MR program was taken as there were not enough female doctors in the government service.

The primary emphasis of the MR program, accounting for the bulk of its budget, is to provide training to doctors and paramedics employed in the government health service. As such, the program leverages a large amount of funding and has extensive influence relative to the amount of resources invested. The involvement of the government may also serve an important legitimization function that provisions through nongovernmental or private agencies would lack.

Table 9.1
Cumulative Numbers of Health Professionals Trained to Provide MR Services in Bangladesh, 1976–95

Year	Doctors	Family Welfare Visitors
1976	3	58
1980	513	920
1985	2614	2627
1990	4814	3846
1994	6436	5045
1995	6561	5103

Sources: Kamal 1992 and BAPSA 1995.

However, not all MRs are conducted in the health facilities where they are meant to take place. Although the training for MR stresses that the procedure needs to take place in strictly sterile conditions, it is speculated that bureaucratic procedures for record keeping and related practices for receiving payments are such that even trained providers conduct the procedure in their own homes. According to one estimate based on the reports of trained MR providers, approximately 241,000 MRs were performed in 1985 (Begum, Kamal, and Kamal 1987). However, only about one-third of these are logged in the official records kept in clinics and hospitals. It has been suggested the highest levels of underreporting are found among untrained providers who are also known to conduct MRs.

Because direct empirical data on incidence of clandestine abortions remain scarce, it is difficult to assess the impact of MR on them. However, it is likely that clandestine abortions are widespread because MR is restricted to early-term pregnancies and almost one in every three clients reports to an MR clinic at a gestational stage when MR is not possible and is hence rejected. Most MR service providers are convinced that women who are rejected as MR cases resort to clandestine abortionists.

LEGAL STATUS

The criminal code on abortion, although long established, is seldom implemented. The Criminal Code of 1860 derived from British colonial law permits abortion only to save a woman's life—the severity of penalty increases after the fetus has "quickened." Any person, including the woman herself, is culpable. However, prosecution under this code is difficult because of three issues: problems of establishing ill intent or motive, problems of identifying specific acts or procedures as illegal, and problems of establishing knowledge of pregnancy.[2] To date there are no recorded cases in criminal history in the ex-British colonies in South Asia.

In the early days of the debate on legalization of abortion in Bangladesh, Sobhan (1980) argued that the criminal code's distinction between procedures conducted early and late in pregnancy may be the "pivot on which legal reform will turn"—that is, the first move to liberalize laws should be to permit early-term abortions.[3] Liberalization of abortion laws in Bangladesh turned in fact on the difficulties of establishing pregnancy. A quotation from the Bangladesh Institute of Law on laws regarding abortion was extracted and included in a widely circulated memo to "dispel any prevailing doubts about the legality" (Government of Bangladesh 1980), which said:

> Many Family Planning Clinics are carrying out the post-conceptive method of "Menstrual Regulation" as a means of birth control which does not come under Section 312 of the Penal Code. Under [the] statutory scheme, pregnancy is an essential element of the crime of abortion, but the use of menstrual regulation makes it virtually impossible for the prosecutor to meet the required proof.

Thus, the laws were liberalized through a reinterpretation rather than reform or amendment to the criminal code. It is worth noting that although the historical setting of criminal law in Bangladesh is similar to the criminal codes in other South Asian countries, Bangladesh remains the only country where the Penal Code of 1860 on abortion has not been reformed—India legalized abortion in 1971, and Pakistan amended the code in 1990 to add the exceptions (in addition to threat to life) of threat to health and in the case of rape (Cook 1993).

The Potential for Legal Reform

The two ways of bringing about reform in the Penal Code of 1860 are by presidential ordinance or a legislative act of the parliament. It appears that the first discussions on legal reform in official circles began in 1975 and were initiated by the Family Planning Division of the government of Bangladesh. Several major changes were instituted in the family-planning program in Bangladesh during this time, including the recruitment of female workers. Several years earlier, in 1972, the restrictions on performance of abortion were lifted to provide services in several urban hospitals to women who were victims of rape by the Pakistani Army during the nine-month-long war of liberation. Abortion services were provided to women even in late-term pregnancy, but this provision was repealed after the issue of war babies was considered resolved.[4]

In the mid-1970s the family-planning directorate initiated a discussion on the legalization of abortion to promote it as a method of family planning. By this time, the liberalization of abortion laws carried out in 1972 had been reversed. The discussion focused on a plea for a presidential ordinance that would legalize abortion. At that time, and even now, reform through presidential ordinance was the preferred option because deliberations in Parliament would draw unwelcome attention to the issue. Discussions at high levels of government concluded that there was no point in attracting attention to the legal code because there had been no known prosecutions under this code. Instead, the government was willing to approve the provision of early pregnancy termination by nongovernmental organizations. These services would be referred to as menstrual regulation and not abortion. Around 1976, training in MR services began on a small scale for government-employed doctors and paramedics. Although the bulk of the training and logistic support (specifically supply of MR kits) are still provided by nongovernmental organizations,[5] the MR program is a de facto part of the government health program because the services are provided in government facilities by government personnel. The memo described earlier, which in effect liberalized abortion laws through a reinterpretation rather than reform, was a necessary component of the program.

Extralegal Sources of Legitimacy

Several opinion surveys conducted in the 1970s suggest two important characteristics of social attitudes regarding abortion—first, that attitudes are conditional upon social and economic realities and are not held in abstraction; second, individuals do not base their position on the legal code alone, suggesting that there are other competing sources of moral authority. The legal code does not refer to religious doctrine, and it is likely that some of this extralegal legitimacy is based on religious interpretations of abortion that I describe later.

Three surveys polled opinions on abortion and were conducted around the time MR was first introduced in Bangladesh but had not become widely known. They showed that Bangladeshis approved of pregnancy termination in a variety of circumstances not permitted by law. Among those polled, the majority endorsed abortion for preservation of a woman's health and life, termination of pregnancies out of wedlock, or as a result of rape, and a smaller minority even approved of termination for spacing and for economic reasons (Table 9.2).

ISLAM AND ABORTION

Contrary to common assumption, Islamic doctrine provides for a range of interpretations, with a considerable degree of tolerance for early-term abortion in some cases. Table 9.3 summarizes the views on abortion in the four major schools

Table 9.2
Abortion Approval by Circumstances under Which Approved

Reasons for Which Abortion is Approved	Ahmad, 1975	Rosenberg et al., 1978-79	Chowdhury (1980)
Mother's Health or Mother's life	14	53	95
Defer Child	70	30	48
Economic Reasons	17	32	16
Pre-marital conceptions	88	79	-
Rape	89	66	43
Any reason	6	-	12
Breastfeeding		65	
Grandmother		61	
Widow with many children/ no husband		31	
Acceptable reason but without husband's permission		12	
Survey Population	All Women	Doctors	Elite women

Note: Dates indicate time of survey.
Sources: Ahmad 1979; Rosenberg et al. 1981; Chandhury 1980.

of Islamic jurisprudence and in one small sect where the laws are liberal. With regard to abortion early in the term or before ensoulment, most schools permit, dislike, or consider it loathsome but do not forbid outright. All except the Zaidi sect prohibit abortion after ensoulment.

Although the Koran makes clear distinction between stages of life and the Hadith (guidelines from the Prophet Mohammad) says ensoulment occurs 120 days after conception, neither the Koran not any Hadith have an unequivocal position on abortion. Islamic scholars thus turn to jurisprudence for guidance on this issue.

Most Islamic schools of jurisprudence also define the beginning of life as occurring after ensoulment of the fetus and not at conception. Ensoulment is sometimes related to or even equated with quickening or movement of the fetus (Sachedina 1990). It is evident that the determination of when ensoulment occurs is critical to the debate on abortion in Islam.

Table 9.3
Islamic Jurisprudence and Abortion

School of Jurisprudence (Shari' a)	Region where dominant	Followers of	Position on Abortion
Hanafi (Sunni)	Ottoman and Central Asia and South Asia	Jurist Abu Hanifa	Permitted before ensoulment; forbidden after
Maliki (Sunni)	North Africa	Malik ibn Annas	disliked before 40 days of conception; prohibited after
Hanbali (Sunni)	Arabian peninsula	Ahmed bin Hanbali	considered loathsome; prohibited
Shafii (Sunni)	Indonesia and rest of the world	Al Shafi'i	some interpretations permit before 120 days; others don't permit at all
Zaidi (Shi'i)		small Shi'i sect	permitted unconditionally if preceding quickening

Note: Five categories of Islamic position on human action are: obligatory, recommended, permitted, disapproved but not forbidden, absolutely forbidden.
Sources: Sachedina 1990; Sarour 1991.

It is important that all schools of jurisprudence make a clear distinction between early and late abortion. MR is primarily conducted early in pregnancy and may well derive some of its legitimacy from this fact. The distinction between early and late abortion, marked by the sign of quickening, is also found in the criminal code as discussed earlier. There is some anthropological evidence from Bangladesh in which respondents who favored menstrual regulation reportedly believed that at the early stage when MR is performed, the embryo has no life (Aziz and Maloney 1985, 171).

More relevant than the text of Islamic writings is fear of opposition from the more political Islamic groups. Although the issue of abortion has not yet taken center stage in any political arena, opposition to women's liberation and involvement in public life is a common rallying point for Islamic politics in Bangladesh. In recent years, Islamic opposition to women's emancipation has taken the form of virulent attacks on organizations that provide credit to women (Amin and Hossain 1995).

FOLK KNOWLEDGE ABOUT REPRODUCTIVE PHYSIOLOGY

Dixon-Mueller (1988, 137) speculates that some cultural attributes may have contributed to the success of the widespread acceptability of MR:

> The clinical practice of MR coincides with indigenous practices and beliefs pertaining to menstrual regularity.... The ambiguity in folk belief about the period between delayed menses and the positive identification of a pregnancy coincides with an ambiguity of legal and medical interpretation as well.

This assessment of the state of women's knowledge of reproductive physiology rests mostly on the assumption that Bangladesh must be like other traditional cultures where evidence of such beliefs are found, backed to some extent by anthropological data. In fact, very few studies directly address the issue of folk knowledge about reproductive physiology in Bangladesh. Blanchet's study (1984), which focuses on rituals and symbolic meaning related to pregnancy and birth, is an exception.

Blanchet's findings about folk beliefs rest on the ritual similarities related to onset of menstruation and pregnancy. Dixon-Mueller (1988) argues that women may perceive menstruation as a sign of the ability to bear children. Maloney, Aziz, and Sarker (1981) provide similar evidence on perceptions of normal menstruation as a sign of health and of irregular periods as potentially polluting and unacceptable, particularly in association with contraception.

Assuming for the moment that folk beliefs are important, unchanging, and have a strong influence on health-seeking behavior, the conclusion that menstruation is a sign of good health overemphasizes one dimension in isolation. Other aspects of the same belief system may agitate against women seeking menstrual regulation. For instance, although menstrual induction is a folk practice, there is also a fixed belief that it is a "strong procedure" with potentially harmful consequences for fertility and should be administered sparingly. For instance, Blanchet (1984) describes a condition that was locally described as *bhadok* in her study area, a condition that is said to affect young, nulliparous women. It causes severe abdominal pain and is said to be caused by a "hardened ball of blood stuck in the womb" (37). *Bhadok* is believed to be treatable with indigenous herbs, but these are never used as a treatment before marriage, presumably also because they would cause the loss of virginity and fertility.

More relevant for what such belief systems might imply for health-seeking behavior, clinic data indicate that women are, by and large, aware of their pregnancy status when they seek MR. In general, clinic records show no indication that women seek MR as a general measure of health or for any reason other than pregnancy. Although a relatively high proportion of clients are refused services either because their pregnancy could not be ascertained (10.8 percent) or they had come too late in the pregnancy (18 percent), these were mostly associated with lactation or long-standing history of menstrual irregularity. In the case of patients who were asked to come back later, it was because the woman was assumed to be too early in the term for a clinical diagnosis of pregnancy status (Kamal et al. 1993). Although the legal status of MR requires that objective laboratory tests cannot be conducted to establish pregnancy duration, it is common for practitioners to assess pregnancy duration by a physical examination of the uterus. MR providers do not conduct urine or blood tests to establish pregnancy for an MR client because they may become part of the record and have legal ramifications. In summary, MR is a widely accepted procedure, but it is not generally sought for purposes other than to obviate a birth.

The expressions used in Bangladesh by clients who come for an MR are also indicative of how the procedure is perceived. My interviews with service providers revealed that the most commonly used term for MR is "to get rid of the fetus (or stomach)." More euphemistic expressions, such as "wash out the uterus" or "clean out the stomach," reflect notions of pollution and cleansing associated with the procedure of menstrual induction. These terms are specific to pregnancy and are rarely used for conditions in its absence.

One factor that makes the link between MR and pregnancy very explicit is that although services are suppose to be provided for free, it is common to charge for MR at rates prorated according to the term of the pregnancy. In a set of villages in which I have been conducting a long-term study on family and fertility, the rate for MR is Tk 100 per month of pregnancy.[6] Though difficult to document because they are illegal, such rates are reported to be charged when MR is conducted in private clinics or in the private practice of government providers. As mentioned earlier, there is a suggestion in the data on MR that the majority of abortions are not done in government clinics. In general, there is probably a considerable influence of changing fertility patterns on the state of knowledge about reproductive physiology in the general population. Studies of ritual meaning and traditional practices, although relevant for other purposes, may not be too revealing for the purpose of understanding why MR came to be widely accepted. Women's menstrual patterns change because of changing fertility. In natural fertility, long-lactating and poorly nourished women, menstrual histories may be unreliable for the assessment of pregnancy because women spent relatively less time in states where they menstruated regularly—first, extreme nutritional deprivation can cause delayed onset of menses; second, long periods of lactation result in several months of amenorrhea associated with each live birth; and third, repeated births meant repeated episodes of the absence of menses for each woman.

In Bangladesh, prior to the deliberate control of fertility through contraception, women had an average of seven births. Combined with a mean duration of breastfeeding of twenty-eight months, resulting in approximately nine months of amenorrhea, this meant that each birth could be associated with nineteen months without menstrual cycles. That is, a woman who has seven births will not menstruate for eleven of her reproductive years. With the reduction of fertility to 3.5 births, the time that an average woman now spends either in a pregnant or lactating state is down to 5.5 years (the mean duration of breastfeeding has remained relatively unchanged).[7] Thus, women's "menstrual careers" have changed substantially with the decline of fertility. It is likely that as these changes in menstruation occur, there will be change in how menstruation is understood and perceived by women. It is unlikely that beliefs will remain static while the actual experience changes so radically with changing fertility.

DISCUSSION

In Bangladesh the advent of a new technology for early pregnancy termination created an opportunity to make safe and effective MR services widely available; this probably played a part in giving widespread legitimacy to the procedure of abortion, which providers were previously hesitant to perform and would do so only in secrecy. The use of a new and distinct terminology for early versus late termination probably contributed to the legitimization of MR.

The use of a different word for abortion is only a small part of the story. It was important that menstrual regulation was given the benefit of a more liberal interpretation of the legal code through a government circular at an early stage of the program. The provision of services by the government is legitimization in and of itself. It appears that although the government was cautious and tentative in the initial years of the program and introduced services experimentally, probably out of fear of religious opposition, it gained confidence when there was no opposition to speak of. MR services are now available in governmental health facilities all over Bangladesh.

It is probably significant the program costs relatively little when one considers the extensive services that are available. The MR organizations operate as catalytic agents, and with relatively low levels of resources invested, it leverages a very large amount of manpower employed by the government. The MR program provides training and logistic support to government service providers.

There is relatively little controversy about the MR program in Bangladesh. Although there is some sense that a clearer legal mandate on abortion would improve services, there is hesitation about drawing attention to the issue because doing so might call unwelcome attention to the ambiguity in the law. There appears to be a general consensus that despite the ambiguous legal status, the government and the MR program are providing an important service to women.

There is a growing perception in feminist circles of a threat to women's freedoms from a rising tide of Islamic fundamentalism. Although the fundamentalist movement is largely political, it is vocal in its opposition to all aspects of women's freedom. Organizations such as Grameen Bank and BRAC, and their women's credit and children's education programs in particular, have been under attack as agents of Christianity. Although the family-planning program has not come under direct attack on the same scale, probably because it is a long-standing governmental program and as a matter of policy maintains an open dialogue with the religious groups, a public debate on abortion is still believed to be too risky (Maleka Begum, personal communication, March 10, 1996). Indeed, the demand for abortion rights has never been, and is not likely to be, a demand of the women's movement in Bangladesh in the near future.

For legal and political settings such as Bangladesh, where the situation of women's rights remains constrained by religious laws and a conservative social setting, efforts at legal reform on abortion may well be premature. Although the experience of other countries has not come into the discussion among relevant circles in Bangladesh, recent events in Indonesia lend some support to the belief that efforts at greater legal clarity may have adverse effects. Hull, Sarwono, and Widyantoro (1992) have shown how attempts at clarifying the laws on abortion and reforming health care systems only created more legal ambiguity.

I have argued in this chapter that there is relatively little support for Dixon-Mueller's suggestion that the success of the program rests on ambiguity in folk belief about MR. On the contrary, there is evidence that greater knowledge and clearer messages on MR availability and timing would help to further reduce the number of clandestine abortions that are performed now.

More relevant than confused beliefs about reproductive physiology in the population is the deliberate use of new terminology to create a distinction between early and late abortion; this has served the purpose of legitimizing early termination of pregnancy, whereas late termination is considered dangerous, illegal, and perhaps even immoral. Such a distinction is probably more important to policy makers and service providers than to the women who come to terminate unwanted pregnancies—clients continue to ask for their "stomach to be washed out or cleaned" or for the doctor to "get rid of the fetus." Few come asking simply for their menses to be resumed or displaying other confused notions about menstrual regularity. The legal and medical ambiguity regarding abortion and MR is a deliberate and consciously engineered, but it is unclear that there are similar ambiguities on the matter of reproductive physiology in folk belief.

There is evidence in Bangladesh, as in many other settings, that people form their own moral position on abortion and condition it on social and economic realities rather than rigid interpretations of the legal code. A more liberal acceptance of abortion than what the legal code allows may be attributed in part to a diversity of religious interpretation that can be derived from the Koran. In addition to the diversity of opinions within Islamic jurisprudence on the general topic of abortion, it is likely that all the major schools of thought make an important distinction between early and late abortion—one that can be invoked to make a convincing case for early termination.

In addition to the range of opinions within Islamic jurisprudence playing a part in the public policy on abortion, there is a general principle in Islam that leaves many moral decisions as a matter to be resolved by the individual in his or her personal relationship with God (Sachedina 1990). Women who decide to terminate a pregnancy with an MR do so not because they are casual about contraception and MR but because of other overriding concerns such as the social retribution related to unwed motherhood, costs of raising unwanted children, health costs of mistimed children, and so on. In this process of individual decision making, MR as a method for early termination may derive legitimacy from the unlikely source of Islamic jurisprudence.

NOTES

1. MR refers to pregnancy termination by vacuum aspiration in the early stages of pregnancy.

2. Hull, Sawano, and Widyantoro (1993) have reported a similar situation in Indonesia where the criminal code provided a range of punishments for abortion but failed to define illegal abortion either in terms of gestational age or procedure used, thus making prosecution rare.

3. The specific words of the Penal Code of 1860, Section 312, as quoted in Sobhan (1980) are as follows:

> 312. Whoever voluntarily causes a woman with child to miscarry, shall, if such miscarriage be not caused in good faith for the purpose of saving the life of the woman, be punished with imprisonment of either description for a term which may extend to three years, or with fine, or with both; and, if the woman be quick with child, shall be punished with imprisonment of either description for a term which may extend to seven years, and shall also be liable to fine.
>
> Explanation—A woman who causes herself to miscarry, is within the meaning of this section.
>
> 313. Whoever commits the offence defined in the last preceding section without the consent of the woman, whether the woman is quick with child or not, shall be punished with transportation for life, or with imprisonment of either description for a term which may extend to ten years, and shall also be liable to fine.
>
> 314. Whoever, with intent to cause the miscarriage of a woman with child, does any act which causes the death of such woman with child, shall be punished with imprisonment of either description for a term which may extend to ten years, and shall also be liable to fine.

4. The liberalization of abortion laws was accompanied by relaxation of adoption laws as well that permitted foreign nationals to adopt war babies. According to Malcolm Potts (personal communication, 1999), who led the International Planned Parenthood Federation (IPPF) team to attend raped women in Bangladesh, credit needs to go to a handful of gynecologists in Bangladesh who picked up MR with such alacrity and who had been motivated by seeing years of suffering and death among women trying to control their fertility.

5. The Menstrual Regulation Training and Service Project is a nongovernmental organization that coordinates the supply of MR kits and training of government service

providers all over Bangladesh. It works in close collaboration with the government; its principal training centers are located in major government-run medical centers.

6. Although MR in general refers to early-term abortions, usually before the sixth week, that are conducted by manual vacuum aspiration, in Bangladesh it can be conducted as late as the twelfth week of pregnancy by using appropriately large syringes and cannulas.

7. I have calculated these numbers based on fertility, amenorrhea, and breast-feeding data available from the Demographic and Health Surveys (Mitra et al. 1994).

REFERENCES

Ahmad, Raana. 1979. "Attitude towards Induced Abortion in Bangladesh." *The Bangladesh Development Studies* 7 (4): 97–108.

Amin, Sajeda, and Sara Hossain. 1995. "Women's Reproductive Rights and the Politics of Fundamentalism: A View from Bangladesh." *The American University Law Review* 44 (4): 1319–43.

Aziz, K.M.A., and C. Maloney. 1985. *Life-Stages, Gender and Fertility in Bangladesh.* Dhaka: International Centre for Diarrhoeal Research, Bangladesh.

Bangladesh Association for the Prevention of Septic Abortion (BAPSA). 1985. *MR Newsletter,* no. 1. Dhaka, Bangladesh.

Begum, Syeda Firoza, Haidary Kamal, and G. M. Kamal. 1987. *Evaluation of MR Services in Bangladesh.* Dhaka: Bangladesh Association for Prevention of Septic Abortion.

Blanchet, T. 1984. *Meanings and Rituals of Birth in Rural Bangladesh.* Dhaka, Bangladesh: Dhaka University Press.

Chaudhury, R. H. 1980. "Attitudes towards Legalization of Abortion among a Cross-Section of Women in Metropolitan Dacca." *Journal of Biosocial Science* 12 (4): 417–28.

Cook, Rebecca J. 1993. "International Human Rights and Women's Reproductive Health." *Studies in Family Planning* 24 (2): 73–86.

Dixon-Mueller, Ruth. 1988. "Innovations in Reproductive Health Care: Menstrual Regulation Policies and Programs in Bangladesh." *Studies in Family Planning* 19 (3): 129–40.

Government of Bangladesh. 1980. Memorandum no. 5-14/MCH-FP/Trg 80/358/1 (96), 25 January.

Hull, Terence H., Sarsanto W. Sarwono, and Ninuk Widyantoro. 1993. "Induced Abortion in Indonesia." *Studies in Family Planning* 24 (4): 241–51.

Kamal, Ghulam Mustafa, ed. 1992. *Proceedings of the International Symposium on Antiprogestins.* Publication no. 7. Dhaka: Bangladesh Association for Prevention of Septic Abortion.

Kamal, Haidary, et al. 1992. *Utilization of Reproductive Health Care Services in Dhaka City.* Dhaka: Bangladesh Association for the Prevention of Septic Abortion.

Kamal, Haidary, Altaf Hossain, Syeda Firoza Begum, and Gholam Mustafa Kamal. 1993. *Prospects of Menstrual Regulation Services in Bangladesh.* Dhaka: Bangladesh Association for the Prevention of Septic Abortion.

Maloney, Clarence, K. M. Ashraful Aziz, and Profulla C. Sarker. 1981. *Beliefs and Fertility in Bangladesh.* Dhaka: International Center for Diarrhoeal Disease Research, Bangladesh.

Mitra, S. N., M. Nawab Ali, Shahidul Islam, Anne R. Cross, and Tulshi Saha. 1994. *Bangladesh Demographic and Health Survey: 1993–94*. Dhaka: National Institute of Population Research and Training.

Rochat, R. W., S. Jabeen, and M. J. Rosenberg. 1981. "Maternal and Abortion Related Deaths in Bangladesh, 1978–1979." *International Journal of Obstetrics and Gynecology* 19 (2): 155–64.

Rosenberg, Michael J., et al. 1981. "Attitudes of Rural Bangladesh Physicians toward Abortion." *Studies in Family Planning* 12 (8, 9): 318–21.

Sachedina, Zulie. 1990. "Islam, Procreation and the Law." *International Family Planning Perspectives* 16 (3): 107–11.

Serour, G. I. 1992. "Antiprogestins: Ethical Issues." In *Proceddings of the International Symposium on Antiprogestins*, ed. G. M. Kamal. Dhaka, Bangladesh: Bangladesh Association for the Prevention of Septic Abortion.

Sobhan, Salma. 1980. *Legal Status of Women in Bangladesh*. Dhaka: Bangladesh Institute of Law and International Affairs.

Chapter 10

The Impact of Reproductive Health Policy Changes on Fertility, Abortion, and Contraceptive Use in Romania

Florina Serbanescu, Leo Morris, and Paul Stupp

Until recently, Romania was the setting of the most rigorously enforced pronatalist policy among all the communist countries of Central and Eastern Europe (David 1992; Stephenson et al. 1992). A restrictive law issued in 1966 reversed the legal status of abortion decreed in 1957 and permitted modern contraceptive use and induced abortion for only very limited medical and social reasons. Although extreme measures were taken to enforce compliance with the law and a new decree issued in 1985 further restricted access to abortion and contraception, the resultant fertility increase in the long term was far below expectations of the government. After an initial surge in fertility in 1967–68 to 3.6 births per woman, a rate more than twice the 1966 level, the total fertility rate (TFR) fell to 2.9 in 1970 and continued to decrease slowly to 2.2 in 1980–84 and stabilized around 2.3 births per woman during the 1985–89 period.

We would like to acknowledge all the organizations that contributed to the various phases of the Romania Reproductive Health Survey (RRHS). The survey was conducted by the National Institute for Mother and Child Care, with technical assistance from the Division of Reproductive Heath, National Center for Chronic Disease Prevention and Health Promotion, Centers for Disease Control and Prevention. (DRH/CDC).

The funding for the RRHS was provided by the U.S. Agency for International Development through the Centre for Development Population Activities, the U.N. Population Fund through the local U. N. Development Program (UNDP) office, the Romanian Ministry of Health through the National Academy of Science, and U. N. Children's Fund (UNICEF). We thank Alin Stanescu for contributions in the finalization of this chapter.

This survey could not have been done without the collaboration of other organizations: the National Commission of Statistics, the Association of Public Health and Management, and the District Sanitary Directorates.

In the absence of modern contraception, illegal abortions, most of them self-induced or induced by lay persons, were widely used to avert unwanted births. Although the extent of the prevalence of illegal abortions was impossible to assess, the dramatic effect on women's health was obvious to government officials but concealed from the public for many years. The true scope of the impact this policy had on reproductive health came to worldwide attention only after the December 1989 revolution and the change of government. During the last decade of communist rule (1979–89), Romania had the highest maternal mortality rate in Europe, a rate ten times higher than that of any other European country, and most of these maternal deaths were abortion related (Stephenson et al. 1992). The magnitude of abortion complications is difficult to quantify, but unofficial estimates suggest that nearly 20 percent of the 4.9 million women of reproductive age are thought to have impaired fertility (United Nations Population Fund 1990). The high number of unwanted pregnancies resulting in children abandoned in overcrowded orphanages by families who had been too frightened to attempt an illegal abortion but who were too poor to afford to raise their child was another shocking disclosure (Nachtwey 1990). The dramatic experience of Romania has proved once again how reproductive health can be affected through restrictive laws.

On December 26, 1989, during the revolution, abortion and contraception were legalized when the restrictive law was revoked after public pressure was applied on the interim government. Abortion became available on request through twelve weeks of pregnancy, and the requirement that it be approved by a medical committee was eliminated. The previous legal provision to provide abortions up to twenty-four weeks only in the cases of rape, incest, and endangerment of the woman's life if the pregnancy were to be continued was maintained. Clinics were inundated by women seeking abortions, but the newly created national family-planning program was constrained by severe economic problems, deficient infrastructure, and resistance to modern contraception by both the public and the health care providers. Consequently, the legally induced abortion rate reached the highest level in the world—almost 200 per 1,000 women aged 15–44 in 1990 (Ministerul Sanatatii 1993), a rate seven times higher than that in the United States. But despite a spectacular decline, from 170 per 100,000 live births in 1989 to 84 per 100,000 in 1992, the maternal mortality rate remains the highest in Europe.

In Romania, information about contraceptive use is not routinely collected; thus, little is known about knowledge, attitudes, and perceived effectiveness of contraceptive methods at the national or regional level. According to non-population-based studies (Johnson, Horga, and Androbache 1993; Yip et al. 1993), the prevalence of modern contraceptive use is low, and women mostly rely on traditional family-planning methods that have high failure rates leading to high levels of unintended pregnancy.

The objective of this chapter is to compare selected aspects of fertility, planning status of pregnancies, and use of abortion and contraception before and after the December 1989 revolution, when the laws restricting abortion and contraceptive use were abolished. The liberalization of abortion in Romania provided an ideal situation to study the impact of changing policy on fertility and contraceptive patterns.

DATA SOURCE

This analysis is based on data obtained from the national Romania Reproductive Health Survey (RRHS) conducted in 1993. This nationwide probability survey of reproductive health is the first to be carried out in Romania since 1978. The 1993 RRHS was a household-based survey designed to collect information from a representative sample of women of reproductive age throughout Romania. The population from which the respondents were selected included all women between the ages of fifteen and forty-four, regardless of marital status, who were living in Romania between July and December 1993.

The survey used a stratified sample design with independent samples for Bucharest, the capital city, and the interior, which is divided into forty administrative districts called *judets.* Bucharest, together with the surrounding Agricultural Sector of Ilfov, is the equivalent of a judet. The 1992 census was used as the sampling frame (Comisia Nationala Pentru Statistica 1992). Because the numbers of urban and rural households in the interior were roughly equal, the interior sample was designed to be self-weighting. Based on the percentage of households with at least one woman fifteen to forty-four years of age and on a projected response rate of 90 percent, a sample of 12,387 households was selected from which to obtain complete interviews for approximately 5,000 women. Although it included 11 percent of the total population, Bucharest was oversampled to represent 22 percent of the sample and to allow independent estimates (Serbanescu and Morris 1995). Survey results were weighted to adjust for the oversampling of households in Bucharest and to compensate for randomly selecting only one woman from households with more than one eligible woman.

Of the 12,387 households selected, 5,283 included at least one fifteen- to forty-four-year-old woman. Of this number, 4,861 were successfully interviewed, for a response rate of 92.0 percent. Only 1.1 percent the of selected women refused to be interviewed, whereas another 6.1 percent could not be located. Response rates were slightly better in Bucharest and other urban areas (93 percent) than in rural areas (89 percent). Interviews, conducted at the respondents' homes by trained female interviewers, generally lasted thirty to fifty minutes. The age distribution, marital status distribution, and fertility experience of the RRHS sample closely reflected that of the female population as a whole (Comisia Nationala Pentru Statistica 1993a; Serbanescu and Morris 1995).

The RRHS questionnaire covered a wide range of topics related to reproductive health in Romania: a history of all pregnancies and births (including pregnancies ending in abortion) and the planning status of the pregnancies, family planning (knowledge and history of use of contraceptive methods, reasons for use of less effective methods of contraception, pregnancy intentions, and fecundity), maternal and child health (health information about the most recent pregnancy and birth and the use of maternal and child health services), young adult reproductive health (information about premarital sexual experience and pregnancy among women fifteen to twenty-four years old), women's health (health behavior and use of women's health services), reproductive health knowledge and attitudes (especially regarding birth control pills and intrauterine devices [IUDs]), knowledge about acquired immune deficiency syndrome (AIDS) transmission and prevention, and socioeconomic characteristics of women and their husbands or families. The questionnaire also included a monthly calendar of pregnancies, segments of contraceptive use, and reasons for discontinuing use over a five-year period beginning in January 1988.

DATA ANALYSIS

Using the information recorded in the pregnancy histories, we examined two consecutive three-year periods before and after the restrictive law was repealed in December 1989 and calculated age-specific fertility, induced abortion, and pregnancy rates for two 36-month periods, June 1987–May 1990 and June 1990–May 1993.[1] The total pregnancy rate (TPR), TFR, and total induced abortion rate (TIAR) for these two periods were computed by accumulating the age-specific rates for each event. The TPR, TFR, and TIAR may be interpreted as the average number of events of each type (pregnancies, births, and induced abortions) per woman that a group of women would experience during their reproductive ages, fifteen to forty-four, if they experienced the age-specific rates for a given period.

Using the information obtained on the monthly calendar portion of the questionnaire, we estimated contraceptive prevalence rates by method for the same two periods and twelve-month contraceptive failure and discontinuation rates by method.

RESULTS

After abortion became legal, the TFR dropped sharply to below replacement level, from 2.3 live births per woman for the period 1987–90 to 1.5 live births for 1990–93. Although the TIAR doubled, from 1.7 to 3.4 abortions per woman for the same periods, there was a notable difference in the TFR between urban and rural residents: notably, urban women had almost one child less than did rural women (Table 10.1). Also, in the second period, the abortion rate for urban women was 9 percent higher than the rate for rural women. Education was inversely related to both the fertility rate and the induced abortion rate. The least

Table 10.1
Total Fertility Rates (TFR) and Total Induced Abortion Rates (TIAR) per Woman, by Selected Characteristics

Characteristics	TFR		TIAR	
	1987-1990*	1990-1993**	1987-1990*	1990-1993**
Total	**2.3**	**1.5**	**1.7**	**3.4**
Residence				
Urban	2.0	1.2	1.7	3.5
Rural	2.8	2.1	1.6	3.2
Education Level				
Primary	3.5	2.3	2.0	4.7
Secondary incomplete	2.4	1.7	1.8	3.2
Secondary complete	1.9	1.3	1.5	3.1
Postsecondary & University	1.2	1.1	1.4	2.5
Marital Status				
Ever Married	4.1	3.0	2.1	4.7
Never Married	1.2	1.5	0.7	1.0

* From June 1987 to May 1990.
** From June 1990 to May 1993.
Source: Romania Reproductive Health Survey 1993.

educated women consistently reported the highest rates of fertility and abortion, and although their TFR dropped by one third, from 3.5 to 2.3, their TIAR more than doubled, reaching almost five lifetime induced abortions per woman after the change in legislation. The more highly educated women had a 28 percent decline in fertility, and their induced abortion rate doubled.

The striking decline in fertility in the second three-year period is associated with both a continuous increase in the abortion rate and an increase in the pregnancy rate. Not only did the induced abortion rate increase in the second period, but the pregnancy rate was also 30 percent higher. The change in the TPR in the same direction as that in the TIAR suggests that the use of abortion as the primary means of fertility control tends to increase the pregnancy rate because it speeds up the return of exposure to the risk of conception by shortening the duration of pregnancy and the postgestational anovulatory period. It also suggests a high level of unintended pregnancies, which were almost always terminated through the use of legally induced abortions, and little impact of contraceptive practices in preventing these pregnancies, either because of low prevalence or because of high failure rates.

All age-specific fertility rates declined sharply, except those for women aged forty to forty-four, whose rate was very low in both periods (Table 10.2). Almost 70 percent of the TFR can be attributed to women aged twenty to twenty-nine in both periods of time. Fertility trends for women younger than thirty years of age are particularly important in Romania, where by the age of twenty-nine, 90 percent of the women have already given birth to their first child and the median

Table 10.2
Age-Specific Fertility Rates and Age-Specific Induced Abortion Rates per 1,000 Women Aged 15–44 before and after the Change in Legislation

Age at Pregnancy Outcome	All Women Age Specific Fertility Rates 1987-1990*	1990-1993**	Percent Change(%)	All Women Age Specific Induced Abortion Rates 1987-1990*	1990-1993**	Percent Change(%)
15-19	61	49	-20	10	32	+220
20-24	182	129	-53	63	153	+143
25-29	128	83	-35	82	209	+155
30-34	53	33	-38	65	167	+157
35-39	23	12	-48	52	79	+52
40-44	6	5	-17	65	40	-23
Total (Per Woman)	**2.3**	**1.5**	**-35**	**1.7**	**3.4**	**+100**

Age at Pregnancy Outcome	Married Women Age Specific Fertility Rates 1987-1990*	1990-1993**	Percent Change	Married Women Age Specific Induced Abortion Rates 1987-1990*	1990-1993**	Percent Change
15-19	363	307	-15	57	178	+212
20-24	262	195	-26	88	225	+156
25-29	133	86	-35	84	221	+163
30-34	54	34	-37	66	168	+155
35-39	23	13	-43	53	81	+53
40-44	6	6	0	66	40	+39
Total (Per Ever Married Woman)	**4.2**	**3.2**	**-24**	**2.1**	**4.6**	**+119**

* From June 1987 to May 1990.
** From June 1990 to May 1993.
*** Excludes exposure, births, and abortions occurring before the date of first union for ever married women.
Source: Romania Reproductive Health Survey 1993.

age at the first live birth is twenty-two years. Although the greatest decrease in fertility occurred among women thirty to thirty-four and thirty-five to thirty-nine years of age, their low age-specific fertility rates in the most recent period accounted for only 11 percent and 4 percent, respectively, of the overall fertility.

A comparison of age-specific marital fertility rates and marital induced abortion rates for the two periods reveals that marital fertility rates for all age groups were higher than fertility rates for all women and induced abortion rates for married women were higher than those for all women (Table 10.2) and, by implication, higher than those for unmarried women. These findings are consistent with another survey finding, that only 5 percent of pregnancies are terminated before the date of first union, and illustrate that abortion is primarily associated with married women in Romania. This pattern is opposite to that seen in the United States, where abortion rates are much higher among unmarried women (Koonin, Smith, and Ramick 1993). Because most women are married by age twenty-five (87 percent), marital abortion rates differ little from abortion rates for all women aged twenty-five and above.

Data on the planning status of all pregnancies in the two periods demonstrate significant changes. For each pregnancy outcome after 1987, women were asked a series of questions to determine whether the pregnancy was planned (desired at the time it occurred), mistimed (wanted at a later time), or unwanted. Both mistimed and unwanted pregnancies are classified as unintended pregnancies. The respondents were asked to recall accurately their thoughts at the moment they found out about their pregnancies. Although some women may have been reluctant to report induced abortion and some rationalized their decision postpartum, many women were clearly willing to report unwanted conceptions. After the repeal of the restrictive law, both mistimed and unwanted pregnancies increased by one-third; indeed, 67.5 percent of pregnancies were reported as unintended (Table 10.3). The planning status is strongly correlated with pregnancy

Table 10.3
Planning Status of All Pregnancies Reported by Women Aged 15–44 with at Least One Pregnancy in the Last Five Years, by Selected Characteristics

	1988-1990*			1990-1993**		
Characteristics	Planned	Mistimed	Unwanted	Planned	Mistimed	Unwanted
Total	**49.0**	**9.7**	**41.3**	**32.5**	**12.7**	**54.8**
Residence						
Urban	45.8	10.7	43.5	27.1	13.4	59.5
Rural	54.6	7.9	37.5	40.3	11.6	48.1
Pregnancy Outcome						
Live Birth	81.3	6.4	12.3	86.0	6.0	8.0
Miscarriage/SB/EP	71.7	7.8	20.5	74.3	3.9	21.8
Induced Abortion	3.4	14.2	82.4	3.7	16.6	79.7
Age Group						
15-19	75.8	15.5	8.7	57.3	24.5	18.2
20-24	59.5	15.9	24.6	46.1	21.7	32.2
25-29	49.4	8.2	42.4	28.8	10.5	60.7
30-34	30.7	2.0	67.3	15.5	2.6	81.9
35-44	20.9	1.4	77.7	12.1	0.7	87.2
Education Level						
Primary	43.8	5.1	51.1	25.6	4.8	69.6
Secondary incompl.	53.6	9.7	36.7	35.1	14.3	50.6
Secondary complete	52.1	11.7	36.2	36.0	17.0	47.0
Postsecondary & Univ.	41.9	18.0	40.1	31.9	16.4	51.7

Note: Age groups refer to the age of the woman at the time of pregnancy.
* From January 1988 to May 1990.
** From June 1990 to May 1993.
Source: Romania Reproductive Health Survey 1993.

outcome. For both periods, more than 95 percent of the women whose pregnancy ended in induced abortion reported their pregnancy to be unintended. It should also be noted that a relatively high proportion of women whose pregnancy ended in miscarriage or stillbirth in the most recent period had reported it as an unwanted conception (21.8 percent); this percentage is almost three times that of women with live births who reported an unwanted pregnancy. One can only speculate that some of these outcomes may have been induced abortions reported as spontaneous abortions or stillbirths.

The study of contraceptive prevalence before and after the change in legislation shows a 20 percent increase. Moreover, 70 percent of the increase seen is the result of higher prevalence of traditional methods despite recent efforts to promote modern contraceptive use. It is noteworthy, however, that the increase in modern contraceptive use among all women is almost entirely due to increase usage of IUDs—from 0.6 percent to 1.7 percent—and condoms—from 1.8 percent to 2.7 percent—whereas the other methods' usage does not show any significant change (i.e., the pill prevalence of 2.3 percent remains unchanged).

At the time of the survey, 40.6 percent of all women of reproductive age reported using a contraceptive method. For women who were currently in union, the prevalence of contraceptive use was 57.3 percent (Table 10.4). The prevalence was 43.4 percent for traditional methods: 35 percent for couples using

Table 10.4
Current Use of Specific Contraceptive Methods by Marital Status, All Women Aged 15–44

		Marital Status		
Current Use & Method	Married/ Total	Previously In Union	Never Married	Married
Currently Using Any Method	**40.6**	**57.3**	**14.3**	**5.1**
Traditional Method	30.6	43.4	8.9	3.5
Withdrawal	24.5	35.0	5.6	2.6
Calendar	6.1	8.4	3.3	0.9
Modern Method	10.4	13.9	5.4	1.6
Condom	3.1	4.1	1.8	0.1
IUD	3.0	4.3	1.1	1.0
Pills	2.3	3.2	0.9	0.5
Tubal Ligation	1.0	1.4	1.5	0.0
Spermicides	0.5	0.8	0.0	0.0
Injectables	0.0	0.0	0.0	0.0
Other	0.1	0.1	0.2	0.0
Not Currently Using	**59.3**	**42.7**	**85.7**	**94.8**
Total	100.0	100.0	100.0	100.0
Number of Cases (Not Weighted)	(4,861)	(3,542)	(277)	(1,042)

Source: Romania Reproductive Health Survey 1993.

withdrawal and 8.4 percent for women using the calendar method. Only 13.9 percent of women in union were using modern contraceptives, and the IUD, the condom, and the pill were the contraceptives most commonly used. Less than 2 percent were contraceptively sterilized even though 92 percent of fecund women in union who had two or more children did not want any more children.

Contraceptive prevalence is highest in Transylvania (67.2 percent), highest among women twenty-five to thirty-four years of age (65.9–69.3 percent) and positively correlated with education level (Table 10.5). The percentage of all contracepting women who use modern methods is higher in urban areas, in

Table 10.5
Current Use of Traditional and Modern Contraceptive Methods by Selected Characteristics, Women in Union Aged 15–44

Characteristics	Any Method	Traditional Methods	Modern Methods	Percent of Current Users Using Modern Methods	Unweighted No. of Cases
Total	**57.3**	**43.4**	**13.9**	**24**	**3,542**
Residence					
Urban	58.7	42.0	16.7	28	2,312
Rural	55.1	45.7	9.4	17	1,230
Region					
Bucharest	53.1	32.8	20.4	38	764
Vallahia	52.1	42.0	10.1	20	1,148
Tansylvania	67.2	48.0	19.2	29	1,029
Moldova	53.1	44.4	8.7	16	601
Age Group					
15-19	39.9	33.4	6.5	16	105
20-24	52.8	41.4	11.4	22	569
25-29	65.9	48.4	17.5	27	724
30-34	69.3	49.3	20.0	29	746
35-39	57.3	42.8	14.5	25	785
40-44	44.4	36.8	7.6	17	613
Education Level					
Primary	45.4	38.6	6.6	15	940
Secondary incompl.	56.7	46.4	10.4	18	972
Secondary complete	64.1	43.9	20.2	32	1,202
Postsecondary & Univ.	71.3	47.1	24.2	34	428
Number of Living Children					
0	31.8	22.8	9.0	28	442
1	60.0	44.5	15.5	26	1,092
2	67.2	51.1	16.1	24	1,319
3	54.1	41.0	13.1	24	398
4+	44.6	37.0	7.6	17	290
Socioeconomic Status					
Low	51.0	42.7	8.3	16	1,280
Medium	61.3	46.3	15.0	24	1,821
High	60.2	38.7	28.1	47	441

Source: Romania Reproductive Health Survey 1993.

Bucharest and Transylvania, among the more highly educated women, and among those with fewer children. However, in no group does the prevalence rate for using modern methods surpass 28 percent.

The low prevalence of modern contraceptive use does not reflect the lack of awareness of modern methods. Almost all women currently in union (95 percent) had heard of at least one modern method, and no significant differences in the level of overall modern contraception awareness by residence and educational level surfaced. However, the level of knowledge of specific modern methods varied. The most widely known modern methods were the condom, the pill, and the IUD (80 percent or greater awareness), and the least known were injectables, vasectomy, and the use of the diaphragm, known by 16 percent, 13 percent, and 9 percent, respectively. Not only was the overall awareness high, but 85 percent of women in union also knew at least one place where they thought they could obtain a modern method. The knowledge of where to go for a family-planning method was affected by residence and education: rural residents and less educated women were less likely to have such information (data not shown).

Although the overall level of family-planning awareness was high, for the most widely known contraceptive methods there was a serious gap between awareness of the method and knowledge of where the procedure or product could be obtained; the gap ranged from nine percentage points for tubal ligation to more than thirty percentage points for the IUD and the condom.

Additional questions designed to explore attitudes and opinions about modern methods revealed a high level of misinformation and preconceptions. When users of traditional methods were asked how important were several specified reasons for not using a modern method, the results ranged from 70.6 percent to 11.5 percent (Table 10.6). Most women stated that fear of side effects, partner

Table 10.6
Percentage of Women in Union 15–44 Years of Age Using Traditional Methods Who Reported the Following Specified Reasons as Important for Not Using a Modern Method

Reason Given			Traditional Method			
	Total	**(SE)**	**Withdrawal**	**(SE)**	**Calendar**	**(SE)**
Fear of Side Effects	70.6	(1.4)	70.5	(1.6)	71.0	(3.0)
Partner Prefers Traditional Methods	67.3	(3.1)	(1.3)	68.0	(1.4)	64.3
Little Knowledge of Other Methods	61.1	(1.7)	63.9	(1.8)	49.4	(3.0)
Difficult To Obtain	38.4	(1.8)	38.2	(1.9)	39.5	(3.2)
Cost	34.3	(1.7)	35.9	(1.9)	27.6	(2.8)
Doctors' Recommendation	24.2	(1.6)	22.1	(1.6)	33.0	(3.3)
Religious Beliefs	11.5	(1.2)	11.7	(1.4)	10.6	(2.1)
Unweighted No. of Cases	(1,509)		(1,180)		(329)	

Note: Standard errors (SE) were estimated using SUDAAN.

Source: Romania Reproductive Health Survey 1993.

preference, and little knowledge about modern methods influenced their decision to not use a modern method. About one-third cited the difficulty of obtaining modern contraceptives or their cost. One-fourth acknowledged as an important reason that their physician recommended that they not use a modern method.

Almost two-thirds of traditional method users believed that their method was equally as effective as or even more effective than the pill or the IUD (Table 10.7). Surprisingly, this belief was not affected by education. These findings highlight the lack of correct information about modern contraceptives and highlight women's trust in the traditional methods historically practiced in Romania (Santow 1993).

The women's trust in traditional methods is not justified if one considers the high failure rates associated with these methods. Life table analysis of segments of contraceptive use begun since the change in legislation showed that for both withdrawal and the calendar method, approximately 30 percent resulted in pregnancy within twelve months of initiating use. Three-fourths of the twelve-month discontinuation rate for these methods is accounted for by method failure (Table 10.8). The condom also had a high failure rate of 21.5 percent, which accounted for almost half of the reasons for which this method was discontinued. The IUD and the pill failure rates at twelve months are comparable to rates published in the literature. If, as is usually the case, some women did not report pregnancies ending in abortions and if they had been using contraception at the time of conception, the failure rates reported here are minimum estimates, and the true rates are probably somewhat higher than those shown in Table 10.8.

The low prevalence of modern method use contrasts with the high proportion of women in union, throughout all socioeconomic subgroups, who desired to limit their fertility. Of the women who were currently in union, almost 60 percent did not want to have any more children, 5 percent wanted to wait at least

Table 10.7
Opinion of Women 15–44 Years of Age Using Traditional Methods Concerning Effectiveness of Current Method Compared with Effectiveness of the Pill or IUD by Education

Education Level	Effectiveness of Current Method									
	More Effective	SE*	Equally Effective	SE	Less Effective	SE	Don't Know	SE	Total	Number of Cases
Total	**32.7**	**(1.4)**	**29.8**	**(1.5)**	**18.9**	**(1.1)**	**18.6**	**(1.5)**	**100.0**	**(1,505)****
Primary	34.9	(2.9)	21.8	(2.4)	15.7	(2.1)	27.6	(2.9)	100.0	(350)
Secondary Incompl.	29.8	(2.4)	30.1	(2.7)	18.5	(2.0)	21.6	(2.4)	100.0	(446)
Secondary Complete	32.0	(2.1)	34.1	(2.4)	21.6	(1.8)	12.3	(1.6)	100.0	(519)
Postsec & University	36.9	(4.2)	35.6	(3.9)	19.2	(3.0)	8.3	(2.0)	100.0	(190)

* Standard errors (SE) were estimated using SUDAAN.

** Four women did not answer this question.

Source: Romania Reproductive Health Survey 1993.

Table 10.8
Twelve-Month Life Table Contraceptive Failure and Discontinuation Rates by Method; All Segments of Contraceptive Use Initiated after the Change in Legislation

	Failure		**Discontinuation**		
Method	Failure Rates	Standard Error*	Discontinuation Rates	Standard Error*	Percent of Discontinuation Due to Contraceptive Failure
Total	**25.9**	**(1.4)**	**38.8**	**(1.4)**	**66.7**
Traditional Methods					
Withdrawal	30.0	(1.9)	38.3	(1.9)	78.3
Calendar	30.7	(3.5)	41.0	(3.5)	74.9
Modern Methods					
Pills	2.4	(2.9)	38.9	(4.3)	6.2
IUD	4.1	(2.3)	14.2	(5.4)	28.9
Condom	21.5	(3.9)	46.9	(4.2)	45.8

* Standard errors were estimated using a design effect of 2.0 applied to the survival standard errors generated by the Lifetest SAS procedure.

Source: Romania Reproductive Health Survey 1993.

two years before having a child, and only 10 percent wanted a child in the near future. Almost 20 percent thought they could not become pregnant and cited as the main reason either their failure to conceive in the last two years without using contraception, gynecological surgery other than contraceptive sterilization, or partner subfecundity. If we exclude these subfecund women from the denominator, then 73 percent did not want to have any more children, and this proportion increased to more than 92 percent for women with two or more children. However, these fecund women, despite their intention to terminate childbearing, used mostly traditional methods, and only 15 percent of them expressed a desire to use a modern method in the future. Less than 1 percent expressed an interest in surgical contraception. Those not interested said their most important reason for lack of interest was fear of side effects (27 percent), fear of surgery (17 percent), or "they never thought about it" (16 percent).

DISCUSSION

In this study we have compared fertility, abortion, pregnancy rates, and contraceptive prevalence before and after a change in government policy that legalized abortion and modern contraception. Variations in these rates by social and demographic characteristics have also been examined to help identify the subgroups of women most likely to have experienced major changes in fertility and the extent to which contraceptive practice has or has not influenced these changes.

Our analysis indicates that the concept of family planning was, and still is, poorly developed in Romania, and the change in legislation did not translate into a significant increase in contraceptive use; almost half of the couples are not using any method, and of those who do, most are using traditional methods and induced abortion when the method fails. Because of an overwhelming desire to limit family size, Romanian couples have decreased their fertility below replacement level, mostly through the use of abortion.

Overall, the TFR decreased by 35 percent and the TIAR doubled. The extremely high rate of abortion appears to be the principal determinant of the decline in fertility because no significant changes have occurred in the prevalence of contraceptive use or contraceptive mix. The increased use of abortion as the primary means of fertility regulation has also had an escalating effect on the pregnancy rate, mostly on mistimed and unwanted pregnancies, because it hastens the woman's return to the risk of conception. Increased use of abortion may also explain the slight increase seen in the use of withdrawal and the calendar methods, which would not be expected to be affected by the policy change. Because a pregnancy resulting in abortion returns a woman to risk of conception more quickly than does a pregnancy carried to term, it also increases the time during which she has the opportunity to use contraception. Because women have continued to use traditional methods, which have very high failure rates, more unintended pregnancies occur, and consequently, more abortions take place.

The low prevalence of more effective contraceptives contrasts with a high level of family-planning awareness; almost all women who were currently in union declared that they had heard about at least one modern method, and 85 percent knew where to get the procedure or product. Unfortunately, an awareness of the source was not enough to change contraceptive behaviors, especially when suspicion and misconceptions about modern methods are not uncommon among both the public and the health care professionals.

The effect of switching from the use of illegal, unsafe abortions to legal abortions is dramatically reflected in the decline of the maternal mortality ratio (MMR). After many years of high rates of maternal mortality, more than 85 percent abortion related, the MMR decreased between 1989 and 1992 from 170 to 60 per 100,000 live births, a decrease entirely due to the abrupt decline in the abortion-related deaths (Serbanescu and Morris 1995). Even with this decline, induced abortion is still associated with a relatively high risk of death, mainly because of the continuing use of unsafe abortions. Because the use of illegal abortion was a routine for many women in the past and because nonmedical abortion providers might be more accessible, more affordable, or more familiar, the practice of illegal abortion is likely to continue, especially among women who seek abortion beyond the legal gestational limit of twelve weeks.

In a society that favors a small family size and that has historically relied on traditional family-planning methods and induced abortion to control fertility, reversing the restrictive policy on abortion and modern contraception has resulted in an increase in abortion rates and a decline in fertility but no significant increase in modern contraceptive use throughout all socioeconomic subgroups. The rational approach to reduce abortion and achieve family size preferences is to promote and provide contraceptive services to prevent unintended pregnancies.

Limited sex and contraceptive education, mistrust and misinformation about modern methods, lack of adequately trained providers, shortage or uneven distribution of contraceptive supplies, and in some instances legal constraints are major reasons for the continued high rates of unintended pregnancy. Sex education was removed from the school curriculum in the early 1980s and contraceptive counseling was forbidden; the few efforts that have been made to introduce sex and contraceptive education in the secondary schools' curriculum have been constrained by the resistance of both teachers and parents and the lack of adequate training for teachers.

Only 4 percent of the women said that they first heard about contraception from their mother, and less than 3 percent cited a teacher when asked this question in the survey. Overall, the major source of information about any contraceptive method was a friend or acquaintance (45 percent), followed by mass media (19 percent) and health care providers (10 percent). Even though one in five women mentioned mass media, since 1990, when uncensored publications have multiplied, mass media have played a minor role in contraceptive educational efforts. This minor role is due to financial constraints, little interest in health issues relative to the freedom to pursue political and economic topics for the first time, and lack of specialists able to educate the public about family planning in nontechnical terms.

Postabortion counseling is virtually unknown, and prenatal services, though highly attended (94 percent), do not address postpartum contraceptive needs. Although an increasing number of physicians and nurses are involved in family planning activities in addition to their other tasks, recent Ministry of Health regulations (Ministerul Sanatatii 1994) reduced the availability of providers by requiring six months of continuous training in order to obtain "family planning competency." At the present time, only gynecologists may "officially" prescribe contraceptives and insert IUDs. Unfortunately, their contraceptive counseling skills are considerably prejudiced by limited time and motivation. Even when there is a high level of awareness for some methods (e.g., condom, pill, IUD), their use is hampered by mistrust and misconceptions that are sometimes nourished by the medical community because of their lack of experience in family planning, limited access to available scientific literature, or the fear of losing income often associated with performing induced abortion (Hord et al. 1991).

The availability of modern contraceptive methods continues to be an issue of great concern. Newly opened family-planning clinics have very few, if any, contraceptive supplies, and their main source is international donors. Although large quantities of contraceptive supplies (condoms, IUDs, pills, and barrier devices) have been imported by the Ministry of Health, these commodities are exclusively distributed through the central state pharmaceutical system, and family-planning providers are often unaware of their existence. The absence of contraceptive logistics and managerial skills further contributes to shortages and uneven distribution of these supplies.

Permanent methods of contraception are not promoted, and legal provisions to support voluntary sterilization are absent. Previous legislation, which allowed tubal occlusion only for women with five or more children, for women older than forty-five years of age, or for very limited medical reasons, has yet to be modified. The survey shows that of the 1.4 percent of women in union who reported tubal ligation as their method of contraception, only one in six had their procedures performed since the change in government policy in December 1989. Less than 4 percent of fecund women in union who did not want any more children expressed interest in surgical contraception. The lack of interest in tubal ligation was also documented by other studies (Johnson, Horga, and Androbache 1993; Rochat 1991). Male sterilization is widely unknown, even among health professionals, and often is confused with castration.

For family-planning efforts to meet the needs of Romanian couples, better accessibility to modern contraceptives has to be ensured. A full range of quality contraceptive methods should be available to couples who want to space or limit their children. Active educational programs should be instituted for both the public and the health care providers. Information should also be made available on the health benefits of contraception (Peterson and Lee 1989). The education process should include men as well as women, and age-appropriate sex and contraceptive education should be initiated in schools. Policy makers and program managers should make an effort to decentralize the responsibility of providing services and should encourage the training of general practitioners, nurses and social workers as service providers or counselors. Because the most common reason for using contraception and abortion is to have no more children, permanent methods of contraception should be promoted.

METHODOLOGIC APPENDIX

Estimates of Induced Abortion

Before examining fertility differentials by characteristics of women and trends over time, we compared the level of reporting of pregnancy outcomes in the survey with national counts provided by official statistics (Comisia Nationala Pentru Statistica 1993b). This step was essential not only for analyzing fertility but also for interpreting contraceptive failure rates that depend on complete reporting of pregnancies (Jones and Forrest 1992). Expansion factors based on the sampling fraction for each survey domain were used to convert the survey results into national-level estimates in order to make comparisons with the external data.

Whereas in 1988–89 the number of abortions reported in both the survey and in official statistics is almost identical, the survey estimates are lower for 1990–91 but slightly higher for 1992 and the first half of 1993 (Serbanescu and Morris 1995). The decline in official statistics after 1991 might be due to the recent opening of private clinics that perform abortions and do not report to the Ministry of Health. On the other hand, the level of reporting in the survey, for abortions occurring in 1992 and 1993, may have become more complete as the negative implications of the previous illegality of abortion have faded to the past. Also, recall of more recent events has probably contributed to better response on abortions occurring in 1992 and 1993.

Overall, for 1990–92, it is estimated that 81 percent of abortions reported by official sources were also reported in the survey. This estimate compares with only 35 percent reported in the 1988 National Survey of Family Growth in the United States (Jones and Forrest 1992). Reporting in the survey may actually be greater than 81 percent because some of the difference between abortion reporting in the survey and official statistics may be due to double counting of an unknown magnitude in the official statistics.[2] Because the official reporting system in Romania has some overreporting built into the system and has recently been subject to an unknown amount of underreporting, we did not attempt to adjust the survey estimates.

NOTES

1. This time frame was chosen because any woman with a live birth due or occurring after May 1990 would have been eligible for a first-trimester abortion after the change in legislation on December 26, 1989.

2. In Romania, health care services are provided through predominantly state-subsidized "neighborhood type" clinics, and services are generally free of charge if accessed through the proper administrative steps and guidelines. If patients want to bypass the neighborhood clinic or the referral process, health care is not free and can be very expensive. Abortion, however, is not subject to these regulations and can be obtained in any hospital without referral, as an outpatient procedure at a standard cost equivalent to 5 percent of the average monthly salary. If, for any reason, postabortion care has to be extended overnight, no additional costs will be charged. Conversely, if any readmission for postabortion complications is necessary, proper referral is required, or the costs for hospitalization and treatment will be entirely supported by the patient. In order to avoid these high costs of readmission, some providers admit these cases as new abortions and charge only the standard cost. Such "readmissions" may therefore be recorded in official statistics as new abortions, and thus the abortion will be counted twice.

REFERENCES

Comisia Nationala Pentru Statistica. 1992. Recensamintul Populatiei si Locuintelor din 7 Ianuarie 1992. Rezultate Preliminare. Bucuresti, Romania.

———. 1993a. Population and Housing Census, 1992. Estimated general results from 3 percent sample (English language summary). Bucuresti, Romania.

———. 1993b. Principalele Fenomene Demografice in Anul 1992. Informatii Statistice Operative no.1. Bucuresti, Romania.

David, H. P. 1992. "Abortion in Europe, 1920–91: A Public Health Perspective." *Studies in Family Planning* 23 (1): 1.

Hord C., H. P. Henry, F. Donnay, and M. Wolf. 1991. "Reproductive Health in Romania: Reversing the Ceausescu Legacy." *Studies in Family Planning* 22 (4): 231.

Johnson, B. R., M. Horga, and L. Androbache. 1993. "Contraception and Abortion in Romania." *Lancet* 341 (April 3): 875–78.

Jones, E. F., and J. D. Forrest. 1992. "Underreporting of Abortion in Surveys of U.S. Women: 1976–1988." *Demography* 29 (1): 113.

Koonin, L. M., J. C. Smith, and M. Ramick. 1993. "Abortion Surveillance—United States, 1990." In Centers for Disease Control and Prevention Surveillance Summaries, December 17, MMWR 42 (SS-6): 29–58.

Ministerul Sanatatii. 1993. Buletin de Statistica Sanitara pe Anul 1992. Centrul de Calcul si Statistica Sanitara, Bucuresti, Romania.

———. 1994. *Nota Metodologica* no. 16166/March 21.

Nachtwey, Y. 1990. "Romania's Lost Children." *New York Times Magazine*, 29.

Peterson, H. B., and N.C. Lee. 1989. "The Health Effects of Oral Contraceptive: Misperceptions, Controversies, and Continuing Good News." *Clinical Obstetrics and Gynecology* 32 (2): 339–55.

Rochat, R. 1991. "Women's Health, Family Planning, and Institutionalized Children in Romania." Unpublished report to USAID/Trust Through Health. Cambridge, Mass.: Harvard University.

Santow, G. 1993. "Coitus Interruptus in the Twentieth Century." *Population and Development Review* 19 (4): 767.

Serbanescu, F., and L. Morris. 1995. Reproductive Health Survey, Romania, 1993 Final Report. Bucharest and Atlanta: Institute for Mother and Child Care and Division of Reproductive Health, Centers for Disease Control and Prevention.

Stephenson, P. A., M. G. Wagner, M. Bedea, and F. Serbanescu. 1992. "The Public Health Consequences of Restricted Induced Abortion—Lessons from Romania." *American Journal of Public Health* 82 (10): 1328–31.

United Nations Population Fund. 1990. Report on Mission to Romania, March 5–15. New York: United Nations Population Fund.

Yip, R., et al. 1993. "Romania National Nutrition Survey, 1991." English language final report. Atlanta: Centers for Disease Control and Prevention.

Chapter 11

Determinants of Abortion and Contraceptive Behavior in Russia

Inge Hutter

For decades, Russian women who wanted to avoid having an unwanted child had almost no alternative to abortion (Willekens and Scherbov 1995). Women have, on average, five abortions in their lifetime, two of which are illegal (Popov, Visser, and Ketting 1993). Based on 1985–86 data, Russia appeared to have the highest total abortion rate of all republics of the former Union of Soviet Socialist Republics (USSR): 4.62 (Avdeev 1994). Based on 1989 data, an average of 3.97 abortions for Russian women was estimated (Blayo 1993, based on national statistics). Twenty abortions by the same woman have been reported (Manuilova 1991). On average, a woman has two abortions per live birth (Willekens and Scherbov 1995).

This chapter focuses on the determinants of abortion and contraceptive behavior in Russia. We look at the reproductive behavior of Russian women from what has been called a process-context approach (see Willekens 1990, 1992; de Bruijn 1992, 1993, 1996; Hutter 1996). That is, abortion and contraceptive behavior are seen as being shaped by individual perceptions and motivations that in turn are based on the information that individuals derive from the context in which they live. This context is hierarchical and multilevel and includes the historical (time), the ecological and economic (facilitating and constraining factors for behavior), the social context (institutions), and the cultural context (cultural meaning systems). In this chapter, we situate Russian abortion and contraceptive behavior within the political institutional context, which is described in a historical perspective. Subsequently, constraints and facilitating factors are described. We report the information provided by health institutions and the more specific Information Education and Communication (IEC) activities, and we describe the influence of the immediate social context.

ABORTION AND CONTRACEPTIVE BEHAVIOR

Russia has reached a level of total fertility well below replacement. Total fertility rate (TFR) declined from 2.63 in 1958–59 to 1.97 in 1969–70, 1.55 in 1992, and 1.2 in 2000. For decades, the main methods of regulating fertility were induced abortion and traditional contraceptive methods. Only recently have modern contraceptives started to play a role.

Abortion Behavior

The total number of abortions in Russia, as indicated by data[1] from the USSR Ministry of Health—only published officially since 1988 (Popov 1991)—reached a maximum of 5.4 million in 1965. The number decreased, stabilized around a level of 4.5 million, and from the late 1980s onward declined again. The 1992 figure indicated a total number of 3.2 million abortions (Avdeev, Blum, and Troiskaya 1994; Kulakov 1995). In rural areas, the number is assumed to be three to four times higher than in urban areas (Popov 1991).

Even these figures are believed to be underestimates. They do not include abortions performed in commercial clinics, so-called mini-abortions, or illegal abortions (Popov 1993). The number of illegal abortions[2] is difficult to assess. According to the official estimates by the USSR Ministry of Public Health (1989), the total number of abortions would increase by 13 percent if abortions performed outside the health care centers were to be included (cited by Popov 1991). Others, however, mention higher additional numbers of abortion. Khomassuridze (1989, 1990, cited by David 1992) has estimated the unrecorded private abortions as approaching double the official number; Popov (1991) has estimated an additional 50 to 70 percent, that is, an additional 10 to 11 million; whereas Remennick (1991) thinks an additional 30 to 40 percent would be more realistic. The arguments behind these estimates, however, are not provided. Illegal abortions are reported to be conducted especially in rural areas and among teenagers and unmarried women (Grebesheva 1992).

The underestimate of the number of abortions also can be due to the exclusion of so-called mini-abortions, that is, vacuum aspiration in the early weeks of pregnancy or menstrual regulation. Mini-abortions have been performed since the early 1980s but have only been officially accepted since 1988 (Khomassuridze 1993). In 1988, an estimated 10 to 11 percent of all induced abortions were performed by means of these mini-abortions (Khomassuridze 1993; Popov 1993). This estimate is also disputable. Remennick (1991), for example, thinks that the actual number is much higher, and Kulakov (1995) has estimated that about 25 percent of all unplanned pregnancies in Russia are interrupted by means of mini-abortions.

The observed decline in the number of abortions in recent years might be related to three factors. It might be a statistical trick—mentioned as such by

Avdeev (1994)—that is, it is due to the exclusion of mini-abortions. The decline might also be related to either the decreasing proportion of women in the reproductive ages due to a change in age structure or an increase in the use of modern contraceptives (Remennick 1991; Khomassuridze 1993; Avdeev 1994; Willekens and Scherbov 1994).

What are the characteristics of women who obtain an abortion? Official statistics and local surveys both show that most abortions are performed among older women. In 1991, 71 percent of all legal (and thus registered) abortions were performed among women aged twenty to thirty-four and 19 percent among women aged thirty-four and over. Only ten percent of all abortions were performed among teenagers (Remennick 1991; Popov 1994).[3] Recent years, however, show an increase in abortions among teenagers and primigravidae (Russian Family Planning Association 1994; Char'kova 1994; Kulakov 1995).

Most women (87 percent) attending an abortion clinic are married (Schneiderman and Kharkova 1988, cited by Remennick 1991). Abortion is commonly sought to stop childbearing (Khomassuridze 1993) or as a spacing method after the first pregnancy. In most young families, the birth of the first child is not postponed. For example, the average interval between marriage and the first birth, among women who married in 1970–74, was 1.38 years (Remennick 1991; Darsky 1992, 1993, cited by Willekens and Scherbov 1994). A study in St. Petersburg and Kaluga in 1989 indeed indicated that only 2 to 5 percent of the women had an abortion before their first child (Turner 1992; Char'kova 1994). Similarly, a survey in Ulyanovsk indicated that most first pregnancies (85 percent) resulted in live births, whereas second pregnancies were usually terminated by an abortion (Denisov 1994). Again, these figures might be biased because abortions of first pregnancies might be more likely to take place outside the recorded official statistics. Estimates by the Ministry of Public Health in 1989 indicated that 14 percent of all induced abortions among adolescents (<17 years) and 16 percent of all induced abortions among primigravidae were illegal (Popov 1991). Ryan (1987) thinks that the percentage of illegal abortions among abortions of first pregnancies is much higher: about 70 to 90 percent.

The health status of Russian women is affected by this high rate of abortion. In 1980, 35 percent of maternal mortality was due to abortions performed outside the hospital (Khomassuridze 1993). In 1989, this figure was still 31 percent (Popov 1993). An estimated 10 to 15 percent of all Russian married couples do have infertility problems (Kulakov 1995). A survey among female adolescents reported that almost 60 percent of the girls who had obtained an abortion experienced physical problems afterwards, while 9 percent of them complained about depression (Safonova 1991). Although the health effects of mini-abortions are less severe, problems such as hemorrhage and inflammatory complications still occur (Kulakov 1995). Several authors state that Russian women often do not know how hazardous induced abortions can be to their health.

Contraceptive Behavior

A couple of surveys on the use of contraceptives have been conducted in Russia. We shall refer to them briefly in order to indicate changes in relation to time. The results of the surveys should be interpreted with care, as the quality of data is not always clear. For example, we do not know who was included in the Moscow Sample Surveys in the period from the 1960s to the 1980s. The 1990 Goskomstat survey—the first large-scale survey on contraceptive use in the USSR—for example, has been reported as not being entirely representative as, according to some experts, exemplary citizens were overrepresented (Willekens and Scherbov 1994). The authors of the 1991 survey among 8,059 women living in the big cities in Russia and Ukraine (Lehert et al. 1992; Visser et al. 1993) also emphasized that their sample was not representative, as mainly young and highly educated women responded to the appeal in a monthly journal to participate. The survey in St. Petersburg and Kaluga, conducted in 1989 by the Demographic Unit of the State Committee (Turner 1992; Char'kova 1994), seems to be more representative. More than 4,000 women (a sample of 1,813 women in the age group of eighteen to forty-nine years, an additional sample of 1,428 women in an abortion clinic and 1,556 women in a maternity clinic after delivery) were interviewed about their reproductive history and their ideas about problems with contraceptives.

The Moscow Sample Survey was conducted in the period 1965–83. The 1965–66 survey indicated that the majority of all people using contraceptive methods relied on withdrawal and condoms. The 1978 figures reveal that besides withdrawal, the traditional methods of rhythm and douches were frequently applied. Modern methods such as intrauterine devices (IUDs), the diaphragm, and the pill were rarely used. In 1983, the picture was still the same, although the use of IUDs increased to 10 percent. The pill and diaphragm continued to play a minor role (Popov 1991).

Popov (1993) and Popov, Visser, and Ketting (1993) reviewed the surveys conducted in Moscow, Saratov, and Tartu in the period 1976–84 and the large-scale 1990 Goskomstat survey, with regard to knowledge of, attitude toward, and practical usage of modern contraceptives (KAP studies).The results of the first studies reflected the results of the Moscow Sample Surveys. The Goskomstat survey revealed that 57 percent of Russian women in the age group of fifteen to forty-nine years never used modern contraceptives. But only 6 percent appeared to be without any contraceptive knowledge.

The survey conducted in St. Petersburg and Kaluga in 1989 (Turner 1992; Char'kova 1994) revealed a contraceptive prevalence rate (CPR) of 68 percent. This figure is quite high. Only half of all these women, however, used modern contraceptives: mostly IUD (34 percent) and condoms (14 percent), whereas only 5 percent used the pill. Compared with the older women in the sample, younger women used the pill more frequently, but they preferred the rhythm method.

The older women in the sample preferred IUDs. Condoms were used by not more than 16 percent in any age group.

The 1991 survey by Lehert et al. (1992) and Visser et al. (1993) indicated a clear trend among younger women (<25 years) toward the use of modern contraceptives such as IUDs (35 percent) and the pill (10 percent). In general, among all respondents, the use of traditional methods still prevailed. The women most likely not to use modern contraceptives were aged fifteen to twenty, unmarried, living in rural areas, and not very educated. Although the authors emphasized that the sample was not representative (see previous remarks), they reported the results as being a positive general trend for the near future.

Sterilization is still rarely used. In 1992, 3 out of 1,000 women of reproductive age had a sterilization. Several authors expect this method to play a major role in the future (Popov 1994; Char'kova 1994). The 1985 Socio-Demographic Sample Survey, that is, the microcensus conducted among 5 percent of the population, for example, indicated that 50 percent of women aged 26 years and 90 percent of women aged thirty-seven did not intend to have any more children (Andreev and Darsky 1992; Willekens and Scherbov 1994).

Avdeev (1994) estimated a CPR for the entire USSR of 34.8 percent in 1979 and 31.4 percent in 1988. In 1979, traditional methods made up for more than 80 percent, whereas in 1988 their share had decreased to 40 percent. IUD increased to more than 40 percent, whereas the other 20 percent was made up by an increase in pill and condom usage (Avdeev 1994, 144).

THE HISTORICAL, POLITICAL, AND SOCIAL CONTEXT

In this section, we situate Russian abortion and contraceptive behavior within its political institutional context, which is described in a historical perspective. In addition, we describe the information provided by health institutions, the IEC activities, and the influence of the immediate social context.

Political Institutions in Historical Perspective

People typically act on (incomplete) information that is situated in a hierarchical multilevel context. In the case of abortion and contraceptive behavior of Russian women, information from political and governmental institutions—molded in laws, formal rules, and prohibitions—has played a major role. In order to understand the current situation, we view the political context in a historical perspective.

In Tsarist Russia, induced abortions were considered to be murder. Both the doctor and the woman involved could be imprisoned and lose their civil rights. Illegal abortions, however, are believed to have been common. After the 1917 revolution, abortion remained prohibited up to 1920. During this period, under the conditions of political disturbance, civil war, famine, and epidemics, even more illegal abortions are assumed to have been performed (Popov 1993; Stloukal 1993).

Abortions were legalized in 1920. The main aim was to decrease the number of induced abortions outside the hospitals or, as Stloukal (1993, 8) states, "Apparently, it was the feeling that legislative punishment was useless and only drove the abortion practices underground that prompted the government to adopt relevant measures." Punishment of either the physician or the woman involved was abolished. Abortions were conducted free of charge in Soviet hospitals by a doctor on the woman's request. From 1920 onward, induced abortion became the principal method of family planning. It has been estimated that in the 1920s one out of three pregnancies were terminated (Remennick 1991; Khomassuridze 1993; Popov 1993; Stloukal 1993; Avdeev 1994).

The legalization of abortion has been related to several societal background factors: to conditions of hunger, famine, poverty, illiteracy, and unemployment—leading to illegal abortions—but also to the upsurge of egalitarian ideas, the wide involvement of women in the labor market, communal facilities for children, and Marxist ideology (Remennick 1991; Lorimer 1946, cited by Stloukal 1993; Avdeev 1994).

Legalization was considered to be a temporary measure. Under the conditions of poverty, which were inherited from the past, abortion was allowed. But the increase in unwanted children and the decline in fertility were considered to be atypical of socialism. It was believed that improved socioeconomic conditions would lead to lower levels of abortion and higher birth rates. This doctrine hampered interest in modern contraception (Stloukal 1993; Avdeev 1994).

The phenomenon, however, was not temporary. The number of abortions continued to increase, and fertility declined further. In 1924, therefore, measures were taken to discourage women from having abortions: abortions were no longer performed free of charge. In the late 1920s and early 1930s, access to abortion was gradually restricted. For example, Communist Party members were denied access to legal abortion, abortions of first pregnancies were forbidden, abortion was allowed only in the first three months of pregnancy, a minimum of six months was required between two operations, and curettage without anesthesia was prescribed (Avdeev 1989, cited by Stloukal 1993).

Abortions were forbidden altogether in 1936. The legalization in 1920 was justified as a measure related to the social chaos of that time. The 1936 law was introduced with the argument of protecting women's health but, in reality, it was related to Stalin's policy to increase the Soviet population for the labor force and the army (Khomassuridze 1993; Popov 1993; Stloukal 1993; Avdeev 1994; Ruevekamp 1994). Besides the prohibition of abortion, all activities involving spreading the use of contraceptive methods were stopped. Pronatalist measures, like family allowances, taxes for couples without children, and special assistance during pregnancy, were taken. At the same time, as Stloukal (1993) reports, traditional sex roles within the family were reestablished, divorces were more difficult to get, and the concept of the glory of motherhood was (re)introduced. The number of legal abortions did indeed decline but, at the end of the 1930s, illegal abortions had replaced them (Popov 1993; Stloukal 1993; Khomassuridze 1993).

In the late 1940s and early 1950s, the number of illegal abortions rose significantly, accompanied by a rise in morbidity and mortality of young women. Due to this high morbidity and mortality and due to the process of de-Stalinization (after the death of Stalin in 1953), abortion was legalized again in 1955 (Popov 1993; Khomassuridze 1993). The new law aimed at "providing the opportunity for women to solve the question of their motherhood themselves, and also with the purpose of preventing any harm to health caused by abortion out of hospital" (Popov 1993, 24). In addition, as Stloukal (1993) reports, the unequal sex structure of the Soviet population after World War II, making women work in places traditionally not meant for them, helped to create an environment in which abortion was again allowed.

From 1955 onward, the number of abortions gradually increased, reaching a maximum of 5.4 million in 1965. But the legalization of abortion interfered with the pronatalist policy of the Soviet government (for a more detailed discussion of this pronatalist policy, see Stloukal 1993 and Boelens 1996). The unwanted child was still considered a temporary phenomenon. Only in the 1960s did it become clear that the number of abortions could be reduced only by the introduction of reliable methods of contraception (Avdeev 1994; Avdeev, Blum, and Troiskaya 1994; Kulakov 1995).

In the period 1956–70, attempts were indeed made to replace abortion with effective contraception. In 1974, however, the Soviet Ministry of Public Health issued a formal instruction in which the use of oral contraceptives was prohibited (which was in line with the pronatalist policy). This standpoint against the pill was reinforced in the mid-1980s, when the ministry issued a number of directives, one of them stating: "The long-term use of pills can have as a result a serious destruction of the main internal organs. It is prohibited to speak about pills in lectures on contraceptive use" (Popov, Visser, and Ketting 1993, 232). The pill kept this negative image for years—an image created by health authorities and the Soviet media—and was associated with moral deterioration and the sexual promiscuity of the West (Remennick 1991).

In the early 1980s, the Ministry of Public Health started to pay increased attention to contraception, in particular the manufacturing of IUDs and the importation of oral contraceptives. But the pronatalist policy continued—in 1981, for example, financial and social measures were taken to stimulate the birth of second and third children At the same time, to reduce the incidence of illegal abortions, the same ministry tried to broaden the legal grounds for abortion and to increase the accessibility of abortion services. In 1987, abortion up to twenty-nine weeks was permitted on juridical, genetic, vital, broad medical, and social grounds and, after authorization by a commission of local physicians, also on request (Popov 1993; Stloukal 1993; Avdeev 1994).

With regard to abortion among young women, the law on abortion in the 1980s stated that a girl under eighteen years could not have a legal abortion unless she was accompanied by her mother (Ryan 1987). Publications in the 1990s mention that underage girls should sign a letter to their parents about possible harmful effects of an abortion at a young age (Spanjer 1991; Popova 1992).

Concern over the high levels of abortion grew in the late 1980s, particularly with perestroika, and modern contraceptives received more attention. The proposed shift from abortion, for decades *the* method of Russian family planning, to contraceptives was clearly illustrated by the title of the conference in Tbilisi in October 1990, organized by the United Nations Population Fund (UNFPA), the World Health Organization (WHO), the International Planned Parenthood Federation (IPPF), and the Zhordian Institute of Human Reproduction: "From Abortion to Contraception."

Gradually, the need to use modern contraceptives was recognized. In January 1989, for example, the Soviet Family Health Association (SFHA) was founded. The organization aimed at the provision of family-planning services, with particular encouragement being given to the use of oral contraceptives and IUDs. Besides establishing family-planning centers, the SFHA aimed at organizing lectures, conducting research, assessing the demand for contraceptives, providing sex education for adolescents, providing training of medical personnel, and conducting clinical trials of new contraceptives, such as Norplant (Manuilova 1990). With the dissolution of the USSR, the regional sections of SFHA became national family-planning associations, and the SFHA became the international association named Family and Health (Taniguchi 1991).

In April 1990, President Gorbachev urged the Supreme Soviet to formulate and adopt a resolution on measures to improve both women's status and maternal and child health care. He made a special point of saying that family planning should be the most important aspect of caring for women's health. As a result, a special committee was established by the Supreme Soviet to deal with the problems of women's, family, and maternal and child health care.

In December 1991, with backing of the Russian government, the nongovernmental Russian Family Planning Association (RFPA) was established. The RFPA, accepted as a member of the IPPF in 1993, works together with governmental services and institutions and participates in the State Family Planning Program coordinated by the Russian Ministry of Health. The RFPA focuses on establishing other branches and special Youth Centers, on training experts, and on sexual education (Russian Family Planning Association 1994).

Sterilization, which had been prohibited since 1939, was legalized in 1990. It is true that women had the theoretical possibility of sterilization, but only in a local hospital near her residence and only after a lot of necessary conditions were met. Often even the necessary equipment was missing (Popov 1994). In 1993, a second version of the order on sterilization came out, limiting sterilization to a specific group of people. Sterilization (both female and male) is considered a method of family planning "only to be performed in response to a written declaration by the person concerned, who must be at least 35 years of age or have at least two children; however when there are medical indications, and subject to the person's consent, there are no criteria as regard to age or number of children" (Fluss 1994, 9).

Constraints and Facilitating Factors

Information from political institutions—molded in laws, formal rules, and prohibitions—shaped the constraining and facilitating factors for abortion and contraceptive behavior of Russian women. For example, the legalization of abortion in 1955 made abortions easy to obtain in state hospitals. In 1968, in the period when an attempt was made to replace abortion with effective contraceptives, IUDs were manufactured in huge quantities (Moffet 1987). The 1974 formal instruction of the Soviet Ministry of Public Health prohibited the use of oral contraceptives, thereby determining the availability of this specific contraceptive method. The increased attention of the same ministry for contraception in the early 1980s led to the manufacturing of IUDs and the importation of oral contraceptives.

Abortion services, thus, have been widely available. Abortions are conducted in state clinics for a small fee. Abortion is so widespread that more than three thousand gynecologists and obstetricians perform abortions full time, and more than twenty thousand women a day are absent from work because of an abortion (Leshkevitch 1990, cited by David 1992; Baranov and Baklayanov 1990, cited by Remennick 1991).

Most studies indicate that money is not a constraining factor for legal abortion behavior. Other factors, such as quality of care and services, however, do play a role. State hospitals do not provide anesthesia to all women: anesthesia is for the rich and for those who have the right connections (David 1992; Ruevekamp 1994). In addition, in state abortion clinics there are "assembly lines" of women, all of them wanting an abortion. As a result, women seek abortions outside the hospital, usually for a fee but with proper anesthesia (Remennick 1991; David 1992, cited by Pine 1993). Moreover, such abortions are less time-consuming—there is no waiting list—and women do not need a medical reason for absence from work. The costs have been estimated to be one-fourth to one-fifth of a woman's average monthly income (David 1992). Considering the current economic circumstances, money might nowadays be a constraining factor in access to what are called "illegal abortions," which are typically performed by physicians after work. Performing illegal abortions was and still is a lucrative addition to the normal salary of gynecologist (Ruevekamp 1994), and this might be a reason for low physician interest in encouraging the use of modern contraceptives (Pine 1993).

There have been (and still are) many constraints on contraceptive behavior. The surveys that were briefly reviewed in an earlier section indicated that one of the major reasons for the scant use of modern contraceptives was that the methods were not available. In the mid-1980s, contraceptives from the retail outlets met only 20 percent of the demand. In 1988, this situation had not really changed: official data indicated that the supplies met 25 percent of the demand. That is, 20 percent of the demand for oral contraceptives, 30 percent of the demand for IUDs, and 11 percent of the demand for condoms were met. The unmet need for family planning was thus very large. In 1990, the importation of pills increased sharply, but the supply still did not meet half of the demand. Shortage of hard currency is another constraint in buying contraceptives. Nowadays, for example, imported low-dose pills are sold at free-market prices (Remennick 1991; Komyssova 1992; Khomassuridze 1993; Avdeev 1994; Boelens 1996). Together with the dramatic downturn in the Russian economy, this often makes contraception prohibitively expensive.

Besides the availability and costs of modern contraceptives, the quality of those methods that were available was often low. In the 1980s, for example, oral contraceptives were imported from Eastern Europe, namely Hungary, the German Democratic Republic, Poland, and Bulgaria. Most of them were high-dose pills inducing many side effects. From the beginning of the 1990s, oral contraceptives were imported from Germany and the Netherlands (Moffet 1987; Spanjer 1991; Turner 1992; Popov 1993; Khomassuridze 1993; Avdeev 1994; Ruevekamp 1994).

Condoms have been produced locally, but official data indicate that the USSR produced only 11 percent of the demand. Locally made condoms are known to be of low quality: they leak and burst during use and are known to be very unpleasant in use as they are made of thick, dark rubber. Russian made condoms are called "galoshes" (rubber boots), and men are reported to refuse to wear them (Moffet 1987; Popov 1991; Spanjer 1991; Turner 1992; Ruevekamp 1994).

IUDs have been manufactured in the USSR since 1968. These locally made IUDs were rarely used due to their poor quality: they fitted badly or were inserted by poorly trained doctors. Once accepted, the rate of discontinuation (in a group aged eighteen to twenty-four) was about 25 percent. Due to the poor quality, the IUD factory closed down. From 1987 onwards, IUDs were imported from Yugoslavia and Finland (Manuilova 1990; Turner 1992; Khomassuridze 1993; Popov 1993; Avdeev 1994).

Most authors mention the lack of modern contraceptive methods (especially in rural areas) and the low quality of available methods as major reasons for the low level of contraceptive use and the high level of abortions. None of them, however, identifies this as the one-and-only reason. The traditional orientation of the health services, the absence of training of physicians and nurses, the lack of IEC activities, the lack of proper sex education, and the low involvement of men in reproductive decision making are other reasons mentioned. Moreover, factors related to the motivation of women themselves are mentioned: lack of knowledge of contraceptives, negative opinions on contraceptives, fear of health consequences, and the perception of abortion as a routine procedure (Manuilova 1990; Remennick 1991; Komyssova 1992; Grebesheva 1992; Visser, Bruyniks, and Remennick 1993; Visser, Remmenick, and Bruyniks 1993; Visser et al. 1993; Khomassuridze 1993; Popov, Visser, and Ketting 1993; Ruevekamp 1994).

Health Institutions

Information from political institutions has also determined the amount and type of information available in health institutions. For example, the 1974 formal instruction of the Soviet Ministry of Public Health and its reinforcement in the mid-1980s, emphasizing the negative health effects of oral contraceptives, made physicians in health institutions develop a negative attitude toward this particular method.

Few studies take the attitudes of physicians and other medical personnel into account. Most of them focus on attitudes toward modern contraceptives, often in relationship to abortion. Not much attention has been paid to attitudes toward abortion itself.

A survey among Russian physicians, mostly gynecologists and obstetricians, reveals that the majority (67 percent) rejected the reliance on induced abortion and preferred modern contraceptives (Visser, Remennick, and Bruyniks 1993). But this also means that more than 30 percent did not reject abortion as a method to terminate unwanted pregnancies. Unfortunately, no in-depth information about this specific group and their ideas is available. Ruevekamp (1994), for example, reported that some doctors claim that "an abortion a year" would be good for the female constitution. Of all physicians, 38 percent (particularly physicians working in rural areas) thought that some women would prefer to have an abortion rather than use contraceptives. Abortion was perceived by 73 percent of the physicians as being hazardous to health (Visser, Remennick, and Bruyniks 1993; Visser, Bruyniks, and Remennick 1993).

The physicians most frequently prescribed IUDs and oral contraceptives to their patients. They thought these two methods to be most suitable. But, as the authors concluded, they tended to overestimate several risks and benefits of the two methods. In addition, they showed a lack of knowledge and some misperceptions. Only about half of them knew how the pill worked. Moreover, even vaginal douches (by 49 percent) and abstinence (44 percent) were seen as being unsafe. Based on these results, the authors stress the importance of training physicians in the field of contraceptive methods (Visser, Remennick, and Bruyniks 1993; Visser, Bruyniks, and Remennick 1993).

Information Education Communication Activities

Institutions may provide for specific information on reproductive health, that is, health education or IEC activities, which is deliberately provided to people in order to change (or reinforce) their attitudes and behavior. Here, we focus on information about reproduction, family planning, and sexual education.

Changes have taken place in Russian society, including those regarding sexual relationships. Several authors reported on the earlier conservative sexual attitudes, even called "Victorian" by some of them (Helgeson 1982; Boelens 1996). Nowadays, sexual relationships start at an earlier age. Sixty-five percent of the girls and eighty-five percent of the boys start sexual relationships before they are eighteen years old (Komyssova 1992). A survey in 1989 indicated that 30 percent of the respondents still disapprove of boys having sexual relationships before marriage (40 percent for girls). Respondents thought the present change to premarital sexual relationships to be a result of, among other things, ideological changes: the decline of morality in society, the lack of sexual education and knowledge about the consequences among youngsters, and the change to the idea that love is the same as sex. Young people, respondents felt, wanted to imitate the West, to show their independence, and to be more free (Bodrova and Mytil 1992). Kon (1992), however, argues that recent changes, such as the earlier sexual initiation, the acceptance of premarital sexuality, and cohabitation, are just universal generational changes that were not generated by glasnost but were only accelerated and made visible by it.

However, the need for information and sex education, especially among young people, is evident (Grebesheva 1992; Visser et al. 1993). Popova (1992, 12) concludes that despite the earlier age in sexual relationships "our children, teenagers and adults have little knowledge of their anatomy and physiology." In a public opinion survey in Russia in 1991, 87 percent of the youngsters said their parents had never talked to them about sexuality (Kon 1992).

Since the early 1930s, sexual education and sex research had been absolutely forbidden. In 1981, some schools in Moscow started with sexual education for children aged fifteen to sixteen. In 1983, a course called "The Ethics and Psychology of Family Life" was introduced in schools (Moffet 1987; Kon 1992). According to Komyssova (1992), however, this program has failed to increase students' knowledge, as most young people still use unreliable sources of information.

This actual information on contraceptives was, for a long time, only available in women's clinics. It was only in 1992 that a training program was started for social workers in middle and higher educational establishments (Grebesheva 1992).

Nowadays, the most important sources of information about reproductive health are the Ministry of Health, specifically the Russian Center for Family Planning, and the nongovernmental RFPA. Other nongovernmental organizations, such as the International Fund for the Protection of Mothers and Children, the Russian Contraception Society, the International Women's Center, and the Moscow Center for Forming Sexual Culture in Youth, play a minor role. In the rural areas, midwives are thought to be an important source of information (Popova 1992; Kulakov 1995).

The Immediate Social Context

The immediate social context, or microcontext, is assumed to play a crucial role in providing the information on which people base their decisions and behavior: "Most people are more inclined to gather information in their immediate environment rather than elsewhere and will sooner consult sources of information which are easily accessible" (Willekens 1992, 270). Very few studies report the influence of the immediate social context on abortion and contraceptive behavior of Russian women. These studies all focus on contraceptive use. Studies on the influence of significant others on abortion behavior have not been found.

In the studies by Turner (1992) and Char'kova (1994), women—in their contraceptive decision making—did not rely so much on information provided by clinics but rather on advice from friends and acquaintances. Similarly, in the studies by Lehert et al. (1992) and Visser et al. (1993), friends were an important source of information, especially among not very educated women (better educated women relied more on written information). Parents turned out to be irrelevant, although they were a little bit more important for women aged fifteen to twenty. Among these younger women, however, the peer group especially was an important source of information. The partner was not considered to be an important source: he was mentioned by only 1 percent.

More than half of the respondents, however, said that the partner was actively involved in the decision making. Most respondents also said that both partners were responsible for the prevention of pregnancy (Lehert et al. 1992). These results contrast with those from other studies (Knaus 1981, cited by Boelens 1996; Ruevekamp 1994), which conclude that most men still regard reproductive matters as a woman's affair. Gynecologists admit to never seeing couples coming together to the clinic. Men are not willing to use condoms, and (unmarried) women are afraid to be considered a prostitute if they take the responsibility. The involvement of men in reproductive matters, therefore, is badly needed (Ruevekamp 1994).

Women's Own Motivations

In this section, we study the attitudes of Russian women themselves to abortion and contraceptive behavior. What are the perceived consequences of abortion, and what are the perceived consequences of contraceptive behavior? And how do women weigh these consequences against each other? In other words, what are the attitudes of women themselves?

Very few studies report the reasons, as perceived by Russian women themselves, for induced abortion. At the end of the 1980s, the following reasons were mentioned for not wanting a child: inadequate living space, insufficient child care centers, and family difficulties (drinking husbands in particular). The financial burden ranked very low. Nowadays, given the economic circumstances, financial considerations might play a more important role. Although most young couples prefer to live independently, housing shortages still form an obstacle. In one study, only about 20 percent of the couples get an apartment at the time of marriage, whereas 25 percent of the marriage cohorts still lived with the parents, mostly the husband's, after eleven years (Volkov 1992, 1994, cited by Boelens 1996).

Other authors stated that induced abortion is just routine behavior (Komyssova 1992; Remennick 1991; Ruevekamp 1994). Remennick, for example, concludes that one of the reasons for induced abortion is the "socio-psychological tolerance of the population toward induced abortion, its perception as a routine medical procedure" and "induced abortion has been seen as a routine, although unpleasant, medical procedure, something like removing a tooth" (Remennick 1991, 841, 844).

In the interviews conducted by Ruevekamp, respondents relate abortion behavior to other living conditions: "If every other thing is also rotten, like queuing for food, working all day and having an uninterested and often drunken husband at home in the evening... abortion does not stand out as more horrible than other problems we have to live with" (Ruevekamp 1994, 22).

Do Russian women prefer to use contraceptives rather than have an abortion? The few surveys on this topic are not unanimous. Studies in the 1980s indicated that most women wanted to use contraceptives. Very few had a preference for abortion (Remennick 1991; Popov, Visser, and Ketting 1993). Interviews in maternity clinics among recent abortion acceptors in the 1980s, however, indicated that respondents believed that contraceptives were harmful to health (of either the husband or wife) and that these risks did outweigh the risks of induced abortion (Sannikov et al. 1987, cited by Remennick 1991). In the studies by Lehert et al. (1992) and Visser et al. (1993), women preferred the regular use of contraceptives to the termination of an unwanted pregnancy by induced abortion. The majority judged abortion to be more dangerous. Only 7 percent, mostly older women, thought that the regular use of contraceptives was more dangerous.

There are more surveys that deal with the perceived consequences of contraceptives. In the previously mentioned studies conducted in the 1980s, the major reasons for not using modern contraceptives were the unavailability of the methods and lack of information, whereas minor reasons were dangers to health, the unwillingness of the husband to use a contraceptive, and disappointment with previously used methods. The results also indicated that women perceived traditional methods as being more reliable, more convenient, and less hazardous to health than IUDs and the pill (Popov, Visser, and Ketting 1993; Visser et al. 1993). The fact that IUDs lacked reliability might be due to the high expulsion rate of the IUD type used, the Lippes Loop (Remennick 1991).

In the studies by Lehert et al. (1992) and Visser et al. (1993), some of the questions from earlier surveys were repeated. Some changes, reflecting the trend among youngsters toward the use of modern contraceptives, took place. The respondents, mostly younger, educated women living in big cities, preferred to use IUDs or the pill. At this time, the method perceived to be most reliable and the most convenient was the IUD. Still, 18 percent found traditional methods to be the most reliable and convenient. Moreover, condoms and traditional methods were considered to be least hazardous to health. The studies by Turner

(1992) and Char'kova (1994) reported a similar finding: only 2 percent of all women using modern contraceptives thought that the oral pill was not harmful. This negative attitude regarding the safety of the pill can still be found even among young Russian women who have migrated to Israel (Remennick et al. 1995).

DISCUSSION

In summary, the abortion and contraceptive behavior of individual Russian women has been shaped by the following factors: political and governmental institutions—their information molded in rules, laws, and prohibitions; legalized induced abortion; and discouraged use of contraceptives. As a consequence, abortion services became widely available, and abortions could be obtained for a small fee. To indicate the magnitude of the influence of political institutions on individual abortion behavior, we refer to Stloukal (1993, 22) who remarks: "Within the context of totalitarian socialism, the right to abortion was scarcely even an individual right, at least not in the Western sense."

Changes are taking place, though, and especially among younger people, a trend toward the use of modern contraceptives, such as IUDs and the pill, has been reported. This shift from abortion, for decades *the* method of family planning, to contraceptives is difficult. As Popov (1993, 25) states, there is "a general cultural and mental resistance of the entire society to make a shift away from 'post-hoc' family planning strategies to preventive ones."

There has also been a general lack of sex education and proper information about contraceptives, especially among youngsters. Nowadays, the Ministry of Health, specifically the Russian Center for Family Planning, and the non-governmental RFPA are new sources of information, developing IEC activities on family planning and sexual education.

All these contextual factors affected the motivation of individual Russian women. But to really understand the abortion behavior of Russian women, we need to go beyond Knowledge, Attitudes, and Practices (KAP) surveys and study abortion behavior as the outcome of a process of individual decisions and actions. We need information on the process of decision making (why and under what conditions do women decide to have an abortion), the individual's subjective representation of this decision process (what are perceived consequences of abortion, what are the considerations leading to women "keeping" a pregnancy, and what are the considerations leading to discontinuation; what is the perceived ease in undergoing an abortion or using contraceptives), and the influence of people in the immediate social context (who is involved in the decision to have an abortion or to use contraceptives). This requires the adoption of a micro-approach, that is, the application of small-scale qualitative research such as participant observation and in-depth interviews.

ACKNOWLEDGMENTS

This chapter has been made possible by a fellowship of the Royal Netherlands Academy of Arts and Sciences. I want to thank Frans Willekens and Peter Boelens of the Population Research Center, University of Groningen, for their useful comments on earlier versions of this chapter and the translation of Russian articles (Peter).

NOTES

1. Between 1929 and 1988, no official or representative data on methods of fertility regulation were published. Regarding the quality of official data after 1988, Popov states that they "leave much to be desired in the way of accuracy, reliability and completeness" (Popov 1991, 376).

2. The literature often reports on "illegal abortions." A clear definition, however, usually is not given. The term creates confusion because abortion in Russia is legal. Authors sometimes use it to refer to abortions performed outside the hospital. More often, however, authors (e.g., Popov) seem to refer to unregistered abortions (which can be performed inside as well as outside the hospital)—in other words, to abortions performed without an official notification and that Remennick (1991) calls semilegal abortions. In this paper we reproduce the concepts as applied by authors themselves.

3. Safonova (1991) reports a higher percentage of abortions being performed among women in the age group of fifteen to nineteen years, that is, 15 to 21 percent.

REFERENCES

Andreev, E. M., and L. E. Darsky. 1992. "Prospects of Russian Population in the Former USSR." Paper presented at the KNAW colloquium "The Population of the Former USSR in the 21st Century," organized by the Royal Netherlands Academy of Sciences and the Population Research Center, University of Groningen, September 29–October 2, Amsterdam.

Avdeev, A. 1994. "Contraception and Abortions: Trends in the USSR and Prospects for the 1990s." In *Demographic Trends and Patterns in the Soviet Union before 1991*, ed. W. Lutz, S. Scherbov, and A. Volkov, 131–46. London: Routledge.

Avdeev, A., A. Blum, and I. Troiskaya. 1994. "Histoire de la statistique de l'avortement en Russie et en URSS jusqu'en 1991" (History of Abortion Statistics in Russia and USSR until 1991). *Population* 49 (4–5): 903–33.

Blayo, C. 1993. "Le Role d l'avortement dans les pays d'Europe Centrale en Orientale." In *Proceedings of the International Population Conference, Montreal*, Vol. 1. Liège, Belgium: International Union for the Scientific Study of Population.

Bodrova, V., and A. Mytil. 1992. "L'opinion publique et l'education sexuelle en USSR." *Population* 47 (1): 204–11.

Boelens, P.L.R. 1996. "Fertility Trends and Patterns in Russia, Byelorussia and Ukraine." Working paper, Population Research Center, University of Groningen, the Netherlands.

Char'kova, T. L. 1994. "Problems of Fertility Regulation in Russia" (in Russian). *Rossiiskoe Zdravoochranenie* 2: 32–35.

David, P. 1992. "Abortion in Europe, 1920–91: A Public Health Perspective." *Studies in Family Planning* 23 (1): 1–22.

de Bruijn, B. J. 1992. "The Concept of Rationality in Social Sciences." Postdoctorale Onderzoekersopleiding Demographie paper no. 9. Amsterdam: University of Amsterdam.

———. 1993. "Interdisciplinary Backgrounds of Fertility Theory." Postdoctorale Onderzoekersopleiding Demographie paper no 16. Amsterdam: University of Amsterdam.

———. 1996. "Contribution to a Theory of Choice for Population Studies and Population Policy." Ph.D. diss., University of Groningen, the Netherlands.

Denisov, B. 1994. "The Second Birth Interval." Unpublished paper, Simbirsk Demographic Lab, Ulyanovsk Branch of Moscow University. Mimeographed.

Fluss, S. S. 1994. "Reproductive Health Legislation in Central and Eastern Europe: New Developments." *Entre Nous* 25 (May): 9–10.

Grebesheva, I. 1992. "Abortion and the Problems of Family Planning in Russia." *Planned Parenthood in Europe*, 21 (2): 8.

Helgeson, A. 1982. "Demographic Policy." In *Soviet Policy for the 1980s*, ed. A. Brown and M. Kaser, 118–45. London: Macmillan.

Hutter, I. 1996. "Induced Abortion and Contraceptive Use in Russia: State of the Art and Need for a Micro-Approach." Working paper 96–5, Population Research Center, University of Groningen, the Netherlands.

Khomassuridze, A. G. 1993. "Abortion and Contraception in the USSR." In *Progress Postponed: Abortion in Europe in the 1990s*, ed. K. Neumann, 78–91. London: International Planned Parenthood Federation.

Komyssova, N. 1992. "Family Planning in the Russian Federation." *Planned Parenthood in Europe* 21 (2): 7.

Kon, I. S. 1992. "Culture and Sexuality in the Former USSR." *Planned Parenthood in Europe* 21 (2): 2–4.

Kulakov, V. I. 1995. "Abortion and Infertility in Russia." *Planned Parenthood in Europe* 24 (2): 10–12.

Lehert, P., I. Pavlenko, L. Remennick, and A. Visser. 1992. "Contraception in the Former USSR: Recent Survey Results on Women's Behaviour and Attitudes." *Planned Parenthood in Europe* 21 (2): 9–11.

Manuilova, I. 1990. "Family Planning in the USSR. The Role of the Soviet Family and Health Association (SFHA)." *Planned Parenthood in Europe* 19 (2): 9–13.

———. 1991. "A Major Challenge." *Integration (Japanese Organization for International Cooperation in Family Planning)* 29 (September): 4–5.

Moffet, J. 1987. "Sex and Birth Control in the USSR." In *Soviet/East European Survey, 1985–1986*, ed. V. Mastny, 323–30. Durham, N.C.: Duke University Press.

Pine, R. N. 1993. "Achieving Public Health Objectives through Family Planning Services." *Reproductive Health Matters* 2 (November): 77–83.

Popov, A. A. 1991. "Family Planning and Induced Abortion in the USSR: Basic Health and Demographic Characteristics." *Studies in Family Planning* 22 (6): 368–77.

———. 1993. "A Short History of Abortion and Population Policy in Russia." *Planned Parenthood in Europe* 22 (2): 23–25.

———. 1994. "Sterilization in Post-Soviet Russia,"*Planned Parenthood of Europe* 23 (3): 25–26.

Popov, A. A., A. P. Visser, and E. Ketting. 1993. "Contraceptive Knowledge, Attitudes and Practice in Russia during the 1980s." *Studies in Family Planning* 24 (4): 227–35.

Popova, V. 1992. "Youth Work Initiatives in Moscow." *Planned Parenthood of Europe* 21 (2): 12.

Remennick, L. I. 1991. "Epidemiology and Determinants of Induced Abortion in the U.S.S.R." *Social Science and Medicine* 33 (7): 841–48.

Remennick, L. I., D. Amir, Y. Elimelech, and Y. Novikov. 1995. "Family Planning Practices and Attitudes among Former Soviet New Immigrant Women in Israel." *Social Science and Medicine* 41 (4):569–77.

Ruevekamp, D. 1994. "The Urgent Need for Quality Improvement in Russia." *Planned Parenthood Challenges* 2: 22–23.

Russian Family Planning Association. 1994. "FPA: Russian Family Planning Association (RFPA)." *Planned Parenthood in Europe* 23 (2): 35–36.

Ryan, M. 1987. "Illegal Abortions and the Soviet Health Service." *British Medical Journal* 294 (6569): 525–27.

Safonova, T. 1991. "Planirovanie semi i zdorove materi i rebenka v sovremennom obschchestve" (Family Planning and Maternal and Child Care in Present-Day Society). *Sovetskoe Zdravookhranenie* 9: 48–52.

Spanjer, J. M. 1991. "Eurothema's. Liefde, lust en lijden in Oost-Europa" (Eurothemes: Love, Lust and Suffering in Eastern Europe). *Nederlands Tijdschrift voor Geneeskunde* 135 (12): 528–30.

Stloukal, L. 1993. *The Politics of Population Policy: Abortion in the Soviet Union*. Working Papers in Demography no. 43. Canberra: The Australian National University.

Taniguchi, H. 1991. "The Agenda for Family Planning in the USSR." *Integration (Japanese Organization for International Cooperation in Family Planning)* 29 (September): 2–3.

Turner, R. 1992. "Russian Fertility is Low, despite Early Age at First Birth and Lack of Effective Contraceptive Methods." *Family Planning Perspectives* 24 (5): 236–37.

Visser, A. P., N. Bruyniks, and L. Remennick. 1993. "Family Planning in Russia: Experience and Attitudes of Gynaecologists." *Advances in Contraception* 9 (2): 93–104.

Visser, A. P., I. Pavlenko, L. Remennick, N. Bruyniks, and P. Lehert . 1993. "Contraceptive Practice and Attitudes in Former Soviet Women." *Advances in Contraception* 9 (1): 13–23.

Visser, A. P., L. Remennick, and N. Bruyniks. 1993. "Contraception in Russia: Attitude, Knowledge and Practice of Doctors." *Planned Parenthood in Europe* 22 (2): 26–29.

Willekens, F. J. 1990. *Beweging in de demografie* (Movement in Demography). Oratie. Rijksuniversiteit Groningen (University of Groningen, the Netherlands).

———. 1992. "Models of Man in Demography." In *Dynamics of Cohort and Generations Research,* ed. H. A. Becker, 253–81. Amsterdam: Thesis Publishers.

Willekens, F. J., and S. Scherbov. 1995. "Demographic Trends in Russia." In *Population and Family in the Low Countries,* ed. H. van der Brekel and F. Deven, 177–230. Norwell, Mass.: Kluwer Academic Press.

Chapter 12

Abortion Legislation in Mexico in the Face of a Changing Sociodemographic and Political Context

Susana Lerner and Guadalupe Salas

The purpose of this chapter is to illustrate the variety of legal measures in effect in the states composing Mexico, noting the grounds on which abortion is permitted and the sanctions that are established in the light of Mexico's sociodemographic context and the recent political debates held in the country. It represents an exploratory attempt to systematize some of the principal facts and arguments that form part of the most recent social and political context within which abortion legislation is framed.

After summarizing the major changes that have occurred in demographic and population policies over the last sixty years, an attempt is made in the second and third sections to estimate the incidence of abortion in the country and to describe the diversity of current laws. The fourth section discusses the major sociopolitical movements that have attempted to modify abortion laws, as well as some of the main positions, arguments and attitudes involved in the debate. The final section contains some preliminary thoughts showing that the analysis of the role of legislation is a complex and broad dimension, not only because of the large variety of social, economic, and political forces involved in it but also because of the contradictions at the legal and action levels.

This text addresses the prevailing situation in Mexico up to 1995 and does not include changes that have occurred since 2000 and modified the legal status in some states. Nevertheless, the conclusions are the same, as the main forces underlying and explaining these changes are the ones considered and referred in the political and social context analyzed.

The authors wish to express their gratitude to Susan Beth Kapilian for the translation of this chapter.

DEMOGRAPHIC CONTEXT AND POPULATION POLICIES RELATED TO ABORTION

In the past sixty years, Mexico's population dynamics have undergone a rapid transformation that led to two scenarios that have characterized the pattern of its demographic transition. The first period, from 1940 to 1970, a scenario of intense demographic expansion,[1] was marked by a drastic drop in mortality that began in the late 1930s and the maintenance of high levels of fertility. An average of more than six live births per woman, a great value placed on having a large family, a limited and selective use of modern contraceptive methods (it is estimated that around 18 percent of married women practiced some form of fertility control between 1960 and 1974), and a likely low incidence of voluntary abortions are, among other indicators, evidence of the legitimacy and prevalence of a social and cultural logic with a high preference for numerous offspring.

This demographic expansion was associated with major socioeconomic changes that included institutional programs and actions in the areas of education, health, and infrastructure within a context of social inequalities. During this period, the state took a pronatalist, laissez-faire position on fertility matters, This position was legally and politically grounded in the 1936 and 1947 population laws and led to the prohibition of the distribution of contraceptive methods and abortion, the latter penalized legally since 1871, a position that was maintained in the 1931 penal code and is still in effect.

The second period, from 1970, saw the beginning of a clear and massive decline in fertility that intensified toward the end of that decade and a scenario of "intense actions in the area of fertility regulation" as a result of the changes made to the Mexican Population Law in 1974 and the actions and will of the state to intervene directly in this sphere by implementing the Family Planning Program (FPP) in 1976. During this period, the practice of abortion has, however, continued to be prohibited.

Eighty percent of the rapid decrease in fertility during the first years of this period has been attributed to the extension of contraceptive practices (Bronfman, López, and Tuirán 1986; Juárez et al. 1989).[2] But changes in the preference for a smaller family (around three children), a high prevalence of use of modern contraceptive methods (63 percent in 1992), and an important increase in sterilization (43 percent in 1992, as opposed to 9 percent in 1976), coexist with a significant proportion (25 percent) of women who do not wish to get pregnant again but who do not use any contraceptive method to avoid it, a still considerable urban–rural gap both in terms of family size (fewer than two children) as well as contraceptive prevalence (45 percent in rural areas, as compared with 70 percent in urban zones in 1992), and virtually no lengthening of the first birth interval (Lerner and Quesnel 1994; Consejo Nacional de Población 1995).

Although the institutionalization of family-planning services and the public and social legitimization of the regulation of procreation have played a decisive role in changes affecting fertility, it is also undeniable that these programs were implemented at a time in which the necessary social, economic, and cultural conditions existed among the population for modifying their reproductive preferences and practices and for favoring the acceleration and mass spread of the process that perhaps would have occurred in a different way and at a different pace (Lerner and Quesnel 1994).

In this regard, through the modification of the Mexican Constitution involving the 1974 Population Law and the implementation of the various family-planning programs as of 1976, the principal aim of state intervention in the reproductive process—besides cutting back high fertility levels—has been to greatly reduce the dangers associated with high-risk pregnancies and to avoid unwanted pregnancies, thus decreasing hopefully the need for abortion.

It is stressed that population policies seek to contribute to a reduction in the incidence of abortion through family-planning programs, widening access to reproductive health services, and encouraging the provision of comprehensive sexual education programs (Consejo Nacional de Población 1995). In this regard, Mexico's population policies have maintained a position of dissociating abortion from the instruments designed by such policies for the purpose of cutting back population growth rates. Therefore, induced abortion is not viewed as a family planning method or as part of the actions geared at achieving decreases in fertility; neither is it included as part of the actions conducted by the state to protect maternal health during the gestation process, a basic principle that is also part of the Mexican national health program and associated policies.

A significant part of the public debates on the decriminalization[3] of abortion have positioned the discussion in the context of population policies, social and demographic concerns, and public health problems. This implies a consideration of the deficiencies and limitations related to reproductive technology; high levels of maternal deaths due to abortion practices; inadequate and insufficient conditions of maternal health services and the quality of such services; poor access of a vast part of the population to health and family-planning services; cultural differences in reproductive preferences and expectations; lack of knowledge about the consequences of sexual relations that still persists among wide sectors of the population; and, among other concerns, the limited scope and meaning of the fundamental right of men and women to determine the number and spacing of their children.

WHAT DO WE KNOW ABOUT THE INCIDENCE OF ABORTION?

Owing to the illegal and clandestine nature of abortion in Mexico, the moral and social pressures to which women are subjected, the conditions under which abortions are performed, and the conceptual and methodological problems inherent in the different techniques for registering this phenomenon, the information sources and estimates available on the incidence of induced abortions in Mexico are rather deficient and unreliable. Available estimates from different sources show extremely large variations:

- The country's major newspapers indicate an incidence of between 50,000 and six million during the 1976–82 period (Núñez and Palma 1990).
- Hospital admission records provide the lowest estimate: in 1985 slightly under 110,000 women were admitted for an abortion. This figure refers to intentional and spontaneous abortions and only to the population that resorts to health institutions in the case of complications (Núñez and Palma 1990).
- The most recent information obtained from fertility surveys, the aim of which is not to gain detailed, ad hoc knowledge about abortion, also indicates significant differences. The Mexican National Fertility and Health Survey (Dirección General de Planificación Familiar 1988) reveals that 14 percent of the total number of women of childbearing age have had at least one intentional or spontaneous abortion throughout their reproductive life, which means that nearly 2,700,000 women have had an abortion at one time or another. Of these, only 13 percent (350,000) admitted to having had an intentional abortion. Based on this data, an annual rate of 12.2 abortions per 1,000 women of childbearing age has been estimated for the year 1986, which in absolute numbers represents a total of almost 250,000 abortions. If only women who have ever experienced a pregnancy are taken into account, it is estimated that nearly a quarter of them (23 percent) have had at least one abortion, a figure that rises to 34 percent in the older age groups (forty-five to forty-nine years old). In addition, it is observed that women with a higher level of schooling tend to have abortions more frequently than those with a lower educational level, and a lower incidence is also found among those residing in rural areas (Dirección General de Planificación Familiar 1988).[4]
- On the other hand, the Mexican National Survey on Demographic Dynamics (Instituto Nacional de Estadística, Geografía e Informática 1992) shows a small decrease in the incidence of abortion or at least in reporting this phenomenon: around 20 percent of pregnant women of childbearing age had had an abortion. Among the youngest ones (fifteen to nineteen years old) the proportion is 10 percent; it rises to 45 percent among older women (forty-five to forty-nine years). Based on this source, the Mexican National Population Council estimates the number of annual abortions for the 1990–92 period at approximately 220,000 (Consejo Nacional de Población 1995).
- The findings of the Reproductive Health Survey (Núñez and Palma 1990) conducted in 1989 in four neighborhoods of the metropolitan area of Mexico City,[5] the main objective of which was to test a methodology for obtaining data on induced abortions, revealed that one out of every five women stated that they had had an abortion at some time in their reproductive life, an incidence that increases to one out of every three when ever pregnant women are considered.

These estimates provide a very broad idea of the possible magnitude of abortion. Its impact as a social and public health problem can be illustrated considering at least the following facts: although in 1980 abortion ranked tenth as a cause of maternal mortality, it rose to third place in 1990 (Langer 1994); maternal mortality related to abortion ranges from 60,000 to 80,000 deaths a year, and morbidity attributable to the same cause is estimated to be as high as 240,000 women with complications of differing types and importance (Karchmer 1994).

MEXICAN LEGISLATION IN THE AREA OF ABORTION

As in many other Latin American countries, the origin of Mexican legislation that was in effect during the colonial period until the middle of the nineteenth century can be found in Spanish legislation. Its restrictive concepts were in turn inherited from canon law and later from the Napoleonic Code. During this period, the Catholic Church enjoyed considerable prerogatives, among which was that of imposing sanctions for violations of the standards set by Catholicism. It wasn't until 1855, during Benito Juárez's presidency and due to his influence, that ecclesiastical jurisdiction was abolished, and in 1874 the Laws of Reform were established, proclaiming the separation of church and state. Under the rule of Maximilian of Hapsburg (1864–67), the Napoleonic Code was enforced in Mexico; this later led to the issuing of the Mexican Penal Code in 1871, which was in effect—with numerous modifications—from 1872 to 1931, when the current Penal Code was established. This code, in turn, has undergone various changes, but in the case of the laws on abortion, they have remained unchanged (Margadant 1982).

On the other hand, Mexico does not have a single series of federal legislative measures concerning abortion. On the contrary, a wide variation in laws can be observed at the state level[6] owing to the diversity of conditions under which abortion is penalized and the sanctions set for it. Before discussing current penal legislation, it seems relevant to consider at least two elements of the legal framework in which this legislation is set.

As a result of changes observed in the demographic and epidemiological transition and in population policies at the national level and due also to the international debate held on these topics, two important legal modifications were introduced. The first of these was made to the Mexican Constitution (fourth article) for the purpose of maintaining five principles: the right of all individuals to decide freely, responsibly, and on the basis of proper information, about the number and spacing of their children; the duty of parents to safeguard the right of their children to physical and mental health; the promotion of equal rights for men and women; the inclusion of women in economic development; and subsequently, in 1983, the right to health protection.

The second one refers to the Civil Code, where it is stipulated that legal status (as a subject of rights and obligations) is acknowledged for any individual who is born live and who remains alive for twenty-four hours or who remains alive for a shorter period but is brought, alive, before an official of the Registrar's Office. Notwithstanding the above, the "individual is protected by law as of the moment of his or her conception"; therefore, in the Penal Code, abortion is given the status of a punishable crime.

The concept of abortion is defined by the Penal Code of the Federal District as the "death of the product of conception at any time during pregnancy." According to this concept, "time of gestation" differs from that contained in medical and international definitions and, with the exception of the state of Tlaxcala, which establishes as a limit "before the moment at which the fetus becomes viable," the rest of the states—like the Federal District—fail to stipulate any time period. In this sense, it should be added that all legislation protects an "interest," and in the case of the crime of abortion, the interest being protected is life in gestation.

From the preceding paragraphs, it is relevant to underline the contradiction between the continuance of this abortion legislation and human reproductive rights included, more recently, in the Mexican Constitution. This discrepancy in the laws has led various specialists in this field to underline the illegal, contradictory, and unconstitutional nature of the existing norms regarding abortion (Pérez Duarte 1994).[7]

PROFILE OF PENAL LEGISLATION IN THE STATES OF MEXICO

Abortion legislation is included in the Penal Code of each of the states comprising the country.[8] The reference terms for analyzing the different legislative measures in effect at the state level are the concepts and assumptions of the legislation included in the Penal Code of the Federal District, given that the laws of most of the states use it as a guide either partially or fully. Table 12.1 shows the similarities and differences among the states according to types of abortion and the sanctions that are stipulated in each case and the average number of years of imprisonment, thus giving a full panorama of the diversity of Mexican abortion laws in force up to 1995.

Abortions that are consented to or self-induced refer to those practiced with the consent of the woman or those that are performed by the woman herself. The Penal Code of the Federal District stipulates a sanction of from one to three years imprisonment for the person who performs the abortion, regardless of the method employed (Table 12.1, column 1). In this case sixteen states follow the norm established in the Federal District and fifteen do not. Of the latter, four assign an average term of imprisonment that is shorter than that established for the Federal District, whereas eleven stipulate a longer period. In addition, in five states a fine is added to the sanction. The least severe state is Tlaxcala, with a sanction ranging from fifteen days to two months imprisonment, except when the abortion provider does so regularly for a living, in which case the punishment is from two to three years imprisonment. In contrast, the state of Baja California Sur has a maximum penalty of eight years, five more than in the Federal District.

Table 12.1

Comparison of Mexican State Abortion Laws According to Type of Abortion and Sanctions Set for Each (Average Number of Years' Imprisonment)

STATE	CONSENTED TO OR SELF-INDUCED ABORTION		(3) HONORIS CAUSA EXTENUATING CIRCUMSTANCES FOR THE WOMAN	(4) INVOLUNTARY ABORTION	(5) INVOLUNTARY ABORTION INVOLVING VIOLENCE	(6) ABORTION IN THE EXERCISE OF A RIGHT PREGNANCY BY RAPE	(7) ABORTION IN DEFENSE OF NECESSITY	(8) ABORTION DUE TO GENETIC OR CONGENITAL MALFORMATIONS	(9) ABORTION DUE TO A PREGNANCY BY ARTIFICIAL INSEMINATION
	(1) SANCTION PERSON INDUCING IT	(2) SANCTION THE WOMAN							
DISTRITO FEDERAL	*2.0*	*3.0*	*0.75*	*4.5*	*7.0*	*a*	*b*		
AGUASCALIENTES	=	=	=	=	=	=	=		
BAJA CALIFORNIA	3.0	1.25		5.5	=	=			
B. CALIFORNIA SUR	4.5	1.25				=	=		
CAMPECHE	=	=	2.0	=	=	=	=		
COAHUILA	3.5	3.5		=	6.0*	c	=	d	
COLIMA	=	=		5.5	8.0	e	=	d	f

The thirty-one states are compared with the Federal District. The sanction refers to the average number of years of imprisonment. When an asterisk (*) follows the number, this indicates that in addition, the law stipulates the payment of a fine. The equal sign (=) means that the sanction is equal to the one set in the Federal District. The blank spaces indicate that no law exists for that particular ground.

[a]Not sanctioned.

[b]Not sanctioned if the abortion is performed on the recommendation of the attending physician, with the judgment of another physician when possible, and when the delay does not endanger the life or health of the mother.

[c]Not sanctioned if the abortion is performed at a gestational age of ninety days or less.

[d]Not sanctioned when it is performed with the consent of the mother and father, when applicable, and if in the judgment of two physicians there is sufficient reason to suppose that the fetus has genetic or congenital malformations that would lead to the birth of a child with serious physical or mental impairments.

[e]Not sanctioned if the abortion is performed within the first three months of pregnancy and if the woman gives her consent or whoever should legally provide such consent does so.

[f]Not sanctioned if the abortion is performed within the first three months of pregnancy and if said pregnancy is the result of improper artificial insemination and if the woman gives her consent or whoever should legally provide such consent does so.

Table 12.1 *(continued)*

	(1)	(2)	(3)	(4)	(5)	(6)	(7)	(8)	(9)
CHIAPAS	=	2.0		=	=	c	=	g	
CHIHUAHUA	1.54	2.54		=	=	c	=		h
DURANGO	=	1.75		=	=	c	=	d	
GUANAJUATO	=	2.0*	1.25	6.0*		=			
GUERRERO	=	2.0	0 .66	5.5	8.0*	=		d	i
HIDALGO	3.0*	2.0	=	5.5		=	j		
JALISCO	=	2.0	0.66	=	5	=	=k		
MÉXICO	3.0*	2.0*	1.25	5.5*		=	=		
MICHOACÁN	3.0*	2.0*	1.25	5.5*		=	=k		
MORELOS	=	=	=	=	=	=	=		
NAYARIT	=*	2.0*	0.66	=*	=*	=	=k		
NUEVO LEÓN	=	0.75		=	7.5	=	=k		
OAXACA	3.5	=	1.25	5.5	8.0	l	=	m	
PUEBLA	=	=	=	=	=	=	=	m	
QUERÉTARO	=	2.0	0.66	5.5	8.0	=			
QUINTANA ROO	1.62*	1.04	1.25	5.5		=	=	n	
SAN LUIS POTOSÍ	=	0 .75		=	6.5	=	=k		
SINALOA	=	1.75		=	=	=	=o		
SONORA	3.5	3.5		3.5		=	=		

[g]Not sanctioned when it can be determined that the fetus is suffering from genetic or congenital malformations that necessarily lead to the birth of a child with serious physical or mental impairments, after a medical report is filed by the attending physician and the judgments of other physicians are heard when possible, and when the delay does not endanger the life or health of the mother.

[h]Not sanctioned when the pregnancy is the result of artificial insemination that was not desired or consented to by the woman, providing that the abortion is performed at a gestational age of no more than ninety days.

[i]Not sanctioned when the pregnancy is the result of improper artificial insemination, in which case the substantiation of the facts by the Ministerio Público will be sufficient for authorizing the abortion.

[j]Not sanctioned when the woman's health is seriously endangered. No other requirement is mentioned.

[k]It adds: "or serious injury to her health."

[l]Not sanctioned if the victim, by herself or by means of her legal representatives, decides to have an abortion, with medical intervention and within the three months following the time of the rape.

[m]Not sanctioned when the abortion is based on serious eugenic grounds in the judgment of two experts.

[n]Not sanctioned when one of the parents has a hereditary, chronic, contagious, or incurable disease that, in the judgment of the attending physician, presupposes the abnormal birth of the fetus.

[o]It adds: "and when the mother has consented to it."

Table 12.1 *(continued)*

TABASCO	=	=	=	=	=	=	=	
TAMAULIPAS	3.0	=	=	=	=	=	=k	
TLAXCALA	0 .10	0 .10		5.0	8.0	=	=k	
VERACRUZ	3.5*	3.5*		=*	6.0*	c	=	d
YUCATÁN	3.0	=	=	5.5	7.5	=	=	p
ZACATECAS	1.3	1.3	0.66	=	=	=	=	

[p]Not sanctioned when the abortion is based on serious eugenic grounds.
Source: Salas 1991.

As regards the sanction specified for the woman in this type of abortion (column 2), nineteen states impose an average sanction shorter than that set by the D.F. (three years), whereas in one of them this sanction is applied only when the woman has had a self-induced abortion (Durango). On the other hand, only three states set a longer period of imprisonment, two of them with an additional fine aside from the sanction, and nine states have sanctions equal to that of the Federal District. The states that have established the most severe sanctions are Coahuila and Veracruz, whereas Tlaxcala has set the least severe sanction.

It is interesting to observe that the Federal District stipulates a longer period of imprisonment for the woman who performs an abortion on herself or who consents to one than for the third party who performs it, except when the person is qualified to do so; this condition can also be observed in five states. The opposite is true of thirteen states, and the rest specify the same sanction for both parties involved.

An *honoris causa abortion* reflects, in effect, an extenuating circumstance affecting punishment and refers to certain characteristics of the pregnant woman, which in the case of the Federal District are as follows: a woman who is of ill repute and was able to conceal the fact that she was pregnant, which was the result of an illicit union. The differences observed among states (column 3) are that six states specify a longer term of imprisonment than the Federal District; another five establish a shorter term, one of which adds a fine to the prison sentence; seven impose the same penalty as the Federal District; and thirteen (the greatest number of states) do not explicitly concede any type of reduction in the sentence to the woman. With regard to extenuating circumstances, certain states add as a fourth condition that the abortion be performed within the first five months of gestation; some mention, in a generic fashion, the extenuating circumstance of "concealing her dishonor" (four states); two states consider a series of conditions and attributes of the woman who had an abortion; and just one state accepts as an extenuating circumstance the fact that the fetus has serious genetic or congenital malformations, that the pregnancy was the result of rape, and that the abortion was performed at a gestational age of no more than ninety days.

Involuntary abortions and *involuntary abortions involving violence* include the cases in which abortion is induced without the consent of the woman. These are the types of abortions for which the most severe penalties are established: from three to six years in prison and from five to eight years if physical or moral violence was involved. With this norm, the intention is to protect the rights of the woman: her freedom to make her own decisions and, related to this, her right to motherhood.

In the case of involuntary abortions (column 4), seventeen states establish a sentence equal to that of the Federal District and twelve set a longer one, whereas only one stipulates a lesser sentence. Aside from the sentence itself, five states add the payment of a fine. The maximum sanction is eight years imprisonment in eight states and the shortest sentence is one year, in the state of Sonora.

The most severe sanction is set for the person who induces the abortion using physical or moral violence (column 5), with the exception of seven states that do not include this sanction explicitly in their legislation, although four of them form part of the group of states that establish a very long sentence for involuntary abortions. The shortest prison term to be found is three years, in the states of Coahuila and Veracruz, and the longest one, ten years, is set in the state of Tlaxcala.

Culpable abortion and *abortion in the exercise of a right* are not punished, because the former is the result of imprudent or accidental acts committed by the woman and the latter is the consequence of criminal behavior in which the woman was a victim (rape and incest). Although culpable abortion is not punished in any of the states, in three of them (Chiapas, Nuevo León, and San Luis Potosí) the penal ordinances do not specifically include it.[9] In the case of abortion in the exercise of a right, all thirty-one states allow it, although five stipulate as a condition that it be performed at a gestational age of no more than ninety days. In other states, certain conditions are added such as: substantiation of the facts by the Ministerio Público (the office of the state attorney general), which authorizes that the abortion be performed (the state of Guerrero); the consent of the victim or that of her legal representatives; and that the abortion be performed by a physician within three months of the date on which the rape occurred (states of Oaxaca and Colima) (column 6).

An abortion in defense of necessity involves a situation in which the life of the pregnant woman is endangered in the opinion of the attending physician, and with the exception of the state of Quintana Roo, the judgment of a second physician is also required (column 7). In this case, the abortion is not punished and is justified as a means for protecting a more important interest: the health or life of the woman. Nevertheless, there are still three states that do not include abortions in defense of necessity in their laws or whose norms in this regard are unclear. Two other states also require that the Ministerio Público be notified (Baja California Sur) and that the mother give her consent (Sinaloa).

Regarding this type of abortion, eight states broaden the grounds for the same and include danger of grave injury to the woman's health. These states have the most progressive type of legislation in all of Mexico; for them, the protection of the woman's health is a greater interest than the life of the fetus.

Other causes of abortion: In this group are the following three types of abortion not included in the legislation of the Federal District but specified in that of certain states.

Abortion due to genetic or congenital malformations is allowed, without punishment, in only ten states, with variations in terms of the requirements for its application: the report of two physicians (in five states); the consent of both the mother and father (in four states); and, in only one state, the sole condition that one of the parents be suffering from a hereditary, chronic, contagious, and incurable disease that, in the judgment of the physician, will lead to an abnormal birth. In just one state, Yucatán, requirements are not included (column 8).

Abortion due to a pregnancy caused by artificial insemination is not punished in three states when the pregnancy is due to improper insemination or when such insemination was not consented to or desired by the woman in question. In two of these states, in order for the abortion to be unpunishable, it must be performed at a gestational age of no more than ninety days; in the third state, the Ministerio Público must substantiate the facts and authorize that the abortion be performed (column 9).[10]

Abortion due to financial motives is only included without punishment in the state of Yucatán and is subject to the condition that the pregnant woman have grave and justified economic motives and at least three children. It is interesting to add that in two states, this type of abortion was not punishable until the 1960s (Chihuahua and Chiapas).

Lastly, another sanction in addition to those mentioned previously is called *aggravating circumstances with regard to the qualification of the participant in the crime.* This involves individuals who are trained to perform abortions (medical and paramedical personnel) who are precisely the persons who would be expected to be in a position to perform the least risky abortions. The additional penalty consists of suspension from professional practice for a period of two to five years in the Federal District.

With the exception of two states, the rest sanction personnel with formal or empirical training. The differences between them show that four states establish a shorter term of suspension from professional practice than that stipulated for the Federal District. In four other states, a more drastic sanction is applied, involving permanent suspension from professional practice for persons who regularly perform abortions or for second offenders, and in another state (Baja California) a term of imprisonment of three to ten years is established, as well as suspension from professional practice for two to five years, and if the person is a second offender, permanent suspension is mandated.

The previous description illustrates the wide range of factors that come into play in the legal process involving either the women that resort to abortion, the providers of it, or the persons in charge of establishing the penalties. Nevertheless, it should be stressed that most women are not aware of the legal situation or at least under what circumstances abortion may be legal; in general, even when they request this right, it will be denied to them. In addition, this panorama is particularly relevant for the debate on the possibilities of legal changes, as it clearly evinces the ambiguity of circumstances, the permissiveness or severeness of the enforcement of the laws, and above all, the diverse obstacles or requirements that must be fulfilled to avoid or reduce the sanctions established by the different states.

In sum, as can be seen in Table 12.1, in all states the types of abortion that are not punishable are the same as those established in the Penal Code of the Federal District: in the case of rape, as a result of imprudent or accidental acts committed by the women, or when the life of the pregnant woman is endangered. In twenty-one states other significant changes introduced to decriminalize abortion are related to genetic or congenital malformations of the fetus (ten states), to grave injury to the woman's health (eight), and to pregnancy by artificial insemination (three). Most of the changes introduced in the legislation at the state level have taken place since the late 1970s.

THE SOCIOPOLITICAL CONTEXT OF ABORTION

We present below a summarized and simplified review of some of the main positions held and arguments wielded during the most recent period, from 1976 to 1995. This does not deny the fact that the current debate is part of an older, more generalized process that includes a wide range of different viewpoints and actions of the various groups being considered over time.

The Position of the Roman Catholic Church

The main opposition to changing the laws and policies related to abortion is found in the Catholic hierarchy.[11] The dominant position of the Catholic Church is characterized by permanent and categorical opposition to abortion as well as a growing and constant direct and indirect intervention in any attempt to modify abortion legislation. This position is shared by different conservative groups, which, in an organized manner, have managed to thwart the different initiatives undertaken by other religious and citizens groups.[12] Moreover, unlike its position concerning abortion, it is interesting to observe the position of this institution, and of the groups associated with it, regarding the actions undertaken by the state in the sphere of fertility control; although at the level of discourse, categorical opposition prevails, such opposition is silent, tolerant, and permissive at the level of family-planning actions. A similar situation that has arisen more recently is noted with regard to the use of condoms as a preventive measure against sexually transmitted diseases and acquired immune deficiency syndrome (AIDS).

In contrast, it appears that the *behavior* of the population in the realm of abortion is not influenced by the predominant doctrine, even though the majority of the population considers itself to be Catholic. On the contrary, the population puts certain procedures and behavior patterns into play in order to contradict sanctioned behaviors while at the same time maintaining its religious beliefs and practices.

A complex web of political, economic, and social factors explains the significant influence of the Church in blocking the modification of existing legislation. These include (1) the ability or lack of ability to negotiate and, especially, the political will of the state to achieve a more tolerant and permissive attitude by the Catholic Church with regard to the decriminalization of abortion and the respect for human rights guaranteed in the Mexican Constitution; (2) the social and political conditions and interests of the other groups that participate in these initiatives and the costs they are willing or not willing to pay that lead them to the need to create alliances with the Church; (3) the national and international religious interests and pressures forming part of the process;[13] and (4) the capacity for organized and agglutinant mobilization of the key sectors of the population that are in favor of decriminalizing abortion.

Political Actors and Social Movements

One of the means for gaining knowledge about the political debate on abortion has been by analyzing the way in which it has been dealt with in the press. We shall summarize some of the main findings of the detailed analysis conducted by Tarrés (1994) for the 1976–89 period and complemented with other sources. As this author rightly states, the relevance of this type of approach lies in considering the press as a means of dialogue between the ruling sectors and civil society, which helps identify the positions and arguments of the different actors and deduce their interrelationships. In this study, the author defines four key periods in terms of efforts geared at modifying abortion legislation.

1. The first (from late 1976 to 1979) was influenced by the modification of the Mexican Population Law, the implementation of a population policy and the family-planning programs, and the creation of the Mexican National Population Council. This was a crucial time owing to the drastic change that occurred in the government's position, as it meant direct interference and control by the state in the sphere of reproduction. In this period, the creation of the Interdisciplinary Group on Abortion, an initiative of the government, expressed the interest and intention of the government to deal with the issue of abortion and its legislation as a procedure for generating public policies in this regard.[14] This situation was accompanied by other initiatives—which were conflicting and which did not go beyond the discussion stage—presented in 1979 before the Chamber of Deputies by the Communist Party and the Partido de Acción Nacional (Party for National Action) (Leal 1994). In turn, this period coincided with the growing mobilization of feminist groups, whose basic demand was precisely the liberalization of abortion. In view of the change of government the country was

undergoing at that time, the presidential candidate did not deem it advisable to face the situation and decided to postpone his recommendations.

2. The second period (1980) occurred as part of the feminist movement and was supported by the leftist coalition, which presented the Draft of a Law on Voluntary Motherhood before the Chamber of Deputies. The rejection of this proposal arose from the chamber's majority party (the Partido Revolucionario Institucional, or PRI) which was opposed to all initiatives and alliances with the left, an attitude that was supported by the other conservative parties, which are, to a large extent, allied with the PRI. This situation coincided with the implementation of the 1977 political reforms that made it possible for opposition parties to be represented in the Chamber of Deputies. This fact was extremely significant for the left and led it to put off the discussion about abortion, a political cost they were not willing to pay. This period ended with the segmentation of feminist groups. At this time, the church also began a process of social mobilization and the creation of the pro-life movement.

3. The third period (1983) was especially significant because it began with a proposal by the president then in office to extend the grounds for unpunishable abortion contained in the 1931 Penal Code to include eugenic grounds, grave financial motives, and improper artificial insemination. The draft legislation was derived from the demands of wide sectors of the population. However, it was not successful owing to the adverse political climate generated mainly by the economic crisis, the elections, and the strengthening of the opposition as well as the lack of articulation of the feminist movement. This period, as was the case of the previous ones, clearly illustrated the importance of presidentialism in Mexico and the exercise of the political will of the president to promote or cancel reforms according to specific political interests. In addition, it demonstrated the logic of power on the part of the representatives of the political parties that paid more attention to critical situations involving oppositions or alliances, exhibiting their weak commitment to the question of abortion and the demands of society. This position (of rejection) was subordinated to the interests of the party.

4. The fourth period (1989), right in the middle of the campaign of Mexico's future president, was characterized by the closing of clandestine clinics where abortions were performed, with violent acts against women who had abortions and the medical and paramedical providers who worked there. This was accompanied by a large-scale mobilization of opposition to these actions from different sectors of society, including part of the political groups that had previously opposed abortion, while the church and conservative groups such as the pro-life movement maintained their position.

Since then, other legislative attempts to modify the contents of legislation have also been unsuccessful. Among these, the most important was the proposal—and approval—of reforms to the Penal Code of the state of Chiapas, intended to introduce, for the first time, the broadest types of considerations for decriminalizing abortion due to causes other than rape or risks to the health of the mother, such as those related to family planning with the agreement of both members of a couple and the case of unwed mothers. However, through very intense mobilization at the national as well as state levels, the top echelons of the Catholic clergy and conservative organizations made the Chiapas legislature suspend the implementation of the new code, and the articles of the previous one remained in effect (De la Barreda Solórzano 1994; Fontanive and Damián 1994).

As regards civil social movements, organized nongovernmental women's groups deserve special recognition. Their active, permanent, and continued work in both national and international forums has contributed significantly to maintaining and providing an incentive for public discussions on abortion and to promoting changes to the laws. Their participation in the decriminalization of abortion can be explained, to a large extent, by their more liberal ideological stance, their gender identity, and their greater commitment to social realities, but this does not imply that they indiscriminately accept the practice of abortion, as has been interpreted by conservative groups opposed to them.

The main arguments for decriminalization made by these groups are as follows: (1) the problem of social justice and public health represented by the practice of induced abortions; (2) the respect for the freedom of choice and decision that is contained in the current legal framework, that is, the defense of reproductive rights, which implies both the right to a wanted pregnancy and to a risk-free birth and the right to terminate an unwanted pregnancy; (3) the nonsubordination of these rights and of responsibility in the area of reproductive health to particular interests of political, religious, and other groups; (4) the reduction in the levels of maternal morbidity and mortality in order to avoid a greater number of orphans and the disintegration of the family; and (5) the need to provide suitable postabortion care so as to reduce the number of instances in which abortion is resorted to, because such care is lacking when abortion is performed clandestinely, and in view of the stigmatization to which women who decide to terminate a pregnancy are subjected. The disparities in and dissatisfaction with the quality of maternal child care and health care in general are also a central issue in their demands.

Their most recent attempts have been geared at achieving a proposal that encompasses the greatest possible consensus, without overlooking the opinions of some of the more conservative sectors, which sometimes coincide in considering the problem of social justice and the health risks involved in abortion (Mercado 1994). Lastly, as part of the social context of abortion, a very high priority is to include the opinions voiced by women, especially those who have had voluntary abortions.

DISCUSSION

Two main questions can be addressed. What is the overall panorama that can be observed in Mexico with regard to abortion legislation? What are some of the preliminary thoughts that arise from that panorama and from the sociopolitical context in which it is situated?

Of the thirty-two entities (thirty-one states and the Federal District) that make up the country, none has permissive or liberal legislation, that is, in none is no justification at all is required for obtaining an abortion. Similarly, no state has prohibitive laws that punish abortions performed under any circumstances. Mexico is among the countries that have mixed laws, that is, legislation indicating in what cases and under what conditions abortion is considered to be lawful. The heterogeneous situation observed reveals that only three states, accounting for 10 percent of the country's total population, have highly restrictive legislation, because they allow abortion only in the case of rape; in twenty-one states, representing 66 percent of the population, abortion is also permitted when the life of the woman is endangered. The rest—eight states representing 24 percent of the total population—also include cases in which the woman's health is impaired. In addition to these grounds, some states allow abortion under other circumstances, such as eugenic grounds (ten states), artificial insemination not authorized by the woman (three states), and grave financial conditions, providing that the woman have at least three children (one state). Moreover, in a good number of states (nineteen), extenuating circumstances of a moral nature are included (concealment of the pregnancy on the part of the woman, a good reputation, and in cases in which the pregnancy is the result of an illicit union).

Thus, in Mexico, we cannot speak of abortion legislation as if there were one single set of laws for the whole country; on the contrary, throughout the country we find practically the entire range of legal grounds that are considered for abortion according to the world review done by Tietze (1987), with the exception of intentional abortions freely requested by the woman.

This picture clearly indicates that in the formulation of legal measures, social, economic, and cultural considerations that lead women to choose to terminate their pregnancies are not taken into account, except in one state as mentioned previously. An attempt was made to delve into the possible associations among the current laws according to a grouping of types of abortion and some demographic and social indicators and other indicators of the strength of different political forces.

This exercise did not suggest a correlation among these characteristics and the conditions under which abortion is permitted and suggests that the role of legislation is complex. Even a superficial consideration of the situation in one of these states highlights the need and importance of following a qualitative approach. Thus, the state of Tlaxcala, according to some quantitative indicators, can be characterized by a medium degree of marginalization, with the predominance of conservative forces and relatively modern demographic behavior. At the same time, as can be seen in Table 12.1, Tlaxcala is the state with the shortest term of imprisonment for women who have an abortion, and these sentences can be commuted for low fines in the case of consensual induced abortions. Induced abortions are permitted in cases of rape and risk to the health and life of the woman and are severely punished when performed without her consent. Therefore, it is possible to characterize this state as one with a much less restrictive norm due to the changes introduced in its abortion laws and probably due to a liberal woman who was elected governor. It would seem that by means of her political will, changes in the laws were achieved, and although abortion has not been decriminalized, at least a more flexible legal norm has been attained.

With regard to the sanctions included in the laws, it is noted that in all cases in which abortion is not permitted, the laws call for imprisonment of the woman and the abortion provider(s). In no case are there sanctions for the man jointly responsible for the pregnancy and the decision to have an abortion, with the exception of situations involving rape and incest. This gender inequality is not surprising, although it *is* questionable because it is related to the unfair and unequal assignment of responsibilities for reproductive behavior.

In the case of consensual or induced abortions, criminal liability would seem to be an overt affront to the exercise of the human rights recognized throughout the world and to the individual guarantees included in the Mexican Constitution, especially reproductive rights and those related to health. In this regard, the laws only respect the right of the woman to desired motherhood when the abortion is performed without her consent (involuntary abortions and involuntary abortions involving violence) and when the pregnancy is the consequence of a criminal act such as rape (abortion in the exercise of a right). Similarly, in the latter case it is paradoxical and questionable that abortion is only allowed when the woman was not willing to engage in the sexual intercourse that resulted in the pregnancy, whereas in cases in which she consented to engaging in sexual relations and later clearly expressed her desire to terminate the pregnancy, such a decision is punished.

With regard to honoris causa abortions, although the extenuating circumstances tend to protect the woman who commits the crime, they implicitly express, and tend to encourage, false morals geared at protecting questionable ethical values, although they are defended by conservative groups.[15] Given such arguments, it would seem that women's possibilities of receiving sex education, having access to contraceptive methods, and in general exercising their right to free and responsible sexuality and reproduction are practically nonexistent.

It would appear that the greater severity of the sanction applied to providers, especially qualified personnel, is being justified as a means for exerting pressure that could dissuade them from resorting to performing induced abortions or at least encourage them to do so less frequently. But, paradoxically, it has turned out that this prohibition has contributed significantly to the performance of abortions not only clandestinely but also by untrained or insufficiently trained personnel or, in the absence of such personnel, by the woman herself, with very high economic, health, and social costs. This is an unforeseen adverse consequence of the legal measure.

Regarding the central issue of adolescent pregnancy and adolescents' desire to terminate it, not only is there no specific legislation suited to the needs of this group, but until very recently adolescents were also not provided with information or access to family-planning services that took their specific needs into account.

A perverse aspect that is not dealt with in this chapter but that is most significant is jurisprudence of abortion law. Although Mexico has restrictive, rather intolerant legislation, when it is applied, as is aptly demonstrated by some jurists, penal sanctions are imposed on very few women if we consider the large number of abortions that are performed in this country.[16]

In this sense, although the debate has centered mainly around the legal status of abortion, little is known about how it is performed, both from the viewpoint of its jurisdiction and from that of compliance on the part of the medical agents that take part in it. What is obvious is that the penalization of abortion has not managed to prevent abortions.

Finally, it is appropriate to include a general conclusion involving the need to frame an analysis of the problems related to abortion as an issue of social justice, of high risks to health, and of respect for human rights. It is also necessary to know more about the dynamics and features of this phenomenon, which are central issues for justifying, promoting, and effecting changes in existing abortion legislation. To this must be added the illegality and unconstitutionality of current abortion laws in Mexico that are inconsistent with the existing right to free decisions regarding reproduction. Nevertheless, as we have sought to show in this chapter, the political will of the rulers and their commitment to hearing and responding to the demands and needs of the population are what ultimately will make it possible to achieve changes in the laws. In order to achieve this goal, the participation of the population and of the different social forces—regardless of whether they are opposed or not to the decriminalization of abortion—is extremely important, and here the main focus should be the interests of society and not the particular concerns of certain groups.

NOTES

1. This demographic expansion involved a doubling of the annual population growth rate, which went from 1.7 percent in the 1930s to 3.4 percent between 1960 and 1970.

2. In 1969 the total fertility rate was estimated at 6.3 children per woman. In 1980 that figure had dropped to 4.6 and decreased further, reaching 3.4 in 1990 and 3.0 in 1995.

3. A legal term that may not necessarily imply complete legalization but rather the elimination of certain sanctions set for abortion.

4. The 1981 Rural Survey on Family Planning revealed that one out of every five women of childbearing age has had at least one abortion.

5. It must be noted that the findings of this survey are not comparable to the other surveys mentioned previously because they involve very different universes and objectives.

6. Mexico is a federal republic composed of thirty-one free and sovereign states, each with its own constitution and laws, and the Federal District.

7. Thus, for example, it is noted that if every individual has the right to decide freely, responsibly, and on the basis of proper information, about the number and spacing of his

or her children, that implies both not having them and having them beyond the limits—ideals or program goals—established in population policies geared at reaching particular levels of population growth. Clearly this right is not taken into account by abortion law, which denies the possibility of resorting freely to a voluntary abortion.

8. The analysis included in this section is a synthesis of a more extensive article written by one of the authors of this paper (Salas 1991). The information sources are the Penal Codes of each state and the official gazette of the Mexican government (*Diario Oficial*) revised up to 1995.

9. This may be due to the fact that it is already considered a condition of imputability in the chapter on crimes in general.

10. These states justify this type of abortion for the sake of modernity or reality, despite the fact that in Mexico the practice of artificial insemination is virtually nonexistent.

11. In this section, we shall refer only to the dominant position of the ecclesiastical hierarchy, which does not mean that we fail to recognize the plurality of positions held within this institution and the important initiatives and actions carried out by other religious groups such as Catholics for Free Choice with regard to the decriminalization of abortion.

12. A testimony of this fact is the recent campaign these groups conducted on the occasion of the past World Conference on Women, which tended to misinform the public and give inaccurate reports of the agreements reached at that conference that were signed by the Mexican Delegation. Both the delegation and the women's groups that participated in it responded to this campaign at length (Tuirán 1995).

13. In this regard, it is sufficient to consider the positions of the ecclesiastical authority and of conservative groups in the International Conference on Population and the World Conference on Women in Cairo.

14. This group acknowledged the severity of current legislation, which, instead of reducing the incidence of abortion, made women get them under unsanitary, unsafe, and clandestine conditions, leading to serious social and health problems on a national level.

15. An example of this is the erroneous accusation and false interpretations made by these groups on the occasion of the Beijing Conference, claiming that the Mexican delegation accepted abortion as a birth control method, sexual rights, and the decriminalization of abortion, which leads to an encouragement of "sexual promiscuity and acts against 'good manners, public morals, and traditional values upholding the family'" (Tuirán 1995, 12).

16. Of the estimated 250,000 induced abortions that were performed from 1988 to 1989, eight guilty sentences were passed in the first year, and two in the second (which implied imprisonment for the women, although they were able to leave prison by posting bail) (De la Barreda Solórzano 1991).

REFERENCES

Bronfman, M., E. López, and R. Tuirán.1986. "Práctica anticonceptiva y clases sociales en México: la experiencia reciente." *Estudios Demográficos y Urbanos* 1 (2): 165–203.

Consejo Nacional de Población. 1995. *Programa Nacional de Población 1995–2000.* Mexico City, D. F.: Consejo Nacional de Población.

De la Barreda Solórzano, L. 1991. *El delito del aborto.* Mexico City, D. F.: Grupo Editorial Miguel Angel Porrúa.

———. 1994. "Tres intentos abortados." In *Razones y pasiones en torno al aborto,* ed. A. Ortiz Ortega, 41–43. Mexico City, D. F.: Population Council, Mexico.

Dirección General de Planificación Familiar, Secretaria de Salubridad y Asistencia. 1988. *Encuesta Nacional de Fecundidad y Salud, ENFES 1987.* Mexico City.

Fontanive, A., and D. Damián. 1994. "Chiapas, una mirada hacia atrás." In *Razones y pasiones en torno al aborto,* ed. A. Ortiz Ortega, 133–38. Mexico City, D. F.: Population Council, Mexico.

Frejka, T., and L. Atkin. 1990. "The Role of Induced Abortion in the Fertility Transition in Latin America." Paper presented at the International Union for the Scientific Study of Population/Centro Latino Americano de Demografia/Centro de Estudios en Población Seminar on the Fertility Transition in Latin America, April 3–6, Buenos Aires.

Instituto Nacional de Estadística, Geografía e Informática. 1992. *Encuesta nacional sobre la dinámica demográfica ENADID 1992.* Aguascalientes, Mexico: Instituto Nacional de Estadistica.

Juárez, F., et al. 1989. *Les tendances récents de la fécondité au Mexique.* Paris: Centre de Recherche et de Documentation Sur l'Amérique Latine.

Karchmer K. S. 1994. "El riesgo de abortar: algo que se oculta." In *Razones y pasiones en torno al aborto,* ed. A. Ortiz Ortega, 163–65. Mexico City, D. F.: Population Council, Mexico.

Langer, A. 1994. "La mortalidad materna en México: la contribución del aborto inducido." In *Razones y pasiones en torno al aborto,* ed. A. Ortiz Ortega, 149–53. Mexico City, D. F.: Population Council, Mexico.

Leal, L. 1994. "Falta de voluntad política para tratar el aborto." In *Razones y pasiones en torno al aborto,* ed. A. Ortiz Ortega, 73–74. Mexico City, D. F.: Population Council, Mexico.

Lerner, S., and A. Quesnel. 1994. "Instituciones y reproducción. Hacia una interpretación del papel de las instituciones en la regulación de la fecundidad en México." In *La población en el desarrollo contemporáneo de México,* ed. F. Alba and G. Cabrera, 85–118. Mexico City, D. F.: El Colegio de México.

Margadant, Guillermo F. 1982. *Introducción a la historia del derecho mexicano.* Mexico City: Editorial Esfinge.

Mercado, P. 1994. "Sí se puede: una labor conjunta." In *Razones y pasiones en torno al aborto,* ed. A. Ortiz Ortega, 87–89. Mexico City, D. F.: Population Council, Mexico.

Núñez, L., and Palma, Y. 1990. "El aborto en cifras." *Demos,* No. 3, 31–32.

Ortiz Ortega, A. 1994. "Yo no queria abortar." In *Razones y pasiones en torno al aborto,* ed. A. Ortiz Ortega, 233–55. Mexico City, D. F.: Population Council, Mexico.

———., ed. 1994. *Razones y pasiones en torno al aborto.* Mexico City, D. F.: Population Council, Mexico.

Pérez Duarte, A. 1994. "El aborto en nuestra república." In *Razones y pasiones en torno al aborto,* ed. A. Ortiz Ortega, 34–40. Mexico City, D. F.: Population Council, Mexico.

Salas, G. 1991. "La legislación del aborto en la República Mexicana: un estudio comparativo." Paper presented at the Round Table on the Sociodemographic Aspects of Abortion in Mexico, Sociedad Mexicana de Demografía, Mexico City, D. F., Mexico.

Tarrés, M. L. 1994. "Qué publica la prensa nacional sobre el aborto?" In *Razones y pasiones en torno al aborto,* ed. A. Ortiz Ortega, 98–109. Mexico City, D. F.: Population Council, Mexico.

Tietze, C. 1987. *Informe mundial sobre el aborto.* Madrid: Ministerio de Cultura, Instituto de la Mujer.

Tuirán, R. 1995. *Mesa redonda. Cuarta Conferencia Mundial sobre la Mujer, Pekín 1995.* Mexico City, D. F.: Sociedad Mexicana de Demografía, Mexico.

Chapter 13

The Role of Pharmacists and Market Herb Vendors as Abortifacient Providers in Mexico City

Susan Pick, Martha Givaudan,
Marsela Alvarez Izazaga, and María Elena Collado

In Mexico in 1990 there were 22.5 million women of reproductive age facing a maternal mortality rate of 5.8 deaths per 10,000 births. Maternal mortality is a principal health problem in the country, much of which could be prevented through easier access to quality family-planning services and the implementation of sex education programs for children at an early age (Declaración de México para una maternidad sin riesgo 1995). In 1994 it was estimated that 6.7 million women between the ages of fifteen and forty-four needed access to family-planning services or needed to change their traditional birth control methods, such as rhythm and withdrawal, to more effective methods.

Of the estimated total pregnancies in 1990, 23 percent were unwanted births, and 17 percent ended in abortion. The number of abortions conducted each year in Mexico has reached an estimated 850,000 (López García 1993, 2), and complications from abortions make up the fourth largest cause of maternal mortality. It is estimated that some 42 percent of abortions result in complications. The most common methods for inducing abortions in the country are injections, herbs, or a combination of the two. In the specific case of Mexico City, between 75,000 and 100,000 women get abortions each year, and one out of every ten dies from the abortion.

As discussed in chapter 12, abortion in Mexico is illegal in most cases. Laws vary from state to state; the most liberal law, in the state of Yucatán, allows abortion for family size/socioeconomic reasons, and several states allow abortion for fetal defects. Most states, including Mexico City, prohibit abortion except when continuing the pregnancy would endanger the woman's life and when the pregnancy is the result of rape.

The Mexican law is doubly unrelated to reality—not only are illegal abortions not prosecuted, but it can also be very difficult for a woman to obtain an abortion even when she fits into one of the categories of noncriminal abortion. For example, until very recently, a woman who was pregnant as a result of rape had to wait until the rapist was convicted to have a legal abortion. Because a trial can take a year to complete, the woman would either have to have the child or obtain an illegal abortion. In states where the law is more liberal, both women and doctors are unlikely to be aware of the conditions under which abortion is legal. Even if a woman knows her rights, she may have trouble finding a doctor who will perform a legal abortion because the impression persists among doctors that abortion is an illegal practice that is performed only by disreputable practitioners.

More qualitative aspects of abortion in Mexico have remained largely unexplored. One area that demands study is how women abort. As in most countries with restrictive abortion laws, wealthy women have access to quality providers at clandestine clinics in Mexico or through travel to a country where the procedure is legal. However, it is less well understood how women from lower socioeconomic strata find an abortion provider.

Pharmacies have been identified as a principal source of general medical care for the poor in Latin America. Specifically, studies have shown that a large percentage of contraceptives and remedies for sexually transmitted diseases are obtained through pharmacies directly without a doctor's prescription (Lande and Blackburn 1989, 3). Pick de Weiss et al. (1988) found that 52 percent of adolescents using some form of contraceptive had obtained the method in a pharmacy. Two recent studies have shown that as many as 250,000 Brazilian women abort annually using the over-the-counter ulcer drug misoprostol (brand name Cytotec), which they purchase in pharmacies (Brooke 1993).

Market herb vendors are another common source of information and medication for reproductive health problems. A study of women who had entered the Hospital General de México for abortion complications showed that 36 percent had aborted using herbal remedies or teas and 22 percent had used pharmaceutical injections. These were the two methods of aborting that women cited most frequently (Rivera 1990, 5). According to a study of Mexican women who had recently had an abortion, 75 percent had attempted to self-induce an abortion using herbs, injections, or some combination of these methods before turning to someone else (either a doctor or another type of practitioner) to perform the abortion (Pick de Weiss and David 1990, 716).

In the absence of safe, legal abortion services in Mexico, the emergence of alternatives such as pharmaceutical or herbal abortifacients is logical if not inevitable. Because available information confirms that pharmacy workers and sellers of herbal methods are likely abortion method providers for Mexican women, IMIFAP (the Mexican Institute for Family and Population Research) conducted a study with the following goals:

1. To assess pharmacists' and herb vendors' knowledge and attitudes regarding abortion and contraceptives

2. To determine what information and medications are distributed to clients
3. To measure perceptions of and attitudes toward clients who request contraceptives and abortifacients

Although the project goals included gathering information about pharmacy workers and herb vendors' roles as contraceptive as well as abortifacient providers, this chapter concentrates on the results related to abortion.

METHODOLOGY

Owing to abortion's illegality, it is difficult to obtain accurate information from providers. Therefore, two different methods were used. The first (referred to in the text as the questionnaire), which was funded by the World Health Organization's Program for Research on Abortion in Mexico City, was a cross-sectional survey consisting of guided field interviews.

The study sample was chosen randomly from the total number of pharmacies and markets identified through a census and direct physical observation in three Mexico City "delegations" (districts). In the pharmacies and markets chosen, a total of 181 pharmacy workers and forty-one market herb vendors were interviewed.

The sample of pharmacy workers is representative for this group in Mexico City and, by extension, other large cities in Mexico. The sample of market herb vendors is not representative.

To obtain a more in-depth picture of pharmacists' and market herb vendors' interaction with clients, a second methodology was implemented independently by IMIFAP (referred to in the text as "role-playing visits"). Young, female interviewers visited each of the pharmacies and markets where the questionnaire had been applied and requested assistance from the same individual interviewed for the questionnaire according to a previously developed guide. They requested information about drugs or herbs that would provoke menstruation and then requested details about possible side effects, what to do if it did not work, and how much it would cost.

The group of subjects interviewed in pharmacies are described as "pharmacy workers" (PWs), and the group interviewed in markets as "market herb vendors" (MHVs). These two terms encompass a wide variety of experiences and qualifications. A pharmacy worker could be anyone from a professionally trained pharmacist to a clerk. Likewise, a market herb vendor could be someone who only sells the herbs or someone who is an herbalist, that is, who collects herbs and has greater knowledge of their properties.

RESULTS

Subjects' Knowledge Regarding Abortion

The subjects had a low level of general knowledge about abortion and pregnancy. One-third of pharmacy workers and over half of market herb vendors did not know that the safest time to induce an abortion is during the first trimester.

Almost equal percentages of pharmacy employees (62.8 percent) and herb vendors (64.3 percent) said that there are methods that will induce an abortion. However, the two groups mentioned different methods when asked to specify. Almost all pharmacy workers (88.7 percent) mentioned injections, 23.6 percent mentioned pills, and 4.7 percent mentioned herbs or surgical abortion (a method that would require surgical intervention such as curettage or suction). Among herb vendors, a large majority named herbs (94.1 percent), followed by injections and surgical abortion.

It is interesting that so few in either group mentioned surgical abortion as an option. It seems that this was due not to ignorance that such methods exist but to a tendency to mention methods accessible to the provider, because many subjects mentioned surgical methods during the role-playing visits as an option if the primary method of an injection or an herbal preparation did not work.

A substantial majority of the drugstore salespersons and herb vendors said they had obtained their knowledge regarding abortion through work experience or written materials. Fewer than 20 percent of either group had acquired the information in school or courses.

Information and Medications Given to Clients

Substantial majorities of both pharmacy workers (87.2 percent) and market herb vendors (76.9 percent) reported on the questionnaire that clients have asked them for help in provoking an abortion. When asked what methods clients have requested, a majority of pharmacy employees answered injectable drugs, and most herb vendors said their clients have asked for herbal preparations. Almost 20 percent of both groups said that clients ask for "whatever I provide," indicating that these individuals do not only supply what clients request but also take a more active role in actually prescribing abortifacients.

On the questionnaire, subjects were not directly asked whether they provide abortive methods to clients, owing to the issue's sensitivity. However, in the role-playing visits, 39.8 percent of PWs recommended some method for aborting, 42 percent recommended nothing, and 18.2 percent said that abortive methods do not exist. Among MHVs, 65.9 percent recommended a method, and 34.1 percent did not.

Out of the PWs who recommended a method, most recommended injections, followed by pills, curettage, and herbs. In the markets, all the vendors who recommended a method recommended herbs, and some subjects also recommended pills.

Medications Recommended in Pharmacies

The medication most prescribed by PWs was Metrigen, followed by Quinine, Benzoginestril, Lutoginestril, Prostigmine, Syntocinon, and Calgluquina. These medications are briefly described in the following section.

It is interesting that Cytotec was not mentioned by any of the pharmacists surveyed. In other countries, notably Brazil (Brooke 1993), this drug has become one of the most common methods used by women to abort illegally. This medication is widely available in Mexican pharmacies as an ulcer drug and was mentioned by several users to the authors but not by the pharmacists.

The most frequently prescribed medication was Metrigen, an injection containing estrogen and progesterone. Metrigen is normally used to restore the menstrual cycle in women who lack one of these hormones. Pharmaceutical literature indicates that Metrigen has a long list of contraindications, including that it can have adverse effects on blood pressure and circulation and should not be given to women with diabetes, hypertension, epilepsy, liver problems, or migraines (Diccionario de especialidades farmacedticas 1981). In addition, one source mentioned that if taken during the early stages of pregnancy, Metrigen can cause virilism in a female fetus (Dr. M. Rodriguez, personal communication 1990). Metrigen in any dose cannot cause an abortion. Lutoginestryl F contains the same formula as Metrigen. Many pharmacy workers prescribed Metrigen for both a pregnancy test and an abortifacient or for just a pregnancy test, though pharmaceutical literature states that it is not effective for either.

The second most commonly mentioned method was quinine, a medication primarily taken for malaria that can, however, provoke an abortion. According to one of our sources, the amount of quinine necessary to provoke an abortion could also cause death. The toxic side effects of quinine include disturbances in hearing and sight, nausea, vomiting, abdominal pain, delirium, and fainting spells (Diccionario de especialidades farmacedticas 1981, 799). Unlike Metrigen, quinine was prescribed consistently as an effective method for aborting. Calgluquina, which contains gluconate of quinine, is important to mention here. Only two PWs prescribed this medication, but it was mentioned by several others as highly effective, so effective that it was apparently taken off the market a few years ago. As one PW said, "There is no medicine for aborting. Before there was Calgluquina that was used for aborting, but the health authorities realized and they took it off the market." Apparently, Calgluquina was implicated in women's deaths as well. As one subject said, "Before, there was a medicine called Calgluquina but since it was very effective they discontinued it, because many women even bled to death."

Another hormonal injection, Benzoginestryl, was also prescribed as an abortifacient. This medication is used to correct irregular menstrual cycles and to treat frequent miscarriages. Side effects can include swelling of the breasts, edemas, and hemorrhages when the medication is stopped. It cannot cause abortions. Prostigmine is indicated for treating muscle spasms. It provokes smooth muscle activity and therefore can cause uterine contractions and potentially abortion. Side effects include intestinal blockage, slowing of the heart's action, nausea, and vomiting (Diccionario de especialidades farmacedticas 1981, 786; personal conversations).

Herbs Recommended in Markets

One third of MHVs gave the names of the abortive herbs they prescribed, whereas 35.9 percent did not provide names although they did prescribe herbs. The reasons most commonly given for not providing the names were a fear of punishment or to keep the composition of the herbal combination secret and protect the business.

Out of the individuals who prescribed herbs, six combined the herbal preparation with a medication, while the rest prescribed exclusively herbs. The medications prescribed in combination with herbs were not manufactured pharmaceuticals but drugs extracted from natural sources.

It was not practical to quantify how many subjects mentioned each type of herb because the numbers are too small, as many as ten or twelve herbs were often prescribed in combination, and we know too little about most of the herbs to reach a conclusion about the combination's effectiveness. Herbal remedies often consisted partially of common kitchen herbs such as basil, cloves, marjoram, and parsley, some of which apparently can have abortive or menstruation inducing properties in sufficient concentrations (Martínez 1991, 476, 464).

Two herbs—*zoapatle* (*Montanoa tomentosa*) and *ruda* (*Ruta graveolens;* in English, rue)—were more commonly mentioned and are known to have abortive properties. Therefore, more detailed information is offered regarding these two plants. Out of the thirteen MHVs who gave the names of the herbs or preparations they prescribed, over 50 percent prescribed both *zoapatle* and *ruda,* 23.1 percent prescribed *zoapatle* but not *ruda,* and the same number *ruda* but not *zoapatle.* In some of these cases, *ruda* and/or *zoapatle* were the only herbs prescribed; in others, they were combined with as many as nine or ten other herbs.

Zoapatle has been used both to cause abortions and to facilitate labor at least since the sixteenth century (Lozoya and Lozoya 1982, 193). The Mexican name for this herb was *cihuapatli,* "women's medicine," and it was widely enough used for colonial Spanish scholars to comment on it extensively. The exact way in which *zoapatle* works has not been determined. Apparently, it works like an oxytocin to cause contractions and also changes the hormonal balance in the uterus. In addition, the herb has been shown to have potential anti-implantive characteristics, which suggests that it could potentially work as a contraceptive as well as an abortifacient and labor inducer (Lozoya 1976, 164–65). This study's results demonstrate that it is still widely known and used in Mexico as an abortifacient. If excessive doses are given, hypertonicity of the uterus can occur.

Ruda is also an effective abortifacient according to Martínez (1991, 283). This same source mentions that excessive doses of the herb can cause gastroenteritis and even poisoning. In addition, very high doses can cause uterine hemorrhaging (Guerin et al. 1985, 28). We do not have information on the potential effects of combining *ruda* and *zoapatle,* which was the most common situation found in this study. We do not know whether the two herbs are seen to complement each other or if they are prescribed together to ensure that if one herb isn't effective for a certain woman, the other will be.

Knowledge of Potential Side Effects

When subjects were asked what side effects could be caused by the methods prescribed, the responses were not very detailed, and not one subject mentioned preexisting conditions that could contraindicate the medication or herbal preparations prescribed. Three-quarters of the PWs who mentioned side effects at all said that cramps and bleeding would be the principal side effects, and a few mentioned vomiting and dizziness. One PW mentioned death as a potential result of taking the medication prescribed (which, in this case, was Syntocinon). The responses to this question show a certain level of either ignorance or negligence among pharmacy workers regarding the side effects that could be caused by the medications they prescribe. This negligence is particularly glaring in the case of quinine. As mentioned earlier, the dose of quinine needed to cause an abortion can be fatal; however, not one of the pharmacy workers who prescribed quinine mentioned the possibility that it could cause the woman's death.

Among MHVs, little information was given regarding the side effects that the herbal preparations prescribed could cause. Out of the MHVs who mentioned side effects, 71.4 percent referred to bleeding and cramps and the rest to vomiting and dizziness or nervous ailments. Again, not one asked the client about preexisting conditions or mentioned more serious effects such as tetanization of the uterus, poisoning, or death, all of which can be caused by high doses of the herbs prescribed.

Prices of Pharmaceuticals and Herbs Prescribed

The majority of the medications prescribed by PWs cost between $.30 and $3.00 (all prices are presented in U.S. dollars). The price exceeded $3.00 in less than 20 percent of the cases. The prices given in markets for herbal preparations were considerably higher. Over half of the MHVs who gave a price for the herbs or herbal preparations that they recommended mentioned a price between $13.00 and $23.00. The substantial price differences between pharmaceuticals and herbal preparations is likely due to price controls on pharmaceuticals. Herbs are not subject to this kind of regulation. However, even herbs are much less expensive than surgical methods of abortion.

Subjects' Beliefs and Opinions Regarding Abortion

The interviewees were asked several questions about the church's role with regard to abortion. A majority of both MHVs and PWs said that a woman who aborts can be considered a "good Christian"; however, opinions were divided in both groups on whether women should consider the church's stance when deciding to abort and whether the church should continue to condemn the practice of abortion. In general, PWs saw the church's position as less relevant in the question of abortion than did the MHVs.

The two groups' opinions were more similar on the question of what role the government should play with regard to abortion. Approximately one out of every ten PWs and MHVs said that abortion should be legalized, and about 20 percent of PWs and 10 percent of MHVs said that abortion should be legal in some cases such as rape or danger to the mother's health.

A slightly more negative general attitude toward a woman who has an abortion was observed in herb vendors than in pharmacy workers. The most negative attitudes toward a woman who aborts were found among the MHVs and PWs with the least education.

It is important to note that the beliefs subjects expressed on the questionnaire were not necessarily consistent with their actions in a concrete situation (the role-playing visits). The belief that a woman who aborts is "bad" did not prevent either MHVs or PWs from prescribing an abortifacient. Almost half of PWs who had a negative image of a woman who aborts recommended an abortifacient during the role-playing visits, as did over 50 percent of MHVs.

It was difficult to classify the subjects' attitudes during the role-playing visit as "negative," "positive," or "neutral" because the reactions were so diverse and complex. Instead, we attempted to organize the responses into categories that reflected the dominant modes of interaction with clients. We identified five different types of interactions: popular, legal, emotional, instructional, and economic.

These different types of interactions show that PWs and MHVs take on a wide variety of functions with respect to abortion. Some see the transaction in principally commercial terms of buying and selling; others incorporate an emotional involvement that results in their assuming some responsibility for the problem in conjunction with the woman who is asking them for help.

More MHVs than PWs expressed "popular" beliefs, which is logical because herb vendors' work involves magical or nonscientific beliefs and practices, whereas pharmacy workers are more closely tied to mainstream medical practices. In addition, more MHVs than PWs were primarily concerned with the economic aspect of the transaction. This finding is supported by the high prices that MHVs charged, which leads one to believe that some MHVs make a healthy profit out of women's desperate situations.

The presence or lack of emotional involvement is an important element for a woman who faces an unwanted pregnancy in a society where abortion is a criminal act. The significance of this type of involvement stems from the fact that illegal abortion's damage to a woman's health is not limited to physical scars but also can include mental and emotional effects. Approximately the same proportion of PWs and MHVs showed emotional involvement.

DISCUSSION

Pharmacy workers and market herb vendors are providers of abortive (or pseudo-abortive) methods for their clients. Many of these individuals do not only provide the herbs and pharmaceuticals women request but also take an active role in recommending methods to their clients. In this sense, pharmacy workers and market herb vendors assume the role of a medical provider with regard to abortion; however, their knowledge is inadequate to support this role.

Fewer than 20 percent of either group had learned what they know about abortion and contraception in formal courses. Instead, the majority learned through their work experience. The implications of "learning through work experience" may be different for the two groups studied. Among pharmacy workers, the fact that their information regarding abortion comes from experience rather than formal courses seems to have resulted in a common pool of false knowledge shared by the majority of this group. On the other hand, the market herb vendors' knowledge of herbal abortive methods seemed more accurate overall (they prescribed herbs that could potentially cause an abortion, whereas the pharmacy workers prescribed injections that were clearly ineffective) in spite of this group's lower general level of formal education. Therefore, it seems that herb vendors' knowledge of abortive methods has little to do with formal education and should not be discounted merely because they learned through empirical experience.

Most medications recommended in pharmacies are not effective. Pharmacy workers seem to share a common pool of false knowledge, in which menstruation-inducing hormonal injections are confused with medications that could actually cause an abortion. Quinine was the one effective medication recommended by a significant number of pharmacy workers. However, this drug is also extremely toxic, and the dose required to induce an abortion can cause death.

On the other hand, the herbs recommended have the potential to be effective, although we do not have enough information to determine whether the exact preparations prescribed would have caused an abortion or to calculate what other effects these preparations could have.

The study also found that provider attitudes to abortion do not have a predictable impact on their actions. We found that a negative opinion about women who abort did not have any significant impact on whether subjects provided abortive methods. In fact, the herb vendors had more negative attitudes *and* were more likely to provide an abortifacient than pharmacy workers.

Three types of recommendations can be derived from this study: recommendations for policy changes, for training programs, and for further research. The principal policy recommendation stemming from this study is that abortion should be legalized and regulated so that women can receive safe, inexpensive abortions from qualified personnel in clinics and hospitals. We hope that the results presented here will help achieve abortion law reform.

Before legislative change takes place, training programs for women and providers could improve the situation. Women are going to abort no matter what the law says, as has been proven in all societies where abortion is illegal. Therefore, punishing providers of clandestine methods (no matter how incompetent) without providing a better option is not necessarily helpful. However, the following topics could be covered in an educational program, preferably as part of wider courses on reproductive health and family planning:

1. Courses could give some perspective on the abortion issue in Mexico by explaining the factors that can result in an unwanted pregnancy and confronting the beliefs that women who abort must be "bad" or "prostitutes," as well as providing statistics that show illegal abortion's extent in Mexico. This type of information could encourage pharmacy workers and market herb vendors to treat clients seeking abortions more humanely.
2. For pharmacy workers, courses could cover the ineffectiveness of Metrigen and other injections prescribed in this study as abortifacients and the dangers of prescribing quinine as an abortifacient due to its toxicity.
3. The case of the herb vendors is more difficult to address because we do not know how effective or how dangerous the herbal methods can be.
4. Finally, in training programs with both groups, the importance of family planning for clients who request abortifacients should be stressed as an attempt to prevent repeat abortions. Pharmacy workers and market herb vendors should learn to automatically discuss contraceptive methods with women who want to abort.

Regarding research, it would also be useful to expand this type of study to other kinds of abortion providers, including, if possible, those who perform surgical methods (curettage, catheter insertion, etc.).

It would also be useful to compare results from Mexico City with other parts of the country and of Latin America to attempt to determine why certain methods are common in specific countries or regions. Comparative studies might also provide some information about variations in mortality rates from illegal abortion.

REFERENCES

Brooke, J. 1993. "Ulcer Drug Tied to Numerous Abortions in Brazil." *New York Times.* May 19.

Declaración de México para una maternidad sin riesgo (1995). Cocoyoc, Morelos, Mexico.

Diccionario de especialidades farmacedticas. 1981. Cocoyoc, Mexico: Ediciones PLM.

Guerin, H. P., A. Guyot, S. Rastein, and P. Thiebaut. 1985. *Plantas Medicinales.* Barcelona: Ediciones Daimon.

Lande, R. E., and R. Blackburn. 1989. "Pharmacists and Family Planning." *Population Reports,* Series J, no. 37, 1–31.

López García, R. 1994. "El aborto como problema de salud pública." In *Maternidad sin riesgos en Mexico,* 85–90. Mexico City, D. F.: Comite Promoter por una Maternidad sin Riesgos en Mexico.

Lozoya, X., ed. 1976. *Estado actual del conocimiento en plantas medicinales mexicanas.* Mexico City, D.F.: Instituto Mexicano para el Estudio de las Plantas Medicinales.

Lozoya, X., and M. Lozoya. 1982. *Flora medicinal de México.* Mexico City, D.F.: Instituto Mexicano del Seguro Social.

Martínez, M. 1991. *Las plantas medicinales de México.* 6th ed. Mexico City, D. F.: Ediciones Botas.

Pick de Weiss, S., R. Díaz Loving, P. Andrade Palos, and L. Atkin. 1988. "Adolescents in Mexico City: A Psychosocial Study of Contraceptive Methods and Unintended Pregnancy." Internal report presented to the Pan American Health Organization.
Pick de Weiss, S. and H. David. 1990. "Illegal Abortion in Mexico: Client Perceptions." *American Journal of Public Health* 80 (6): 715–16.
Rivera, A. 1990. "Abortos inducidos en México." *Doblejornada* (July): 5.

Chapter 14

The Social Pressure to Abort

Chantal Blayo and Yves Blayo

The power to procreate is a power that women have rarely been allowed to exercise freely. All societies have traditionally obliged their womenfolk to use it for one purpose only, the production of as many children as possible. Numerous rules have been laid down to this end, rules that have been more or less tacit, more or less coercive, and more or less well accepted by women, depending on the country and the period. The proscriptions and constraints linked to this essential female function have shaped the status of women. These proscriptions included those of inducing a pregnancy termination. For a long period, legislation on abortion was concerned solely with outlawing the practice, exception only being made where a pregnancy endangered the life of the mother, which sometimes gave the right to a legal abortion.

Unrestricted access to induced abortion is a very recent possibility, available to women in almost all the industrialized countries and in a few other countries but that is still denied them in many other parts of the world (see chapters 1 and 2 for further details on the current legal situation). Legislative repression of abortion is, of course, accompanied by a multitude of social pressures against having access to abortion.

We have become used to thinking that societies are more likely to stigmatize women who have abortions than encourage them to abort. However, now that the survival of societies is no longer linked to a high level of fertility, it is reasonable to wonder if the social pressure against the use of abortion has not given way to a pressure in the opposite direction, a change that has occurred in parallel with the liberalization of the laws on abortion. In other words, has the proscription of abortion really been replaced by a freedom to abort or not abort, or have new pressures, this time favorable to abortion, emerged?

We attempt to reply to this question by distinguishing societies according to whether they perceive a need to limit the growth of their population, and according to whether they are favorable to abortion as a means of limitation of births. We then examine whether the pressure in favor of abortion, when it exists, is directed just at women whose families are considered already large enough or also at women whose pregnancy is judged to be undesirable for other reasons. Finally, we review the channels through which these social pressures operate.

PRESSURE LINKED TO THE MALTHUSIANISM OF THE WESTERN EUROPEAN COUNTRIES: THE EXAMPLE OF FRANCE

In recent years, fertility in most of the industrialized countries has reached very low levels that have often been attributed to individual factors. Yet the factors commonly invoked by couples in these countries (housing conditions, inadequate income, desire for leisure) to explain why they do not want another child were not perceived to be brakes on fertility in the past and are still not in other societies; if they are today, it is simply because the social and cultural environment has changed.

Societies have always established a norm of fertility compatible with their goals, and it is this norm that set limits to the choices of couples. Production and economic growth, and their corollary, the need for an ever greater consumption by individuals, are what characterize the contemporary industrial societies; the new values are those that make possible a constant increase in output, sales, and consumption (competitive spirit, individualism, ambition). Everything becomes a commodity, and new needs have to be created so as to produce new goods; there is a conflict, or even a contradiction, between satisfying these new needs and the existence of a family that is too large.

A new system of values has taken shape. Society now tolerates all forms of behavior likely to favor a lower fertility, even those that had formerly been disapproved of, such as female labor, abortion, informal union, and childbearing out of wedlock.

The reduced desire for children is thus the consequence of a social pressure that seeks to limit women's completed fertility to a number of children compatible with the new socially desirable forms of behavior. The rules that a social system imposes may be freely respected by individuals, to the point that they rationalize their attitudes a posteriori by choices that they believe are personal; but they are rules nonetheless, as can be proved by seeing if they are easy to break.

We wanted to verify that the social milieu exerts a real pressure on women's reproductive behavior. To this end, a survey was conducted in France to observe the women in the most marginal position (that is, those who deviated the most from the existing norms in this field), because it is always easier to measure the pressure on those who resist than on those who acquiesce; so the women questioned, in 1988, were those whose behavior is becoming rare, namely, women who had just given birth to a third or higher-order child, plus those whose behavior was starting to become common, women who had just had a child out of wedlock. These women with this kind of "marginal" behavior were questioned to see if they had been the target of social reprobation, and if so, what form it had taken.

Praise for the small-family model, rejection of large families, encouragement to use very effective means of contraception, and finally incitement to abort are all means by which pressure is applied to limit family size.

The women who had failed to respect the fertility norm were first asked if they had been criticized for this. For 91 percent of mothers with at least three children, at least one member of their family, professional or neighborhood or social networks had said to them at the time of the last birth: "I hope you're not going to have any more." A list was then drawn up of the phrases, unfavorable to their pregnancy, commonly heard by pregnant women, and these same women were then asked if they had been addressed to them. During their last pregnancy or pregnancies, 64 percent had heard: "You're mad" or "Do you realize, its madness the way things are today" or finally "You're mad to have another one," and 73 percent had been told: "Having them isn't everything, you've got to provide for them" or "You've got to be able to give them a good future." Much less frequent, and increasingly rare with increased birth order, were positive or congratulatory remarks: "That's terrific," "Congratulations," or "You're very brave." Finally, 55 percent of these women reported having been aware of a hostility toward large families, often looked on, they felt, with pity or contempt. In addition, these women came under strong pressures, in particular from the medical profession, to adopt effective methods of contraception.

It is worth bearing in mind that this high frequency of expressions of disapproval directed at pregnant women who were already mothers of several children was observed in France in 1988, that is, in a country where overpopulation is hardly a problem. These expressions coexist, however, with pronatalist attitudes; some groups, a very small minority, have even gone so far as to form anti-abortion commando units that enter hospitals with the aim of preventing abortions from being performed, though such actions have never reached the level of violence that has been observed in the United States. Although French society is increasingly homogeneous, this is a subject on which it remains divided, as in all transitional periods.

The members of a woman's surroundings who disapprove of her new pregnancy may even suggest to her that she have an abortion. The incitement to have an abortion increases rapidly with the number of live births by the woman, and women pregnant with a sixth or higher-order child have *all* been "invited" to terminate the pregnancy. This invitation is less frequent when the woman's family is smaller; but the proportions found (22, 33, and 67 percent for three, four, and five live births, respectively) are far from negligible, particularly when one considers that these attitudes are being expressed in a country where abortion was the object of social censure and punishable by law until 1975 and that discussion of the bill to liberalize abortion provoked stormy debates. Since then, the spread of Malthusian attitudes has swept away those traditional values, overcoming the last remaining scruples of the social body.

A request for a voluntary termination of a pregnancy made at the very end of the authorized period of gestation, when there is no objective reason for such a slow response, may be a further sign of pressure from a husband or family in favor of having an abortion, a pressure that the woman resists by putting herself in a position in which the doctor has to refuse the operation; proof to this effect is the relief expressed by women when they are told of the refusal. We have heard of this phenomenon in a number of hospitals where abortions are performed.

A relaxation in contraceptive practice, followed by an abortion that is itself followed by a new pregnancy, is the sort of situation that causes despair among those who believe that a better diffusion of contraception will remove the need for abortions. However, such a situation is often due to the existence of a pressure to limit fertility, which the woman initially resists before giving in and then resisting again.

In a country with a very low population growth such as France, the pressure to abort is thus an extension of the pressure to prevent conception, which occurs when a woman adopts, or attempts to adopt, a fertility behavior that does not respect the prevailing norms. Society in this case is reacting not against an excessive population growth but against family sizes that pose a threat to mass consumption.

PRESSURE LINKED TO THE DESIRE TO LIMIT POPULATION GROWTH: THE EXAMPLE OF CHINA

By contrast, the desire to curb the growth of population leads some countries to encourage couples to limit their fertility. This is a field in which constraints can be imposed by law or regulation, but putting them into practice requires the cooperation of at least part of the social body, even in an extremely authoritarian country like China.[1] In the absence of official regulations, the role of the different social groups is even more apparent.

At the start of 1979, Chinese couples were invited, more or less firmly, to pledge to have only one child; in return for this undertaking they would receive a one-child certificate that entitled them and their child to a certain number of advantages but subjected them to penalties should they have a second child or more. Officially no penalty existed for the couples who refused to accept the one-child certificate, but parents who did not cooperate faced an extremely strong social pressure, accompanied by informal penalties.

Collective responsibility, a traditional feature of imperial China, has lead in modern China to a reinforcement of mutual surveillance and to the pressure that the group can bring to bear on couples who might be tempted to disregard the family-planning rules, forcing them to abort an unauthorized pregnancy.

According to Chen and Kols (1982), the higher proportion of holders of the one-child certificate in towns was due in part to the practice of denying profits for a month to all certificate holders in a work group each time one of their number broke the agreement. This acted as a powerful incentive to continue using contraception and, in the case of contraceptive failure, was responsible for a very strong pressure and an atmosphere of denunciation to prevent the conception from ending in a birth likely to penalize all the members of the group.

In addition, the economic incentives in a village were to be linked to the village's meeting targets for birth control. Even if the village was successful in other areas of activity, it would automatically lose the chance of receiving "advanced" status for industrial or agricultural production, whereas its cadres would become ineligible for bonuses and promotions. The same system was imposed on the work units of the urban zones.

As a result, the standard of living of the entire population of a village, including that of its cadres, is influenced by the behavior of couples who fail to respect the birth plan drawn up for the village. This naturally leads some local authorities to use forced abortion and sterilization to make sure that the number of births does not exceed the planned quota. According to Peng Xizhe (1991), persuasion and education are the principal official birth control methods, but, reportedly, coercive measures were used at the local level when persuasion alone did not work.

The use of coercion stems from the strong pressure exerted on the basic-level family-planning workers by the higher echelons, but the Chinese authorities take the view that social and political pressure is acceptable in order to avoid birth rates soaring in the already densely populated districts and provinces. The cadre responsibility system reinforces the pressure.

Each local cadre has responsibility for between ten and twenty households and signs a contract with the hierarchy guaranteeing that none of them will have an unplanned birth. The results incur bonuses or penalties. Because of this system, the cadres exert strong pressures to fulfill the planned birth targets, pressures that sometimes even include forcing women to have abortions. Those cadres who prove unable to exert such pressures either incur penalties, resign (Parish 1984), or supply their superiors with inaccurate reports.

Subsequently, couples of certain villages would be authorized to have a second child if their first was a girl and if all the couples of the village had respected the norms for reproduction. This policy, known as *dunühu,* was experimented in Heilongjiang in 1984, made general in 1986, and adopted formally in 1988. In the villages with no unplanned births, couples with just a girl are allowed to have a second child when she reaches the age of six; in 1987, 37 percent of the villages of the province, in which the control of unauthorized pregnancies had been particularly effective, were in this position.

In 1988, a quota of second births was allocated to the villages of Liaoning Province that satisfied six conditions, including the absence of unplanned births, use of contraception by all women of childbearing age, and the establishment of an effective system of population control. Eighty percent of the villages in the province were authorized to apply the *dunühu* policy. Under this policy, an unauthorized pregnancy resulted in the suspension of the quota of second births until it was terminated, and if an unauthorized birth did occur, all second births were prohibited for one year. Such a policy cannot but heighten the pressure that the village community exerts on individuals.

The flexibility introduced in the course of time to the one-child policy is very relative, however, and some are in favor of radical measures. Kuang Ke (1989, in Aird 1990), of the provincial school of the Communist Party of Jiangsu Province, called for a new population policy involving compulsory termination of pregnancy for women under twenty-five, for second pregnancies less than five years after the first, and for all subsequent pregnancies; he advocated the creation in every county of a population police force, under the supervision of a population commission. Anyone who subverted the law by not having an abortion, by concealing pregnancies, or by accepting bribes would face prison or other punishments, including the death penalty. The author added that the coercive measures of the current population policy, such as the demolition of houses; felling of trees; confiscation of cattle, tractors, and other major items of farm machinery; and the refusal to register new births are unscientific and serve only to hinder production and impair the accuracy of birth statistics, whereas compulsory abortion is entirely in accord with the spirit of the constitution. It is significant that this article was authorized to be published.

All these pressures have met with opposition, indicating that the traditional values have not completely disappeared and that they are responsible for pressures in the opposite direction. That said, it is certainly true that a large part of Chinese society has supported the politicians in the wielding of pressure to impose abortion.

PRESSURE LINKED TO MALTHUSIANISM AND TO A REJECTION OF OTHER FORMS OF CONTRACEPTION: THE EXAMPLE OF THE EASTERN EUROPEAN COUNTRIES

Contraception, abortion, and sterilization are complementary or conflicting methods for reducing fertility. In some cases the group encourages or imposes abortion when the population resists contraception, but in other cases the group favors one method of birth control over another or certain members of the group who have the power to favor a particular method impose the type that benefits them most. This is the situation observed today in the European countries of the former communist bloc.

We have witnessed the unsatisfactory state of family planning in Albania and Latvia.[2] The number of abortions there is very high, and the spread of contraception has been slow. When the pill is available, it is sold expensively in pharmacist's shops. The intrauterine device (IUD) is not very popular, and although less costly for women than hormonal contraception, is less profitable for certain suppliers than the latter. Having an abortion is cheaper than taking the pill, but above all, and this is the most important point, abortions are an indispensable source of income for the medical establishments and gynecologists who are underemployed, too numerous, and at present the only ones with the right to perform abortions and prescribe contraceptives. In Latvia we were told that a reduction in the number of abortions performed in a provincial hospital posed a serious budgetary threat. The IUDs that are supplied free by humanitarian organizations only replace abortion when they are stolen and resold. Supplies of the pill are usually imported and earn no profit for any group, except the pharmacists who resell them. Under these conditions, modern contraception is slow to spread.

We were present when an Albanian doctor, the head of a hospital gynecological service, requested funds from the United Nations Population Fund (UNFPA) to improve the equipment used to perform abortions but who refused, laughingly, the various contraceptives offered by UNFPA—condoms that he "daren't" offer to women; the pill, which is usually "*dangerous*"; and IUDs that were to be "reserved" for a small number of women. At the end he added that Albanian women "preferred" the abortions they underwent, without anaesthetic, in his hospital, because they were "strong women."

Pressure from doctors, reinforced by that of the populations, is thus responsible for a distrust among women for modern contraceptive methods. To varying degrees, the same situation is observed in almost all the countries of Eastern Europe.

Moreover, contrary to the situation in Western Europe, abortion has always been a favored means of birth control in these countries, where it has faced little competition from traditional masculine contraception, which is little used. The fact that the man seldom took responsibility for contraception obliged the woman to abort; nowadays, although the woman could be responsible for the contraception, economic factors and pressure from the medical profession are added to the pressure from the husband to have her abort. This explains why in this part of the world the mean number of abortions per women is the highest, always greater than one abortion per women, often two or three and even reaching six abortions per woman in Romania (see, for example, the chapter by Serbanescu and others in this volume).

Changes in the law, whether in the sense of repressing or liberalizing abortion, have had little influence on this phenomenon, and the pressure to abort remains more or less the same. Only maternal mortality has reflected the modifications to the sanitary conditions under which abortions are performed, depending on whether they are clandestine or legal.

PRESSURE LINKED TO THE REJECTION OF CERTAIN PREGNANCIES

The pressure to abort can be exerted not just when the size of the family is judged to be adequate but also when the social group refuses to accept the birth of certain categories of children or births to certain categories of women.

The French survey mentioned earlier revealed that a termination of pregnancy had been suggested, implicitly or explicitly, to 36 percent of women giving birth out of wedlock. Pregnancies of unmarried women are socially much more acceptable today than in the past, but this proportion makes clear that certain values have not yet completely disappeared. Mention can be made of another French survey, conducted in 1976 in a Bordeaux hospital, among women who had just had a legal abortion (Fresel Lozey 1980). Among the reasons given by the unmarried women for having an abortion are the difficulties for a single woman, more sociological than financial, of motherhood (45 percent of the answers) and also the hostility from friends, family, and neighbors and the attitudes of rejection that result (17 percent of the answers). In all then, some pressure (direct or indirect) had been exerted on 62 percent of the unmarried women who had aborted.

A woman has only to fail to respect the norms for the group to manifest its disapproval and pressure her to have an abortion. More than half the women pregnant with a third or higher-order child (55 percent) were criticized by at least one member of their network who thought they were too young or too old to bear children.

There are other selective abortions that are encouraged or imposed, all which seek to prevent the birth of certain categories of children: these include female babies, which are much more often terminated than males in China, South Korea, and India, something that has become possible thanks to prenatal diagnosis, plus the attempts to avoid the birth of children who are imperfect or believed to be so.

The ability to identify the sex of the fetus enables the husband and the family to put pressure on the woman to have an abortion if the fetus is female. The large number of abortions of female fetuses in India led the authorities to pass a law against selective abortion in 1996 and against unlicensed use of sex-determination techniques in 2000. Pressure from the family and society will continue, however, as long as the sociocultural context is not modified and a girl is less valued than a boy. In China, the obsession with male births has, of course, been reinforced by the one-child policy. In these countries, as in South Korea, the sex ratio of births is very high, providing evidence that such pressures have a real impact.

The birth-planning program in China contains two parts: control of population growth and improvement in population quality. In 1980, the Chinese authorities considered denying the right to reproduce to the developmentally disabled and the mentally ill, hemophiliacs, and individuals suffering from achro-

matopsy (color blindness) or various genetic defects. A regulation to prohibit the severely mentally retarded from reproducing, the first in the country, was introduced in Gansu Province on November 23, 1988. The individuals in question had to be sterilized before marriage, and severely retarded women who became pregnant were to have compulsory abortions. Administrative and economic penalties were to be imposed on those with the direct responsibility for a birth in this category of individuals.

The potential for drift is always present. A draft law called "Eugenics and Health Protection" submitted to the Chinese National Popular Assembly in December 1993 advocated the use of abortion and sterilization to avoid further births of inferior quality. Individuals suffering from hepatitis, venereal disease, or mental illness that could be transmitted to their offspring would not be allowed to marry until they had been cured; pregnant women with an infectious disease or whose fetus had been diagnosed as defective would be offered an abortion, and couples would have to be sterilized. Shortly afterwards, the Chinese authorities revised the terms of this project: the new law would not be compulsory; the mentally handicapped and carriers of hereditary diseases would not be forced to have abortions or accept sterilization; the word *eugenics* was removed from the text, as was all mention of "births of inferior quality," and the title was changed to "Draft Law on Natal and Health Care."[3]

A paper prepared for the International Symposium on Population and Sustainable Development held in Peking in September 1995 (Yang and Yi 1995) advocated an "alternative population policy" with the double objective of limiting the growth of the population and improving its quality. The illiterate would not have the right to reproduce, and any pregnancy in this group would have to be terminated; individuals who had received just a primary education could have only one child, and those in the highest category of education could have as many children as they liked.

The temptation to apply eugenics is not confined to China; Singapore provides numerous similar instances, and the countries of the West are not immune from the dangers of drift. The mere proliferation of prenatal examinations is responsible for generating an insidious but real pressure from members of the medical profession in favor of abortion. Some categories of women are more exposed than others, such as older women or women with acquired immune deficiency syndrome (AIDS).

DISCUSSION

It is a characteristic of transitional periods that older traditional values persist among some groups. It is not therefore surprising that a country can simultaneously contain groups that are hostile to abortion and others that encourage it. Given that women belong to several groups, they are liable to be exposed to contradictory pressures.

Social pressure can work in favor of a policy, as has happened in China with some of the groups concerned, as seen earlier, or it can run counter to a policy: a case in point is the attitude of families in India whose preference for male births is opposed by the authorities or again the opposition of certain groups to the one-child policy in China.

When the pressure in favor of abortion has the aim of limiting the size of families, the social body as a whole participates. In the French survey, the members of the women's networks who had suggested an abortion were, in order of frequency with which they are reported, the mother, then doctor, colleague, and husband. Less frequently mentioned are neighbors, in-laws, brothers, and sisters.

In half of the cases, at least two individuals had encouraged the woman to accept an abortion, and in a quarter of cases the number was at least three. The number of people bringing this pressure to bear did not depend on the number of live births the woman had had.

Where a pressure to abort exists on grounds of eugenics, it usually originates with members of the medical profession. Similarly, as has been seen, responsibility for favoring abortion as a means of birth control in Eastern Europe can again be attributed to the medical profession, though also to husbands.

It is the husband, but also the family, who exerts the greatest pressure when family rules are at stake, because if these rules are not respected, it is the family as a whole that is likely to be rejected by society. In the countries mentioned earlier, a woman who refuses to abort a female fetus faces being rejected by her husband and by her family.

Pressure from husbands, pressure from the medical profession, pressure from the family, pressure from neighbors, pressure from political parties, pressure from colleagues—under these conditions how much autonomy does a woman have? It is true that women have often been prevented and are often still prevented from having an abortion when they want one, but it is also true that the new freedom to have an abortion can turn into a constraint.

NOTES

1. For a fuller discussion, see Yves Blayo, *Des politiques démographiques en Chine* (Paris: Editions de l'Institut National d'Etudes Démographiques, forthcoming).

2. In the course of missions carried out for the United Nations Population Fund in 1993, 1994, and 1995.

3. Population Headliners (Economic and Social Commission for Asia and the Pacific, Bangkok), January 1994 and February 1994.

REFERENCES

Aird, John S. 1990. *Slaughter of the Innocents, Coercive Birth Control in China*. Washington, D.C.: The AEI Press.

Chen, Pi-chao, and Adrienne Kols. 1982. "La population et la planification des naissances dans la République populaire de Chine." *Population Reports,* series J, nE 25: 46. Baltimore, Md.: The Johns Hopkins University.

Frezel Losey, Michel. 1980. "L'avortement: incidence de la contraception et motivations. Une enquête à Bordeaux." *Population Reports* nE 3: 545–64. Baltimore, Md.: The Johns Hopkins University.

Parish, William L. 1984. "The Family and Economic Change." *China: The 80's Era,* ed. Norton Ginsburg and Bernard A. Lalor, 222–42. Boulder, Colo., and London: Westview Press.

Peng, Xizhe. 1991. *Demographic Transition in China, Fertility Trends since the 1950s.* Oxford: Clarendon Press.

Yang, Yaochen, and Yang Yi. 1995. "Universally Increasing Education and the Alternative Population Policy in China." Paper prepared for the International Symposium on Population and Sustainable Development, September 27–29, Beijing.

Chapter 15

Concluding Remarks: The Role of Ambiguity

Alaka Malwade Basu

This book hopes to fill an important gap in the contemporary literature on abortion. On the one hand, in the demographic literature, abortion research tends to concentrate on demographic matters (estimates, data availability, program factors, and so on) and, especially, on the role of abortion in historical and contemporary fertility declines. On the other hand, the literature on abortion in other disciplines tends to fall in one of the two following categories:

1. Medical and safety aspects of abortion
2. The pro-choice versus pro-life debate in the United States and, in the context of Catholicism, outside the United States

The present book belongs to a somewhat different category. Its strength lies in the fact that it tries to understand and place in context some of the personal realities that underlie the fifty million or so abortions that are believed to occur annually worldwide. It is not about the reproductive health implications of abortion in a medical or clinical sense, although the scale of the reproductive health problem was indicated in the statistical overview by Singh, Henshaw, and Berentsen. The urgent need for safe and easy access to abortion and, even more so, family-planning services in many parts of the developed and developing world was well brought out in this chapter, even though the authors had to contend with much incomplete and unavailable information.

This shortage of information is not surprising. As the chapter by Kulczycki argued, abortion research has never been a priority with researchers or funders, partly because it is difficult terrain methodologically but also partly because the very collection of data on abortion represents a political decision. In any case, even when research findings are available, they are often woefully underused to inform policy. Abortion policy is so highly politicized and must answer to so many ideological constituencies that what academic research suggests is good for or wanted by women or families rarely takes center stage in its formulation. Kulczycki rightly underscored the need for more attention to abortion research and the need for policy to then seek guidance from such research.

Unsatisfactory statistical data, however, represent only a part of the problem of missing information. As Mundigo emphasized, abortion research is one of the subjects most in need of and most lacking in cross-disciplinary approaches that address the many levels at which the problem may be posed. Particularly lacking are microlevel studies that look at the lives of the women, couples, and households that seek abortion, often at great financial, physical, and social cost, and at the societies, states, and pressures that facilitate or constrain this search for abortion. The present volume has tried to address some of these gaps with anthropological and historical data from many parts of the world.

I should reiterate at this point that this is not a polemical book about the moral debate on abortion. In particular, it does not enter the pro-choice versus pro-life debate that dominates discussions on abortion in the United States of America and that in turn have such profound effects on policy in other parts of the world. This focus is missing from the present volume both because it tends to overwhelm most discussions on the ethics of abortion policy in the Western world and because it turns out to not be a major concern in those parts of the world that are not dominated by the Catholic Church politically. Indeed, even the contemporary position of the church on the abortion issue may be challenged, as the activities of organizations like Catholics for Free Choice indicate.

Instead, many of the chapters in this volume have tried to understand the moral imperatives that guide the search for abortion from the perspective of the abortion seekers (and, to a lesser extent, abortion providers) themselves. The wealth of material on this matter from the microlevel research that has been reported here tells us very strongly that the act of abortion is rarely easy. Most cultures are very conscious of the conflicting emotions it can arouse, and most have therefore developed a number of rationales to lessen the emotional or moral pain of the act. At the same time, the presence of these moral arguments to justify abortion does not mean that they are merely arguments to justify otherwise sinful or unworthy behavior; several non-Christian cultures genuinely lack any explicit injunctions against abortion as a specific form of behavior.

In the introductory chapter, John and Pat Caldwell reflected on many of the issues raised in this book. They pointed in particular to the wide variation in abortion levels, attitudes to abortion, and abortion policies worldwide, variations that belie the kind of publicity given to particular viewpoints in forums such as the International Conference on Population and Development.

The Caldwells' chapter also summarized many of the key findings of the chapters in this book. But here, in a concluding piece, I would like to pull out a few unexpected strands that emerge from the chapters and that give the book a nuance that much of the contemporary rhetoric on abortion does not sufficiently acknowledge. These nuances concern sticky questions to do with agency, especially as derived from legal or medical access to abortion and with the assumed role of education in affecting agency.

ABORTION RESTRICTIONS AND INDIVIDUAL AGENCY

A key semiphilosophical question that the chapters in this volume raise is one connected to issues of female autonomy. The pro-choice abortion debate in the United States of America has its analogue in the literature on the rest of the world that posits that access to safe abortion services is an essential component of policies that seek to increase women's autonomy. Conversely, the absence of such services is often viewed as a proxy for the unreasonable constraints on the lives of women who desperately need some control over their own bodies and selves.

Both these propositions are broadly valid and supported in many parts of the chapters in this book. But the chapters included here are important because they also suggest that the matter is less straightforward than these propositions allow. In particular, they demonstrate that societal norms, religious norms, legal strictures, and poor medical services have, both historically and today, never been a complete barrier to the successful practice of abortion. This is not to suggest that such barriers have not often led to unsafe abortions or to unwanted births. It is to suggest that societies and individuals have often developed strategies to overcome these barriers without explicitly challenging them. This leads to the curious combination of restrictive norms or laws and a fair amount of individual agency in the resort to abortion, all this while simultaneously paying at least lip service to these norms. Indeed, it is not only the individual, the family, or society that finds ways of getting around such barriers; the state itself may often be a willing partner in these strategies to terminate a pregnancy without breaking the law, written or unwritten.

Several of the papers in this volume describe these weapons of subversion. And in doing so, they illustrate a major strength of the anthropological method of enquiry in this area of study—few of these findings could have emerged from a survey that asked women if they had ever had an abortion or even a miscarriage.

Most of these subversive strategies exploit, even if unconsciously, the ambiguities of language and of what may be called "cultural biomedicine." They hinge around the uncertainties that can surround the following questions:

1. When is a delayed menstrual period a pregnancy?
2. When is a pregnancy a form of life?
3. When does the life in a womb acquire a "soul"?

Many of the chapters comment on this scope for ambiguity in the answers to these questions and on the ways in which cultures can and do encourage such ambiguity, of which there are broadly two. First, the restoring of menses is not seen as having to do anything with terminating a pregnancy. Second, pregnancies (or rather, delayed menses) are not seen as having a clear relationship with the beginning of life. The presence of a life in the womb is seen as beginning with symptoms and under conditions that are only marginally related to the menstrual cycle. In such understandings, what Western medicine may call an "abortion" is not an abortion at all until there is a culturally defined pregnancy and a life that can be aborted.

To begin with, under many circumstances, a delayed menstrual period is seen as just that—a delayed menstrual period, the causes of which may have nothing at all to do with pregnancy. Instead, the delay is often seen to indicate some other health problems, problems that may in fact later *prevent* a much-wanted pregnancy. Elisa Levin brings this out very nicely in her description of the "cleaning the belly" that restoring regular, healthy menstrual flow is seen to involve. Needless to say, this action of restoring menstruation to its regular, "healthy" state is not perceived as having anything to do with abortion, which women, as well as the traditional healers who help them restore menses, are strongly against. In this formulation abortion is not only illegal but also morally abhorrent and against all societal norms.

The chapter by Elisha Renne provides further illustration of such resort to ambiguous language to legitimize what Western medicine sees as an abortion. In her study area in Northern Nigeria, many potential abortifacients are referred to as medicines that "put a pregnancy to sleep" or "make a pregnancy lie down," the intent being to later reactivate such a sleeping pregnancy at a more fortuitous time. And even when an abortion is explicitly sought, it is often sought by women who seek the right to an abortion using the protection of the Koran. In her survey, women who had attended Islamiyya classes were significantly more likely to say that abortion was allowed by Islam if a pregnancy threatened the life of the mother. The exact determination of a threat is, of course, open to debate, an ambiguity that can again be useful for legitimizing resort to abortion within a religious framework.

Cultural ideas about human growth facilitate abortion even more simply in Amy Stambach's Tanzanian study. Here a delayed menstrual period signifies nothing more than a "grain of sand," which can proceed to a real pregnancy and fetus only with continued nourishment from both parents, which is to say, continued intercourse with a socially acceptable genitor so that the flesh, blood, and bones that go to make up a life can be generated. Once this happens, abortion is naturally frowned upon. But as long as all that occupies a womb is a few grains of sand or even *nyama* (meat) that does not yet have a sufficient input from the male, it is hardly a human life that is being destroyed when attempts are made to reinstate regular menses.

The State, Society, and Organized Religion: The Representation and the Reality

Women, or indeed families, are not alone in finding ways to get around normative, legal, or religious proscriptions on abortion. Even while endorsing these proscriptions in principle, both organized religion and the state machinery may in practice make it much easier for women to obtain an abortion than a simple perusal of religious or legal views on abortion would imply. They tend to do this in two ways—first, by ignoring or at least not actively prosecuting the abortion seeker, and second, by exploiting the ambiguities and loopholes of most religious and legal doctrines on this matter.

To begin with the state and the legal status of abortion, it is interesting to note that even the meager data available suggest that abortion levels are high in countries with restrictive abortion laws. The very fact that evidence of substantial levels of abortion exists also suggests another interesting point—that this knowledge is not often used by the state to actually prosecute abortion seekers or providers. That is, there is not a one-to-one correlation between a country's laws on abortion and how many abortions take place, and there is not a one-to-one correlation between the severity of its anti-abortion legislation and the level of overcrowding in its jails. In other words, most nations tend to turn a blind eye to abortions as long as they remain sufficiently discreet. For example, Lerner and Salas mention that though an estimated 250,000 induced abortions took place in Mexico during 1988–89, there were only ten convictions for abortion, and even here the imprisonment was waived on bail. The rarity of actual convictions is also highlighted by the publicity given to individual cases. For example, Nepal, which has had, until very recently, one of the world's most restrictive laws on abortion, has attracted much attention from political activists highlighting the personal histories of two women in jail for abortion.

All this is not to suggest that such discreet abortions are easy, safe, or cheap; indeed, the very opposite is usually true, but not always. For example, although a relatively conservative Buddhist priesthood has been able to repeatedly block attempts to liberalize abortion law in Sri Lanka, excellent-quality abortion services are provided by private practitioners. These services are safe, relatively openly available, and not threatened by the law in any obvious way. But they are expensive, and their very expense serves as one more means to penalize the poor through supposedly egalitarian legislation.

In any case, in other parts of the world with restrictive abortion legislation, low levels of prosecution have led to a less happy situation even for the rich in many cases. Not only are clandestine services expensive as they are in Sri Lanka, but they are also generally unsafe and provided by a variety of often dubious sources. The papers in this volume chronicle some of these unconventional sources and the strategies they employ to help women to abort unplanned pregnancies. The most prominent of these providers are the herbalists or other variants of local healers. All societies have traditionally had what may be called home remedies to induce abortions; what the microlevel research reported in this volume highlights is the continued relevance of these home remedies in many parts of the developing world and the increasing sophistication of the providers of these local medicines. Anarfi, for example, describes a popular selling strategy that bypasses legal prohibitions in Ghana. Herbalists prescribe "tonics" that they warn women "not to take if pregnant" because they may lead to a miscarriage. In plain language what this translates into is, of course, the advertisement of an abortifacient, and girls and women with unwanted pregnancies interpret this message accordingly.

But not all local abortifacients may be classified as quack medicine, and at least some of the chapters in this volume wonder if they explain the discrepancy between contraceptive and fertility rates that standard surveys often uncover in developing countries. The chapters by Anarfi, Renne, and Levin take some of the claims of the local herbalists seriously enough to try to compile some kind of list of popular local abortifacients and to call for increased biomedical research into their efficacy. Some of them may indeed turn out to have a larger and safer potential for inducing abortions than do the currently available surgical as well as chemical procedures.

In many countries, after the traditional healer and the local midwife, the next level of unofficial abortion service provider is often the pharmacist. That the pharmacist plays doctor in a variety of settings is well documented. Pick and colleagues report an innovative survey of pharmacy workers and market herb vendors in Mexico City and find a wide range of professional knowledge and skills embodied in these categories. They discovered a widespread willingness to prescribe abortifacients among both groups, abortifacients that are surprisingly potentially more dangerous and less effective in the case of the relatively "educated" pharmacists than those prescribed by the herbalists. In addition, many pharmacists are amateur herbalists, and some herbalists also recommended "modern" pills.

Although all these unofficial abortion service providers provide a much-needed service in legally restrictive societies, they are, of course, not in the business for purely altruistic reasons. They usually make a neat profit. The formal medical profession that provides the relatively safe illegal services for abortion in these societies often has even more gain in this regard, and it is not surprising that the gains usually outweigh the risks. But there is more that can be said about the medical profession and its role in the abortion debate, and a later section returns briefly to this subject.

So much for the state and the law. How do the state and the individual reconcile the frequent contradictions between strict adherence to an organized religion and simultaneous resort to abortion? The key to this question lies in the possible multiple interpretations of most religious doctrine. These are not just abstract possibilities. As some of the papers discuss, not only have there been changing interpretations over time of the same subject within a major religion, but even at a particular time, there is also often no one unassailable interpretation that exists. For example, there have been historical changes in views on ensoulment and hominization within the Catholic Church, changes that are now being reexamined by individuals and organizations who wish to remain Catholic while at the same time breaking free of some of its contemporary injunctions.

As for the simultaneous existence of more than one interpretation of religious teaching on a matter, there are several examples in the contemporary world of different branches of a religion having quite different views on correct behavior. Buddhism, for example, exists in two major forms—the more restrictive Theravada, or southern branch, which still influences policy in countries such as Sri Lanka, and the relatively liberal Mahayana, or northern form of the religion, which exists in Korea and Japan. Hinduism, too, means different things to different people on several matters, and this very difference has aided a policy perspective that can have an avowedly Hindu nationalist government nevertheless make no move to change the country's liberal abortion laws.

Sajeda Amin's chapter in this volume describes the legal and religious ambiguities that help Bangladesh actively promote what it resolutely calls "menstrual regulation." On the latter, four of the five schools of Islamic jurisprudence do not outrightly forbid abortion in the early stages of a pregnancy, that is, before ensoulment. Moreover, there is not complete agreement on when ensoulment occurs. The leeway that this ambiguity provides has been further strengthened by medical technology. The development of the procedure for menstrual regulation, being relatively safe, easy, and inexpensive, has made it easier for the health and family-planning program to exploit the ambiguity in the meaning of a missed period by the relatively simple method of not doing a pregnancy test for menses that are delayed by only a few weeks. But, as Amin points out, it is the state that exploits this ambiguity. Women themselves know enough reproductive physiology to be aware that a missed period is likely to herald a pregnancy and usually treat a menstrual regulation as a means of terminating this pregnancy if it is unwanted.

Female Education and Abortion

The chapters in this volume, and the ones on African countries in particular, also raise the complicated related issue of the relationship between female education and abortion. The vast demographic literature on the universal and unmitigated demographic merits of girl's education gets some more ambiguous nuances in this volume. In the process, the question of women's increased autonomy as the crucial mediator in the relation between education and desired demographic outcomes is also painted in more shades of gray than is usually the case. This subject is therefore worth diverting into, however briefly.

Whether schooling or education raises or reduces recourse to abortion depends on the net effect of contrary and competing effects of education—some of these raise and others reduce the possibility of abortions. This net effect is, of course, contingent on the nature of the schooling or education and the life-cycle stage of the educated woman, but some of the present chapters highlight the difficulties of predicting it even *within* a particular education or life-cycle category, so strong are the modifying influences of cultural and social circumstances of the kind not captured easily by the standard survey.

To pull out just a few examples of some of these perplexities, how can education increase the incidence of abortion? As already mentioned, this increase may be mediated by different factors among young girls and older women. In the former, the most important determinant of increased abortion appears to be the increase in premarital sexual activity associated with schooling. All the chapters examining Africa discuss this issue. However, in many cases, this is not an increase in sexual activity per se but just an increase in sexual activity *before* marriage, predicated by the later age at marriage of girls who attend secondary school. One part of the debate about schoolgirls and abortion among Amy Stambach's Chagga respondents centers around the feeling that the later marriage of schoolgirls in a sense subverts the natural order of things because these girls are biologically ready for sex, pregnancy, and childbearing but lack the social and institutional supports to bear and rear children. Schools do not take kindly to pregnant students, so abortion is often the only way to continue with schooling. The pressure to abort is reinforced by the parental aspirations that send girls to school in the first place: a "modern" marriage, usually in a church and usually to an unmarried man—both of which are greatly hampered by a premarital pregnancy or child.

Educated, older, and married women, on the other hand, face a different set of reasons to abort. At times these are related to the lower fertility goals associated with education, lowered goals that are not yet met through efficient contraception. Educated women are also more likely to disregard norms about postpartum abstinence or lactation so that the chances of a pregnancy too soon after a previous delivery are increased. If cultural norms about birth interval lengths have not changed, then abortion is often the only way to deal with possibly breaking them. In turn, their education often makes it easier for them to seek and find satisfactory services for an abortion. But it is interesting that these norms about desirable birth intervals have in many cases (see Renne's chapter in this volume) changed, with the approval of religious leaders, in the direction of there being less moral opprobrium attached to short intervals. This often makes abortions now less necessary than they were a few decades ago when the changes in postpartum sexual behavior first began.

In her chapter, Elisha Renne also suggests a surprising rise in attitudes *favorable* to abortion among some of the women in her Nigerian study who attended Islamic education classes; the standard understanding is that modern Western education increases the legitimacy of abortion, whereas traditional religion reinforces its undesirability. These Islamiyya-schooled women now find themselves in the position of interpreting Islamic teachings for themselves rather than through intermediaries and also find themselves more able to develop Islamic attitudes that condone abortions under some circumstances. For example, women who had attended Islamiyya classes in her study were significantly more likely to say that abortion was allowed if the mother's life was threatened, than were women who had not attended such religious classes. They were also more aware of the ambiguity of Islamic opinion about when life begins. Given this new ability to reformulate a problem and to reanalyze possible solutions with a greater and more personal knowledge of the Koran, it is hardly surprising that religious education for women was actively opposed by men when it first entered the Hausa community.

ABORTION ACCESS AND INDIVIDUAL AGENCY

Although access to safe and affordable abortion can in principle be assumed to mean an increase in the choices open to women, in the field this access often comes with many strings attached. Worse, it may sometimes bestow a completely illusory autonomy, being used instead to actually constrain women's choices in the opposite direction. That is, although the pressure to not abort is strong in many societies, in others there may well be an undue pressure on women to abort. As the chapter by Blayo and Blayo points out, these pressures may come from the state, the medical profession, society in general, or the family. The last two are particularly difficult to separate out from the woman's own desires, and Blayo and Blayo report on an interesting survey in which French women who had exceeded societal norms about correct family size were interviewed about the status of their last pregnancies and reactions to them. The implicit and often explicit disapproval that these women faced also included advice on the virtue of an abortion by family, friends, and doctors, and those women who went ahead with their pregnancies often needed some reserves of courage to draw upon.

The chapter by Blayo and Blayo also reflects upon the great pressure that many societies exert on women to abort specific *kinds* of pregnancies—those of the "wrong" sex in particular. Easy and legal access to abortion may also sometimes play against the interests of women's autonomy because it in fact *increases* state control over reproductive strategies. At one extreme there is the state pressure to abort unauthorized pregnancies exerted by local cadres in China, as described by Blayo and Blayo. This pressure is more direct and more often articulated in a country like China. But it may also exist in more insidious forms as suggested by the chapters on Eastern Europe and the former Soviet Union. In these cases, perhaps pressures to abort were exerted not so much by easy access to abortion as by difficult access to effective contraception. That is, perhaps it is the sin of omission and not the sin of commission that should be laid at the door of Soviet and Eastern European public policy before the late 1980s.

Hutter's chapter certainly supports such an interpretation. The (inadequate) data on Russia suggest that during the 1960s and 1970s, the high incidence of abortion (reaching a peak of 5.4 million in 1965, which is itself probably an underestimate) is better understood by looking at the low level of effective contraceptive use. Even more revealing is survey information from this period on knowledge of and attitudes to modern contraception—such knowledge is uniformly half-baked, and attitudes are uniformly negative among women, who often see modern contraception as much more dangerous to health than abortion. Although the state was instrumental in the spread of this kind of misinformation, its actual source must certainly be the medical profession. As for the motives of the medical profession itself, one may be generous and blame its own limited exposure to developments in contraceptive technology, or one may be less charitable and wonder if a steady stream of abortions helped to fill its own coffers.

Indeed, this kind of ambiguity continues in most analyses of the role of the medical profession in the abortion debate. Perhaps it is a question of a no-win strategy—if medical practitioners encourage legal abortions, they are guaranteeing their own survival in the official medical system; if they do not, they are guaranteeing their own income through private and illegally provided services. Other actions by them may be similarly questioned. For example, the medical profession in India has been consistently against training paramedical personnel to perform even menstrual regulation (MR), whereas in neighboring Bangladesh, the entire MR program runs on the paramedics. Is the Indian resistance a genuine concern with women's health, or is it a resistance to relinquishing control? One could argue endlessly on these issues—perhaps the best answer is that actions do not necessarily predict motives, and a case-study approach has more local insights to offer.

In any case, the Russian data in Hutter's chapter do suggest that liberalized abortion policy was not merely a device to benefit the state and the medical profession. At least in the first phase of liberalization in 1920, a major concern seems to have been with the large number of illegal and unsafe abortions that took place in Tsarist Russia. Also articulated was a concern for poverty, which necessitated lower fertility. And a lower emphasis on modern contraception is much more understandable given the limited developments in this area at that time. In 1936, however, the Stalinist concern about unacceptably low population growth retracted many of the liberal provisions of the 1920 legislation and clamped down on any activities that promoted contraception. Needless to say, illegal and unsafe abortions again climbed sharply, and 1955 again saw an attempt to deal with the health implications of this trend with a liberalization of abortion access.

Serbanescu and colleagues' paper on Romania is an even stronger indictment of the direct impact of misguided abortion policy. The authors graphically relate the abnormally high maternal mortality and morbidity in Romania during 1979 to 1989 to the illegal abortions that continued to flourish in an environment in which access to safe abortion was denied but many pregnancies remained unwanted. The reversal of restrictive abortion laws in 1989 in turn were reflected in a dramatic decline in the maternal mortality rate from 170 per 100,000 live births in 1989 to 60 in 1992.

Both Hutter and Serbanescu and colleagues point to the future with some hope and some pessimism. The hope arises from the slowly climbing levels of contraceptive use that should eventually reduce the reliance on induced abortion. But they also reflect on the fact that the rise in modern contraception is so slow—and much of it is due to a rise in the use of traditional methods. It appears that Eastern Europe and the former Soviet Union need a major change in contraceptive *ideology,* from one in which abortions are perceived as so much more safe and effective to one in which modern contraceptives are seen as the more desirable key to control over one's sexuality and fertility.

But can effective and widespread contraception ever completely end the need for abortion? The answer seems to be that it cannot. There will continue to be situations in which pregnancies occur that are unwanted enough to justify (at least in the abortion seeker's eyes) resort to abortion. Prior contraceptive use is not always possible; in some circumstances it may have unhappy connotations that preclude its use. Particularly troubling is the confusion in adolescent minds between sexual desire or opportunity and the need to appear chaste. Being armed with contraceptives can give the wrong message in an unsure or new relationship. Although sexuality and contraceptive education and information should make the need for abortion more and more distant, the problems are more acute and complicated than an authoritarian state, religion, or society may acknowledge. And shutting off access to abortion may only serve to drive abortions underground, even if access to contraception is not simultaneously denied as well.

In any case, there does seem to be the curious combination of a wanted pregnancy but an unwanted birth. The post-Cairo reproductive health approach, which assumes that the slogan "every birth a wanted birth" is equivalent to "every pregnancy a wanted pregnancy," may be missing certain important nuances. For example, a pregnancy is often the strategy employed to cement a relationship or to test a relationship. In both cases, once the relationship has been confirmed or *because* it has not been affirmed by the pregnancy, the birth that would result from such a wanted pregnancy may become unwanted or infeasible to deal with. The correct and long-term policy response would be to educate women to prevent a pregnancy unless a birth is actually desired, but there will always be the desperate cases in which denial of access to abortion can only endanger the health, welfare, and very lives of women and children.

Moreover, being able to correctly predict if a birth will be wanted may not be such a benign thing after all. For example, it is one thing to equate a wanted pregnancy with a wanted birth because one is indifferent to the sex of one's child. But it is quite a different matter if this happens because one is able to engineer the sex of a fetus. In that case, all one has done is what may metaphorically be called a *preconception abortion.* This is not a far-fetched description. Medical technology is rushing to serve public demands, and it appears that we are not far from the day in which a sex-selective abortion will be unnecessary not because sex preferences for births die out but because sex-selective *pregnancies* are possible. The ethical ramifications of this and of reproductive (and especially abortion) technology in general are mind-boggling to say the least. It is hoped that this volume contributes to a sorting out of some of these ramifications through its microlevel demonstration that there are few absolutes—in values or ideology—to which one can turn. The path to a more sympathetic understanding of reproductive behavior and a more effective and sensitive policy to influencing such behavior may then become less thorny.

This volume, therefore, seeks to provide an in-depth analysis of the cultural and moral imperatives for abortion and the ways in which all the key players—women, families, society, and the state (including religion)—are willing agents of change at the same time that they are seemingly locked into a network of constraints. For this reason, it is hoped that it will attract a wide readership.

About the Editor and Contributors

ALAKA MALWADE BASU is Associate Professor of Demography in the Department of Sociology at Cornell University. She is a demographer by training with a special interest in the social and cultural underpinnings of demographic behavior. She has served as the chairperson of the Committee on Anthropological Demography of the International Union for the Scientific Study of Population and as a member of the Panels on Reproductive Health and on Population Projections of the National Research Council, Washington, D.C. Her recent publications include (edited with R. Jeffery) *Girls Schooling, Women's Autonomy and Fertility Change in South Asia* (1996), (edited with P. Aaby) *The Methods and Uses of Anthropological Demography* (1998), and articles in *Population and Development Review, Population Studies, Demography, Studies in Family Planning, Cambridge Journal of Economics,* and *Development and Change.*

SAJEDA AMIN is a Senior Associate in the Policy Research Division of the Population Council in New York. Previously she was a research fellow at the Bangladesh Institute of Development Studies in Dhaka, Bangladesh. Her field of interest is family and gender issues in population. She is currently working on a project on transitions to adulthood in Bangladesh and Egypt with special focus on work, school, and marriage. Her recent publications appear in *International Journal of Population Geography, Demography, Population Development Review, Population Studies,* and *Journal of The Royal Statistical Society Series A.*

JOHN K. ANARFI is Associate Professor of Social Demography at the Institute of Statistical, Social and Economic Research. His main research interests are in the areas of migration, sexuality, HIV/AIDS, and reproductive health.

KATHLEEN BERENTSEN was a Senior Research Assistant at the Alan Guttmacher Institute from 1998 to 2000. She provided extensive research and data processing support on the subject of abortion statistics worldwide while working at the Institute. She has a first degree in the social sciences and a master's degree in genetic counseling. She is currently working at Columbia University.

CHANTAL BLAYO and YVES BLAYO are professors of demography at the Institut Nationale d'Etudes Demographiques in Paris. They have published widely in the areas of fertility and reproductive health.

JOHN C. CALDWELL is Emeritus Professor of Demography at the Australian National University, Canberra, and head of the university's Health Transition Centre. He and his wife PAT CALDWELL have carried out research on behavior affecting demographic outcomes in Africa, Asia, and Australia over the past four decades.

MARÍA ELENA COLLADO is a social psychologist with a master's degree from the Universidad Autonoma Metropolitana (UAM). She is a specialist in qualitative methodologies and their application to the development and evaluation of health and education programs. Collado collaborated in IMIFAP from 1993 to 1999 in the research department and is currently a Professor of Psychology at the Universidad Autonoma Metropolitana (UAM).

MARTHA GIVAUDAN is currently a doctoral student in Psychology at the University of Tilburg in Holland and the Executive Vice President of IMIFAP. She is a Clinical psychologist with ten years of experience at the National Institute of Perinatalology in the areas of child development research and teenage pregnancy. She has authored or coauthored more than twenty books and didactic materials in the area of family life education and health and has published more than fifty articles in specialist journals and book chapters. She is a former Executive Secretary of the Inter-American Society of Psychology (SIP) for Mexico, Central America, and the Caribbean.

STANLEY K. HENSHAW is a Senior Fellow at the Alan Guttmacher Institute. Dr. Henshaw has carried out research on the subject of abortion over the past thirty years. He has focused particularly on the United States and other developed countries but has also done work on abortion in developing countries. He has served in an advisory role to the World Health Organization for more than ten years. He has published extensively on the subject of abortion statistics and has also written on abortion laws and policies as well as other factors affecting abortion.

INGE HUTTER is an Associate Professor at the Population Research Centre, University of Groningen, the Netherlands. She is an anthropologist and demographer by training. Her recent publications include *Being Pregnant in Rural*

South India: Nutrition of Women and Well-Being of Children (1994) and *Fertility Change in India* (1996), and she has also been published in *Tropical Medicine and International Health.*

MARSELA ALVAREZ IZAZAGA is a psychologist with a master's degree in social psychology from Universidad Nacional Autonoma de Mexico (UNAM). She has been an Associated Investigator at Instituto Nacional de Ciencias Médicas y Nutrición "Salvador Zubirán" and a Professor at both Universidad Intercontinental Mexico and Instituto Nacional de Actualizacion y Capacitacion Educativa (INACE).

ANDRZEJ KULCZYCKI is Assistant Professor in the Department of Epidemiology and International Health, University of Alabama at Birmingham. Earlier, he was on the faculty of health sciences at the American University of Beirut and was a research associate at the School of Public Health, University of Michigan. He holds degrees from the universities of Michigan, London, and Durham. Dr. Kulczycki's research and teaching centers on reproductive health and demography with a strong international emphasis and merges both social science and public health perspectives. He has worked in Kenya, Mexico, Poland, and Lebanon. His publications include *The Abortion Debate in the World Arena* (1999) and articles in *Women in the Labour Market in Changing Economies: Demographic Issues, Genus, The Lancet,* and *Population and Development Review.*

SUSANA LERNER is Professor and Researcher at Centro de Estudios Demográficos y de Desarrollo Urbano, El Colegio de México. She has a B.A. in sociology and an M.A. in demography from El Colegio de México. Her recent publications include *Fertility and the Male Life-Cycle in the Era of Fertility Decline* (2000).

ELISE LEVIN is a doctoral candidate in anthropology at Northwestern University, studying childbearing decisions and family formation in Guinea, West Africa. Other publications are a chapter in *Regulating Menstruation* (forthcoming) and an article in *Africa Today,* a special issue on sexuality and reproduction in Africa.

LEO MORRIS is the Chief of the Behavioral Epidemiology and Demographic Research Branch, Division of Reproductive Health at the Centers for Disease Control and Prevention, Atlanta, Georgia.

AXEL I. MUNDIGO is currently Director of International Programs at the Center for Health and Social Policy, New York, and co-chair of the Reproductive Health Committee of the International Union for the Scientific Study of Population. After his retirement from the World Health Organization in 1995, Dr. Mundigo undertook a worldwide evaluation of the Reproductive Health and Population Program of the Ford Foundation and of the MacArthur Foundation

Brazil Population Program in 1998. From 1983 to 1995, Dr. Mundigo headed the Social Science Research Unit of the Special Program of Research, Development and Research Training in Human Reproduction of the World Health Organization in Geneva, Switzerland. Among his recent publications are *Promoting Reproductive Health* (2000) and *Abortion in the Developing World* (1999) and articles in *Culture Health and Sexuality* (2000) and *Human Evolution* (1999).

SUSAN PICK has been a professor at the National University of Mexico since 1975 and in 1985 established the Mexican Institute for Family and Population Research, a nongovernmental organization working to develop and implementing research-based health and life skills education programs. She is on the executive board of the International Association of Applied Psychology and has served on the Committee for International Relations in Psychology of the American Psychological Association. She has directed research, training, and advocacy work in sexuality and life skills education, prevention of violence against women, maternal and child health, and sensitization of health personnel. She has carried out projects in Mexico and several other countries with the help of funding from over ninety national and international agencies. She was awarded the Mexican National Prize for Young Researchers in the Social Sciences in 1991. Her recent publications include articles in *Reproductive Health Matters* and *American Psychologist.*

ELISHA P. RENNE is Assistant Professor in the Department of Anthropology and the Center for Afro-American and African Studies at the University of Michigan. Her research focuses on fertility and reproductive health; gender relations; religion and social change; and the anthropology of development, specifically in Nigeria. Recent publications include *Regulating Menstruation: Beliefs, Practices, Interpretations* (2001) and *Population and Development Issues: Ideas and Debates* (2000) as well as articles in *Ethnology* and *Africa Today.*

GUADALUPE SALAS is currently the Personal Assistant to the General Director of Population Studies at the Consejo Nacional de Población. Salas has a master's degree in demography and has worked as an attorney-at-law. For the last twenty years Salas has been dedicated to research on induced abortion as well as reproductive health in general.

FLORINA SERBANESCU is at the Centers for Disease Control, Atlanta.

SUSHEELA SINGH is Director of Research at The Alan Guttmacher Institute, New York. She earned her doctorate in sociology from University of California at Berkeley and worked until 1984 at the World Fertility Survey. During her career as a social scientist, she has written or cowritten numerous articles and publications on sexual behavior, fertility, family planning, maternal and child health, teenage pregnancy, and abortion. She coauthored *Hopes and Realities: Closing the*

Gap between Women's Aspirations and Their Reproductive Experiences, based on the institute's investigation of the reproductive behavior and health care needs of women worldwide. She also coauthored *Into a New World: Young Women's Sexual and Reproductive Lives,* an investigation of adolescents in fifty-three countries. With colleagues at The Alan Guttmacher Institute, she has also conducted several investigations on the incidence of abortion in Latin America, Asia, and Nigeria, including the effects of unsafe abortion on women's health. She has served on committees of the International Union for the Scientific Study of Population and on the National Institutes of Health Study Section on Population.

AMY STAMBACH is Assistant Professor of Educational Policy Studies and Anthropology at the University of Wisconsin–Madison. She holds affiliations in the African Studies Program and the Women's Studies Program. Stambach's research and publications focus on the cultural context of schooling in East Africa. Research projects in northern Tanzania explore gendered and generational transformations associated with secondary schooling; the cultural reworking of educational policies at local, national, and international levels; and the history of colonial ethnographies in local conceptualizations of education. Her recent publications include *Lessons from Mount Kilimanjaro: Schooling, Community, and Gender in East Africa* (2000) and articles in *Anthropological Quarterly* and *Civil Society and the Political Imagination in Africa.*

PAUL STUPP is the team leader of the Demographic Research and Program Evaluation Team, Division of Reproductive Health at the Centers for Disease Control and Prevention. Dr. Stupp earned his doctorate degree from Princeton University.

Index

D